Social Performance

This pathbreaking volume makes a powerful case for a new direction in cultural sociology and for social scientific analysis more generally. Taking a "cultural pragmatic" approach to meaning, the contributors suggest a new way of looking at the continuum that stretches between ritual and strategic action. They do so by developing, for the first time, a model of "social performance" that applies not only to micro- but to macro-sociology. This new model is relevant not only to contemporary analysis but to comparative and historical issues, and it is as sensitive to power as it is to cultural structures. The metaphor of performance has long been used by sociologists and humanists to explore not only the social world but literary texts, but this volume offers the first systematic and analytical framework that transforms the metaphor into a social theory and applies it to a series of fascinating large-scale social and cultural processes – from September 11 and the Clinton/Lewinsky Affair, to the South African Truth and Reconciliation Commission and Willy Brandt's famous "kneefall" before the Warsaw Memorial. Building on works by Austin and Derrida on the one side, and Durkheim, Goffman and Turner on the other, *Social Performance* offers a new perspective that will be of great interest to scholars and students alike in the social sciences, humanities, and theatre arts.

JEFFREY C. ALEXANDER is the Lillian Chavenson Saden Professor of Sociology and also Chair of the Sociology Department at Yale University. He is the author of *The Meanings of Social Life: A Cultural Sociology* (2003), *Cultural Trauma and Collective Identity* (with Eyerman, Giesen, Smelser, and Sztompka) (2004), and the editor (with Philip Smith) of *The Cambridge Companion to Durkheim* (2005).

BERNHARD GIESEN holds the chair for macro-sociology in the Department of History and Sociology at the University of Konstanz (Germany) and is a Visiting Professor in the Department of Sociology at Yale University. Among the more than twenty books he has written and edited are *The Intellectuals and the Nation: Collective Identity in a German*

Yankee/Appr. 8/25/06

Axial Age (Cambridge 1998) and *Triumph and Trauma* (2004).

JASON L. MAST is a Doctoral Candidate in Sociology at the University of California, Los Angeles, and a Visiting Fellow at Yale University's Department of Sociology and its Center for Cultural Sociology.

Cambridge Cultural Social Studies

Series editors: JEFFREY C. ALEXANDER, *Department of Sociology, Yale University, and* STEVEN SEIDMAN, *Department of Sociology, University of Albany, State University of New York.*

Titles in the series

ARNE JOHAN VETLESEN, *Evil and Human Agency*

ROGER FRIEDLAND AND JOHN MOHR, *Matters of Culture*

DAVINA COOPER, *Challenging Diversity, Rethinking Equality and the Value of Difference*

KRISHAN KUMAR, *The Making of English National Identity*

RON EYERMAN, *Cultural Trauma*

STEPHEN M. ENGEL, *The Unfinished Revolution*

MICHÈLE LAMONT AND LAURENT THÉVENOT, *Rethinking Comparative Cultural Sociology*

RON LEMBO, *Thinking through Television*

ALI MIRSEPASSI, *Intellectual Discourse and the Politics of Modernization*

RONALD N. JACOBS, *Race, Media, and the Crisis of Civil Society*

ROBIN WAGNER-PACIFICI, *Theorizing the Standoff*

KEVIN MCDONALD, *Struggles for Subjectivity*

S. N. EISENSTADT, *Fundamentalism, Sectarianism, and Revolution*

PIOTR SZTOMPKA, *Trust*

SIMON J. CHARLESWORTH, *A Phenomenology of Working-Class Experience*

LUC BOLTANSKI, Translated by GRAHAM D. BURCHELL, *Distant Suffering*

MARIAM FRASER, *Identity without Selfhood*

(list continues at end of book)

Social Performance

Symbolic Action, Cultural Pragmatics, and Ritual

EDITED BY

Jeffrey C. Alexander

Bernhard Giesen

Jason L. Mast

CAMBRIDGE
UNIVERSITY PRESS

CAMBRIDGE UNIVERSITY PRESS
Cambridge, New York, Melbourne, Madrid, Cape Town, Singapore, São Paulo

Cambridge University Press
The Edinburgh Building, Cambridge CB2 2RU, UK

Published in the United States of America by Cambridge University Press, New York

www.cambridge.org
Information on this title: www.cambridge.org/9780521674621

© Cambridge University Press 2006

First published 2006

Printed in the United Kingdom at the University Press, Cambridge

A catalogue record for this publication is available from the British Library

ISBN-13 978-0-521-85795-6 hardback
ISBN-10 0-521-85795-3 hardback

ISBN-13 978-0-521-67462-1 hardback
ISBN-10 0-521-67462-X paperback

Life itself is a dramatically enacted thing.
                                        Erving Goffman

Contents

Figures

Tables

Contributors

JEFFREY ALEXANDER is the Lillian Chavenson Saden Professor of Sociology at Yale University, and was also Chair (to July, 2005) of the Sociology Department. With Ron Eyerman, he is Co-Director of the Center for Cultural Sociology. He works in the areas of theory, culture, and politics. An exponent of the "strong program" in cultural sociology, Alexander has investigated the cultural codes and narratives that inform diverse areas of social life. His most recent paper in this area is "Cultural Pragmatics: Social Performance between Ritual and Strategy," *Sociological Theory*, 22. He is the author of *The Meanings of Social Life: A Cultural Sociology* (Oxford, 2003), *Cultural Trauma and Collective Identity* (with Eyerman, Giesen, Smelser, and Sztompka, University of California Press, 2004), and the editor (with Philip Smith) of *The Cambridge Companion to Durkheim* (2005). In the field of politics, Alexander is finishing a book called *Possibilities of Justice: The Civil Sphere and Its Contradictions*, which includes discussions of gender, race, and religion, as well as new theorizing about civil power, communication, and social movements.

DAVID E. APTER is the Henry J. Heinz Professor Emeritus of Comparative Political and Social Development and Senior Research Scientist at Yale University. He has taught at Northwestern University, the University of Chicago (where he was the Executive Secretary of the Committee for the Comparative Study of New Nations), the University of California (where he was Director of the Institute of International Studies), and Yale University where he holds a joint appointment in political science and sociology and served as Director of the Social Science Division, Chair of Sociology, and was a founding fellow of the Whitney Humanities Center. He has done field research on development, democratization, and political violence in Africa, Latin America, Japan, and China. His book, *Choice and the Politics of Allocation* (1971) received the

Woodrow Wilson award for the best book of the year in political science and international studies.

RON EYERMAN is Professor of Sociology and Co-Director (with Jeffrey Alexander) of the Center for Cultural Sociology as Yale University. He has published two books with Cambridge University Press, *Cultural Trauma Slavery and the Formation of African American Identity* (2002) and *Music and Social Movements* (1998). His most recent research concerns the development of a "meaningful" sociology of the arts.

BERNHARD GIESEN holds the chair for macro-sociology in the Department of History and Sociology at the University of Konstanz (Germany) and is an Associate Professor in the Department of Sociology at Yale University. He has held visiting positions at the Department of Sociology at the University of Los Angeles, the Committee for Social Thought (Chicago), the Department of Sociology at New York University, and the Center for Advanced Studies at Stanford University. Bernhard Giesen works in the areas of cultural and historical sociology and sociological theory and has extensively published on social evolution, postmodern culture, and collective identity and more recently on collective memory, collective trauma, intergenerational conflict, and collective rituals. Among the more than twenty books he has written and edited are *The Intellectuals and the Nation. Collective Identity in a German Axial Age* (Cambridge 1998) and *Triumph and Trauma* (Boulder 2004).

TANYA GOODMAN recently completed her Ph.D. in Sociology at Yale University. She is currently a Visiting Lecturer at Yale Law School, teaching a research seminar on the South African Truth and Reconciliation Commission. She is also engaged in a project under a grant from the United States Institute of Peace, which uses multi-media technology to develop a set of teaching and research tools for scholars and practitioners interested in truth commissions. Her research interests lie in the fields of cultural sociology, social change, and the contexts of peace, war, and social conflict on both a global and local scale.

KAY JUNGE (1960) graduated from Bielefeld University (Germany) and got his doctoral degree from Justus-Liebig University in Giessen. In 1999 he became an Assistant Professor in the Department of History and Sociology at the University of Konstanz. He has published mainly in the fields of historical and theoretical sociology and is currently working on a book on the sociology of law.

JASON L. MAST is a Doctoral Candidate in Sociology at the University of California, Los Angeles, and a visiting fellow at Yale University's Department of Sociology and its Center for Cultural Sociology. Aided by a grant from the Mellon Foundation for Writing Performance History, he is completing his dissertation on the social dramatic processes at play in the Clinton/Lewinsky Affair. He is also writing an ethnography of street performers, in which he examines how discourse shapes interactions between strangers in public spaces.

VALENTIN RAUER graduated at Humboldt University Berlin (Germany) and recently completed his dissertation in Sociology at Konstanz University (Germany). Since 2000 he has been Research Fellow in an interdisciplinary research group "Norms and Symbols" at the University of Konstanz (Germany) under a grant of the German Scientific Society (DFG). His fields of interests are cultural sociology, migration, the public sphere, and social performance. He has published in the fields of migration, (trans-)national identity, and collective memory. Future projects include papers on transnational rituals of reconciliation.

ISAAC REED is Doctoral Candidate in Sociology at Yale University. His dissertation concerns the theoretical logic of interpretive sociology, and aims to provide a new epistemological footing for qualitative, cultural, and historical work in the social sciences by developing an explanatory framework commensurate with the interpretive nature of sociological work. His fields of interest are social theory, cultural sociology, sex and gender, historical sociology, and the sociology of popular culture. Future projects include papers on gender and power at the Salem witch trials, and on the cultural sociology of sport, as well as continuing theoretical work on sociological interpretation and validity.

Introduction: symbolic action in theory and practice: the cultural pragmatics of symbolic action

Jeffrey C. Alexander and Jason L. Mast

The question of theory and practice permeates not only politics but culture, where the analogue for theory is the social-symbolic text, the bundle of everyday codes, narratives, and rhetorical configurings that are the objects of hermeneutic reconstruction. Emphasizing action over its theory, praxis theorists have blinded themselves to the deeply embedded textuality of every social action (Bourdieu 1984; Swidler 1986; Turner 2002). But a no less distorting myopia has affected the vision from the other side. The pure hermeneut (e.g., Dilthey 1976; Ricoeur 1976) tends to ignore the material problem of instantiating ideals in the real world. The truth, as Marx (1972: 145) wrote in his tenth thesis on Feuerbach, is that, while theory and practice are different, they are always necessarily intertwined.

Theory and practice are interwoven in everyday life, not only in social theory and social science. In the following chapters, we will see that powerful social actors understand the conceptual issues presented in this introduction in an intuitive, ethnographic, and practical way. In the intense and fateful efforts to impeach and to defend President Clinton (Mast, ch. 3), for instance, individuals, organizations, and parties moved "instinctively" to hook their actions into the background culture in a lively and compelling manner, working to create an impression of sincerity and authenticity rather than one of calculation and artificiality, to achieve verisimilitude. Social movements' public demonstrations (Eyerman, ch. 6) display a similar performative logic. Movement organizers, intensely aware of media organizations' control over the means of symbolic distribution, direct their participants to perform in ways that will communicate that they are worthy, committed, and determined to achieve acceptance and inclusion from the larger political community. And during South Africa's transition from apartheid to democracy (Goodman, ch. 5), perpetrators' confessions and victims' agonistic retellings of disappeared relatives, displacement, and torture before a Truth and Reconciliation Commission stimulated interest and identification amongst local and global audiences, and initiated a pervasive sense of national catharsis. These examples, and the others that follow, show how social actors, embedded in collective representations and working through symbolic and material means, implicitly orient towards others as if they were actors on a stage seeking identification with their experiences and understandings from their audiences.

Towards a cultural pragmatics

Kenneth Burke (1957 [1941]) introduced the notion of symbolic action. Clifford Geertz (1973a) made it famous. These thinkers wanted to draw attention to the specifically cultural character of activities, the manner in which they are expressive rather than instrumental, irrational rather than rational, more like theatrical performance than economic exchange. Drawing also from Burke, Erving Goffman (1956) introduced his own dramaturgical theory at about the same time. Because of the one-sidedly pragmatic emphases of symbolic interactionism, however, the specifically cultural dimension of this Goffmanian approach (Alexander 1987) to drama made hardly any dent on the sociological tradition, though it later entered into the emerging discipline of performance studies.

In the decades that have ensued since the enunciation of these seminal ideas, those who have taken the cultural turn have followed a different path. It has been meaning, not action, that has occupied central attention, and deservedly so. To show the importance of meaning, as compared to such traditional sociological ciphers as power, money, and status, it has been necessary to show that meaning is a structure, just as powerful as these others (Rambo and Chan 1990; Somers 1995). To take meaning seriously, not to dismiss it as an epiphenomenon, has been the challenge. The strong programs in contemporary cultural sociology (Alexander and Smith 1998; Alexander and Sherwood 2002; Smith 1998; Edles 1998; Jacobs 1996; Kane 1997; Somers 1995; Emirbayer and Goodwin 1996; Sewell 1985) have followed Ricoeur's philosophical demonstration that meaningful actions can be considered as texts, exploring codes and narratives, metaphors, metathemes, values, and rituals in such diverse institutional domains as religion, nation, class, race, family, gender, and sexuality. It has been vital to establish what makes meaning important, what makes some social facts meaningful at all.

In terms of Charles Morris's (1938) classic distinction, strong programs have focused on the syntactics and semantics of meaning, on the relations of signs to one another and to their referents. Ideas about symbolic action and dramaturgy gesture, by contrast, to the pragmatics of the cultural process, to the relations between cultural texts and the actors in everyday life. While the latter considerations have by no means been entirely ignored by those who have sought to sustain a meaning-centered program in cultural sociology, they have largely been addressed either through relatively ad hoc empirical studies (Wagner-Pacifici 1986) or in terms of the metatheoretical debate over structure and agency (Sewell 1992; Kane 1991; Hays 1994; Alexander 1988, 2003a; Sahlins 1976). Metatheory is indispensable as an orienting device. It thinks out problems in a general manner and, in doing so, provides more specific, explanatory thinking with a direction to go. The challenge is to move downward on the scientific continuum, from the presuppositions of metatheory to the models and empirical generalizations upon which explanation depends. Metatheoretical thinking about structure and agency has provided hunches about how this should be done, and creative empirical studies show that it can be, but there remains a gaping hole between general concepts and empirical facts. Without providing systematic mediating concepts, even the most fruitful empirical efforts to bridge semantics and pragmatics (e.g., Sahlins 1981; Wagner-Pacifici 1986; Kane 1997) have an ad hoc character, and the more purely metatheoretical often produce awkward, even oxymoronic circumlocutions.[1]

Cultural practices are not simply speech acts. Around the same time Goffman was developing a pragmatic dramaturgy in sociology, John Austin (1975) introduced ordinary language philosophy to the idea that language could have a performative function and not only a constative one. Speaking aims to get things done, Austin denoted, not merely to make assertions and provide descriptions. In contrast to simply describing, the performative speech act has the capacity to realize its semantic contents; it is capable of constituting a social reality through its utterance. On the other hand it can fail. Given that a performative may or may not work, that it may or may not succeed in realizing its stated intention, Austin keenly observed, its appropriate evaluative standard is not truth and accuracy, but "felicitous" and "unfelicitous."

When Austin turned to investigating felicity's conditions, however, like Goffman he stressed only the speech act's interactional context, and failed to account for the cultural context out of which particular signs are drawn forth by a speaker. This philosophical innovation could have marked a turn to the aesthetic and to considerations of what makes actions exemplary (Arendt 1958; Eyerman and Jamison 1991; Ferrara 2001); instead, it led to an increasing focus on the interactional, the situational, and the practical (e.g., Goffman 1956; Searle 1961; Habermas 1984; Schegloff 1987). Austin's innovation, like Goffman's dramaturgy, had the effect of cutting off the practice of language from its texts.

Saussure would have agreed with Austin that *parole* (speech) must be studied independently of *langue* (language). However, he would have insisted on the "arbitrary nature of the sign," that, to consider its effectiveness, spoken language must be considered in its totality, as both *langue* and *parole*. A sign's meaning is arbitrary, Saussure demonstrated,[2] in that "it actually has no natural connection with the signified" (1985: 38), i.e., the object it is understood to represent. Its meaning is arbitrary in relation to its referent in the real world, but it is also arbitrary in the sense that it is not determined by the intention or will of any individual speaker or listener. Rather, a sign's meaning derives from its relations – metaphorical, metonymic, synecdochic – to other signs in a system of sign relations, or language. The relations between signs in a cultural system are fixed by social convention; they are structures that social actors experience as natural, and unreflexively depend on to constitute their daily lives. Consequently, an accounting of felicity's conditions must attend to the cultural structures that render a performative intelligible, meaningful, and capable of being interpreted as felicitous or infelicitous, in addition to the mode and context in which the performative is enacted.

In this respect, Saussure's sometimes errant disciple, Jacques Derrida, has been a faithful son, and it is in Derrida's (1982a [1971]) response to Austin's speech act theory that post-structuralism begins to demonstrate a deep affinity with contemporary cultural pragmatics. Derrida criticized Austin for submerging the contribution of the cultural text to performative outcome. Austin "appears to consider solely the conventionality constituting the *circumstance* of the utterance [*énoncé*], its contextual surroundings," Derrida admonished, "and not a certain conventionality intrinsic to what constitutes the speech act [locution] itself, all that might be summarized rapidly under the problematic rubric of 'the arbitrary nature of the sign'" (1988: 15). In this way, Derrida sharply criticized Austin for ignoring the "citational" quality of even the most pragmatic writing and speech; that words used in talk cite the seemingly absent background cultural texts from which they derive their meanings. "Could a performative utterance succeed," Derrida asked, "if its formulation did not repeat a 'coded' or iterable utterance, or in other words, if the formula I pronounce in order to open a meeting, launch a ship or a marriage were not identifiable as conforming with an iterable model, if it were not then identifiable in some way as a 'citation'?" (1988: 18)

Because there can be no determinate, trans-contextual relation of signifier and referent, difference always involves *différance* (Derrida 1982b). Interpreting symbolic practice – culture in its "presence" – always entails a reference to culture in its "absence," that is, to an implied semiotic text. In other words, to be practical and effective in action – to have a successful performance – actors must be able to make the meanings of culture structures stick. Since meaning is the product of relations between signs in a discursive code or text, a dramaturgy that intends to take meaning seriously must account for the cultural codes and texts that structure the cognitive environments in which speech is given form.

Dramaturgy in the new century emerges from the confluence of hermeneutic, post-structural, and pragmatic theories of meaning's relation to social action. Cultural pragmatics grows out of this confluence, maintaining that cultural practice must be theorized independently of cultural symbolics, while, at the same time, remaining fundamentally interrelated with it. Cultural action puts texts into practice, but it cannot do so directly, without "passing go." A theory of practice must respect the relative autonomy of structures of meaning. Pragmatics and semantics are analytical, not concrete distinctions.

The real and the artificial

One of the challenges in theorizing contemporary cultural practice is the manner in which it seems to slide between artifice and authenticity. There is the deep pathos of Princess Diana's death and funeral, mediated, even in a certain sense generated by, highly constructed, commercially targeted televised productions, yet so genuine and compelling that the business of a great national collectivity came almost fully to rest. There are the Pentagon's faked anti-ballistic missile tests and its doctored action photographs of smart missiles during the Iraq war, both of which were taken as genuine in their respective times. There is the continuous and often nauseating flow of the staged-for-camera pseudo-event, which Daniel Boorstin (1962 [1961]) flushed out already in the 1960s. Right along beside them, there is the undeniable moral power generated by the equally "artificial" media event studied by Daniel Dayan and Elihu Katz (1992) – Sadat's arrival in Jerusalem, the Pope's first visit to Poland, and John F. Kennedy's funeral.

Plays, movies, and television shows are staged "as if" they occur in real life, and in real time. To seem as if they are "live," to seem real, they are increasingly shot "on location." National armies intimidate one another by staging war games, completely artificial events whose intention not to produce a "real" effect is announced well before they occur but which often alter real balances of power. Revolutionary guerrilla groups, like the Zapatista rebels from Chiapas, Mexico, represent powerful grassroots movements that aim to displace vast material interests and often have the effect of getting real people killed. Yet the masses in such movements present their collective force via highly staged photo-marches, and their leaders, like subcommander Marcos, enter figuratively into the public sphere, as iconic representations of established cultural forms.

The effort at artificially creating the impression of liveness is not in any sense new. The Impressionist painters wanted to trump the artificiality of the French Academy by moving outside, to be closer to the nature they were representing, to paint *en plein air*. The Lincoln–Douglas debates were highly staged, and their "real influence" would have been extremely narrow were it not for the hyperbolic expansiveness of the print media (Schudson 1998). The aristocracies and emerging middle classes of the Renaissance, the period marking the very birth of modernity, were highly style-conscious, employing facial makeup and hair shaping on both sides of the gender divide, and engaging, more generally, in strenuous efforts at "self-fashioning" (Greenblatt 1980). It was the greatest writer of the Renaissance, after all, who introduced into Western literature the very notion that "the whole world's a stage, and we merely actors upon it."

Despite a history of reflexive awareness of artificiality and constructedness, such postmodern commentators as Baudrillard (1983) announce, and denounce, the contemporary interplaying of reality with fiction as demarcating a new age, one in which pragmatics has displaced semantics, social referents have disappeared, and only signifiers powered by the interests and powers of the day remain. Such arguments represent a temptation, fueled by a kind of nostalgia, to treat the distinction between the real and artificial in an essentialist way. Cultural pragmatics holds that this vision of simulated hyper-textuality is not true, that the signified, no matter what its position in the manipulated field of cultural production, can never be separated from some set of signifiers (cf. Sherwood 1994).

The relation between authenticity and modes of presentation is, after all, historically and culturally specific.[3] During the Renaissance, for instance, the theatre, traditionally understood to be a house of spectacle, seduction, and idolatry, began to assume degrees of authenticity that had traditionally been reserved for the dramatic text, which was honored for its purity and incorruptibility. The relation between authenticity and the senses shifted during this time as well. With its close association with the aural eroding, authenticity became an attribute of the visual. The visual displaced the aural as the sense most closely associated with apprehending and discerning the authentic, the real, and the true. The aural, on the other hand, was increasingly presumed to "displace 'sense,'" and language to "dissolve into pure sound and leave reason behind" (Peters 2000: 163).

It is difficult to imagine a starker example of authenticity's cultural specificity than Donald Frischmann's (1994) description of the Tzotzil people's reaction to a live theatrical performance staged in their village of San Juan Chamula, in Chiapas, Mexico in 1991. Frischmann describes how, during the reenactment of an occurrence of domestic violence, the audience was taken by "a physical wave of emotion [that] swept through the entire crowd" nearly knocking audience members "down onto the floor." During a scene in which a confession is flogged out of two accused murderers the line separating theatrical production and audience completely disintegrated: "By this point in the play, the stage itself was full of curious and excited onlookers – children and men, surrounding the actors in an attempt to get a closer look at the stage events, which so curiously resembled episodes of *real life* out in the central plaza" (1994: 223, italics in original).

Cultural pragmatics emphasizes that authenticity is an interpretive category rather than an ontological state. The status of authenticity is arrived at, is contingent, and results from processes of social construction; it is not inseparable from a transcendental, ontological referent. If there is a normative repulsion to the fake or inauthentic, cultural pragmatics asserts that it must be treated in an analytical way, as a structuring code in the symbolic fabric actors depend on to interpret their lived realities.

Yes, we are "condemned" to live out our lives in an age of artifice, a world of mirrored, manipulated, and mediated representation. But the constructed character of symbols does not make them less real. A talented anthropologist and a clinical psychologist recently published a lengthy empirical account (Marvin and Ingle 1999) describing the flag of the United States, the "stars and stripes," as a totem for the American nation, a tribe whose members periodically engage in blood sacrifice so that the totem may continue to thrive. Such a direct equation of contemporary sacrality with pre-literate tribal life has its dangers, as we are about to suggest below, yet there is much in this account that rings powerfully true.

Nostalgia and counter-nostalgia: sacrality then and now

For those who continue to insist on the centrality of meaning in contemporary societies, and who see these meanings as in some necessary manner refractions of culture structures, the challenge is the same today as it has always been: How to deal with "modernity," an historical designation that now includes postmodernity as well? Why does it remain so difficult to conceptualize the cultural implications of the vast historical difference between earlier times and our own? One reason is that so much of contemporary theorizing about culture has seemed determined to elide it. The power–knowledge fusion that Foucault postulates at the center of the modern episteme is, in fact, much less characteristic of contemporary societies than it was of earlier, more traditional ones, where social structure and culture were relatively fused. The same is true for Bourdieu's habitus, a self that is mere nexus, the emotional residue of group position and social structure that much more clearly reflects the emotional situation of early societies than the autonomizing, reflexive, deeply ambivalent psychological processes of today.

Culture still remains powerful in an a priori manner, even in the most contemporary societies. Powers are still infused with sacralizing discourses, and modern and postmodern actors can strategize only by typifying in terms of institutionally segmented binary codes. Secularization does not mean the loss of cultural meaning, the emergence of completely free-floating institutions, or the creation of purely self-referential individual actors (cf. Emirbayer and Mische 1998). There remains, in Kenneth Thompson's (1990) inimitable phrase, the "dialectic between sacralization and secularization." But action does not relate to culture in an unfolding sort of way. Secularization does mean differentiation rather than fusion, not only between culture, self, and social structure, but within culture itself.

Mannheim (1971 [1927]) pointed out that it has been the unwillingness to accept the implications of such differentiation that has always characterized conservative political theory, which from Burke (1790) to Oakeshott (1981 [1962]) to contemporary communitarians has given short shrift to cultural diversity and individual autonomy. What is perhaps less well understood is that such unwillingness has also undermined the genuine and important insights of interpretively oriented cultural social science.

For our modern predecessors who maintained that, despite modernization, meaning still matters, the tools developed for analyzing meaning in traditional and simple societies seemed often to be enough. For instance, late in his career Durkheim used descriptions of Australian aboriginal clans' ceremonial rites to theorize that rituals and "dramatic performances" embed and reproduce the cultural system in collective and individual actions (1995: 378). The Warramunga's ceremonial rites that honor a common ancestor, Durkheim argued, "serve no purpose other than to make the clan's mythical past present in people's minds" and thus to "revitalize the most essential elements of the collective consciousness" (1995: 379). Similarly, almost a decade after the close of World War Two, Shils and Young (1953) argued that Queen Elizabeth II's coronation signified nothing less than "an act of national communion," and W. Lloyd Warner (1959) argued that Memorial Day represented an annual ritual that reaffirmed collective sentiments and permitted organizations in conflict to "subordinate their ordinary opposition and cooperate in collectively expressing the larger unity of the total community" (279).

These arguments demonstrate a stunning symmetry with Durkheim's descriptions of the ritual process's effects on comparatively simple and homogeneous aboriginal clans. These thinkers jumped, each in his own creative way, directly from the late Durkheim to late modernity without making the necessary conceptual adjustments along the way. The effect was to treat the characteristics that distinguished modern from traditional societies as residual categories. It was in reaction to such insistence on social-cum-cultural integration that conflict theory made claims, long before postmodern constructivism, that public cultural performances were not affective but merely cognitive (Lukes 1975), that they sprang not from cultural texts but from artificial scripts, that they were less rituals in which audiences voluntarily if vicariously participated than symbolic effects controlled and manipulated by elites (Birnbaum 1955).

The old-fashioned Durkheimians, like political conservatives, were motivated in some part by nostalgia for an earlier, simpler, and more cohesive age. Yet their critics have been moved by feelings of a not altogether different kind, by an anti-nostalgia that barely conceals their own deep yearning for the sacred life. In confronting the fragmentations of modern and postmodern life, political radicals have often been motivated by cultural conservatism. From Marx and Weber to the Frankfurt School (Horkheimer and Adorno 1972), from Arendt's (1951) mass society theory to Selznick's (1951, 1952), from Jameson (1991) to Baudrillard, left cultural critics have lodged the nostalgic claim that nothing can ever be the same again, that capitalism or industrial society or mass society or postmodernity has destroyed the possibility for meaning. The result has been that cultural history has been understood allegorically (cf. Clifford 1986, 1988). It is narrated as a process of disenchantment, as a fall from Eden, as declension from a once golden age of wholeness and holiness (Sherwood 1994). The assertion is that once representation is encased in some artificial substance, whether it is substantively or only formally rational, it becomes mechanical and unmeaningful.

The classical theoretical statement of this allegory remains Walter Benjamin's (1968 [1936]) "The Work of Art in the Age of Mechanical Reproduction," veneration (!) for which has only grown among postmodern critics of the artificiality of the present age. Benjamin held that the auratic quality of art, the aura that surrounded it and gave it a sacred and holy social status, was inherently diminished by art's reproducibility. Sacred aura is a function of distance. It cannot be maintained once mechanical reproduction allows contact to become intimate, frequent, and, as a result, mundane. Baudrillard's simulacrum marks merely one more installment in the theoretical allegory of disenchantment. A more recent postmodern theorist, Peggy Phelan (1993: 146), has applied this allegory in suggesting that, because the "only life" of performance is "in the present," it "cannot be saved, recorded, documented, or otherwise participate in the circulation of representations of representations." Once performance is mechanically mediated, its meaningfulness is depleted. The argument here is pessimistic and Heideggerian. If ontology is defined in terms of *Dasein*, as "being there," then any artificial mediation will wipe it away. "To the degree that performance attempts to enter the economy of reproduction," Phelan predictably writes, "it betrays and lessens the promise of its own ontology."

We can escape from such Heideggerianism only by developing a more complex sociological theory of performance. It was Burke (1957, 1965) who first proposed to transform the straightforward action theory of Weber and Parsons, the schema of means–ends–norms–conditions, which simultaneously mimicked and critiqued economic man. This meant taking "act" in a theatrical rather than a nominalist and mundane manner. It meant transforming "conditions" into the notion of a "scene" upon which an act could be displayed. With analytical transformations such as these, cultural traditions could be viewed not merely as regulating actions but as informing dramas, the performance of which could display exemplary motives, inspire catharsis, and allow working through (Burke 1959).

The implications of this extraordinary innovation were limited by Burke's purely literary ambitions and by the fact that he, too, betrayed nostalgia for a simpler society. Burke suggested (1965: 449, italics added), on the one hand, that "a drama is a mode of symbolic action so designed that an audience *might* be induced to 'act symbolically' in sympathy with it." On the other hand, he insisted that, "insofar as the drama *serves* this function it may be studied as a 'perfect mechanism' composed of parts moving in mutual adjustment to one another like clockwork." The idea is that, if audience sympathy is gained, then society really has functioned as a dramatic text, with true synchrony among its various parts. In other words, this theory of dramaturgy functions, not only as an analytical device, but also as an allegory for re-enchantment. The implication is that, if the theory is properly deployed, it will demonstrate for contemporaries how sacrality can be recaptured, that perhaps it has never disappeared, that the center will hold.

Such nostalgia for re-enchantment affected the most significant line of dramaturgical thinking to follow out from Burke. More than any other thinker, it was Victor Turner who demonstrated the most profound interest in modernizing ritual theory, with notions of ritual process, social dramas, liminality, and communitas, being the most famous results (Turner 1969; cf. Edles 1998). When he turned to dramaturgy, Turner (1974a, 1982) was able to carry this interest forward in a profoundly innovative manner, creating a theory of social dramas that deeply marked the social science of his day (Abrahams 1995; Wagner-Pacifici 1986). At the same time, however, Turner's intellectual evolution revealed a deep personal yearning for the more sacred life, which was demonstrated most forcefully in his descriptions of how ritual participants experience liminal moments and communitas (1969).

Turner used these terms to describe social relations and forms of symbolic action that are unique to the ritual process. Derived from the term *limen*, which is Latin for "threshold," Turner defines liminality as representing "the midpoint of transition in a status-sequence between two positions" (1974a: 237). All rituals include liminal phases, Turner argued, in which traditional status distinctions dissolve, normative social constraints abate, and a unique form of solidarity, or communitas, takes hold:

Communitas breaks in through the interstices of structure, in liminality; at the edges of structure . . . and from beneath structure . . . It is almost everywhere held to be sacred or "holy," possibly because it transgresses or dissolves the norms that govern structured and institutionalized relationships and is accompanied by experiences of unprecedented potency. (1969: 128)

During liminal moments, Turner maintained, social distinctions are leveled and an egalitarian order, or "open society" (1974a: 112), is momentarily created amongst ritual participants. Liminal social conditions foster an atmosphere of communitas, in which ritual participants are brought closer to the existential and primordial, and distanced from dependence on the cognitive, which Turner associated with the structured, normative social order. In such moments, the "unused evolutionary potential in mankind which has not yet been externalized and fixed in structure" is released, and ritual participants are free to "enter into vital relations with other men" (1974a: 127–8). Turner's re-enchantment imagery is unmistakable. It combines Marxist, utopian formulations of post-revolutionary, radical equality on the one hand, with Nietzschian (2000 [1927]) formulations of Dionysian social action on the other. Through liminality we may return to an idealized state of simple humanity, a community of equals; the dissolution of structure will initiate the erosion of our socially constructed selves, thus allowing us to explore the potency of our "unused evolutionary potential."

When Turner turned explicitly to theorizing about highly differentiated societies, he moved from an analytical model based on ritual to one based on performance. The concept of liminality weathered this transition. Turner modified it, though, because he recognized that relationships between ritual producers and audiences in post-industrial contexts are more complicated and contingent than those he witnessed in tribal settings. Post-industrial actors demonstrate greater degrees of interpretive autonomy and more control over their solidary affiliations than the tribal members he had lived amongst. Thus, Turner introduced the concept "liminoid" to represent liminal-like moments and communitas-like sentiments that post-industrial actors experience in (ritual-like) social dramas in more individualized ways, and enter into more freely, as "more a matter of choice, not obligation" (1982: 55). Despite these insightful modifications, the spirit of liminality, and the nostalgic sentiments that shaped it, continued to permeate Turner's work. Indeed, both continue to exert a powerful sway in contemporary performance studies, as will be shown below.

If Turner moved from ritual to theatre, his colleague, drama theorist and avant-garde theatre producer Richard Schechner (1977, 1985, 1988), moved from theatre to ritual and back again. Turner's theoretical co-founder of contemporary performance studies, Schechner provided the first systematic insight into the "mutual positive feedback relationship of social dramas and aesthetic performances" (2002: 68). His theorizing also provided a path for understanding failed cultural productions. Yet what he himself hankered after was a way to recreate the wholeness of what Peter Brook (1969) called "Holy Theatre." Schechner, even more than Turner, was animated as much by existential as analytical ambition, and his vision of performance studies was deeply shaped by the nostalgia for re-enchantment embedded in Turner's theorizing. Liminality, in Turner's theorizing, represented the pathway to re-enchantment. Liminality, for Schechner, is the cornerstone of performance studies:

Performance Studies is "inter" – in between. It is intergenric, interdisciplinary, intercultural – and therefore inherently unstable. Performance studies resists or rejects definition. As a discipline, PS [sic] cannot be mapped effectively because it transgresses boundaries, it goes where it is not expected to be. It is inherently "in between" and therefore cannot be pinned down or located exactly. (Schechner 1998: 360)

For Schechner, performance studies is a set of performative acts that, if properly deployed, will catalyze liminality in the broader social arena, destabilize the normative structure, inspire criticism, and reacquaint mundane social actors with the primordial, vital, and existential dimensions of life. Put another way, for Schechner, performance studies is a vehicle for re-enchantment.

Clifford Geertz made a similar move from anthropology to theatricality, employing notions of staging and looking at symbolic action as dramatic representation. Yet it is striking how Geertz confined himself to studying performances inside firmly established and articulated ritual containers, from the Balinese cockfight (1973b), where "nothing happened" but an aesthetic affirmation of status structures, to the "theatre state" of nineteenth-century Bali (1980), where highly rigid authority structures were continuously reaffirmed in a priori, choreographed ways. In Geertz's dramaturgy, background collective representations and myths steal each scene. In the Balinese case, cultural scripts of masculinity, bloodlust, and status distinctions seem to literally exercise themselves through the social actions that constitute the cockfight event, leaving precious little room for the contingencies that accompany social actors' varying degrees of competency and complicity. The structural rigidity in Geertz's dramaturgy is doubly striking when juxtaposed to Turner's and Schechner's emphasis on liminality and the social and cultural dynamism that liminal social actors may initiate.

What characterizes this entire line of thinking, which has been so central to the development of contemporary cultural-sociological thought, is the failure to take advantage of the theoretical possibilities of understanding symbolic action as performance. Fully intertwining semantics and pragmatics can allow for the openness and contingency that is blocked by theoretical nostalgia for simpler and more coherent societies.

In an influential volume that capped the "Turner era," and segued to performance theory, John MacAloon (1984: 1) offered a description of cultural performance that exemplified both the achievements and the limitations to which we are pointing here. Turner's and Geertz's influence cannot be missed: MacAloon defined performance as an "occasion in which as a culture or society we reflect upon and define ourselves, dramatize our collective myths and history, present ourselves with alternatives, and eventually change in some ways while remaining the same in others." Through social performances we tell a story about ourselves to ourselves (Geertz 1973b), and, because performances precipitate degrees of liminality, they are capable of transforming social relations. The communitarian emphasis on holism, on cultural, social, and psychological integration, is palpable.

Taking off from Burke in a different direction, Goffman initiated a second, decidedly less nostalgic line of dramaturgical theory. Half persuaded by game theory and rational choice, Goffman adopted a more detached, purely analytical approach to the actor's theatrical preoccupations. He insisted on complete separation of cultural performance from cultural text, of actor from script. Rejecting out of hand the possibility that any genuine sympathy was on offer, either from actor or from audience, Goffman described performance as a "front" behind which actors gathered their egotistical resources and upon which they displayed the "standardized expressive equipment" necessary to gain results. Idealization was a performative, but not a motivational fact. In modern societies, according to Goffman, the aim was to convincingly portray one's own ideal values as isomorphic with those of another, despite the fact that such complementarity was rarely, if ever, the case.

This cool conceptual creativity contributed signally to understanding social performance, but the instrumental tone of Goffman's thinking severed, not only analytically but in principle, that is ontologically, the possibility of strong ties between psychological motivation, social performance, and cultural text. This opening towards a pure pragmatics of performance was taken up by Dell Hymes in linguistics, and by Richard Bauman in folklore and anthropology. Following also in Austin's emphasis on the performative, Bauman (1986) stressed the need for "highlighting the way in which communication is carried out, above and beyond its referential content."

Earlier in anthropology, this line was elaborated in Milton Singer's (1959) explorations of the "cultural performances" in South Asian societies, which he described as the "most concrete observable units of the cultural structure," and which he broke down into such standard features as performers, audience, time span, beginnings, endings, place, and occasion. This form of Goffmanian, analytical deconstruction has combined with nostalgic theories of liminality to feed forcefully into one of the two broad trends in contemporary performance studies. Explicitly praxis-oriented, this strain of performance theory emphasizes exclusively the pragmatic dimensions of resistance and subversion, while focusing in an exaggerated manner on questions of commodification, power, and the politics of representation (MacKenzie 2001; Conquergood 2002; Diamond 1996; Auslander 1997, 1999). Raising the ghost of Marx's Thesis XI and giving it a Foucauldian twist, this strand argues that an epistemology centered on thickly describing the world represents ethnocentric, "epistemic violence" (Conquergood 2002: 146; cf. Ricoeur 1971; Geertz 1973a). The point of practicing performance studies, they argue, is to *change* the world. Liminality, which represents ideal sites for contestation, and pragmatism, which romanticizes actor autonomy and individual self-determination, are its natural theoretical bedfellows.

This praxis approach is attracted to sites of contestation where performances of resistance and subversion are understood to flourish in the ceremonial and interactional practices of the marginalized, the enslaved, and the subaltern (Conquergood 1995, 2002). Rejecting the "culture as text" model, this approach argues that subaltern groups "create a culture of resistance," a "subjugated knowledge" that must be conceptualized not as a discourse but as "a repertoire of performance practices" (Conquergood 2002:150). As a repertoire of practices, culture is theorized as embodied and experiential, and thus wholly unrecognizable to members of the dominant culture.[4] Citationality in these works is limited to representing strategies that "reclaim, short-circuit, and resignify" the hegemonic code's "signed imperatives" (151). While members of the dominant culture are incapable of recognizing subaltern cultures, savvy agents of resistance are described as capable of creatively citing hegemonic codes in order to play upon and subvert them.

This theoretical constraining of citationality to intra-group representational processes has the effect of attributing to subaltern groups radical cultural autonomy. This would seem to lead ineluctably to the conclusion that such groups' identities are constituted wholly from within, and share no symbolic codes with the dominant culture. Yet for subaltern performances of resistance to occur, in which the dominant culture is creatively played upon and subverted, subversive performers must to some degree have internalized the hegemonic code. And to play upon it creatively and felicitously they must be able to *cite* the code in a deeply intuitive, understanding way. One must be able to communicate through the code as much as merely with or against it. Homi Bhabha expressed this succinctly, "mimicry is at once resemblance and menace" (1994: 86). This approach interprets Foucault as a theorist of subjugated knowledges, Turner as a theorist of subversion,[5] and Butler as a philosopher of a Goffmanian world. It generalizes from empirical examples of resistance to a full-blown pragmatic and cognitivist view of the world.

Whether it is Marxist or Heideggerian, conservative or postmodern, Turnerian or Goffmanian, the blinders of these lines of dramaturgical thinking, while enormously instructive, have also had the effect of leading dramaturgical theory and cultural sociology astray. We will be able to develop a satisfying theory of cultural practice only if we can separate ourselves from both nostalgia and anti-nostalgia. Not only disenchantment but re-enchantment characterizes post-traditional societies (Sherwood 1994; Bauman 1993). If social action can continue to be understood by social actors and social interpreters as a meaningful text – and empirical evidence suggests overwhelmingly that this continues to be the case – then cultural practice must continue to be capable of capturing sacrality and of displaying it in successful symbolic performance. Disenchantment must be understood, in other words, not as the denial of some romanticized ontology, much less as proof that, in the post-metaphysical world of modernity, social actors live only in a deontological way (Habermas 1993). What disenchantment indicates, rather, is unconvincing cultural practice, failed symbolic performance.

An alternative form of dramaturgical theorizing is, however, also beginning to emerge. In contrast to the anti-nostalgic, praxis-oriented strand, a second line of inquiry in performance studies has resisted the allure of pragmatic promises of uber-agency while retaining an interest in liminality and the politics of identity. Aligned with Geertzian dramaturgy and Derridean citationality, this approach emphasizes the culturally structured scripts that social actors orient towards, and that they must act through, if only to subvert the script's normative power (Roach 1996; Taylor 1995). Such arguments show that even performances of resistance depend on and redeploy dominant, hegemonic codes.

Citationality is foregrounded when these empirical investigations hermeneutically reconstruct how past performances, performers, and imagined cultural identities manifest themselves in, or "ghost," performances in the present (Taylor 1995; Roach 1996, 2000; Carlson 2001). Alterity takes place within, not simply against, historically produced cultural contexts (Taylor 1995; Roach 1996). Performers in the present innovate, create, and struggle for social change through small but significant revisions of familiar scripts which are themselves carved from deeply rooted cultural texts – as actors in a production of Macbeth (Carlson 2001: 9), mourning musicians and pallbearers in a New Orleans jazz funeral (Roach 2000), or protesting mothers of Argentina's "disappeared" children (Taylor 1995). In these studies, the imagined past weighs heavily on the present, but actors are shown to be capable of lacing the coded past with significant, at times profoundly dramatic revisions.[6]

In a persuasive analysis of Argentina's "Dirty War," for instance, Diane Taylor concludes that rather than simply a repertoire of practices, culture must be understood as a relatively autonomous system of *"pre*texts" (1995: 300, original italics) from which scripts for practice emerge. Once embodied in actors, she argues, scripts become objects of cognition that are open to circumscribed, coded revisions. To protest the military junta's "disappearing" of the nation's young men, and the sexual violence it visited upon women, Argentine "mothers of the disappeared" – "Los Madres" – staged dramatic performances of resistance in the Plaza de Mayo, the political, financial, and symbolic center of Buenos Aires (Taylor 1995: 286). In their performances, the women of Los Madres enacted a script of Motherhood. Taylor views such self-casting as "highly problematic," suggesting it obscured differences among women and "limited the [Resistance's] arena of confrontation" (1995: 300). Why did the Madres make the "conscious political choice" to assume the Motherhood role, she asks? Why did they perform according to a script that relegated them to "the subordinate position of mediators between fathers and sons," when they could have "performed as women, wives, sisters, or human rights activists"? Her answer rejects the epistemology of pragmatic choice, liminality as existential freedom, and cognitive performativity:

I have to conclude that the military and the Madres reenacted a collective fantasy [in which their] positions were, in a sense, already there as *pre*text or script. Their participation in the national tragedy depended little on their individual position as subjects. On the contrary: their very subjectivity was a product of their position in the drama. (Taylor 1995: 301, original italics)

The performative turn in sociology today

Since the late 1980s, the "strong program in cultural sociology" (Alexander 1996; Alexander and Smith 1993, 1998; Edles 1998; Jacobs 1996, 2000; Kane 1991, 1997; Magnuson 1997; Rambo and Chan 1990; Sherwood 1994; Smith 1991, 1996, 1998) has been demonstrating culture's determinative power and its relative autonomy from the social structure. These studies have corrected tendencies to treat culture as epiphenomenal or as a "tool kit" metaphor (Swidler 1986), as materialist and pragmatic writings suggest. At the turn of the century, cultural sociology takes a performative turn. Born of colloquia at the University of Konstanz in 2002/4, and at Yale University in 2003, the theory of cultural pragmatics (Alexander, ch. 1) interweaves meaning and action in a non-reductive way, allowing for culture structures while recognizing that it is only through the actions of concrete social actors that meaning's influence is realized. The essays comprising this volume represent the efforts of cultural sociologists to further develop cultural pragmatics by examining the theatrical dimensions of social life. They examine the instantiation of culture, even while they resist subsuming meaning to practical pragmatics, on the one hand, or to interactional context, on the other.

In the first chapter, Alexander describes the historical and theoretical shifts that have precipitated the move to performance. The challenges facing turn-of-the-century social order, Alexander argues, stem from the problems of defusion and re-fusion. Ritual has performed the work of solidifying collective identity and embedding the cultural system in individual actions. As social forms of organization have grown more complex and cultural systems more differentiated, however, interaction- and collective-rituals have grown more contingent. The range of potential understandings that govern how social actors relate to ritual processes has dramatically expanded. Ritual producers and leaders no longer *are*, in a totalizing and ontological sense, the unproblematic, authoritative disseminators of meaning and order that they were in the past. The social actors who play ritual leaders have become defused from their roles, and audiences have become defused from ritual productions. Participation in, and acceptance of, ritual messages are more a matter of choice than obligation. The process by which culture gets embedded in action, in fact, more closely resembles the dynamics of theatrical production, criticism, and appreciation than it resembles old fashioned rituals. After establishing the rationale for this epistemological turn, Alexander outlines a theory of cultural pragmatics, and analyzes how the elements in his conceptual model – collective representations, actors, means of symbolic production, *mise-en-scène*, power, and audiences – interact to perform contemporary social realities.

The chapters that follow converse with this historical, theoretical, and conceptual formulation, and each raises and addresses questions of performativity in postmodern social life in a different way. The essay that concludes this volume, Bernhard Giesen's "Performing the sacred: A Durkheimian perspective on the performative turn in the social sciences," provides a major theoretical statement to be placed alongside Alexander's. We have placed these theoretical treatments at the beginning and end of the book in order not to obscure their subtle differences, and to allow their consequential nuances to drift to the fore. Functioning as theoretical bookends to this move to performance, Alexander's formulation of, and theoretical response to, the "problem of fusion" opens the volume, and Giesen's identification of the modes through which the sacred is performed in postmodern life closes it. The chapters between these bookends draw variously from both. We are confident that the conceptual affinities between them, and their differences, will be apparent in subtle ways.

Alexander's and Giesen's theories share fundamental presuppositions: meaning is central to social life; meaning systems demonstrate relative autonomy from the more material social realm; the mechanism that most powerfully structures meaning is the binary opposition that distinguishes the sacred from the profane. Yet Alexander and Giesen approach the performativity of order from different directions. Starting from the *"problem* of fusion," Alexander brings the sacred's constructedness to the fore, and his theory of cultural pragmatics encourages us to investigate how the sacred gets contested and reconstituted through symbolically combative, social dramatic processes (see Alexander, ch. 2, this volume). Giesen accepts that social conditions have become defused; he emphasizes, however, that, despite the sacred's arbitrary nature in theory, it continues to exist in some particular form in each socio-historical moment, articulated via a particular set of values. We know this, Giesen argues, because we *feel the sacred* when we come into contact with it. Giesen offers an index of the modes that cultural performances take in contemporary social life, and provides a phenomenology of how the sacred is experienced in each.

The chapters between these bookends demonstrate, extend, and even contest elements of Alexander's and Giesen's theories. In his essay, "From the depths of despair: performance, counterperformance, and 'September 11,'" Alexander demonstrates how the cultural pragmatic model allows new insight into the socio-historical dynamics that have given rise to contemporary manifestations of the centuries-long conflict pitting the "Arab-Islamic world" against the "West." Understanding terrorism requires that we contextualize its gruesomely violent means and narrow, tactical instrumentality within the cultural frameworks that make such actions seem sensible, even holy, to its practitioners, on the one hand, and alien and barbaric to its victims, on the other. Doing so enables us to examine terrorist acts as meaning-laden symbolic performances enacted with particular goals and audiences in mind. The interpretations of such performances remain contingent and subject to "misreading," despite their directors' efforts, the tightness of scripts, and the quality of execution. The idea that even the most serious-minded action can create an unintended counterperformance highlights this interpretive contingency and its immensely realistic consequences.

In "The cultural pragmatics of event-ness: the Clinton / Lewinsky affair," Jason Mast shows how the cultural pragmatic framework helps explain how a beleaguered American president, adrift in waves of scandal, garnered historically enviable job approval ratings and widespread popular support, even while being investigated by the Office of Independent Council and impeached by the House of Representatives. President Clinton's impeachment in December 1998, Mast explains, was the melodramatic conclusion to a lengthy, emotionally charged, yet highly contingent social dramatic struggle. Clinton's first six years of tenure had been marked by a series of quasi-scandalous yet minor political occurrences that failed to rise to the level of crisis or generalization (Alexander 2003b [1988]). Mast shows how popular culture structures shaped and infused the strategies through which motivated parties dramatized these occurrences into "Monicagate," a political event writ large.

In his chapter, "Social dramas, shipwrecks, and cockfights: conflict and complicity in social performance," Isaac Reed argues that three classic anthropological works, which have been read as paradigmatic statements delimiting how culture should be analytically situated vis-à-vis action, can more fruitfully be read, in light of the cultural pragmatic turn, as representing ideal types of social performance. Reed offers a detailed rereading of Turner's (1974b) social drama of Thomas Becket, Sahlins's Captain Cook shipwreck (1981), and Geertz's (1973b) Balinese cockfight essays. He then shows how, in each of these events, the cultural pragmatic elements that Alexander identifies (ch. 1) interacted in context-specific ways, structuring the principals' dramatic strategies and the kinds of social action audiences were expecting to witness. Reed explains how each particular constellation of cultural pragmatic elements established conflict or complicity, thus demonstrating how the cultural pragmatic approach enlarges our ability to theorize the many ways culture infuses social action and society.

We have framed cultural pragmatics as representing, in part, a theoretical response to the challenges that cultural and social differentiation pose to ritual theory. Tanya Goodman's chapter, "Performing a 'new' nation: the role of the TRC in South Africa," shows that emotionally charged, broadly inclusive rituals remain potent forms of social performance even at the turn of the twenty-first century. When the Truth and Reconciliation Commission (TRC) was created by South Africa's embattled political parties, it was charged with producing two seemingly contradictory performatives. It needed to symbolically produce a deep chasm that could separate the nation's racist past from an idealized democratic future. Yet the TRC also need to unify, or bridge, the deeply divided social relations institutionalized under Apartheid. Goodman examines the dramaturgy that allowed the TRC to accomplish both tasks – the way it cast each hearing's performance, selected staging and props, and oriented to multiple audiences and their potential reactions. The TRC's felicitous use of dramatic elements, Goodman argues, transformed what could have been highly contentious, if not openly violent, proceedings into substantively charged, cathartic rituals of reconciliation, which unfolded against the background of the universalist principles that had been embedded in the Commission's founding legislation.

In his chapter, "Performing opposition or, how social movements move," Ron Eyerman shows how performance theory and cultural pragmatics illuminate a series of issues that contemporary social movements literature overlooks, such as how and what social movements actually *represent*. The lens of performance, Eyerman argues, brings into focus the challenges social movements face in coupling their strategic goals with compelling expressive means. It also provides analytical tools for examining the interplay between movements' general ethics and their specific choreographic practices. Striking a felicitous symmetry between goals, practices, and broad dramatic themes, Eyerman concludes, can move people emotionally, cognitively, morally, and physically; it can facilitate cathexis between movement participants and their causes, and stir empathy and identification in movement audiences.

In "Politics as theatre: an alternative view of the rationalities of power," David Apter sets out to answer two questions: how does the theatricality of politics shape consciousness, and how do politically dramatized meanings shape interpretive action? Apter's answers to these questions place him firmly in the theoretical terrain that Alexander and Giesen travel in their contributions to this volume. Apter's theory, however, represents a more explicitly critical approach to dissecting political theatricality; it is a dramaturgy of suspicion designed to reveal the dramatic techniques employed by those who would take, keep, and exercise power. Apter identifies the dramatic strategies that political "actor-agents" use to integrate and unify individuals into coherent audiences, and the devices they employ to magnify audience loyalties by simultaneously constructing outsiders as morally undeserving of inclusion. Actor-agents contrive heroic pasts, articulate glorious futures, and manipulate genres of intrigue to clarify, concentrate, and intensify public opinion. Apter's argument is bolstered by rich illustrations drawn from fieldwork conducted at different global sites, and from his deep familiarity with literary, theatrical, and political theory.

Valentin Rauer's essay, "Symbols in action: Willy Brandt's kneefall at the Warsaw Memorial," is the clearest representation of how Alexander's theory of cultural pragmatics and Giesen's theory of performing the sacred can inform and enhance one another. In the winter of 1970, West German Chancellor Willy Brandt triggered a decisive shift in German collective identity by falling to his knees before Poland's Warsaw Memorial, a dramatic gesture witnessed by European political leaders and international journalists. Drawing on Giesen's work, Rauer explains how Brandt, embedded in a particularly sacred time and space, actually performed and momentarily embodied the sacred in this single epiphanic gesture. Alexander's complex model of cultural pragmatics, Rauer goes on to show, helps us understand how this single gesture could lead to profound symbolic shifts in German understandings of the nation's past, present, and future.

Contemporary explorations into the theatrical dimensions of social life typically reference Austin's (1975 [1962]) critique of modern language philosophy and Goffman's (1956) drama-based conceptual architecture. In "The promise of performance and the problem of order," by contrast, Kay Junge returns to Hobbes, Hume, Rousseau, and Spencer. Junge queries their work from the perspective of performativity, how they were sensitive to the fragility of social order, the ambiguity of actors' promises, and the tensions between the social interests of groups and their moral identities. In the latter part of his essay, Junge offers a radically different understanding of contract theory. He shows how Hobbes turned to the theatre for metaphors to explain how humanity has escaped chaos and managed to keep the state of nature at bay. Whereas Eyerman (ch. 6, this volume) explores the aesthetics of opposition and dissension, Junge shows that order and consent are matters of performativity as well. Junge concludes by arguing that retooling the contractarian tradition with a cultural pragmatic sensibility can lead to fresh understandings of how political authority is gained and legitimated.

In "Performance art," Giesen systematically reconstructs our understanding of this new artistic fashion. He constructs subgenres of performance art, identifying their productive strategies and representation elements, and comparing these dimensions to earlier movements in art history. According to Giesen, contemporary performance art can be conceived as an intentionally orchestrated, aesthetically stylized action that resists classification, crosses or blurs traditional boundaries, destroys conventions, and exists only momentarily before vanishing. Quintessentially postmodern, performance art is in part about aesthetic alienation. It aims to estrange and subvert the structures of meaning that bind a community and constitute its identity. In the process, however, performance art renders deeply felt cultural orientations visible and hints at their theoretical arbitrariness, thus suggesting that things could be otherwise. Through his analysis, Giesen identifies an aesthetic movement whose tentative and elusive identity is rooted in its practitioners' very rejection of the strategies of identification and classification. In a dialectic of identification and transcendence, performance artists compel the aesthetic sphere (and the political and moral) if not forward, then at least into ceaseless motion. By continually shifting their means of artistic production, and the boundaries between art, artist, and audiences, performance artists alter both the art world's and their audiences' orientations to deeply held meaning structures. By continually reflecting on, and creatively conversing with, the art world's grand narratives, the actions of performance artists parallel, in an expressive medium, the move that the contributors to this volume are making in the intellectual medium. Our message is that traditional, organic understandings of social performances, whether rituals or strategies, must give way to a denaturalized, analytically differentiated, and much more self-conscious understanding that allows us to see every dimension of performance as a possibly independent part.

Cultural pragmatics is a social scientific response to the conditions of a postmetaphysical world, in which institutional and cultural differentiation makes successful symbolic performance difficult to achieve. To develop a theory of cultural practice, we must take these historical limitations seriously. The chapters that follow acknowledge that cultural life has radically shifted, both internally and in its relation to action and social structure. They also demonstrate that, despite these changes, culture can still be powerfully meaningful; it can possess and display coherence, and it can exert immense social effect. To understand how culture can be meaningful, but may not be, we must accept history but reject radical historicism. Life is different but not completely so. Rather than sweeping allegorical theory, we need allegorical deconstruction and analytic precision. We need to break the "whole" of symbolic action down into its component parts. Once we do so, we will see that cultural performance covers the same ground that it always has, but in a radically different way.

Notes

1. See, for instance, Sewell's (1992) theory of structure and agency. We do not in any way disagree with the metatheoretical formulation that text, situation, and agency all play a role in shaping social life. We believe, however, that arguments about this interplay must be much more specific and nuanced, and show how these elements actually interact. We also suggest that the generality of Sewell's formulation disguises the tension between the different formulations of structure and agency he brings together. Any framework that "combines" Giddens with Bourdieu, and the two with Sahlins and Geertz, without providing a new model, has great difficulties. Emirbayer's (1997; Emirbayer and Mische 1998) metatheoretical discussions are more coherent, and much more closely approximate the direction we take cultural pragmatics here; but Emirbayer performs a much more thoroughgoing critique of culturalism than he does of pragmatics. His failure to develop such a correspondingly forceful criticism of pragmatism – from the perspective of culture structure and citational meaning-making – makes his model vulnerable to the reinsertion of the structure–agency dualism.
2. Saussure's *Course in General Linguistics* is a reconstruction of lectures he delivered at the University of Geneva between 1906 and 1911. First published in book form in 1913, the lectures appeared in an English translation in 1959.
3. The attribution of inauthenticity to a performance in public discourse often demonstrates a particular logic: that which is accused of being inauthentic and fake is represented as either threatening a just social order, on the one hand, or as (seductively) trapping people in an unjust one, on the other.
4. "Textocentric" academics (Conquergood 2002: 151), who practice a Geertzian approach to studying social life, are included in the group of ignorant members of the dominant culture.
5. "[Judith] Butler turns to Turner – *with a twist* . . . [She] twists Turner's theory of ritual into a theory of normative performance," McKenzie criticizes (in Phelan 1993: 222–3).
6. Where in her earlier and most influential contributions to performance theory, Judith Butler (1990) presented resistance to gender stereotyping in an exaggeratedly agent-centered manner, she has tried to escape from such an exclusively agent-centered understanding of "resistance" in her later essays (e.g. Butler 1993), emphasizing the kind of citational qualities of performance we are pointing to here.

References

Abrahams, Roger D. 1995. "Foreword to the Aldine Paperback Edition," in Victor Turner. *The Ritual Process: Structure and Anti-Structure*. New York: Aldine de Grayter.

Alexander, Jeffrey C. 1987. *Twenty Lectures: Sociological Theory Since World War II*. New York: Columbia University Press.

1988. *Action and Its Environments: Toward a New Synthesis*. New York: Columbia University Press.

1996. "Cultural Sociology of Sociology of Culture?" *Culture* 10, 3–4: 1–5.

2003a. *The Meanings of Social Life: A Cultural Sociology*. New York: Oxford University Press.

2003b [1988]. "Watergate as Democratic Ritual," reprinted in *The Meanings of Social Life: A Cultural Sociology*. New York: Oxford University Press.

Alexander, Jeffrey C. and Phillip Smith. 1993. "The Discourse of American Civil Society: A New Proposal for Cultural Studies." *Theory and Society* 22, 2: 151–207.

1998. "Cultural Sociology or Sociology of Culture? Towards a Strong Program for Sociology's Second Wind." *Sociologie et Société* 30, 1: 107–16.

Alexander, Jeffrey C. and Steve Sherwood. 2002. "'Mythic gestures': Robert N. Bellah and Cultural Sociology," in *Meaning and Modernity: Religion, Polity, and Self*, ed. R. Madsen, W. M. Sullivan, A. Swidler, and S. M. Tipton. Berkeley: University of California Press.

Arendt, Hannah. 1951. *The Origins of Totalitarianism*. New York: Harcourt, Brace.

1958. *The Human Condition*. Chicago: University of Chicago Press.

Auslander, Philip. 1997. *From Acting to Performance: Essays in Modernism and Postmodernism*. New York: Routledge.

1999. *Liveness: Performance in a Mediatized Culture*. New York: Routledge.

Austin, John L. 1975 [1962]. *How To Do Things with Words*. Cambridge, MA: Harvard University Press.

Baudrillard, Jean. 1983. *In the Shadow of the Silent Majorities, or, The End of the Social, and Other Essays*. New York: Semiotext(e).

Bauman, Richard. 1986. *Story, Performance and Event: Contextual Studies in Oral Narrative*. New York: Cambridge University Press.

Bauman, Zygmunt. 1993. *Postmodern Ethics*. Cambridge, MA: Blackwell.

Benjamin, Walter. 1968 [1936]. "The Work of Art in the Age of Mechanical Reproduction," pp. 217–52, in *Illuminations*. New York: Schocken Books.

Bhabha, Homi K. 1994. *Location of Culture*. New York: Routledge.

Birnbaum, N. 1955. "Monarchies and Sociologists: A Reply to Professor Shils and Mr. Young." *Sociological Review* 3: 5–23.

Boorstin, Daniel. 1962 [1961]. *Image: or, What happened to the American Dream*. New York: Atheneum.

Bourdieu, Pierre. 1984. *Distinction: A Social Critique of the Judgement of Taste*. Cambridge, MA: Harvard University Press.

Brook, Peter. 1969. *The Empty Space*. New York: Avon.

Burke, Edmund. 1987 [1790]. *Reflections on the Revolution in France*. Indianapolis: Hackett Publishing Co.

Burke, Kenneth. 1957 [1941]. *The Philosophy of Literary Form: Studies in Symbolic Action*. New York: Vintage.
   1959. "On Catharsis, or Resolution, with a Postscript." *The Kenyon Review* 21: 337–75.
   1965. "Dramatism." *Encyclopedia of the Social Sciences* 7: 445–51.
Butler, Judith. 1990. *Gender Trouble: Feminism and the Subversion of Identity*. New York: Routledge.
   1993. "Critically Queer." *GLQ* 1: 17–32.
Carlson, Marvin. 2001. *The Haunted Stage: The Theatre as Memory Machine*. Ann Arbor: University of Michigan Press.
Clifford, James. 1986. "On Ethnographic Allegory," pp. 98–121 in *Writing Culture: The Poetics and Politics of Ethnography*. Berkeley: University of California Press.
   1988. *The Predicament of Culture: Twentieth-Century Ethnography, Literature, and Art*. Cambridge, MA: Harvard University Press.
Conquergood, Dwight. 1995. "On Caravans and Carnivals: Performance Studies in Motion." *The Drama Review* 39, 4: 137–42.
   2002. "Performance Studies: Interventions and Radical Research." *The Drama Review* 46, 2: 145–56.
Dayan, Daniel and Elihu Katz. 1992. *Media Events: The Live Broadcasting of History*. Cambridge, MA: Harvard University Press.
Derrida, Jacques. 1978. *Writing and Difference*. Chicago: University of Chicago Press.
   1982a [1972]. "Signature Event Context," in *Margins of Philosophy*. Chicago: University of Chicago Press.
   1982b. "Différance," in *Margins of Philosophy*. Chicago: University of Chicago Press.
   1988. *Limited Inc*. Evanston: Northwestern University Press.
Diamond, Elin ed. 1996. *Performance and Cultural Politics*. New York: Routledge.
Dilthey, Wilhelm. 1976. "The Construction of the Historical World in the Human Studies," pp. 168–245 in *Dilthey: Selected Writings*, ed. H. P. Rickman, Cambridge: Cambridge University Press.
Durkheim, Emile. 1995 [1915]. *The Elementary Forms of Religious Life*. New York: Free Press.
Edles, Laura. 1998. *Symbol and Ritual in the New Spain: The Transition to Democracy After Franco*. New York: Cambridge University Press.
Emirbayer, Mustafa and Jeff Goodwin. 1996. "Symbols, Positions, Objects: Toward a New Theory of Revolutions and Collective Action." *History and Theory* 35, 3: 358–74.
Emirbayer, Mustafa and Ann Mische. 1998. "What is Agency?" *American Journal of Sociology* 103, 4: 962–1023.
Eyerman, Ron and Andrew Jamison. 1991. *Social Movements: A Cognitive Approach*. Cambridge: Polity Press.
Ferrara, Alessandro. 2001. "The Evil That Men Do," in *Rethinking Evil*, ed. Maria Pia Lara. Berkeley: University of California Press.

Frischmann, Donald H. 1994. "New Mayan Theatre in Chiapas: Anthropology, Literacy and Social Drama," in *Negotiating Performance: Gender, Sexuality and Theatricality in Latin/o America*, ed. Diana Taylor and Juan Villegas. Durham: Duke University Press.

Geertz, Clifford. 1973a. "Thick Description: Toward an Interpretive Theory of Culture," in *The Interpretation of Cultures*. New York: Basic Books.

    1973b. "Deep Play: Notes on the Balinese Cockfight," in *The Interpretation of Cultures*. New York: Basic Books.

    1980. *Negara: The Theatre State in Nineteenth-Century Bali*. Princeton: Princeton University Press.

Goffman, Erving. 1956. *The Presentation of Self in Everyday Life*. New York: Doubleday.

Greenblatt, Stephen. 1980. *Renaissance Self-fashioning: From More to Shakespeare*. Chicago: University of Chicago Press.

Habermas, Jürgen. 1984. *The Theory of Communicative Action, Vol. I: Reason and the Rationalization of Society*. Boston: Beacon Press.

    1993. *Justification and Application: Remarks on Discourse Ethics*. Cambridge, MA: MIT Press.

Hays, Sharon. 1994. "Structure and Agency and the Sticky Problem of Culture." *Sociological Theory* 12, 1: 57–72.

Horkheimer, Max and Theodor W. Adorno. 1972. *Dialectic of Enlightenment*. New York: Continuum Publishing.

Hymes, Dell. 1964. *Language in Culture and Society*. New York: Harper & Row.

Jacobs, Ronald. 1996. "Civil Society and Crisis: Culture, Discourse, and the Rodney King Beating." *American Journal of Sociology* 101: 1238–72.

    2000. *Race, Media, and the Crisis of Civil Society*. Cambridge: Cambridge University Press.

Jameson, Frederic. 1991. *The Postmodern Condition, or, The Cultural Logic of Late Capitalism*. Durham: Duke University Press.

Kane, Anne E. 1991. "Cultural Analysis in Historical Sociology: The Analytic and Concrete Forms of the Autonomy of Culture." *Sociological Theory* 9, 1: 53–69.

    1997. "Theorizing Meaning Construction in Social Movements: Symbolic Structures and Interpretation during the Irish Land War, 1879–1882." *Sociological Theory* 15: 249–76.

Lukes, Steven. 1975. "Political Ritual and Social Integration." *Sociology* 2: 289–308.

MacAloon, John. 1984. "Introduction: Cultural Performances, Culture Theory," pp. 1–18, in *Rite, Drama, Festival, Spectacle: Rehearsals Toward a Theory of Cultural Performance*, ed. John MacAloon. Philadelphia: Institute for the Study of Human Issues.

MacKenzie, Jon. 1998. "Gender Trouble: (the) Butler Did It," pp. 217–35 in *The Ends of Performance*, ed. Peggy Phelan and Jill Lane. New York: New York University Press.

    2001. *Perform or Else: From Discipline to Performance*. New York: Routledge.

Magnuson, Eric. 1997. "Ideological Conflict in American Political Culture." *International Journal of Sociology and Social Policy* 17, 6: 84–130.

Mannheim, Karl. 1971 [1927]. "Conservative Thought," in *From Karl Mannheim*, ed. Kurt H. Wolff. New York: Oxford University Press.

Marvin, Carolyn and David W. Ingle. 1999. *Blood Sacrifice and the Nation: Totem Rituals and the American Flag*. New York: Cambridge University Press.

Marx, Karl. 1972. "Theses on Feuerbach," pp. 143–45, in *The Marx–Engels Reader*, 2nd edn., ed. R. Tucker. New York: W. W. Norton & Co.

Morris, Charles Williams. 1938. *Foundations of the Theory of Signs*. Chicago: University of Chicago Press.

Nietzsche, Friedrich. 2000 [1927]. *The Birth of Tragedy*. New York: Oxford University Press.

Oakeshott, Michael. 1981 [1962]. "Rationalism in Politics," pp. 1–36 in *Rationalism in Politics and Other Essays*. New York: Methuen.

Peters, Julie Stone. 2000. *Theatre of the Book, 1480–1880 – Print, Text, and Performance in Europe*. New York: Oxford University Press.

Phelan, Peggy. 1993. *Unmarked: The Politics of Performance*. New York: Routledge.

Rambo, Eric and Elaine Chan. 1990. "Text, Structure, and Action in Cultural Sociology." *Theory and Society* 19: 635–48.

Ricoeur, Paul. 1971. "The Model of the Text: Meaningful Action Considered as a Text." *Social Research* 38: 529–62.

1976. *Interpretation Theory: Discourse and the Surplus of Meaning*. Fort Worth: Texas Christian University Press.

Roach, Joseph. 1996. *Cities of the Dead: Circum-Atlantic Performance*. New York: Columbia University Press.

2000. "Cutting Loose: Burying the 'First Man of Jazz,'" pp. 3–14 in *Joyous Wakes, Dignified Dying: Issues in Death and Dying*, ed. Robert Harvey and E. Ann Kaplan. Stony Brook: Humanities Institute of the State University of New York at Stony Brook.

Sahlins, Marshall. 1976. *Culture and Practical Reason*. Chicago: Chicago University Press.

1981. *Historical Metaphors and Mythical Realities: Structure in the Early History of the Sandwich Islands Kingdom*. Ann Arbor: University of Michigan Press.

Saussure, Ferdinand de. 1985. "The Linguistic Sign," pp. 28–46 in *Semiotics: An Introductory Anthology*, ed. Robert E. Innis. Bloomington: Indiana University Press.

Schechner, Richard. 1977. *Essays on Performance Theory 1970–1976*. New York: Drama Book Specialists.

1985. *Between Theatre and Anthropology*. Philadelphia: University of Pennsylvania Press.

1988. *Performance Theory*. New York: Routledge.

1998. "What is Performance Studies Anyway," pp. 357–62 in *The Ends of Performance*, ed. Peggy Phelan and Jill Lane. New York: New York University Press.

2002. *Performance Studies: An Introduction*. New York: Routledge.

Schegloff, Emanuel A. 1987. "Between Macro and Micro: Contexts and Other Connections," pp. 207–34, in *The Micro-Macro Link*, ed. J. Alexander, B. Giesen, R. Munch, and N. Smelser. Berkeley: University of California Press.

Schudson, Michael. 1998. *The Good Citizen: A History of American Civic Life*. New York: Free Press.

Searle, John. 1961. *Speech Acts: An Essay in the Philosophy of Language*. Cambridge: Cambridge University Press.

Selznick, Philip. 1951. "Institutional Vulnerability in Mass Society." *The American Journal of Sociology* 56: 320–31.

1952. *The Organizational Weapon*. New York: McGraw-Hill.

Sewell, William Jr. 1985. "Ideologies and Social Revolutions: Reflections on the French Case." *Journal of Modern History* 57: 57–85.

1992. "A Theory of Structure: Duality, Agency, and Transformation," pp. 188–201, reprinted in *The New American Cultural Sociology,* ed. Phillip Smith. Cambridge: Cambridge University Press.

Sherwood, Steven Jay. 1994. "Narrating the Social: Postmodernism and the Drama of Democracy." *Journal of Narrative and Life History* 4: 69–88.

Shils, Edward and Michael Young. 1953. "The Meaning of the Coronation." *Sociological Review* 1: 63–81.

Singer, Milton. 1959. *Traditional India: Structure and Change*. Philadelphia: American Folklore Society.

Smith, Philip. 1991. "Codes and Conflict: Toward a Theory of War as Ritual." *Theory and Society* 20, 1: 103–38.

1996. "Executing Executions: Aesthetics, Identity and the Problematic Narratives of Capital Punishment Ritual." *Theory and Society* 25, 2: 235–61.

Smith, Philip, ed. 1998. "The New American Cultural Sociology," pp. 1–14 in *The New American Cultural Sociology*, ed. Philip Smith. Cambridge: Cambridge University Press.

Somers, Margaret R. 1995. "Narrating and Naturalizing Civil Society and Citizenship Theory: The Place of Political Culture and the Public Sphere." *Sociological Theory* 13: 229–74.

Swidler, Ann. 1986. "Culture in Action: Symbols and Strategies." *American Sociological Review* 51: 273–86.

Taylor, Diana. 1995. "Performing Gender: Las Madres de la Plaza de Mayo," pp. 275–305 in *Negotiating Performance: Gender, Sexuality, and Theatricality in Latin/o American*, ed. Diana Taylor and Juan Villegas. Durham: Duke University Press.

Thompson, Kenneth. 1990. "Secularization and Sacralization," pp. 161–81 in *Rethinking Progress: Movements, Forces, and Ideas at the end of the 20th Century*, ed. J. C. Alexander and P. Sztompka. Boston: Unwin Hyman.

Turner, Jonathan. 2002. *Face to Face: Toward a Sociological Theory of Interpersonal Behavior*. Stanford: Stanford University Press.

Turner, Victor. 1969. *The Ritual Process: Structure and Anti-structure*. New York: Aldine De Gruyter.

1974a. *Dramas, Fields, and Metaphors*. Ithaca: Cornell University Press.

1974b. "Religious Paradigms and Political Action: Thomas Becket at the Council of Northampton," pp. 60–97 in *Dramas, Fields, and Metaphors*. Ithaca: Cornell University Press.

1982. *From Ritual to Theater: The Human Seriousness of Play*. New York: PAJ Publications.

Wagner-Pacifici, Robin E. 1986. *The Moro Morality Play: Terrorism as Social Drama*. Chicago: University of Chicago Press.

Warner, W. Lloyd. 1959. *The Living and the Dead: A Study of the Symbolic Life of Americans*. New Haven: Yale University Press.

1

Cultural pragmatics: social performance between ritual and strategy

Jeffrey C. Alexander

From its very beginnings, the social study of culture has been polarized between structuralist theories that treat meaning as a text and investigate the patterning that provides relative autonomy and pragmatist theories that treat meaning as emerging from the contingencies of individual and collective action – so-called practices – and that analyze cultural patterns as reflections of power and material interest. In this chapter, I present a theory of cultural pragmatics that transcends this division, bringing meaning structures, contingency, power, and materiality together in a new way. My argument is that the materiality of practices should be replaced by the more multidimensional concept of performances. Drawing on the new field of performance studies, cultural pragmatics demonstrates how social performances, whether individual or collective, can be analogized systemically to theatrical ones. After defining the elements of social performance, I suggest that these elements have become "de-fused" as societies have become more complex. Performances are successful only insofar as they can "re-fuse" these increasingly disentangled elements. In a fused performance, audiences identify with actors, and cultural scripts achieve verisimilitude through effective *mise-en-scène*. Performances fail when this relinking process is incomplete: the elements of performance remain apart, and social action seems inauthentic and artificial, failing to persuade. Re-fusion, by contrast, allows actors to communicate the meanings of their actions successfully and thus to pursue their interests effectively.

Rituals are episodes of repeated and simplified cultural communication in which the direct partners to a social interaction, and those observing it, share a mutual belief in the descriptive and prescriptive validity of the communication's symbolic contents and accept the authenticity of one another's intentions. It is because of this shared understanding of intention and content, and in the intrinsic validity of the interaction, that rituals have their effect and affect. Ritual effectiveness energizes the participants and attaches them to each other, increases their identification with the symbolic objects of communication, and intensifies the connection of the participants and the symbolic objects with the observing audience, the relevant "community" at large.

If there is one cultural quality that marks the earliest forms of human social organization, it is the centrality of rituals. From births to conjugal relationships, from peaceful foreign relations to the preparation for war, from the healing of the sick to the celebration of collective well-being, from transitions through the age structure to the assumption of new occupational and political roles, the affirmation of leadership and the celebration of anniversaries – in earlier forms of society such social processes tended to be marked by ritualized symbolic communication. If there is one cultural quality that differentiates more contemporary, large-scale, and complex social organizations from earlier forms, it is that the centrality of such ritual processes has been displaced. Contemporary societies revolve around open-ended conflicts between parties who do not necessarily share beliefs, frequently do not accept the validity of one another's intention, and often disagree even about the descriptions that people offer for acts.

Social observers, whether they are more scientific or more philosophical, have found innumerable ways to conceptualize this historical transformation, starting with such thoroughly discredited evolutionary contrasts as primitive/advanced or barbarian/civilized, and moving on to more legitimate but still overly binary distinctions such as traditional/modern, oral/literate, or simple/complex. One does not have to be an evolutionist or to accept the simplifying dichotomies of metahistory to see that a broad change has occurred. Max Weber pitted his contingent historical approach against every shred of evolutionary thinking, yet this decentering of ritual was precisely what he meant by the movement from charisma to routinization and from traditional to value and goal-rational society. Rather than being organized primarily through rituals that affirm metaphysical and consensual beliefs, contemporary societies have opened themselves to processes of negotiations and reflexivity about means and ends, with the result that conflict, disappointment, and feelings of bad faith are at least as common as integration, affirmation, and the energizing of the collective spirit.

Still, most of us who live in these more reflexive and fragmented societies are also aware that, for better and for worse, such processes of rationalization in fact have not completely won the day (Alexander 2003a). There is a continuing symbolic intensity based on repeated and simplified cognitive and moral frames (Goffman 1967, 1974) that continues to mark all sorts of individual and private relationships. More public and collective processes – from social movements (Eyerman and Jamison 1991) to wars (Smith 1993), revolutions (Apter and Saich 1994; Hunt 1984; Sewell 1980), and political transitions (Giesen, this volume; Edles 1998), and even to the construction of scientific communities (Hagstrom 1965) – continue to depend on the simplifying structures of symbolic communications and on cultural interactions that rely on, and to some degree can generate, intuitive and unreflective trust (Sztompka 1999; Barber 1983). It might even be said that, in a differentiated, stratified, and reflexive society, a strategy's success depends on belief in the validity of the cultural contents of the strategist's symbolic communication and on accepting the authenticity and even the sincerity of another's strategic intentions. Virtually every kind of modern collectivity, moreover, seems to depend at one time or another on integrative processes that create some sense of shared identity (Giesen 1998; Spillman 1997; Ringmar 1996), even if these are forged, as they all too often are, in opposition to simplistic constructions of those who are putatively on the other side (Jacobs 2000; Ku 1999; Chan 1999).

At both the micro and the macro levels, both among individuals and between and within collectivities, our societies still seem to be permeated by symbolic, ritual-like activities. It is precisely this notion of "ritual-like," however, that indicates the puzzle we face. We are aware that very central processes in complex societies are symbolic, and that sometimes they are also integrative, at the group, inter-group, and even societal level. But we also clearly sense that these processes are not rituals in the traditional sense (cf. Lukes 1977). Even when they affirm validity and authenticity and produce integration, their effervescence is short-lived. If they have achieved simplicity, it is unlikely they will be repeated. If they are repeated, it is unlikely that the symbolic communication can ever be so simplified in the same way again.

This is the puzzle to which the present chapter is addressed. Is it possible to develop a theory that can explain how the integration of particular groups and sometimes even whole collectivities can be achieved through symbolic communications, while continuing to account for cultural complexity and contradiction, for institutional differentiation, contending social power, and segmentation? Can a theory give full credence to the continuing role of belief while acknowledging that unbelief and criticism are also the central hallmarks of our time?

In order to solve this puzzle, I will develop a systematic, macro-sociological model of social action as cultural performance. In so doing, I will enter not only into the historical origins of theatrical performance and dramaturgical theory (e.g. Turner 2002; Schechner 2002; Auslander 1997; Carlson 1996; Geertz 1980; Goffman 1974; Burke 1965; Austin 1957) but also into the history and theories of social performance.[1] This means looking at how, and why, symbolic action moved from ritual to theatre (Turner 1982) and why it so often moves back to "ritual-like" processes again (Schechner 1976).

The gist of my argument can be stated simply. The more simple the collective organization, the less its social and cultural parts are segmented and differentiated, the more the elements of social performances are *fused*. The more complex, segmented, and differentiated the collectivity, the more these elements of social performance become *de-fused*. To be effective in a society of increasing complexity, social performances must engage in a project of *re-fusion*. To the degree they achieve re-fusion, social performances become convincing and effective – more ritual-like. To the degree that social performances remain de-fused, they seem artificial and contrived, less like rituals than like performances in the pejorative sense. They are less effective as a result. Failed performances are those in which the actor, whether individual or collective, has been unable to sew back together the elements of performance to make them seem connected seamlessly. This performative failure makes it much more difficult for the actor to realize his or her intentions in a practical way.

This argument points immediately to the question of just what the elements of social performance are. I will elucidate these in the section immediately following. Then, with this analytical model of social performance safely in hand, I will turn back to the historical questions of what allowed earlier societies to more frequently make their performances into rituals and how later social developments created the ambiguous and slippery contexts for performative action in which we find ourselves today. Once this historical argument is established, I will come back to the model of performative success and failure and will elaborate its interdependent elements in more detail.

The elements of cultural performance

Cultural performance is the social process by which actors, individually or in concert, display for others the meaning of their social situation. This meaning may or may not be one to which they themselves subjectively adhere; it is the meaning that they, as social actors, consciously or unconsciously wish to have others believe. In order for their display to be effective, actors must offer a plausible performance, one that leads those to whom their actions and gestures are directed to accept their motives and explanations as a reasonable account (Scott and Lyman 1968; Garfinkel 1967). As Gerth and Mills (1964: 55) once put it, "Our gestures do not necessarily 'express' our prior feelings," but rather "they make available to others a sign." Successful performance depends on the ability to convince others that one's performance is true, with all the ambiguities that the notion of aesthetic truth implies. Once we understand cultural performance in this way, we can easily make out the basic elements that compose it.

*Systems of collective representation: background symbols and
foreground scripts*

Marx ([1852] 1962: 247) observed that "just when they seem engaged in rev-
olutionizing themselves and things, in creating something that has never yet
existed," social actors "anxiously conjure up the spirits of the past to their service and borrow from them names, battle cries, and costumes in order to present
the new scene of world history in this time-honored disguise and this borrowed
language." Marx is describing here the systems of collective representations
that background every performative act.

Actors present themselves as being motivated by and towards existential, emotional, and moral concerns, the meanings of which are defined by
patterns of signifiers whose referents are the social, physical, natural, and
cosmological worlds within which actors and audiences live. One part of
this symbolic reference provides the deep background of collective representations for social performance; another part composes the foreground,
the scripts that are the immediate referent for action. These latter can be
understood as constituting the performance's immediate referential text. As
constructed by the performative imagination, background and foreground symbols are structured by codes that provide analogies and antipathies and by
narratives that provide chronologies. In symbolizing actors' and audiences'
worlds, these narratives and codes simultaneously condense and elaborate,
and they employ a wide range of rhetorical devices, from metaphor to synecdoche, to configure social and emotional life in compelling and coherent
ways. Systems of collective representations range from "time immemorial"
myths to invented traditions created right on the spot, from oral traditions
to scripts prepared by such specialists as playwrights, journalists, and speech
writers.

Like any other text, these collective representations, whether background or
foreground, can be evaluated for their dramatic effectiveness. I will say more
about this later, but what is important at this point is to see that no matter
how intrinsically effective, collective representations do not speak themselves.
Boulton (1960: 3) once described theatre as "literature that walks and talks
before our eyes." It is this need for walking and talking – and seeing and
listening to the walking and talking – that makes the practical pragmatics of
performance different from the cultural logic of texts. It is at this conjuncture
that cultural pragmatics is born.

Actors

These patterned representations are put into practice, or are encoded (Hall
1980), by flesh-and-blood people. As Reiss (1971: 138) suggested in his study

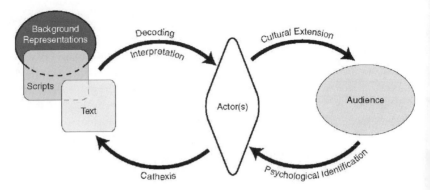

Figure 1.1   Successful performance: re-fusion

of the relation between theatrical technique and meaning in seventeenth-century French theatre, "the actor is as real as the spectator; he is in fact present in their midst." Whether or not they are consciously aware of the distinction between collective representations and their walking and talking, the actor's aim is to make this distinction disappear. As Reiss (1971: 142) put it, the actor's desire is "to cause the spectator to confuse his emotions with those of the stage character." While performers must be oriented to background and foreground representations, their motivations vis-à-vis these patterns are contingent. In psychological terms, the relation between actor and text depends on cathexis. The relation between actor and audience, in turn, depends on the ability to project these emotions and textual patterns as moral evaluations. If those who perform cultural scripts do not possess the requisite skills (Bauman 1989), then they may fail miserably in the effort to project their meanings effectively.

Observers/audience

Cultural texts are performed so that meanings can be displayed to others. "Others" constitute the audience of observers for cultural performance. They decode what actors have encoded (Hall 1980), but they do so in variable ways. If cultural texts are to be communicated convincingly, there needs to be a process of cultural extension that expands from script and actor to audience. Cultural extension must be accompanied by a process of psychological identification, such that the members of the audience project themselves into the characters they see onstage.

There is empirical variation in the extent to which cultural extension and psychological identification actually occur. Audiences may be focused or

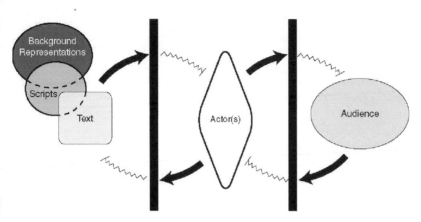

Figure 1.2   Performance failure: de-fusion

distracted, attentive or uninterested (Verdery 1991: 6; Berezin 1997: 28, 35, 250). Even if actors cathect to cultural texts, and even if they themselves possess high levels of cultural proficiency, their projections still may not be persuasive to the audience/observers. Observation can be merely cognitive. An audience can see and can understand without experiencing emotional or moral significa-tion. As we will see in the following section, there are often social explanations of this variability. Audiences may represent social statuses orthogonal to the status of performers. Audience attendance may not be required, or it may be merely compelled. Critics can intervene between performance and audience. There might not be an audience in the contemporary sense at all, but only partic-ipants observing themselves and their fellow performers. This latter condition facilitates cultural identification and psychological extension, though it is a con-dition much less frequently encountered in the complex societies of the present day.

Means of symbolic production

In order to perform a cultural text before an audience, actors need access to the mundane material things that allow symbolic projections to be made. They need objects that can serve as iconic representations to help them dramatize and make vivid the invisible motives and morals they are trying to represent. This material ranges from clothing to every other sort of "standardized expressive equipment" (Goffman 1956: 34–51). Actors also require a physical place to perform and the means to assure the transmission of their performance to an audience.

Mise-en-scène

With texts and means in hand, and audience(s) before them, social actors engage in dramatic social action, entering into and projecting the ensemble of physical and verbal gestures that constitutes performance. This ensemble of gestures involves more than the symbolic devices that structure a non-performed symbolic text. If a text is to walk and talk, it must be sequenced temporally and choreographed spatially (e.g. Berezin 1997: 156). The exigencies of time and space create specific aesthetic demands; at some historical juncture, new social roles like director and producer emerge that specialize in this task of putting text "into the scene."

Social power

The distribution of power in society – the nature of its political, economic, and status hierarchies, and the relations among its elites – profoundly affects the performance process. Power establishes an external boundary for cultural pragmatics that parallels the internal boundary established by a performance's background representations. Not all texts are equally legitimate in the eyes of the powers that be, whether possessors of material or interpretive power. Not all performances, and not all parts of a particular performance, are allowed to proceed. Will social power (Mann 1986) seek to eliminate certain parts of a cultural text? Who will be allowed to act in a performance, and with what means? Who will be allowed to attend? What kinds of responses will be permitted from audience/observer? Are there powers that have the authority to interpret performances independently of those that have the authority to produce them? Are these interpretive powers also independent of the actors and the audience itself, or are social power, symbolic knowledge, and interpretive authority much more closely linked?

Every social performance, whether individual or collective, is affected fundamentally by each of the elements presented here. In the language of hermeneutics, this sketch of interdependent elements provides a framework for the interpretive reconstruction of the meanings of performative action. In the language of explanation, it provides a model of causality. One can say that every social performance is determined partly by each of the elements I have laid out – that each is a necessary but not sufficient cause of every performative act. While empirically interrelated, each element has some autonomy, not only analytically but empirically vis-à-vis the others. Taken together, they determine, and measure, whether and how a performance occurs, and the degree to which it succeeds or fails in its effect. Two pathways lead out from the discussion thus far. The analytic model can be developed further, elaborating the nature of each factor and its interrelations with the others. I will take up this task in a later section. Before doing so, I will engage in a historical discussion. I wish to explore how the analytical model I have just laid out, despite the fact it is so far only presented very simply, already provides significant insight into the central puzzle of ritual and rationalization with which I introduced this chapter and that defines its central question.

The conditions for performativity: historical transformations

The model of performance I am developing here provides a new way of looking at cultural and organizational change over broad spans of historical time. We can see differently how and why rituals were once so central to band and tribal societies and why the nature of symbolic action changed so remarkably with the rise of states, empires, and churches. We can understand why both the theatre and the democratic *polis* arose for the first time in ancient Greece and why theatre emerged once again during the early modern period at the same time as open-ended social dramas became central to determining the nature of social and political authority. We can understand why Romanticism, secularization, and industrial society made the authenticity of symbolic action such a central question for modern times.

Old-fashioned rituals: symbolic performances in early societies

Colonial and modernist thinkers were deeply impressed by the ritualistic processes that explorers and anthropologists observed when they encountered societies that had not experienced "civilization" or "modernity." Some associated the frequency of rituals with the putative purity of early societies (Huizinga [1938] 1950) and others with some sort of distinctively primitive, non-rational mentality (Lévy-Bruhl 1923). Huizinga ([1938] 1950: 14), for example, stressed that rituals create not a "sham reality" but "a mystical one," in which "something invisible and inactual takes beautiful, actual, holy form." Less romantic observers still emphasized the automatic, predictable, engulfing, and spontaneous qualities of ritual life. Weber exemplified this understanding in a sociological manner; it also marked the modern anthropological approach to ritual that became paradigmatic. Turner (1977: 183) defined rituals as "stereotyped" and as "sequestered"; Goody (1986: 21) called them "homeostatic"; and Leach (1972: 334), insisting also on "repetition," expresses his wonderment at how, in the rituals he observed, "everything in fact happened just as predicted" (1972: 199).

Against these arguments for the essential and fundamental difference of symbolic interactions in earlier societies, critical and postmodern anthropologists have argued for their more "conjunctural" (Clifford 1988: 11) quality. Those mysterious rituals that aroused such intense admiration and curiosity among earlier observers, it is argued, should be seen not as expressions of some distinctive essence but simply as a different kind of practice (Conquergood 1992). The model I am developing here allows us to frame this important insight in a more nuanced, less polemical, and more empirically oriented way. Rituals in early societies, I wish to suggest, were not so much *practices* as *performances*, and in this they indeed are made of the same stuff as social actions in more complex societies. In an introduction to his edition of Turner's posthumous essays, Schechner (1987: 7) suggested that "all performance has at its core a ritual action." It is better, I think, to reverse this statement, and to say that all ritual has at its core a performative act.

This is not to deny the differences between rituals and performances of other kinds. What it does suggest, however, is that they exist on the same continuum and that the difference between them is a matter of variation, not fundamental type. Ritual performances reflect the social structures and cultures of their historically situated societies. They are distinctive in that they are fused. Fusion is much more likely to be achieved in the conditions of less complex societies, but it occurs in complex societies as well.

To see why performances in simpler societies more frequently became rituals, we must examine how early social structure and culture defined the elements of performance and related them to one another in a distinctive way. The explanation can be found in their much smaller size and scale; in the more mythical and metaphysical nature of their beliefs; and in the more integrated and overlapping nature of their institutions, culture, and social structures. Membership in the earliest human societies (Service 1962, 1979) was organized around the axes of kinship, age, and gender. Forming collectivities of sixty to eighty members, people supported themselves by hunting and gathering and participated in a small set of social roles with which every person was thoroughly familiar. By all accounts, the subjectivity that corresponded with this kind of social organization resembled what Stanner (1972), when speaking of the Australian Aboriginals, called "dream time." Such consciousness merged mundane and practical dimensions with the sacred and metaphysical to the extent that religion did not exist as a separate form. In such societies, as Service (1962: 109) once remarked, "there is no religious organization" that is "separated from family and band."

The structural and cultural organization of such early forms of societies suggests differences in the kinds of social performance they can produce. The collective representations to which these social performances refer are not texts composed by specialists for segmented subgroups in complex and contentious social orders. Nor do these collective representations form a critical "metacommentary" (Geertz 1973) on social life, for there does not yet exist deep tension between mundane and transcendental spheres (Goody 1986; Habermas 1982–3; Eisenstadt 1982; Bellah 1970). The early anthropologists Spencer and Gillen (1927) were right at least in this, for they suggested that the Engwura ritual cycle of the Australian Arunta recapitulated the actual lifestyle of the Arunta males. A century later, when Schechner (1976: 197) observed the Tsembaga dance of the Kaiko, he confirmed that "all the basic moves and sounds – even the charge into the central space – are adaptations and direct lifts from battle."

The tight intertwining of cultural text and social structure that marks social performances in early societies provides a contextual frame for Durkheim's theoretical argument about religion as simply society writ large. While claiming to propose a paradigm for studying every religion at all times, Durkheim might better be understood as describing the context for social performances in early societies. Durkheim insists that culture is identical with religion, that any "proper" religious belief is shared by every member of the group, and that these shared beliefs are always translated into the practices he calls rituals, or rites. "Not only are they individually accepted by *all members* of that group, but they also belong *to* the group and *unify* it . . . A society whose members are united because they imagine the sacred world and its relation with the profane world *in the same way*, and because they *translate* this common representation into identical practices, is called a Church" (Durkheim [1912] 1995: 41, italics added).[2]

In such ritualized performances, the belief dimension is experienced as personal, immediate, and iconographic. Through the painting, masking, and reconfiguring of the physical body, the actors in these performances seek not only metaphorically but literally to become the text, their goal being to project the fusion of human and totem, "man and God," sacred and mundane. The symbolic roles that define participation in such ritualized performances emerge directly, and without mediation, from the other social roles actors play. In the Engwura ritual (Spencer and Gillen 1927), the Arunta males performed the parts they actually held in everyday Arunta life. When social actors perform such roles, they do not have a sense of separation from them; they have little self-consciousness about themselves as actors. For participants and observers, rituals are not considered to be a performance in the contemporary sense at all but rather to be a natural and necessary dimension of ongoing social life. As for the means of symbolic production, while not always immediately available, they generally are near at hand – a ditch dug with the sharp bones of animals, a line drawn from the red coloring of wild flowers, a headdress made from bird feathers, an amulet fashioned from a parrot's beak (Turner 1969: 23–37).

In this type of social organization, participation in ritual performance is not contingent, either for the actors or the observers. Participation is determined by the established and accepted hierarchies of gender and age, not by individual choices that respond to the sanctions and rewards of social powers or segmented social groups. Every relevant party in the band or tribe must attend to ritual performances. Many ceremonies involve the entire community, for they "regard their collective well-being to be dependent upon a common body of ritual performances" (Rappaport 1968, in Schechner 1976: 211). Turner (1982: 31, original italics) attested that "the *whole* community goes through the *entire* ritual round." Durkheim ([1912] 1995) also emphasized obligation, connecting it with the internal coherence of the audience. In the ritual phase of Aboriginal society, he wrote, "the population comes together, concentrating itself at specific places . . . The concentration takes place when a clan or a portion of the tribe is summoned to come together" ([1912] 1995: 217).

Nor are attendees only observers. At various points in the ritual, those merely watching the ritual performance are called upon to participate – sometimes as principals and at other times as members of an attentive chorus providing remonstrations of approval through such demonstrative acts as shouting, crying, and applause. At key phases in male initiation ceremonies, for example, women attend closely and, at particular moments, play significant ritual roles (Schechner 2002). They express indifference and rejection early in the performance and display physical signs of welcome and admiration in order to mark its end. Even when they do not participate, ritual audiences are hardly strangers. They are linked to performers by direct or indirect family ties.

In terms of the elementary model I have laid out already, it seems clear that such ritualized social actions fuse the various components of performance – actors, audiences, representations, means of symbolic production, social power, and *mise-en-scène*.

It is the actor/audience part of this fusion to which Service (1962: 109) referred when he wrote that "the congregation is the camp itself." Lévi-Strauss (1963: 179) meant to emphasize the same fusing when he spoke of the "fabulation" of ritual as a "threefold experience." It consists "first of the shaman himself, who, if his calling is a true one . . . undergoes specific states of a psychosomatic nature; second, that of the sick person, who may or may not experience an improvement of his condition; and, finally, that of the public, who also participates in the cure, experiencing an enthusiasm and an intellectual and emotional satisfaction which produce collective support." In the studies of shamanistic rituals offered by postmodern performance theorists, we can read their ethnographic accounts as suggesting fusion in much the same way. "They derive their power from listening to the others and absorbing daily realities. While they cure, they take into them their patients' possessions and obsessions and let the latter's illnesses become theirs . . . The very close relationship these

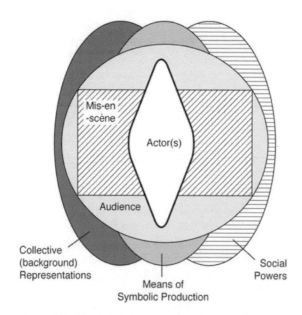

Figure 1.3   The fused elements of performance inside simple social organization

healers maintain with their patients remains the determining factor of the cure" (Trinh 1989, in Conquergood 1992: 44).

With sacred texts tied to mundane society, actors' roles tied to social roles, performance directly expressing symbolic text and social life, obligatory participation, and homogeneous and attentive audiences it is hardly surprising that the effects of ritual performances tend to be immediate and only infrequently depart from the expectations of actors and scripts (cf. Schechner 1976: 205, 1981: 92–4). As Lévi-Strauss attested (1963: 168, italics added), "There is . . . no reason to doubt the efficacy of certain magical practices" precisely because "the efficacy of magic implies *a belief in* magic." Rites not only mark transitions but also create them, such that the participants become something or somebody else as a result. Ritual performance not only symbolizes a social relationship or change; it also actualizes it. There is a direct effect, without mediation.

Anthropologists who have studied rituals in earlier forms of society reported that the tricks of ritual specialists rarely were scrutinized. Lévi-Strauss (1963: 179) emphasized the role of "group consensus" when he began his famous retelling of Boas's ethnography of Quesalid. The Kwakiutl Indian was so unusually curious as to insist (at first) that the sorcerer's rituals indeed were tricks. Yet after persuading ritual specialists to teach him the tricks of their trade, Quesalid himself went on to become a great shaman. "Quesalid did not become a great shaman because he cured his patients," Lévi-Strauss assures us; rather, "he cured his patients because he had *become* a great shaman" (1963: 180, italics added). Shamans effect cures, individual and social, because participants and observers of their performances believe they have the force to which they lay claim. Shamans, in other words, are institutionalized masters of ritual performance. The success of this performance depends, in the first place, on their dramatic skills, but these skills are intertwined with the other dimensions that allow performances to be fused in simple social organizations.

Social complexity and post-ritual performances

Fused performances creating ritual-like effects remain important in more complex societies. There are two senses in which this is true. First, and less importantly for the argument I am developing here, in primary groups such as families, gangs, and intergenerationally stable ethnic communities, role performances often seem to reproduce the macrocosm in the microcosm (Slater 1966). Even inside of complex societies, audiences in such primary groups are relatively homogeneous, actors are familiar, situations are repeated, and texts and traditions, while once invented, eventually take on a time immemorial quality. The second sense in which ritual-like effects remain central, more importantly for my argument here, is that fusion remains the goal of performances even in complex societies. It is the context for performative success that has changed.

   As I noted earlier, historians, anthropologists, and sociologists have analyzed the sporadic and uneven processes that created larger-scale societies in innumerably different ways. There is sharply contrasting theorizing about the causes and pathways of the movement away from simpler social organization in which ritual played a central role to more complex social forms, which feature more strategic, reflexive, and managed forms of symbolic communication. But there is wide consensus that such a transformation did occur, that the processes of "complexification," "rationalization," or "differentiation" (Thrift 1999; Luhmann 1995; Champagne 1992; Alexander and Colomy 1990; Habermas 1982–3; Eisenstadt 1963) produce different kinds of symbolic communications today. Even Goody (1986: 22) spoke confidently of the transition "from worldview to ideology."

   This emphasis on ideology is telling, and it leads directly to the argument about changes in the conditions for performativity that I am making here. Earlier sociological and anthropological investigations into the social causes of the transition from simple forms of social organization emphasized the determining role of economic change. Technological shifts created more productivity, which led to surplus and the class system, and finally to the first distinctive political institutions, whose task was to organize the newly stratified society and to administer material and organizational needs. By the end of the 1950s, however, anthropologists already had begun to speak less of technological changes than shifts in economic orientations and regimes. When Fried (1971: 103) explained "the move from egalitarian to rank society," he described a shift "from an economy dominated by reciprocity to one having redistribution as a major device." In the same kind of anti-determinist vein, when Service (1962: 171) explained movement beyond the monolithic structures of early societies to the "twin forms of authority" that sustained distinctive economic and political elites, he described it as "made *possible* by greater productivity" (1962: 143, italics added). Sahlins (1972) built on such arguments to suggest that it was not the economic inability to create surplus that prevented growth but the ideological desire to maintain a less productivity-driven, more leisurely style of life. Nolan and Lenski (1995) made the point of this conceptual-cum-empirical development impossible to overlook: "Technological advance created the possibility of a surplus, but to transform that possibility into a reality required an ideology that *motivated* farmers to produce more than they needed to stay alive and productive, and *persuaded* them to turn that surplus over to someone else" (1995: 157, italics added). As this last comment makes clear, this whole historiographic transition in the anthropology of early transitions points to the critical role of ideological projects. The creation of surplus depended on new motivations, which could come about only through the creation of symbolic performances to persuade others, not through their material coercion.

The most striking social innovation that crystallized such a cultural shift to ideology was the emergence of written texts. According to Goody (1986: 12), the emergence of text-based culture allowed and demanded "the decontextualization or generalization" of collective representations, which in oral societies were intertwined more tightly with local social structures and meanings. With writing, the "communicative context has changed dramatically both as regards the emitter and as regards the receivers" (1986: 13): "In their very nature written statements of the law, of norms, of rules, have had to be abstracted from particular situations in order to be addressed to a universal audience out there, rather than delivered face-to-face to a specific group of people at a particular time and place" (1986: 13). Only symbolic projection beyond the local would allow groups to use economic surplus to create more segmented, unequal, and differentiated societies. Without the capacity for such ideological projection, how else would these kinds of more fragmented social orders ever be coordinated, much less integrated in an asymmetrical way?

These structural and ideological processes suggest a decisive shift in actors' relation to the means of symbolic production. In text-based societies, literacy is essential if the symbolic processes that legitimate social structure are to be carried out successfully. Because literacy is difficult and expensive, priests "have privileged access to the sacred texts." This allows "the effective control of the means of literate communication," concentrating interpretive authority in elite hands (Goody 1986: 16–17). Alongside this new emergence of monopoly power, indeed because of it, there emerges the necessity for exercising tight control over performance in order to project this ideological control over distantiated and subordinate groups. Evans-Pritchard (1940: 172, italics added) once wrote that, in order to "allow him to *play the part he plays* in feuds and quarrels," the Nuer chief needs only "ritual qualifications." Because the Nuer "have no law or government," or any significant social stratification, obeying their chief follows from the perception that "they are sacred persons" (1940: 173). In his study of the origins of political empires, Eisenstadt (1963: 65) demonstrated, by contrast, that: with the "relative autonomy of the religious sphere and its 'disembeddedness' from the total community and from the other institutional spheres," everything about political legitimation has changed. The sacredness of the economic, political, and ideological elites now has to be achieved, not assigned. As Eisenstadt put it, these elites now "*tried to maintain dominance*" (1963: 65, italics added); it was not given automatically to them. "In all societies studied here, the rulers *attempted to portray* themselves and the political systems they established as the bearers of special cultural symbols and missions. They *tried to depict* themselves as transmitting distinct civilizations . . . The rulers of these societies invariably *tried to be perceived* as the propagators and upholders of [their] traditions [and they] desire[d] to minimize any group's pretensions to having the right *to judge and evaluate* the rulers or to sanction their legitimation" (Eisenstadt 1963: 141, italics added).

The most ambitious recent investigation into pharaonic Egypt finds the same processes at work. "A state imposed by force and coercing its subjects to pay taxes and perform civil and military service," Assmann (2002: 74) wrote, "could hardly have maintained itself if it had not rested on a core semiology that was as persuasive as the state itself was demanding." Reconstructing "the semantics that underlie the establishment of the state" (2002: 75), Assmann finds that in the Old Kingdom Egyptians "clung to the graphic realism of hieroglyphic writing" with an "astounding tenacity." This "aspiration to permanence" meant that state rituals involved "maximum care . . . to prevent deviation and improvisation." Only the lector priest's "knowledge of the script and his ability to recite accurately" could "ensure that precisely the same text was repeated at precisely the same time in the context of the same ritual event, thus bringing meaning, duration, and action into precise alignment" (2002: 70–1). By the time of the Middle Kingdom, Assmann reported (2002: 118–19), "the kings of the Twelfth Dynasty were in a fundamentally different position." Social and cultural complexity had proceeded to such an extent that the pharaonic rulers "had to assert themselves against a largely literate and economically and militarily powerful aristocracy . . . and win over the lower strata." These objectives "could not be achieved by force alone," Assmann wrote, "but only by the power of eloquence and explanation."

The assertion of political power was no longer a matter of apodictic self-glorification, but was accomplished . . . by the power of the word. "Be an artist in speech," recommends one text, "then you will be victorious. For behold: the sword-arm of a king is his tongue. Stronger is the word than all fighting." The kings of the Twelfth Dynasty understood the close links between politics and the instantiation of meaning. (2002: 118–19)

   In terms of the model I am developing here, these empirical accounts suggest de-fusion among the elements of performance: (1) the separation of written fore-ground texts from background collective representations; (2) the estrangement of the means of symbolic production from the mass of social actors; and (3) the separation of the elites who carried out central symbolic actions from their mass audiences. The appearance of seamlessness that made symbolic action seem ritualistic gives way to the appearance of greater artifice and planning. Performative action becomes more achieved and less automatic.

The emergence of theatrical from ritual performance

To this point in our historical discussion, my references to performance have been generated analytically, which is to say they have been warranted by the theoretical considerations presented in the first section. While it seems clear that the emergence of more segmented, complex, and stratified societies created the conditions – and even the necessity – for transforming rituals into performances, the latter, more contingent processes of symbolic communication were not understood by their creators or their audiences as contrived or theatrical in the contemporary sense. There was social and cultural differentiation, and the compulsion to project and not merely to assume the effects of symbolic action, but the elements of performance were still not defused enough to create self-consciousness about the artificiality of that process.

   Thus, when Frankfort (1948: 135–6) insisted on the "absence of drama" in ancient Egypt, he emphasized both the continuing fusion of sacred texts and actors and the relative inflexibility, or resistance to change, of ancient societies (cf. Kemp 1989: 1–16). "It is true," Frankfort conceded, "that within the Egyptian ritual the gods were sometimes represented by actors." For example, an embalming priest might be "wearing a jackal mask" to impersonate the god Anubis. In fact, one of the best-preserved Egyptian texts, the *Mystery Play of the Succession*, "was performed when a new king came to the throne." Nonetheless, Frankfort insists, such performances "do not represent a new art form." He calls them "simply the 'books' of rituals." They may be "dramatic," but "they

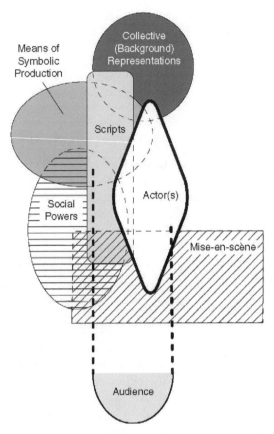

Figure 1.4   The de-fused elements of performance inside complex social organization

certainly are not drama." In drama, the meaning and consequences of action unfold, and in this sense are caused by, the theatrical challenge of *mise-en-scène*: "In drama, language is integrated with action and a change is shown to be a consequence of that action." In Egyptian rites, by contrast, as in Durkheim's Aboriginal ones, the "purpose is to *translate* actuality in the unchanging form of myth . . . The gods appear and speak once more the words they spoke 'the first time'" (Frankfort 1948: 135–6, italics added). It is the actuality of myth that marks ritual.

Only in the Greek city-states did drama in the contemporary sense emerge. The social organizational and cultural background for these developments was crucial, of course, even as the emergence of dramatic performance fed back into social and cultural organization in turn. As compared to the fused and ascriptive hierarchies that ruled urban societies in the Asian empires, in Greece there emerged urban structures of a new, more republican kind. They were organized and ruled by elites, to be sure, but these elites were internally democratic. As Schachermeyr ([1953] 1971: 201) emphasized in his widely cited essay, the historically unprecedented "autonomy of the citizen body" in the Greek cities was accompanied by the equally distinctive "emancipation of intellectual life from Greek mythology." These new forms of organizational and culture differentiation fostered, according to Schachermeyr, a "revolutionary spirit" that engaged in "a constant fight against the monarchical, dictatorial, or oligarchic forms of government."

This marked opening up of social and cultural space focused attention on the projective, performative dimension of social action, subjecting the ritual-ized performances of more traditional life to increased scrutiny and strain (e.g. Plato 1980). In Greek society, we can observe the transition from ritual to per-formance literally and not just metaphorically. We actually see the de-fusion of the elements of performance in concrete terms. They became more than analytically identifiable: their empirical separation became institutionalized in specialized forms of social structure and available to common-sense reflec-tion in cultural life.

Greek theatre emerged from within religious rituals organized around Diony-sus, the god of wine (Hartnoll 1968: 7–31). In the ritual's traditional form, a dithyramb, or unison hymn, was performed around the altar of Dionysus by a chorus of fifty men drawn from the entire ethnos. In terms of the present discus-sion, this meant continuing fusion: actors, collective representations, audiences, and society were united in a putatively homogeneous, still mythical way. In expressing his nostalgia for those earlier, pre-Socratic days, Nietzsche ([1872] 1956: 51–5, 78–9) put it this way: "In the dithyramb we see a community of unconscious actors all of whom see one another as enchanted . . . Audience and chorus were never fundamentally set over against each other . . . An audience of spectators, such as we know it, was unknown . . . Each spectator could quite literally imagine himself, in the fullness of seeing, as a chorist [sic]."

As Greek society entered its period of intense and unprecedented social and cultural differentiation (Gouldner 1965), the content of the dithyramb gradu-ally widened to include tales of the demi-gods and fully secular heroes whom contemporary Greeks considered their ancestors. The background representa-tional system, in other words, began to symbolize – to code and to narrate – human and not only sacred life. This interjection of the mundane into the sacred introduced symbolic dynamics directly into everyday life and vice versa. Dur-ing communal festivals dedicated to performing these new cultural texts, the good and bad deeds of secular heroes were recounted along with their feuds, marriages, and adulteries, the wars they started, the ethnic and religious ties they betrayed, and the sufferings they brought on their parents and successors. Such social conflicts now provided sources of dramatic tension that religious performers could link to sacred conflicts and could perform on ritual occasions.

As the background representations became reconfigured in a more socially oriented and dramaturgical way – as everyday life became subject to such symbolic reconstruction – the other elements of performance were affected as well. The most extraordinary development was that the social role of actor emerged. Thespius, for whom the very art of theatrical performance eventually came to be named, stepped out of the dithyramb chorus to become its leader. During ritual performance, he would assume the role of protagonist, either god or hero, and would carry on a dialogue with the chorus. Thespius formed a traveling troupe of professional actors. Collecting the means of symbolic production in a cart whose floor and tailboard could serve also as a stage, Thespius traveled from his birthplace, Icaria, to one communal festival after another, eventually landing in Athens where, in 492 BC, he won the acting prize just then established by the City Dionysus festival.

During this same critical period of social development, systems of collective representations began for the first time not only to be written down, or to become actual texts, but also to separate themselves concretely from religious life. In fifth-century Athens, theatre writing became a specialty; prestigious writing contests were held, and prizes were awarded to such figures as Aeschylus and Sophocles. Such secular imagists soon became more renowned than temple priests. At first, playwrights chose and trained their own actors, but eventually officials of the Athenian festival assigned actors to playwrights by lot. In our terms, this can be seen as having the effect of emphasizing and highlighting the autonomy of the dramatic script vis-à-vis the intentions or charisma of its creators (cf. Gouldner 1965: 114).

As such an innovation suggests, the independent institution of performance criticism also had emerged, mediating and pluralizing social power in a new way. Rather than being absorbed by the performance, as on ritual occasions, interpretation now confronted actors and writers in the guise of judges, who represented aesthetic criteria separated from religious and even moral considerations. At the same time, judges also represented the city that sponsored the performance, and members of the *polis* attended performances as a detached audience of potentially critical observers. Huizinga ([1938] 1950: 145) emphasized that, because the state did not organize theatrical competitions, "audience criticism was extremely pointed." He also suggested that the public audience shared "the tension of the contest like a crowd at a football match," but it seems clear that they were not there simply to be entertained. The masked performers of Greek tragedies remained larger than life, and their texts talked and walked with compelling emotional and aesthetic force, linking performance to the most serious and morally weighted civic issues of the day. From Aeschylus to Sophocles to Euripedes, Greek tragic drama (Jaeger 1945: 232–381) addressed civic virtue and corruption, exploring whether there existed a natural moral order more powerful than the fatally flawed order of human social life. These questions were critical for sustaining the rule of law and an independent and democratic civil life.

Nietzsche ([1872] 1956: 78–9) complained that, with the birth of tragedy, "the poet who writes dramatized narrative can no more become one with his images" and that he "transfigures the most horrible deeds before our eyes by the charm of illusion." In fact, however, the de-fusion of performative elements that instigated the emergence of theatre did not necessarily eliminate performative power; it just made this power more difficult to achieve. This increased difficulty might well have provided the social stimulus for Aristotle's aesthetic philosophy. In terms of the theoretical framework I am developing here, Aristotle's poetics can be understood in a new way. It aimed to crystallize, in abstract theoretical terms, the empirical differentiation among the elements of performance that pushed ritual to theatre. What ritual performers once had known in their guts – without having to be told, much less having to read – Aristotle (1987) now felt compelled to write down. His *Poetics* makes the natural artificial. It provides a kind of philosophical cookbook, instructions for meaning-making and effective performance for a society that had moved from fusion to conscious artifice. Aristotle explained that performances consisted of plots and that effective plotting demanded narratives with a beginning, middle, and end. In his theory of catharsis, he explained, not teleologically but empirically, how dramas could affect an audience: tragedies would have to evoke sensations of "terror and pity" if emotional effect were to be achieved.

This sketch of how theatre emerged from ritual is not teleological or evolutionary. What I have proposed, rather, is a universally shared form of social development, one that responds to growing complexity in social and cultural structure. Ritual moved towards theatre throughout the world's civilizations in response to similar social and cultural developments – the emergence of cities and states, of religious specialists, of intellectuals, and of needs for political legitimation. "There were religious and ritual origins of the Jewish drama, the Chinese drama, all European Christian drama and probably the Indian drama," Boulton (1960: 194) informed us, and "in South America the conquering Spaniards brought Miracle Plays to Indians who already had a dramatic tradition that had development out of their primitive cults."

Social complexity waxes and wanes, and with it the development of theatre from ritual. Rome continued Greek theatricality, but with the decline of the empire and the rise of European feudalism the ritual forms of religious performance dominated once again. What happened in ancient Greece was reiterated later in medieval Europe, when secular drama developed from the Easter passion plays. In twelfth-century Autun, a center of Burgundian religious activity, an astute observer named Honorius actually made an analogy between the effects of the Easter Mass and the efforts of the ancient tragedians (Schechner 1976: 210; Hardison 1965: 40). "It is known," Honorius wrote, "that those who recited tragedies in theatres presented the actions of opponents by gestures before the people." He went on to suggest that, "in the theatre of the Church before the Christian people," the struggle of Christ against his persecutors is presented by a similar set of "gestures" that "teaches to them the victory of his redemption." Honorius compared each movement of the Mass to an equivalent movement in tragic drama and described what he believed were similar – tightly bound and fused, in our terms – audience effects. "When the sacrifice has been completed, peace and communion are given by the celebrant to the people," he wrote, and "then, by the *Ite, missa est*, they are ordered to return to their homes [and] they shout *Deo gratias* and return home rejoicing." It is no wonder that Boulton (1960) equated such early religious pageants with acting. Suggesting that "the earliest acting was done by priests and their assistants," she notes that "one of the causes of the increasing secularization of the drama was that laymen had soon to be called in to fill in parts in the expanding 'cast'" (1960: 195).

By the early seventeenth century in Europe, after the rise of city-states, absolutist regimes, the scientific revolution, and internal religious reforms, the institution of criticism was already fully formed: "Nearly every play had a prologue asking for the goodwill of the critics" (Boulton 1960: 195). Long before the rise of the novel and the newspaper, theatrical performances became arenas for articulating powerful social criticisms. Playwrights wove texts from the fabric of contemporary social life, but they employed their imagination to do so in a sharply accented, highly stimulating, and provocative manner. The performance of these scripted representations were furnaces that forged metaphors circulating back to society, marking a kind of figure-eight movement (Turner 1982: 73–4; Schechner 1977) from society to theatre and back to society again. Secular criticism did not emerge only from rationalist philosophy or from the idealized arguments in urban cafés (Habermas [1962] 1989) but also from theatrical performances that projected moral valuation even while they entertained. While providing sophisticated amusement, Molière pilloried not only the rising bourgeois but also the Catholic Church, both of which returned his vituperation in kind. Shakespeare wrote such amusing plays that he was patronized as low-brow by the more intellectual playwrights and critics of his day. Yet Shakespeare satirized every sort of conventional authority and dramatized the immorality of every sort of social power. Reviled by the Puritan divines, such Elizabethan drama was subject to strenuous efforts at censorship.

The Restoration comedies that followed were no less caustic in their social ambitions or stinging in their effects. In his study of seventeenth-century drama, Reiss (1971: 122) observed that "the loss of illusion follows when the *mise-en-scène* is designed with no attempt at *vraisemblance*," and he concludes that "the theater relied . . . on the unreality of the theatrical situation itself . . . to maintain a distance" (1971: 144). Taking advantage of performative de-fusion, these playwrights used stagecraft to emphasize artificiality rather than to make it invisible, producing a critical and ironic space between the audience and the mores of their day.

The emergence of social drama

The historical story I am telling here addresses the puzzle at the core of this chapter: Why do ritually organized societies give way not to social orders regulated simply by instrumentally rational action but instead to those in which ritual-like processes remain vital in some central way?

It is vital for this story to see that the emergence of theatre was more or less simultaneous with the emergence of the public sphere as a compelling social stage. For it was, in fact, roughly during the same period as theatrical drama emerged that social drama became a major form of social organization – and for reasons that are much the same.

When society becomes more complex, culture more critical, and authority less ascriptive, social spaces open up that organizations must negotiate if they are to succeed in getting their way. Rather than responding to authoritative commands and prescriptions, social processes become more contingent, more subject to conflict and argumentation. Rationalist philosophers (Habermas [1962] 1989) speak of the rise of the public sphere as a forum for deliberative and considered debate. A more sociological formulation would point to the rise of a public stage, a symbolic forum in which actors have increasing freedom to create and to project performances of their reasons, dramas tailored to audiences whose voices have become more legitimate references in political and social conflicts. Responding to the same historical changes that denaturalized ritual performance, collective action in the wider society comes increasingly to take on an overtly performative cast.

In earlier, more archaic forms of complex societies, such as the imperial orders of Egypt or Yucatán, social hierarchies simply could issue commands, and ritualized ideological performances would provide symbolic mystification. In more loosely knit forms of complex social organization, authority becomes more open to challenge, the distribution of ideal and material resources more subject to contention, and contests for social power more open-ended and contingent. Often, these dramatic contests unfold without any settled script.

Through their success at prosecuting such dramas, individual and collective actors gain legitimacy as authoritative interpreters of social texts.

It is a commonplace not only of philosophical but also of political history (e.g. Bendix 1964) that during the early modern period the masses of powerless persons gradually became transformed into citizens. With the model of social performance more firmly in hand, it seems more accurate to say that non-elites also were transformed from passive receptacles to more active, interpreting audiences.[3] With the constitution of audience publics, even such strategic actors as organizations and class fractions were compelled to develop effective forms of expressive communication. In order to preserve their social power and their ability to exercise social control, elites had to transform their interest conflicts into widely available performances that could project persuasive symbolic forms. As peripheries gradually became incorporated into centers, pretenders to social power strived to frame their conflicts as dramas. They portrayed themselves as protagonists in simplified narratives, projecting their positions, arguments, and actions as exemplifications of sacred religious and secular texts. In turn, they "cast" their opponents as narrative antagonists, as insincere and artificial actors who were only role playing to advance their interests.

These are, of course, broad historical generalizations. My aim here is not to provide empirical explanations but to sketch out theoretical alternatives, to show how a performative dimension should be added to more traditional political and sociological perspectives. But while my ambition is mainly theoretical, it certainly can be amplified with illustrations that are empirical in a more straightforward way. What follows are examples of how social processes that are well known both to historical and lay students of this period can be reconstructed with the model of performance in mind.

(i) *Thomas Becket.* When Thomas Becket opposed the effort of Henry II to exercise political control over the English church, he felt compelled to create a grand social drama that personalized and amplified his plight (Turner 1974: 60–97). He employed as background representation the dramatic paradigm of Christ's martyrdom to legitimate his contemporary script of antagonism to the king. While Henry defeated Sir Thomas in instrumental political terms, the drama Becket enacted captured the English imagination and provided a new background text of moral action for centuries after.

(ii) *Savonarola.* In the Renaissance city-states (Brucker 1969), conflicts between church and state were played out graphically in the great public squares, not only figuratively but often also literally before the eyes of the increasingly enfranchised *populo*. Heteronomy of social power was neither merely doctrine nor institutional structure. It was also public performance. Savonarola began his mass popular movement to cleanse the Florentine Republic with a dramatic announcement in the Piazza della Signoria, where open meetings had taken place already. Savonarola's public hanging, and the burning of his corpse that followed, were staged in the same civil space. Observed by an overflowing audience of citizens and semi-citizens – some horrified, others grimly satisfied (Brucker 1969: 271) – the performance instigated by Savonarola's arrest, confession, and execution graphically drew the curtain on the reformer's spiritual renewal campaign. It is hardly coincidental that Machiavelli's advice to Italian princes offered during this same period concerned not only how to muster dispersed administrative power but also instructions about how to display power of a more symbolic kind. He wished to instruct the prince about how to perform like one so that he could appear, no matter what the actual circumstances, to exercise power in a ruthlessly efficient and supremely confident way.

(iii) *The American Revolution.* In 1773, small bands of anti-British American colonialists boarded three merchant ships in the Boston harbor and threw 90,000 tons of Indian tea into the sea. The immediate, material effect of what immediately became represented in the popular imagination as "the Boston tea party" was negligible, but its expressive power was so powerful that it created great political effects (Labaree 1979: 246ff.). The collective performance successfully dramatized colonial opposition to the British crown,[4] clarified a key issue in the antagonism, and mobilized fervent public support. Later, the inaugural military battle of the American Revolution, in Lexington, Massachusetts, was represented in terms of theatrical metaphor as "the shot heard 'round the world.'" In contemporary memorials of the event, social dramatic exigencies have exercised powerful sway. American and British soldiers are portrayed in the brightly colored uniforms of opposed performers. Paul Revere is portrayed as performing prologue, riding through the streets and shouting, "The Redcoats are coming, the Redcoats are coming," though he probably did not. The long lines of soldiers on both sides are often depicted as accompanied by fifes and drums. Bloody and often confusing battles of the War of American Independence have been narrated retrospectively as fateful and dramatic contests, their victors transformed into icons by stamps and etchings.

(iv) *The French Revolution.* The similar staging of radical collective action as social drama also deeply affected the Revolution in France. During its early days, *sans-culottes* women sought to enlist a promise of regular bread from King Louis. They staged the "momentous march of women to Versailles," an extravagantly theatrical pilgrimage that one leading feminist historian described as "the recasting of traditional female behavior within a republican mode" (Landes 1988: 109–11). As the Revolution unfolded, heroes and villains switched places according to the agonistic logic of dramatic discourse (Furet 1981) and theatrical configuring (Hunt 1984), not only in response to political calculation. No matter how violent or bloodthirsty in reality, the victors and martyrs were painted, retrospectively, in classical Republican poses and togas, as in David's celebrated portrait of Marat Sade (Nochlin 1993).

It was Turner (1974, 1982) who introduced the concept of social drama into the vocabulary of social science more than thirty years ago. For a time, this idea promised to open macro-sociology to the symbolic dynamics of public life (e.g. Moore and Myerhoff 1975, 1977), but with a few significant exceptions (e.g. Edles 1998; Alexander 1988; Wagner-Pacifici 1986) the concept has largely faded from view, even in the field of performance studies. One reason has to do with the triumph of instrumental reason in rational-choice and critical theories of postmodern life. There were also, however, basic weaknesses in the original conceptualization itself. Turner simplified and moralized social performance in a manner that obscured the autonomy of the elements that composed it. Searching for a kind of natural history of social drama on the one hand and for a gateway to ideological communitas on the other, Turner spoke (1982: 75) of the "full formal development" of social dramas, of their "full phase structure." While acknowledging that social complexity created the conditions for social drama, he insisted that it "remains to the last simple and ineradicable," locating it in "the developmental cycle of all groups" (1982: 78). He believed that the "values and ends" of performances were "distributed over a range of actors" and were projected "into a system . . . of shared or consensual meaning" (1982: 75). Social dramas can take place, Turner (1987) insisted, only "among those members of a given group . . . who feel strongly about their membership [and] are impelled to enter into relationships with others which become fully 'meaningful', in the sense that the beliefs, values, norms, and symbolism 'carried' in the group's culture become . . . a major part of what s/he might regard as his/her identity" (1987: 46; for similar emphases, see Myerhoff 1978: 32; Schechner 1987).

However, from the perspective on social dramas I am developing here, this is exactly what does not take place. The elements of social-dramatic performances are de-fused, not automatically hung together, which is precisely why the organizational form of social drama first emerged. Social drama is a successor to ritual, not its continuation in another form.

We are now in a position to elaborate the propositions about performative success and failure set forth in the first section.

Re-fusion and authenticity: the criteria for performative success and failure

The goal of secular performances, whether on stage or in society, remains the same as the ambition of sacred ritual. They stand or fall on their ability to produce psychological identification and cultural extension. The aim is to create via skillful and affecting performance, the emotional connection of audience with actor and text and thereby to create the conditions for projecting cultural meaning from performance to audience. To the extent these two conditions have been achieved, one can say that the elements of performance have become fused.

Nietzsche elegized the "bringing to life [of] the plastic world of myth" ([1872] 1956: 126) as one of those "moments of paroxysm that lift man beyond the confines of space, time, and individuation" ([1872] 1956:125). He was right to be mournful. As society becomes more complex, such moments of fusion become much more difficult to achieve. The elements of performance become separated and independently variable, and it becomes ever more challenging to bring texts into life.

The challenge confronting individual and collective symbolic action in complex contemporary societies, whether on stage or in society at large, is to infuse meaning by re-fusing performance. Since Romanticism, this modern challenge has been articulated existentially and philosophically as the problem of authenticity (Taylor 1989). While the discourse about authenticity is parochial, in the sense that it is specifically European, it provides a familiar nomenclature for communicating the sense of what performative success and failure mean. On the level of everyday life, authenticity is thematized by such questions as whether a person is "real" – straightforward, truthful, and sincere. Action will be viewed as real if it appears *sui generis*, the product of a self-generating actor who is not pulled like a puppet by the strings of society. An authentic person seems to act without artifice, without self-consciousness, without reference to some laboriously thought-out plan or text, without concern for manipulating the context of her actions, and without worries about that action's audience or its effects. The attribution of authenticity, in other words, depends on an actor's ability to sew the disparate elements of performance back into a seamless and convincing whole. If authenticity marks success, then failure suggests that a performance will seem insincere and faked: the actor seems out of role, merely to be reading from an impersonal script, pushed and pulled by the forces of society, acting not from sincere motives but to manipulate the audience.

Such an understanding allows us to move beyond the simplistic polarities of ritual versus rationality or, more broadly, of cultural versus practical action. We can say, instead, that re-fusion allows ritual-like behavior, a kind of temporary recovery of the ritual process. It allows contemporaries to experience ritual because it stitches seamlessly together the disconnected elements of cultural performance. In her performative approach to gender, Butler (1999: 179) insisted that gender identity is merely "the stylized repetition of acts through time" and "not a seemingly seamless identity." Yet seamless is exactly what the successful performance of gender in everyday life makes it appear to be.

"In what sense," Butler (1999: 178) then asks, "is gender an act?" In the same sense, she answers, "as in other ritual social dramas . . . the action of gender requires a performance that is repeated. This repetition is at once a reenactment and reexperiencing of a set of meanings already socially established; and it is the mundane and ritualized form of their legitimation."

In psychological terms, it is this seamless re-fusion that Csikszentmihalyi (1975) described as "flow" (cf. Schechner 1976) in his innovative research on virtuoso performance in art, sport, and games. In the terms I am developing here, what Csikszentmihalyi (1975) discovered in these widely varying activities was the merging of text, context, and actor, a merging that resulted in the loss of self-consciousness and a lack of concern for – even awareness of – the scrutiny of observers outside the action itself. Because of "the merging of action and awareness," Csikszentmihalyi (1975: 38) wrote, "a person in flow has no dualistic perspective." The fusion of the elements of performance allows not only actors but also audiences to experience flow, which means they focus their attention on the performed text to the exclusion of any other possible interpretive reference: "The steps for experiencing flow . . . involve the . . . process of delimiting reality, controlling some aspect of it, and responding to the feedback with a concentration that excludes anything else as irrelevant" (Csikszentmihalyi 1975: 53–4).

Performances in complex societies seek to overcome fragmentation by creating flow and achieving authenticity. They try to recover a momentary experience of ritual, to eliminate or to negate the effects of social and cultural de-fusion. Speaking epigrammatically, one might say that successful performances re-fuse history. They break down the barriers that history has erected – the divisions between background culture and scripted text, between scripted text and actors, between audience and *mise-en-scène*. Successful performances overcome the deferral of meaning that Derrida (1991) recognized as *différance*. In a successful performance, the signifiers seem actually to become what they signify. Symbols and referents are one. Script, direction, actor, background culture, *mise-en-scène*, audience, means of symbolic production – all these separate elements of performance become indivisible and invisible. The mere action of performing accomplishes the performance's intended effect (cf. Austin 1957). The actor seems to be Hamlet; the man who takes the oath of office seems to be the president.

While re-fusion is made possible only by the deposition of social power, the very success of a performance masks its existence. When performance is successful, social powers manifest themselves not as external or hegemonic forces that facilitate or oppose the unfolding performance but merely as sign-vehicles, as means of representation, as conveyors of the intended meaning. This is very much what Bourdieu ([1968] 1990: 211) had in mind when he spoke of the exercise of graceful artistic taste as culture "becoming natural." The connoisseur's poised display of aesthetic judgment might be thought of as a successful performance in the sense that it thoroughly conceals the manner in which this gracefulness is "artificial and artificially acquired," the result of a lengthy socialization resting upon class privilege. "The virtuosi of the judgment of taste," Bourdieu wrote, present their knowledge of art casually, as if it were natural. Their aim is to present "an experience of aesthetic grace" that appears "completely freed from the constraints of culture," a performance "little marked by the long, patient training of which it is the product."

Attacking the hegemonic exercise of sexual rather than class power, Butler (1999) makes a similar argument. The successful performance of gender, she claims, makes invisible the patriarchal power behind it. The difference is that, by drawing upon the theories of Austin and Turner, Butler can explicitly employ the language of performance. "Gender is . . . a construction that regularly conceals its genesis; the tacit collective agreement to perform, produce, and sustain discrete and polar genders as cultural fictions is obscured by the credibility of those productions . . . The appearance of substance is precisely that, a constructed identity, a performative accomplishment which the mundane social audience, including the actors themselves, come to believe and to perform in the mode of belief" (1999: 179).

When post-ritual drama emerged in ancient Greece, Aristotle (1987) explained that a play is "an imitation of action, not the action itself." When refusion occurs, this cautionary note goes unheeded. The performance achieves verisimilitude – the appearance of reality. It seems to be action, not its imitation. This achievement of the appearance of reality via skillful performance and flow is what Barthes ([1957] 1972) described in his celebrated essay on "true wrestling." He insisted that the "public spontaneously attunes itself to the spectacular nature of the contest, like the audience at a suburban cinema . . . The public is completely uninterested in knowing whether the context is rigged or not, and rightly so; it abandons itself to the primary virtue of the spectacle, which is to abolish all motives and all consequences: what matters is not what it thinks but what it sees" ([1957] 1972:15).

How does cultural pragmatics work? The inner structures of social performance

Having elaborated the criteria of performative failure and success, I now turn to a more detailed discussion of the elements and relations that sustain it. I will draw upon the insights of drama theory to decompose the basic elements of performance into their more complex component parts, and I will link these insights to the social dramas that compose the public sphere. To be able to move back and forth between theatrical and social drama enriches both sides of the argument; it also helps document my core empirical claim. Social action in complex societies so often is ritual-like because it remains performative. The social conditions that gave rise to theatre also gave rise to post-ritual forms of symbolic action.

The challenge of the script: re-fusing background representations with contingent performance

Behind every actor's social and theatrical performance lies the already established skein of collective representations that compose culture – the universe of basic narratives and codes and the cookbook of rhetorical configurations from which every performance draws. In a theatrical performance, the actor strives to realize "individual character," as Turner (1982: 94) put it, but he or she can do so only by taking "partly for granted the culturally defined roles supposedly played by that character: father, businessman, friend, lover, fiancé, trade union leader, farmer, poet" (1982: 94). For Turner (1982: 94), "these roles are made up of collective representations shared by actors and audience, who are usually members of the same culture," but we do not have to accept his consensual assumptions to get his point. The ability to understand the most elementary contours of a performance depends on an audience knowing already, without thinking about it, the categories within which actors behave. In a complex social order, this knowledge is always a matter of degree. In contrast with Turner (1982), I do not presume that social performance is ritualistic; I wish to explain whether and how and to what degree.

It is precisely at this joint of contingency or possible friction between background representations and the categorical assumptions of actors and audience that scripts enter into the scene. The emergence of the script as an independent element reflects the relative freedom of performance from background representations. From within a broader universe of meanings, performers make conscious and unconscious choices about the paths they wish to take and the specific set of meanings they wish to project. These choices are the scripts – the action-oriented subset of background understandings. If script is meaning primed to performance, in theatrical drama this priming is usually, though not always, sketched out beforehand. In social drama, by contrast, scripts more often are inferred by actors. In a meaning-searching process that stretches from the more intuitive to the more witting, actors and audiences reflect on performance in the process of its unfolding, gleaning a script upon which the performance "must have" been based.

In such social-dramatic scripting, actors and audiences actively engage in drawing the hermeneutical circle (Dilthey 1976). Performances become the foreground parts upon which wholes are constructed, the latter being understood as the scripts that allow the sense of an action to be ascertained. These scripts become, in turn, the parts of future wholes. It seems only sensible to suggest that an authentic script is one that rings true to the background culture. Thus, as one critic of rock music suggests, "authenticity is often located in current music's relationship to an earlier, 'purer' moment in a mythic history of the music" (Auslander 1999: 71). Yet, while this seems sensible, it would be misleading, since it suggests the naturalistic fallacy. It is actually the illusory circularity of hermeneutic interpretation that creates the sense of authenticity, and not the other way around. A script seems to ring true to the background culture precisely because it has an audience-fusing effect. This effectiveness has to do with the manner in which it articulates the relationship among culture, situation, and audience. Another recent music critic (Margolick 2000: 56) argued against the claim that Billie Holiday's recording of "Strange Fruit" – the now almost-mythical, hypnotic ballad about black lynching – succeeded because lynching was "already a conspicuous theme in black fiction, theater, and art." She had success, rather, because "it was really the first time that anyone had so . . . poetically transmitted the message." The existence of the background theme is a given; what is contingent is the dramatic technique, which is designed to elicit an effective audience response. In our terms, this is a matter of fusing the script in two directions, with background culture on the one side and with audience on the other. If the script creates such fusion, it seems truthful to background representations and real to the audience. The former allows cultural extension; the latter psychological identification.

The craft of script writing addresses these possibilities. The writer aims to "achieve concentration" (Boulton 1960: 12–13) of background meaning. Effective scripts compress the background meanings of culture by changing proportion and by increasing intensity. They provide such condensation (cf. Freud [1900] 1950) through dramatic techniques.

(i) *Cognitive simplification.* "In a play," Boulton (1960: 12–13) wrote, "there are often repetitions even of quite simple facts, careful explanations, addressing of people by their names more frequently than in real conversation and various oversimplifications which to the reader of a play in a study may seem almost infantile." The same sort of simplifying condensation affects the less consciously formed scripts of successful social dramas. As they strive to become protagonists in their chosen narrative, such social performers as politicians, activists, teachers, therapists, or ministers go over time and time again the basic story line they wish to project. They provide not complex but stereotyped accounts of their positive qualities as heroes or victims, and they melodramatically exaggerate (Brooks 1976) the malevolent motives of the actors they wish to identify as their antagonists, depicting them as evildoers or fools.

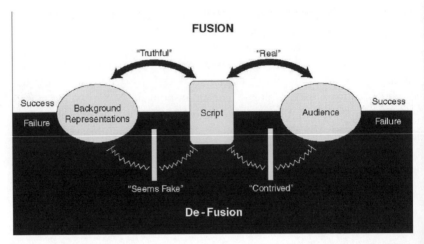

Figure 1.5   Fusion/de-fusion of background representation, script, and audience

Professional speechwriters plotting social dramas are as sensitive to this technical exigency as screen writers and playwrights plotting theatrical ones. In Noonan's (1998) manual *On Speaking Well*, the much-heralded speech writer for Presidents Ronald Reagan and George Bush emphasized time and time again that simplification is the key to achieving the fusion among speaker, audience, and background culture (cf. Flesch 1946). "You should treat the members of the audience as if they're friends," Noonan (1998: 23) instructs, which means "that you're going to talk to them the way you talk to your friends, with the same candor and trust and respect." Noting the "often unadorned quality to sections of great speeches, a directness and simplicity of expression," Noonan (1998: 48) attributes this to the fact that "the speaker is so committed to making his point, to being understood and capturing the truth." Sentences "must be short and sayable," she warns, because "your listeners [are] trying to absorb what you say" (1998: 35). Noonan praised Bush's acceptance speech at the 1988 Republican Convention in terms of this two-way fusion. On the one hand, her script allowed Bush to connect his own life to the background representations of American society. Bush "was not only telling about his life in a way that was truthful and specific [but] was also connecting his life to history – the history of those who'd fought World War II and then come home to the cities, and married, and gone on to invent the suburbs of American, the Levittowns and Hempsteads and Midlands." On the other hand, the script also allowed Bush to fuse speaker with audience: "He was also connecting his life to yours, to everyone who's had a child and lived the life that children bring with them . . . You were part of the saga" (1998: 28–9).

(ii) *Time–space compression*. Responding to the emergence of theatre from ritual, Aristotle (1987) theorized that every successful drama contains the temporal sequence of beginning, middle, and end. In early modern Europe, when ritual was secularized and de-fused once again, the demand for narrative coherence became a stricture that dramatists must stress "three unities" – of action, place, and time (Boulton 1960: 13ff.). Given the material and behavioral constraints on performance, the classic dramatists argued, theatrical action must be clearly of one piece. If the background culture is to be articulated clearly and if the audience is to absorb it, then performance must take place in the confines of one dramatic scene – in one narrative place – and must unfold in one continuous time.

Such social dramas as congressional hearings or televised investigations strive strenuously to compress time and space in the same way. With large visual charts, lead investigators display time lines for critical events, retrospective plottings whose aim is to suggest continuous action punctuated by clearly interlinked causes and effects. Daytime television is interrupted so that the representations of these investigations themselves can unfold in continuous and real, and thus forcefully dramatic time. Ordinary parliamentary business is suspended so that such political-cultural performances, whether grandiose or grandiloquent, can achieve the unity of action, place, and time.

(iii) *Moral agonism*. The fusion achieved by successful scripting does not suggest harmonious plots. To be effective, in fact, scripts must structure meaning in an agonistic way (Benhabib 1996; Arendt 1958). Agonism implies a dynamic movement that hinges on a conflict pitting good against evil (Bataille 1985), creating a wave-like dialectic that highlights the existential and metaphysical contrast between sacred and profane. "Performing the binaries" (Alexander 2003a) creates the basic codes and propels narratives to pass through them. The drama's protagonists are aligned forcefully with the sacred themes and figures of cultural myth and, through this embodiment, become new icons and create new texts themselves. Signaling their antipathy to the profane, to the evil themes and figures that threaten to pollute and to overwhelm the good, one group of actors casts doubt on the sincerity and verisimilitude of another. If a protagonist successfully performs the binaries, audiences will pronounce the performer to be an "honest man," the movement to be "truly democratic," an action to be the "very epitome of the Christian spirit." If the performance is energetically and skillfully implanted in moral binaries, in other words, psychological identification can be achieved and elements from the background culture can be extended dramatically.

Agonistic scripting is exhibited most clearly in grandiloquent performance. Geertz (1973: 420–1) portrayed the Balinese cockfight as "a blood sacrifice offered . . . to the demons," in which "man and beast, good and evil, ego and id, the creative power of aroused masculinity and the destructive power of loosened animality fuse in a bloody drama." Barthes ([1957] 1972: 17) recounted how the wrestler's "treacheries, cruelties, and acts of cowardice" are based in an "image of ignobility" portrayed by "an obese and sagging body" whose "asexual hideousness always inspires . . . a particularly repulsive quality." But performing the binaries is also fundamental to the emergent scripts of everyday political life. In 1980, in the debate among Republican and Democratic candidates for vice president of the United States, the Republican contender from Indiana, Senator Dan Quayle, sought to gain credibility by citing the martyred former president John F. Kennedy. Quayle's opponent, Texas Senator Lloyd Benton, responded with a remark that not merely scored major debating points but also achieved folkloric status in the years following: "Senator, I had the honor of knowing Jack Kennedy, and you're no Jack Kennedy." Speaking directly to his political opponent, but implicitly to the television audiences adjudicating the authenticity of the candidates, Senator Benton wished to separate his opponent's script from the nation's sacred background representations. To prove they were not aligned would block Senator Quayle from assuming an iconic role. As it turned out, of course, while Senator Quayle's debate performance failed, he was elected anyway.

(iv) *Twisting and turning*. Explicating "the general artistic laws of plot development," Boulton (1960: 41ff.) observed that "a play must have twists and turns to keep interest until the end." To keep the audience attentive and engaged, staged dramas "must develop from one crisis to another." After an initial clarification, in which "we learn who the chief characters are, what they are there for and what are the problems with which they start," there must be "some startling development giving rise to new problems." This first crisis will be followed by others, which "succeed one another as causes and effects."

Turner (1974) found almost exactly the same plot structure at work in social drama. He conceptualized it as involving successive phase movements, from breach to crisis, redress, and reintegration or schism. The initial breach that triggers a drama "may be deliberately, even calculatedly, contrived by a person or party disposed to demonstrate or challenge entrenched authority." But a breach also "may emerge [simply] from a scene of heated feelings" (Turner 1982: 70), in which case the initiation of a social drama is imputed, or scripted, by the audience, even when it is not intended by the actors themselves.

The naturalism underlying Turner's dramaturgical theory prevents him from seeing twisting and turning as a contingent effort to re-fuse background culture and audience with performative text. In her revisions of Turner's scheme, Wagner-Pacifici (1986, 1994, 2000) demonstrated just how difficult it is for even the most powerful social actors to plot the kind of dramatic sequencing that an effective script demands. Her study of the 1978 kidnapping and assassination of the Italian prime minister Aldo Moro (Wagner-Pacifici 1986) can be read as a case study of failed performance. Despite Moro's status as the most influential Italian political figure of his day, the popular prime minister could not convince other influential collective actors to interpret his kidnapping in terms of his own projected script. He wished to portray himself as still a hero, as the risk-taking and powerful protagonist in a performance that would continue to demonstrate the need for a historic "opening to the left" and, thus, the necessity to negotiate with his terrorist kidnappers to save his life. Against this projected script, other social interpreters, who turned out to be more influential, insisted that Moro's kidnapping illuminated a script not of romantic heroism but of a tragic martyrdom, which pointed to a narrative not of reconciliation but of revenge against a terrorist left. Wagner-Pacifici herself attributes the failure of Moro's performance primarily to unequal social power and the control that anti-Moro forces exercised over the means of symbolic production. The more multidimensional model I am elaborating here would suggest other critically important causes of the failed performance as well.

The challenge of mise-en-scène: re-fusing script, action, and performative space

Even after a script has been constructed that allows background culture to walk and talk, the "action" of the performance must begin in real time and at a particular place. This can be conceptualized as the challenge of instantiating a scripted text, in theatrical terms as *mise-en-scène*, which translates literally as "putting into the scene." Defining *mise-en-scène* as the "confrontation of text and performance," Pavis (1988: 87) spoke of it as "bringing together or confrontation, in a given space and time, of different signifying systems, for an audience." This potential confrontation has developed because of the segmentation that social complexity rends among the elements of performance. It is a challenge to put them back together in a particular scene.

Rouse (1992: 146) saw the "relationship between dramatic text and theatrical performance" as "a central element in the Occidental theatre." Acknowledging that "most productions here continue to be productions 'of' a preexisting play text," he insists that "exactly what the word 'of' means in terms of [actual] practices is, however, far from clear," and he suggests that "the 'of' of theatrical activity is subject to a fair degree of oscillation." It seems clear that the specialized dramatic role of director has emerged to control this potential oscillation. In Western societies, theatrical performances long had been sponsored financially by producers and had been organized, in their dramatic specifics, by playwrights and actors. As society became more complex, and the elements of performance more differentiated, the coordinating tasks became more demanding. By the late nineteenth century, according to Chinoy (1963: 3, in McConachie 1992: 176), there was "so pressing a need" that the new role of director "quickly preempted the hegemony that had rested for centuries with playwrights and actors." Chinoy (1963) believes that "the appearance of the director ushered in a new theatrical epoch," such that "his experiments, his failures, and his triumphs set and sustained the stage" (1963: 3).

When Boulton (1960:182–3) warned that "overdirected scripts leave the producer no discretion," she meant to suggest that, because writers cannot know the particular challenges of *mise-en-scène*, they should not write specific stage directions into their script. Writers must leave directors "plenty of scope for inventions." Given the contingency of performance, those staging it will need a large space within which to exercise their theatrical imagination. They will need to coach actors on the right tone of voice, to choreograph the space and timing among actors, to design costumes, to construct props, and to arrange lights. When Barthes ([1957] 1972: 15) argued that "what makes the circus or the arena what they are is not the sky [but] the drenching and vertical quality of the flood of light," he points to such directorial effect. If the script demands grandiloquence, Barthes observes, it must contrast darkness with light, for "a light without shadow generates an emotion without reserve" ([1957] 1972: 15).

For social dramas, in which scripts are attributed in a more contemporaneous and often retrospective way, *mise-en-scène* more likely is initiated within the act of performance itself. This coordination is triggered by the witting or unwitting sensibilities of collective actors, by the observing ego of the individual – in Mead's terms, her "I" as compared with her "me" – or by suggestions from an actor's agents, advisers, advance men, or event planners. This task of instantiating scripts and representations in an actual scene underscores, once again, the relative autonomy of symbolic action from its so-called social base. The underlying strains or interest conflicts in a social situation simply do not "express" themselves. Social problems not only must be symbolically plotted, or framed (Eyerman and Jamison 1991; Snow et al. 1986), but also must be performed on the scene. In analyzing "how social movements move," Eyerman (this volume) highlights "the physical, geographical aspects of staging and managing collective actions." In theorizing the standoff, Wagner-Pacifici (2000: 192–3) distinguishes between "ur-texts" and "texts-in-action," explaining how the often deadly standoffs between armed legal authorities and their quarries are triggered by "rules of engagement" (2000: 157) that establish "set points" (2000: 47) in a physical scene, such as barricades. Temporal deadlines also are established, so that the "rhythm of siege" becomes structured by the "clock ticking" (2000: 64). Standoffs are ended by violent assault only when dramatic violations occur vis-à-vis these specific spatial and temporal markers in a particular scene.

The challenge of the material base: social power and the means of symbolic production

While *mise-en-scène* has its own independent requirements, it remains interdependent with the other performative elements. One thing on which its success clearly depends is access to the appropriate means of symbolic production. Goffman's (1956) early admonishment has not been sufficiently taken to heart: "We have given insufficient attention to the assemblages of sign-equipment which large numbers of performers can call their own" (1956: 22–3). Of course, in the more typically fused performances of small-scale societies, access to such means was not usually problematic. Yet even for such naturalistic and fused performances, the varied elements of symbolic production did not appear from nowhere. In his study of the Tsembaga, for example, Schechner (1976) found that peace could be established among the warring tribes when they performed the *konj kaiko* ritual. While the ritual centered on an extended feast of wild pig, it took "years to allow the raising of sufficient pigs to stage a *konj kaiko*" (1976: 198). War and peace thus depended on a ritual process that was "tied to the fortunes of the pig population" (1976: 198).

One can easily imagine just how much more difficult and consequential access to the means of symbolic production becomes in large-scale complex societies. Most basic of all is the acquisition of a venue. Without a theatre or simply some makeshift stage, there can be no performance, much less an audience. Likewise, without some functional equivalent of the venerable soapbox, there can be no social drama. The American presidency is called "the bully pulpit" because the office provides its occupant with extraordinary access to the means for projecting dramatic messages to citizens of the United States.

Once a performative space is attained, moreover, it must be shaped materially. Aston and Savona (1991: 114) remarked that "the shape of a playing space can be altered by means of set construction." There is, in the literal and not the figurative or metaphysical sense, a material "base" for every symbolic production. The latter are not simply shaky superstructures in the vulgar Marxist manner, but neither can cultural performances stand up all by themselves. The *Micro-Robert Poche* (1992) defines *mise-en-scène* as "*l' organization matérielle de la représentation,*" and the means of symbolic production refers to the first half of this definition, the material organization. Still, even the physical platforms of performance must be given symbolic shape. Every theatre is marked by "the style in which it is designed and built," said Aston and Savona (1991: 112), and social dramas are affected equally by the design of their place. During the Clinton impeachment, it was noted widely that the hearings were being held in the old Senate office building, an ornate setting whose symbolic gravitas had been reinforced by the civil theatrics of Watergate decades before.

Yet the design of theatrical space depends, in part, on technological means. In the pre-industrial age, according to Aston and Savona (1991), the "confines" of the "large and inflexible venue" (1991: 114) of open-air theatres placed dramatic limits on the intimacy that performers could communicate, whatever the director's theatrical powers or the artistry of the script. Later, the introduction of lighting "established the convention of the darkened auditorium" and "limited the spectator's spatial awareness to the stage area" (1991: 114). Once attention is focused in this manner, as Barthes ([1957] 1972) also suggested in his observations on spectacle (as mentioned previously), a "space can be created within a space" (Aston and Savona 1991: 114), and greater communicative intimacy is possible.

Equally significant dramatic effects have followed from other technical innovations in the means of symbolic production. The small size of the television as compared with the movie screen limited the use of long-distance and ensemble shots, demanded more close-up camera work, and required more editing cuts to create a scene. Greater possibilities for dramatic intimacy and agonistic dialogue entered into televised performance as a result. The availability of amplification pushed the symbolic content of performance in the opposite way. With the new technological means for electronically recording and projecting the human voice, recordings proliferated and large-scale commercial musicals became amplified electronically through microphones. Such developments changed the criteria of authenticity. Soon, not only concerts but also most non-musical plays needed to be amplified as well, "because the results sound more 'natural' to an audience whose ears have been conditioned by stereo television, high fidelity LPs, and compact disks" (Copeland 1990, in Auslander 1999: 34).

It is here that social power enters into performance in particular ways. Certainly, censorship and intimidation have always been employed to prevent the production and distribution of symbolic communication and, thus, to prevent or control political dissent. What is more interesting theoretically and empirically, however, and perhaps more normatively relevant in complex semi-democratic and even democratic societies, is the manner in which social power affects performance by mediating access to the means of symbolic production (e.g. Berezin 1991, 1994). The use of powerful arc lights, for example, was essential to Leni Riefenstahl's *mise-en-scène* in her infamous propaganda film, *Triumph of the Will*, which reconstructed Adolph Hitler's triumphant evening arrival at the Nuremberg rally in 1933. Whether Riefenstahl had the opportunity to put her imagination into place, however, was determined by the distribution of German political and economic power. Because Hitler's party had triumphed at the level of the state, Nazis controlled the means of symbolic production. As an artist, Reifenstahl herself was infatuated by the Nazi cause, and she wrote a script that cast Hitler in a heroic light. But the tools for making her drama were controlled by others. It was Goebbels who could hire the brilliant young filmmaker and provide her with the means for staging her widely influential work.

In most social-dramatic performances, the effect of social power is even less direct. To continue with our lachrymose example, while the Nazi concentration camps remained under control of the Third Reich, their genocidal purpose could not be dramatized. Performative access to the camps – the critical "props" for any story – was denied to all but the most sympathetic, pro-Nazi journalists, still photographers, and producers of newsreels and films. On the few occasions when independent and potentially critical observers were brought to the camps, moreover, they were presented with falsified displays and props that presented the treatment of Jewish prisoners in a fundamentally misleading way. This control over the means of symbolic production shifted through force of arms (Alexander 2003b). Only after allied troops liberated the western camps did it become possible to produce the horrifying newsreels of dead and emaciated Jewish prisoners and to distribute them worldwide (Zelizer 1998). It would be hard to think of a better example of performance having a material base and of this base depending on power in turn.

As this last example suggests, in complex societies social power not only provides the means of symbolic production but of symbolic distribution as well. The more dependent a dramatic form is on technology, the more these two performative phases become temporally distinct. It is one thing to perform a drama, and even to film it, and it is quite another to make it available to audiences throughout the land. In the movie industry, distribution deals develop only after films are made, for those who represent theatre syndicates insist on first examining the performances under which they intend to draw their bottom line. Similarly, video technology has separated the distribution of social dramas from live-action transmission. Media events (Dayan and Katz 1992; Boorstin 1961) are social performances whose contents are dictated by writers and photographers and whose distribution is decided by corporate or state organization. If the former represent "hermeneutical power" and the latter social power in the more traditional sense, then there is a double mediation between performance and audience. As we will see, there are, in fact, many more mediations than that.

Whether those who "report" media effects are employed by institutions whose interests are separated from – and possibly even are opposed to – those of the performers is a critical issue for whether or not social power affects performance in a democratic way. Because control over media is so vital for connecting performances with audience publics, it is hardly surprising that newspapers for so long remained financially and organizationally fused with particular ideological,

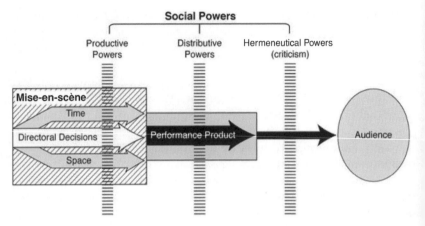

Figure 1.6   *Mise-en-scène* interfacing with social powers

economic, and political powers (Schudson 1981). This fusion allowed those who held hegemonic structural positions to decide which of their performances should be distributed and how they would be framed.

As social power becomes more pluralized, the means of recording and distributing social dramas have been distributed more widely, media interpretation has become more subject to disputation, and performative success more contingent. Even in the "iron cage" of nineteenth-century capitalism, British parliamentary investigations into factory conditions were able to project their often highly critical performances on the public stage. Their hearings were reported widely in the press (Osborne 1970: 88–90), and their findings were distributed in highly influential "white papers" throughout the class system (Smelser 1959: 291–2). Even after Bismarck outlawed the socialist party in late nineteenth-century Germany, powerful performances by militant labor leaders and working-class movements challenged him in "rhetorical duels" that were recorded and were distributed by radical and conservative newspapers alike (Roth 1963: 119–35). In mid-twentieth-century America, the civil rights movement would have failed if Southern white media had monopolized coverage of African-American protest activities. It was critical that reporters from independent Northern-owned media were empowered to record and to distribute sympathetic interpretations, which allowed psychological identification and cultural extension with the black movement's cause (Halberstam 1999).

Differentiating the elements of performance, then, is not just a social and cultural process but a political one as well. It has significant repercussions for the pluralization of power and the democratization of society. As the elements of performance become separated and relatively autonomous, there emerge new sources of professional authority. Each of the de-fused elements of performance eventually becomes subject to institutions of independent criticism, which judge it in relation to criteria that establish not only aesthetic form but also the legitimacy of the exercise of this particular kind of performative power. Such judgments issue from "critics," whether they are specialized journalists employed by the media of popular or high culture or intellectuals who work in academic milieux.

Such critical judgments, moreover, do not enter performance only from the outside. They also are generated from within. Around each of the de-fused elements of drama there have developed specialized performative communities, which maintain and deploy their own critical, sometimes quite unforgiving, standards of judgment. The distance from the first drama prizes awarded by the City Dionysius festival in ancient Greece to the Academy Awards in postmodern Hollywood may be great in geographic, historical, and aesthetic terms, but the institutional logic (Friedland and Alford 1991) has remained the same. The aim is to employ, and deploy, autonomous criteria in the evaluation of social performance. As the elements of performance have been differentiated, the reach of hegemonizing, hierarchical power has necessarily declined. Collegial associations, whether conceived as institutional elites, guilds, or professional associations, increasingly regulate and evaluate the performance of specialized cultural goods. In complex societies, continuous critical evaluations are generated from within every performative medium and emergent genre – whether theatre or feature film, documentary or cartoon, country-and-western song or rap, classical recording, sitcom, soap opera, news story, news photo, editorial, feature, or nightly newscast. Such self-policing devices aim to "improve" the possibilities for projecting performance in effective ways. These judgments and awards are determined by peer evaluations. Despite the power of the studios and mega-media corporations, it is the actors, cinematographers, editors, directors, script and speechwriters, reporters, and costume designers themselves who create the aesthetic standards and prestige hierarchies in their respective performative communities.

In less formal ways, critical interpretive judgments circulate freely and endlessly throughout dramatic life, in both its theatrical and social forms. The public relations industry, new in the twentieth century, aims to condition and structure the interpretations such critics apply. Such judgments are also the concern of agents and handlers, of experts in focus groups, of privately hired pollsters. The more complex and pluralized the society, the tighter this circle of criticism and self-evaluation is wound. Normative and empirical theories of power and legitimacy in the contemporary world must come to terms with how the conditions of performativity have changed everywhere.

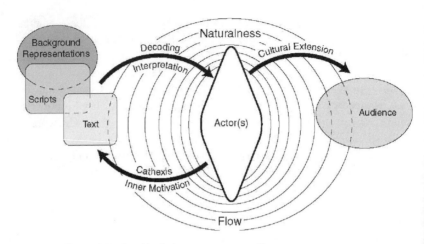

Figure 1.7   Double fusion: text–actor–audience

The challenge of being natural: re-fusing actor and role

Even if the means of symbolic production are sufficient, the script powerfully written, and the *mise-en-scène* skillfully set in place, there is no guarantee that the performance will succeed. There remains the extraordinary challenge of acting it out. Actors must perform their roles effectively, and they often are not up to the task. Thus, while Veltrusky (1964: 84) acknowledges that signifying power resides in "various objects, from parts of the costume to the set," he insists, nevertheless, that "the important thing is . . . that the actor centers their meanings upon himself."

In smaller-scale societies, ritual performers act out roles they have played in actual social life or from sacred myths with which they are intimately famil- iar. In post ritual societies, the situation is much more complex. In theatrical performances, actors are professionals who have no off-screen relation to their scripted role.

In a neglected essay, Simmel (1968: 92) put the problem very clearly: "The role of the actor, as it is expressed in written drama, is not a total person . . . not a man, but a complex of things which can be said about a person through literary devices." In social dramas, actors perform a role they often do occupy, but their ability to maintain their role incumbency is always in doubt; their legitimacy is subject to continuous scrutiny; and their feeling for the role is often marked by unfamiliarity.[5]

As the actor in theatrical drama increasingly became separated from the role, the challenge of double fusion – actor and text on the one side and actor with audience on the other – became a topic of increasing intellectual attention.

When social texts were more authoritative, less contested, and less separated from familiar social roles, professional actors could achieve re-fusion in a more indexical than iconographic way. In what later came to be seen as histrionic, "picture acting," performers merely would point to a text rather than seeking actually to embody it. This overt exhibition of the separation of actor and role could have theatrical purchase (Aston and Savona 1991: 118) only because dramatic texts had a more deeply mythical status than they typically have today. By the late eighteenth century, when sacred and traditional social structures were being reconstructed by secular revolutions (Brooks 1976), this "anti-emotionalist" method came under criticism. In *The Paradox of Acting*, Diderot ([1830] 1957) attacked acting that communicated feelings by gesture rather than embodiment. But it was not until the so-called new drama of the late nineteenth century – when social and culture de-fusion were considerably more elaborate – that the intensely psychological and introspective theatre initiated by Strindberg and Ibsen demanded an acting method that placed a premium on subjective embodiment, or facsimile.

Just as Aristotle wrote the *Poetics* as a cookbook for script-writing once myth had lost its sway, the Russian inventor of modern dramatic technique, Constantin Stanislavski ([1934] 1989), invented "the system" to teach professional actors how to make their artificial performances seem natural and unassuming. He began by emphasizing the isolation of the actor from scripted text. "What do you think?" he admonished the novice actor. "Does the dramatist supply everything that the actors need to know about the play? Can you, [even] in a hundred pages, give a full account of the life of the *dramatis personae*? For example, does the author give sufficient details of what has happened before the play begins? Does he let you know what will happen when it is ended, or what goes on behind the scenes?" ([1934] 1989: 55).

That the answer to each of these rhetorical questions is "no" demonstrates the challenge of re-fusion that contemporary actors face. "We bring to life what is hidden under the words; we put our thoughts into the author's lines, and we establish our own relationships to other characters in the play, and the conditions of their lives; we filter through ourselves all the materials that we receive from the author and the director; we work over them, supplementing them out of our own imagination" (Stanislavski [1934] 1989: 52).

The art of acting aims at eliminating the appearance of autonomy. The ambition is to make it seem that the actor has not exercised her imagination – that she has no self except the one that is scripted on stage. "Let me see what you would do," Stanislavski advised the neophyte, "if my supposed facts were true" ([1934] 1989: 46). He suggested that the actor should adopt an "as if" attitude, pretending that the scripted situation is the actor's in real life. In this way, "the feelings aroused" in the actor "will express themselves in the acts of this imaginary person" – as if she had actually "been placed in the circumstances made by the play" ([1934] 1989: 49; cf. Goffman 1956: 48). If the actor believes herself "actually" to be in the circumstances that the script describes, she will act in a natural way. She will assume the inner motivation of the scripted character, in this way refusing the separation of actor and script. Only by possessing this subjectivity can an artfully contrived performance seem honest and real (Auslander 1997: 29). "Such an artist is not speaking in the person of an imaginary Hamlet," Stanislavski concludes, "but he speaks in his own right as one placed in the circumstances created by the play" ([1934] 1989: 248).

All action in the theater must have an inner justification, be logical, coherent and real . . . With this special quality of *if* . . . everything is clear, honest and above board . . . The secret of the effect of *if* lies in the fact that it does not . . . make the artist do anything. On the contrary, it reassures him through its honesty and encourages him to have confidence in a supposed situation . . . It arouses an inner and real activity, and does this by natural means. ([1934] 1989: 46–7, italics altered)

If social and cultural de-fusion has shifted the focus of theatrical acting, we should not be surprised that the acting requirements for effective social drama have changed in a parallel way. When social and political roles were ascribed, whether through inheritance or through social sponsorship, individuals could be clumsy in their portrayal of their public roles, for they would continue to possess them even if their performances failed. With increasing social differentiation, those who assume social roles, whether ascriptive or achieved, can continue to inhabit them only if they learn to enact them in an apparently natural manner (e.g. Bumiller 2003; Von Hoffman 1978). This is all the more true in social dramas that instantiate meanings without the benefit of a script, and sometimes without any prior clarification of an actor's roles.

It is not at all uncommon, for example, for the putative actors in an emergent political drama to refuse to play their parts. During the televised Watergate hearings in the summer of 1973, even Republican senators who privately supported President Richard Nixon felt compelled to join their fellow Democrats in their expressions of outrage and indignation at the Republican president's behavior (Alexander 2003c; McCarthy 1974). By contrast, during the televised Clinton impeachment hearings in 1998, the Democrats on the House panel distanced themselves from the script, refusing to participate seriously in what Republican leaders tried to perform as a tragic public event (Mast 2003, this volume). Their refusal destroyed the verisimilitude of the social drama. Actors on both sides of the aisle seemed "political," offering what appeared to be contrived and artificial performances. Despite the tried-and-true authenticity of the political script, the political drama failed because the actors could not, or would not, fuse with their parts.

The causal import of acting to performative success is so large that even bad plays can be a great theatrical success. "We know where a bad play has achieved world fame," Stanislavski ([1934] 1989: 52) said, "because of having been re-created by a great actor." Simmel (1968: 93) also emphasized that the "impression of falsehood is generated only by a poor actor." If an actor experiences flow, then he or she has succeeded in fusing with the scripted role. The idea, according to Stanislavski, is "to have the actor completely carried away by the play" so that "it all moves of its own accord, subconsciously and intuitively" ([1934] 1989: 13). Only when flow is achieved can the actor fuse with audience as well. To seem real to an audience, "it is necessary that the spectators *feel* his inner relationship to what he is saying" ([1934] 1989: 249, original italics; cf. Roach 1993: 16–17, 218).

Even the best acting, however, cannot ensure that the audience gets it right.

The challenge of reception: re-fusing audience with performative text

One-sided culturalist and pragmatic theories share one thing in common: each eliminates the contingent relationship between performative projection and audience reception. Viewing performance purely in textual terms, semioticians tie audience interpretation directly to the dramatic intentions of the actors and the culture structure that performance implies. The role of the spectator, according to Pavis (1988: 87), is simply to decipher the *mise-en-scène*, to "receive and interpret . . . the system elaborated by those responsible for the production." If such a theoretical position makes psychological identification and cultural extension seem easy to achieve, then the purely pragmatic position makes it seem virtually impossible. The founder of audience response theory, Iser (1980: 109–10), spoke about "the fundamental asymmetry between text and reader," asserting that the "lack of common situation and a common frame of reference" is so large as to create an "indeterminate, constitutive blank." Speaking in a more historical vein, his French counterpart, Leenhardt (1980), observed that "with the formation of a new reading public," the "organic relationship to the producer has nearly disappeared." The "codes of production of literary works" have now become utterly "alien" to the "spontaneous codes of readers" (1980: 207–8).

It is a mark of social and cultural complexity that the audience has become differentiated from the act of performance. Reception is dictated neither by background nor foreground representations, nor by social power, effective direction, or thespian skill. Yet neither is reception *necessarily* in conflict with them. Every dramatic effort faces uncertainty, but re-fusion is still possible.

Boulton (1960) articulated this contingent possibility when she described the audience as the third side of "the great triangle of responses which is drama."

Will the audience remain apart from the performative experience, or will it be "cooperative," proving itself capable of "submitting itself to a new experience" (1960: 196–97)? Boulton pointed here to the psychological identification of audience with enacted text. By "accepting a sample of life and tasting it," she wrote, an audience is "sharing in the lives of imaginary people not altogether unlike known live persons," (1960: 196–97). It is revealing that the psychoanalyst who created psychodrama, J. L. Moreno, focuses also on the contingent relation between audience and stage and on the manner in which this gap is bridged by identification. "The more the spectator is able to accept the emotions, the role, and the developments on the stage as corresponding to his own private feelings, private roles, and private developments, the more thoroughly will his attentions and his fantasy be carried away by the performance" (Moreno 1975: 48). The paradox that defines the patient-performance is "that he is identifying himself with something with which he is not identical." Overcoming this paradox is the key to therapeutic success: "The degree to which the spectator can enter into the life upon the stage, adjusting his own feelings to what is portrayed there, is the measure of the catharsis he is able to obtain on this occasion."

The audience–performance split also has preoccupied the theatrical avant-garde. Some radical dramatists, such as Brecht (1964) or the Birmingham school of cultural studies (Hall and Jefferson 1976), have sought to accentuate de-fusion, in theory or in practice, in order to block the cultural extension of dominant ideology. By far the greater tendency among radical dramatists, however, has been the effort to overcome the de-fusion that makes theatrical performance artificial and audience participation vicarious and attenuated. Avant-garde performances have tried to create flow experiences, to transform mere theatre into rituals where script, actors, and audience become one. In his 1923 Geneva address, Copeau ([1923] 1955, in Auslander 1997: 16) observed that "there are nights when the house is full, yet there is no audience before us." The true audience is marked by fusion, when its members "gather [and] wait together in a common urgency, and their tears or laughter incorporate them almost physically into the drama or comedy that we perform." Exactly the same language of re-fusion is deployed fifty years later by Brook (1969) when he describes the aim of his "Holy Theatre." Only when the process of "representation no longer separates actor and audience, show and public" can it "envelop them" in such a manner that "what is present for one is present for the other." On a "good night," he comments, the audience "assists" in the performance rather than maintaining "its watching role" (1969: 127).

Postmodern theatrical analysts are acutely aware of the fact that "theatre is attended by the 'non-innocent' spectator whose world view, cultural understanding or placement, class and gender condition and shape her/his response"

(Aston and Savona 1991: 120). Film and television producers and distributors try to protect their investments by targeting specific audience demographics and by staging test runs that can trigger textual readjustments in response. Politicians may be committed vocationally rather than aesthetically and financially to generating an audience, but they display an equally fervent interest in refusing the audience–performance gap. They "keep their ear to the ground" and try to gauge "feedback" from the grassroots in front of whom their social performances are staged. That this testing of the demographics and responses of potential audiences is now conducted by candidate-sponsored scientific polling (Mayhew 1997) does not change the performative principle involved. The goal remains to achieve performative success by overcoming social-dramatic defusion.

If large-scale societies were homogeneous, this segmentation of performance from an audience would be a matter of layering. Performances are projected first to an immediate audience of lay and professional interpreters and only subsequently to the impersonal audience that constitutes the vast beyond (cf. Lang and Lang 1968: 36–77). In real life, however, the problem is much more difficult than this. Audiences are not only separated from immediate contact with performers but also are internally divided among themselves. Even after the intensely observed ritual ceremonies that displayed the political consensus about Nixon's impeachment, poll data revealed that some 20 percent of Americans did not agree that the President was guilty even of a legal violation, much less of moral turpitude (Lang and Lang 1983). In opposition to the vast majority of Americans, this highly conservative group interpreted the impeachment as political vengeance by Nixon's enemies (O'Keefe and Mendelsohn 1974).

Copeau ([1923] 1955) rightly linked the fusion of audience and performance to the internal unity of the audience itself. "What I describe as an audience is a gathering in the same place of those brought together by the same need, the same desire, the same aspirations . . . for experiencing together human emotions – the ravishment of laughter and that of poetry – by means of a spectacle more fully realized than that of life itself" (in Auslander 1997: 16). In complex societies, the main structural barrier to re-fusing social drama and audience is the fragmentation of the citizenry. Social segmentation creates not only different interests but also orthogonal subcultures, "multiple public spheres" (Eley 1992; Fraser 1992), that produce distinctive pathways for cultural extension and distinctive objects of psychological identification. More and less divided by ideology, race, ethnicity, class, religion, and region, citizen-audiences can respond to social performances in diametrically opposed ways (Liebes and Katz 1990). For this reason, group-affirming social dramas are much easier to carry off than universalizing ones. This particularistic strategy informs recent identity politics, but it has always been the default position of social drama in complex societies. When these structured divisions are exacerbated by political and cultural polarization, the seamless re-fusion of audience and performance becomes more difficult still (Hunt 1997).

Whether or not some shared culture framework "really exists" is not, however, simply a reflection of social structure and demographics. It is also a matter of interpretation. Audience interpretation is a process, not an automatic result. For example, Bauman (1989) suggested that a consciousness of doubleness is inherent in the interpretation of performance – that every performance is compared to an idealized or "remembered" model available from earlier experience. In other words, audience interpretation does not respond to the quality of the performative elements per se. Rather, audiences of social and theatrical dramas judge quality comparatively. Scripts, whether written or attributed, are compared to the great and convincing plots of earlier times. Did the fervor over President Reagan's trading of arms for hostages constitute "another Watergate," or did it pale by comparison (Schudson 1992b; Alexander 1987a)? In his role as chair of the House Impeachment Committee, how did Representative Henry Hyde's efforts stack up against Sam Ervin's bravura performance as chair of the Senate Select Committee during the Watergate hearings? How do the participants in today's presidential debates compare to the towering model of the Lincoln–Douglas debates that, according to American mythology (Schudson 1992a), made civil-dramatic history more than a century ago?

When audiences interpret the meaning and importance of social dramas, it is such comparative questions that they keep firmly in mind. If their answers are negative, even those who are within easy demographic reach will be less likely to invest their affect in the performance. For those separated further, neither psychological identification nor cultural extension will likely occur. Fragmented performance interpretations feed back into the construction of subcultures, providing memories that in turn segment perceptions of later performances (Jacobs 2000). If there are some shared memories, by contrast, audiences will experience social drama in a deeper and broadened way. As audiences become more involved, performance can draw them out of demographic and subcultural niches into a more widely shared and possibly more universalistic liminal space.

Conclusion: cultural pragmatics as model and morality

Why are even the most rationalized societies still enchanted and mystified in various ways? The old-fashioned rituals that marked simpler organizational forms

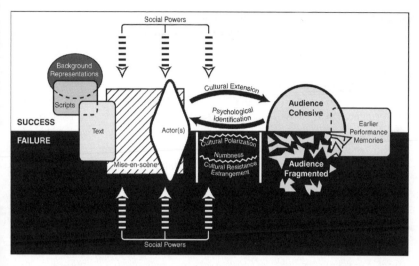

Figure 1.8   Audiences and performance

have largely disappeared, but ritual-like processes most decidedly remain. Individuals and collectivities strategically direct their actions and mobilize all their available resources, but their instrumental power usually depends on success of a cultural kind. This does not mean that the explanation of their success should be purely symbolic. It means that pragmatic and symbolic dimensions are intertwined.[6]

It is such a cultural-pragmatic perspective that has informed this work. I have developed a macro model of social action as cultural performance. In the first section, I proposed that performances are composed of a small number of analytically distinguishable elements, which have remained constant throughout the history of social life although their relationship to one another has markedly changed. In the second section, I demonstrated that, as social structure and culture have become more complex and segmented, so the elements that compose performance have become not only analytically but also concretely differentiated, separated, and de-fused in an empirical way. In the third section, I showed that whether social and theatrical performances succeed or fail depends on whether actors can re-fuse the elements of which they are made. In the fourth section, I explored the challenge of modern performance by investigating the complex nature of the demands that each of its different elements implies.

In simpler societies, Durkheim believed ([1912] 1995), rituals are made at one time and place, after which the participants scatter to engage in activities of a more instrumental and individualistic kind. In complex societies, things are rarely so cut and dried. All actions are symbolic to some degree. In social science, it is best to convert such dichotomous either/or questions into matters of variation. The aim is to discover the invariant structures that vary and to suggest the forces that propel this change over time.

In complex societies, the relative autonomy and concrete interdependence (Kane 1991) of performative elements ensures variation both within and between groups. Even for members of relatively homogeneous communities, performances will range from those that seem utterly authentic to those that seem utterly false, with "somewhat convincing," "plausible," and "unlikely but not impossible" coming somewhere in between. For performances that project across groups, the range is the same, but attributions of authenticity are made less frequently. Such attributions also can be seen to vary broadly across historical time.

It might be worthwhile to offer a figurative rendering of the discussion I have presented here. Figure 1.9 presents a graphical, highly simplified schematization. The x-axis plots the variation in social and cultural structures, from simpler to more complex; the y-axis plots the elements that compose/organize a performance, from fused to de-fused. Three empirical lines are plotted in a hypothetical way. The higher horizontal plot line (a) traces performances that achieve fusion – ritual or ritual-like status – no matter what the degree of social complexity. The lower horizontal plot line (b) graphs failed performances, or those that fail to re-fuse the elements of performance, once again without regard for the state of social complexity. The diagonal plot line (c) graphs the average expectations for successful performance, which decline in stepwise and symmetrical fashion with each increment of social complexity. It has a downward, 45-degree slope, for each increase in social and cultural complexity stretches farther apart – farther de-fuses – the elements of performances, which makes success that much more difficult to achieve. Performances above the diagonal (c) are more successful than expected, given the historical conditions of performance; those below are less.

Wariness about authenticity is intrinsic to the pluralism and openness of complex societies, whether ancient, modern, or postmodern social life. Nietzsche ([1872] 1956: 136) bemoaned that "every culture that has lost myth has lost, by the same token, its natural and healthy creativity." But from a moral point of view, it is often healthy to be skeptical of myths, to see through the efforts of actors to seamlessly re-fuse the elements of performance. When political democracy made its first historical appearance, in ancient Greece, Plato (1980) feared that demagogy might easily sway the *polis* to undertake immoral acts. In terms of the perspective set out here, Plato was an implacable opponent of performance, deeply suspicious of its cultural-pragmatic effects. In one of his dialogues, he portrayed a master of oratory, Gorgias, as bragging about its extraordinary persuasive powers. "You might well be amazed, Socrates, if you

Social and Cultural Complexity

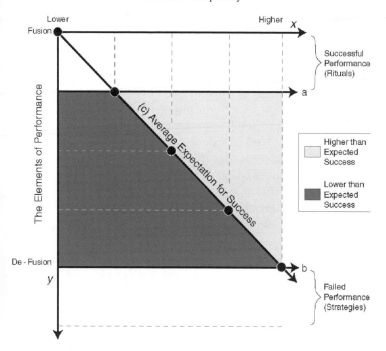

Figure 1.9   The historical conditions of social performance: structured variation

knew . . . that oratory embraces and controls almost all other spheres of human activity . . . The orator can speak on any subject against any opposition in such a way as to prevail on any topic he chooses." Socrates answered caustically, relativizing peformative skill by connecting success to mere audience acceptance. "The orator need have no knowledge of the truth about things," Socrates exclaims; "it is enough for him to have discovered a knack of convincing the ignorant that he knows more than the experts." Socrates continues in an equally sarcastic vein: "What happens is that an ignorant person is more convincing than the expert before an equally ignorant audience. Am I right?" Gorgias responds cynically, asking: "Isn't it a great comfort, Socrates, to be able to meet specialists in all the other arts on equal terms without going to the trouble of acquiring more than this single one?" By this time, Socrates is furious. He acknowledges that orators need "a shrewd and bold spirit together with an aptitude for dealing with men," but he denies that it can be called an art. "Oratory certainly isn't a fine or honorable pursuit," he avows; indeed, "the generic name which I should give it is pandering." As a moral philosopher, Plato sees sincerity as the victim of performance. He insists that "the supreme object of a man's efforts, in public and in private life, must be the reality rather than the appearance of goodness." From the normative point of view, performative fusion must be unmasked, and rational deliberation provides the means. From a cultural-sociological perspective, however, embracing rationality as a norm does not mean seeing social action as rational in an empirical way. Culture is less toolkit than storybook. Why else are critical efforts to question a performance almost always accompanied by creative efforts to mount counterperformances in turn (Alexander 2004)? Re-fusion remains critically important to complex societies. One must insist that social power be justified and that authority be accountable, but one also must acknowledge that even the most democratic and individuated societies depend on the ability to sustain collective belief. Myths are generated by ritual-like social performance (Giesen, this volume). Only if performances achieve fusion can they reinvigorate collective codes, allowing them to be "ubiquitous and unnoticed, presiding over the growth of the child's mind and interpreting to the mature man his life and struggles," as Nietzsche ([1872] 1956: 136–7) astutely observed.

Notes

I am grateful to the members of the Yale-Konstanz seminars for feedback on earlier versions of this essay, and particularly to Bernhard Giesen and Jason Mast.

1. The aim of the present chapter is to develop theory at the middle range. For a more metatheoretical investigation of the intellectual history of performance theory and its relationship to more textual cultural theories, and for the positioning of cultural pragmatics vis-à-vis other contemporary theoretical orientations in the social sciences and humanities, see Alexander and Mast (introduction, this volume).

2. Because Durkheim is the founder of virtually every strong program for cultural analysis in the human sciences (Smith and Alexander, forthcoming), it is particularly unfortunate that he equated socially meaningful symbolic action with ritual rather than conceptualizing ritual as one moment along a continuum of social performance that ranges from fused to defused. One result has been the very broad usage of "ritual" as a synonym for symbolic action (e.g. Goffman 1967; Collins 2004), a usage that camouflages the contingency of symbolic action. Another result has been the restriction of symbolic action to highly integrated and repetitive, i.e. "ritualized," situations, a restriction that conceptualizes acultural, strategic, and materialistic "practices" as taking up the rest of the action space. In his "religious sociology" of aboriginal societies, Durkheim wished to establish the basic elements of a cultural sociology of contemporary life. While he succeeded in laying the foundations for such a theory, he failed to sufficiently differentiate, in an analytical manner, the conditions for symbolic action in simpler and more complex societies. He could not have fully succeeded in his ambition, then, without the kind of differentiated and variable theory of the social conditions for symbolic activity I am presenting here.

3. Normative theorizing about the deliberative aspects of democracy has been allergic to its aesthetic and symbolic dimensions, implicitly equating the latter with anti-democratic, irrationalist commitments. The cultural pragmatics of social performance can provide an important corrective. For their part, Marxian hegemony and Foucauldian power-knowledge perspectives fail to conceptualize the myriad of contingencies that successful symbolic reproduction entails. It is very difficult to hyphenate power with knowledge and to gain the fusion that is indicated by an audience's inability to perceptually differentiate these two dimensions.

4. "The undertaking had all the signs of a well-planned operation . . . The rain had stopped, and some people showed up with lanterns to supplement the bright moonlight that now illuminated the scene . . . As work progressed, a large crowd gathered at the wharf to watch the proceedings in silent approval. It was so quiet that a witness standing at some distance could hear the steady whack-whack of the hatchets . . . 'This is the most magnificent Movement of all,' wrote John Adams in his diary the next day. 'There is a Dignity, a Majesty, a Sublimity in this last Effort of the Patriots that I great admire . . . This Destruction of the Tea,' he concluded, 'is so bold, so daring to form, intrepid, and inflexible, and it must have so important Consequences and so lasting, that I cannot but consider it as an Epocha [sic] in History' " (Labaree 1979: 144–5).

5. The relative autonomy of the "actor" element in contemporary social drama was demonstrated in a world-historical manner by US Secretary of State Colin Powell, whose televised speech to the United Nations Security Council on February 5, 2003, provided the crucial legitimation that allowed America and its allies to launch the Iraq war. By that late date, billions of dollars had been spent already on preparation, American military forces were primed and ready, and the most powerful military and political leaders in the world's most powerful nation were intent on launching the invasion. By their own accounts, however, they felt that they could not do so unless the war was legitimated on the public stage. This legitimation depended on making the case that Saddam Hussein possessed weapons of mass destruction (WMDs) and that their use was imminent. After several failed efforts to prepare for such a performance, those who were directing it decided that only one man could play the critical role. In the following account, the veteran reporter Bob Woodward continually makes resort to performative concepts, including rehearsal, preparation, background scripts, symbolic polarization, actor motivation and skillfulness, *mise-en-scène*, the reading of audience perspective, the role of critics, and audience response.

> [President George] Bush and [National Security Advisor Condoleezza] Rice had asked the CIA to put together the best information in a written document – the "slam dunk" case [for WMDs] that [CIA Director George] Tenet had promised . . . The President was determined to hand the evidence over to experienced lawyers who could use it to make the best possible case. The document was given to . . . Scooter Libby . . . On Saturday, January 25, Libby gave a lengthy presentation in the Situation Room . . . Holding a thick sheaf of paper, Libby outlined the latest version of the case against Saddam . . .

The most important response came from [former presidential assistant] Karen Hughes. As a communications exercise, she said, it didn't work . . . This was a communications problem, not a legal one . . . So who then should present the public case? . . . Powell was the logical choice . . . To have maximum credibility, it would be best to go counter to type and everyone knew that Powell was soft on Iraq [and] when Powell was prepared, he was very persuasive . . . "I want you to do it," Bush told the Secretary of State. "You have the credibility to do it." Powell was flattered to be asked to do what no one else could. Rice and Hughes told Powell that he should get three days for the presentation to the Security Council . . . "No way," Powell said. "I'm doing it once." Okay, [then] it might be three or four hours long. "No, it won't," Powell insisted. "You can't hold these guys for three to four hours." They would fall asleep . . . Powell won agreement that the length and content would be his decision . . . Public expectation was building on Powell's presentation. Newspaper stories and cable television were running with it hard: Will Powell deliver a knockout blow? What does he have? What secrets will finally be let out of the box? Will Saddam be exposed? Will Powell have an Adlai Stevenson moment? Will Saddam fold? Will Powell fold? Powell was well aware that the credibility of the United States, of the president, and his own, were going to be in the Security Council room that day . . . After the final rehearsal in Washington, Tenet announced that he thought their case was ironclad . . . "You're coming with me," Powell said. He wanted Tenet sitting behind him at the U.N. as a visible, on-camera validation of the presentation, as if the CIA director were saying each word himself. Tenet was not the only prop. Powell had a sound and light show, audios and visuals to be presented on large hanging monitors in the Security Council chamber. He even had a teaspoon of simulated anthrax in a small vial to wave around. Millions around the world watched and listened on live television . . . Dressed in a dark suit and red tie, hands clasped on his desk, Powell began cautiously . . . He had decided to add his personal interpretation of the intercepts [of Iraqi military conversations] to his rehearsed script, taking them substantially further and casting them in the most negative light . . . He had learned in the Army that meaning had to be explained in clear English . . . The secretary's presentation took 76 minutes [but] the mixture of understatement, overstatement and personal passion made for riveting television. Mary McGrory, the renowned liberal columnist for the *Washington Post*, and a Bush critic, wrote in the lead column for the next day's op-ed page. . . . "I can only say that he Persuaded me, and I was as tough as France to convince . . . I'm not ready for war yet. But Colin Powell has convinced me that it might be the only way to stop a fiend, and that if we do go, there is reason." (Woodward 2004: 288–312)

6. Twentieth-century linguistic theory – which was central in creating social under-standings of discourse – was marked by a struggle between structuralism and prag-matics. The present theoretical effort can be understood as a sociological extension and reformulation, of the series of fundamentally significant philosophical-linguistic

efforts to transcend this divide, e.g. Bakhtin's (1986) concepts of dialogue and speech genre, Jakobson's dynamic synchrony (1990: 64) and code/message schema (1987: 66), and Morris' (1938) syntactic-semantic-pragmatic model. I am also following upon, while challenging and revising, significant synthetic efforts in sociological theory, e.g. Swidler (1986), Sewell (1992), and most especially Emirbayer and Mische (1998), which is closest to the analytic synthesis I am pursuing here. As these latter efforts suggest, twentieth-century sociological theory was marked by a sharp tension between pragmatic and structural approaches, against which some of my own earlier theoretical efforts were directed as well (Alexander 1998, 1987b, 1987c, 1982–3).

References

Alexander, J. C. 1982–3. *Theoretical Logic in Sociology*. Berkeley: University of California Press.

1987a. "Constructing Scandal." *New Republic*, June 8, no. 3777, pp. 18–20.

1987b. *Twenty Lectures: Sociological Theory Since World War II*. New York: Columbia University Press.

1987c. "Action and Its Environments," pp. 289–318 in *The Micro-Macro Link*, ed. J. C. Alexander, B. Giesen, R. Munch, and N. Smelser. Berkeley: University of California Press.

(ed.). 1988. *Durkheimian Sociology: Cultural Studies*. Cambridge: Cambridge University Press.

1998. "After Neofunctionalism: Action, Culture, and Civil Society," pp. 210–33 in J. C. Alexander, *Neofunctionalism and After*. Malden, Mass.: Blackwell.

2003a. *The Meanings of Social Life: A Cultural Sociology*. New York: Oxford University Press.

2003b. "On the Social Construction of Moral Universals: The 'Holocaust' from War Crime to Trauma Drama," pp. 27–84 in J. C. Alexander, *The Meanings of Social Life*. New York: Oxford University Press.

2003c. "Watergate as Democratic Ritual," pp. 155–78 in J. C. Alexander, *The Meanings of Social Life*. New York: Oxford University Press.

2004. "From the Depths of Despair: Performance and Counter-Performance on September 11th." *Sociological Theory* 21, 1: 88–105.

Alexander, J. C. and P. A. Colomy (eds.). 1990. *Differentiation Theory and Social Change*. New York: Columbia University Press.

Apter, D. E. and T. Saich. 1994. *Revolutionary Discourse in Mao's Republic*. Cambridge, Mass.: Harvard University Press.

Arendt, H. 1958. *The Human Condition*. Chicago: University of Chicago Press.

Aristotle. 1987. *Poetics*. Indianapolis: Hacket.

Assmann, J. 2002. *The Mind of Egypt: History and Meaning in the Time of the Pharaohs*. New York: Metropolitan.

Aston, E. and G. Savona. 1991. *Theatre as Sign-System: A Semiotics of Text and Performance*. London: Routledge.

Auslander, P. 1997. *From Acting to Performance: Essays in Modernism and Postmodernism*. London: Routledge.

1999. *Liveness: Performance in a Mediatized Culture*. London: Routledge.

Austin, J. L. 1957. *How to Do Things with Words*. Cambridge, Mass.: Harvard University Press.

Bakhtin, M. 1986. *Speech Genres and Other Late Essays*. Austin: University of Texas Press.

Barber, B. 1983. *The Logic and Limits of Trust*. New Brunswick, NJ: Rutgers University Press.

Barthes, R. [1957] 1972. "The World of Wrestling," pp. 15–25 in R. Barthes, *Mythologies*. New York: Hill and Wang.

Bataille, G. 1985. *Literature and Evil*. London: Marion Boyard.

Bauman, R. 1989. "Performance," in *International Encyclopedia of Communications*, ed. E. Barnouw. New York: Oxford University Press.

Bellah, R. N. 1970. "Religious Evolution," pp. 20–51 in R. N. Bellah, *Beyond Belief: Essays on Religion in a Post-Traditional World*. New York: Harper and Row.

Bendix, R. 1964. *Nation Building and Citizenship*. New York: John Riley.

Benhabib, S. 1996. *The Reluctant Modernism of Hannah Arendt*. London: Sage.

Berezin, Mabel. 1991. "The Organization of Political Ideology: Culture, State, and Theater in Fascist Italy." *American Sociological Review* 56 (October): 639–51.

1994. "Cultural Form and Political Meaning: State Subsidized Theater, Ideology, and the Language of Style in Fascist Italy." *American Journal of Sociology* 99, 5: 1237–86.

1997. *Making the Fascist Self: The Political Culture of Interwar Italy*. Ithaca: Cornell University Press.

Boorstin, D. 1961. *The Image*. New York: Atheneum.

Boulton, M. 1960. *The Anatomy of Drama*. London: Routledge & Kegan Paul.

Bourdieu, P. [1968] 1990. "Artistic Taste and Cultural Capital," pp. 205–16 in *Culture and Society: Contemporary Debates*, ed. J. C. Alexander and S. Seidman. New York: Cambridge University Press.

Brecht, B. 1964. *Brecht on Brecht*. London: Methuen.

Brook, P. 1969. *The Empty Space*. New York: Avon.

Brooks, P. 1976. *The Melodramatic Imagination: Balzac, Henry James, Melodrama, and the Mode of Excess*. New Haven: Yale University Press.

Brucker, G. A. 1969. *Renaissance Florence*. New York: John Wiley and Sons.

Bumiller, E. 2003. "Keepers of Bush Image Lift Stagecraft to New Heights." *New York Times*, May 16, p. A1.

Burke, K. 1965. "Dramatism." *Encyclopedia of the Social Sciences* 7: 445–451.

Butler, J. 1999. *Gender Trouble: Feminism and the Subversion of Identity*. New York: Routledge.

Carlson, M. 1996. *Performance: A Critical Introduction*. London: Routledge.

Champagne, D. 1992. *Social Order and Political Change: Constitutional Government Among the Cherokee, the Choctaw, the Chickasaw, and the Creek*. Stanford, CA: Stanford University Press.

Chan, E. 1999. "Structural and Symbolic Centers: Center Displacement in the 1989 Chinese Student Movement," pp. 337–54 in *Democratic Culture: Ethnos and Demos in Global Perspective*, ed. M. Berezin and J. C. Alexander (special issue). *International Sociology* 14, 3.

Chinoy, H. K. 1963. "The Emergence of the Director." In *Directors on Directing*, ed. T. Cole and H. K. Chinoy. Indianapolis: Bobbs-Merrill.

Clifford, J. 1988. *The Predicament of Culture: Twentieth-Century Ethnographer, Literature, and Art*. Cambridge, Mass.: Harvard University Press.

Collins, R. 2004. *Interaction Ritual Chains*. New York: Cambridge University Press.

Conquergood, D. 1992. "Performance Theory, Hmong Shamans, and Cultural Politics," pp. 41–64 in *Critical Theory and Performance*, ed. J. G. Reinelt and J. R. Roach. Ann Arbor: University of Michigan Press.

Copeau, J. [1923] 1955. *Notes sur le Métier de Comédien*. Paris: Michel Brient.

Copeland, R. 1990. "The Presence of Mediation." *TDR: The Journal of Performance Studies* 34, 4: 28–44.

Csikszentmihalyi, M. 1975. *Beyond Boredom and Anxiety*. San Francisco: Jossey-Bass.

Dayan, D. and E. Katz. 1992. *Media Events: The Live Broadcasting of History*. Cambridge, Mass.: Harvard University Press.

Derrida, J. 1991. "Différance," pp. 59–79 in *A Derrida Reader: Between the Blinds*, ed. P. Kamuf. New York: Columbia.

Diderot, D. [1830] 1957. *The Paradox of Acting*. New York: Hill and Wang.

Dilthey, W. 1976. "The Construction of the Historical World in the Human Studies," pp. 168–245 in *Dilthey: Selected Writings*, ed. H. P. Rickman. Cambridge: Cambridge University Press.

Durkheim, E. [1912] 1995. *The Elementary Forms of Religious Life*. New York: Free Press.

Edles, L. 1998. *Symbol and Ritual in the New Spain: The Transition to Democracy after Franco*. New York: Cambridge University Press.

Eisenstadt, S. N. 1963. *The Political System of Empires*. New York: Free Press.
    1982. "The Axial Age: The Emergence of Transcendental Visions and the Rise of Clerics." *European Journal of Sociology* 23: 294–314.

Eley, G. 1992. "Nations, Publics, and Political Cultures: Placing Habermas in the Nineteenth Century," pp. 289–339 in *Habermas and the Public Sphere*, ed. C. Calhoun. Cambridge, Mass.: MIT Press.

Emirbayer, M. and A. Mische. 1998. "What is Agency?" *American Journal of Sociology* 103: 962–1023.

Evans-Pritchard, E. E. 1940. *The Nuer: A Description of the Modes of Livelihood and Political Institutions of a Nilotic People*. London: Oxford University Press.

Eyerman, R. and A. Jamison. 1991. *Social Movements: A Cognitive Approach*. London: Polity.

Flesch, Rudolf. 1946. *The Art of Plain Talk*. New York: Harper and Brothers.

Frankfort, Henri. 1948. *Ancient Egyptian Religion*. New York: Harper & Row.

Fraser, Nancy. 1992. "Rethinking the Public Sphere: A Contribution to the Critique of Actually Existing Democracy," pp. 109–42 in *Habermas and the Public Sphere*, ed. C. Calhoun. Cambridge, Mass.: MIT Press.

Freud, S. [1900] 1950. *The Interpretation of Dreams*. London: George Allen & Unwin.

Fried, M. H. 1971. "On the Evolution of Social Stratification and the State," pp. 101–4 in *Political Sociology*, ed. S. N. Eisenstadt. New York: Basic Books.

Friedland, R. and R. R. Alfrod. 1991. "Bring Society Back In: Symbols, Practices, and Institutional Contradictions," pp. 232–63 in *The New Institutionalism in Organizational Analysis*, ed. W. W. Powell and P. J. DiMaggio. Chicago: University of Chicago Press.

Furet, F. 1981. *Interpreting the French Revolution*. Cambridge: Cambridge University Press.

Garfinkel, H. 1967. *Studies in Ethnomethodology*. Englewood Cliffs, NJ: Prentice Hall.

Geertz, C. 1973. "Deep Play: Notes on the Balinese Cockfight," pp. 412–53 in C. Geertz, *The Interpretation of Cultures*. New York: Basic Books.

1980. *Negara: The Theatre State in Nineteenth Century Bali*. Princeton, NJ: Princeton University Press.

Gerth, H. H. and C. W. Mills. 1964. *Character and Social Structure: The Psychology of Social Institutions*. New York: Harcourt, Brace, and World.

Giesen, B. 1998. *Intellectuals and the Nation: Collective Identity in a German Axial Age*. New York: Cambridge University Press.

Goffman, E. 1956. *The Presentation of Self in Everyday Life*. New York: Anchor.

1967. *Interaction Ritual*. New York: Pantheon.

1974. *Frame Analysis*. New York: Harper & Row.

Goody, J. 1986. *The Logic of Writing and the Organization of Society*. Cambridge: Cambridge University Press.

Gouldner, A. 1965. *Enter Plato: Classical Greece and the Origins of Social Theory*. London: Routledge & Kegan Paul.

Habermas, J. 1982–3. *Theory of Communicative Action*. Cambridge, Mass.: MIT Press.

[1962] 1989. *The Structural Transformation of the Public Sphere*. Cambridge, Mass.: MIT Press.

Hagstrom, W. 1965. *The Scientific Community*. New York: Free Press.

Halberstam, D. 1999. *The Children*. New York: Fawcett.

Hall, S. 1980. "Encoding/Decoding," pp. 128–38 in *Culture, Media, Language*, ed. S. Hall, D. Hobson, A. Lowe, and P. Willis. London: Hutchinson.

Hall, S. and T. Jefferson (eds.). 1976. *Resistance Through Rituals: Youth Subcultures in Post-War Britain*. London: Hutchinson.

Hardison, O. B. 1965. *Christian Rite and Christian Drama in the Middle Ages*. Baltimore, MD: Johns Hopkins University Press.

Hartnoll, P. 1968. *A Concise History of the Theatre*. London: Thames and Hudson.

Huizinga, J. [1938] 1950. *Homo Ludens: A Study of the Play Element in Culture*. Boston Mass.: Beacon.

Hunt, D. 1997. *Screening the Los Angeles "Riots."* New York: Cambridge University Press.

Hunt, L. 1984. *Politics, Culture, and Class in the French Revolution.* Berkeley: University of California Press.

Iser, W. 1980. "Interaction Between Text and Reader," pp. 106–19 in *The Reader in the Text: Essays on Audience and Interpretation*, ed. S. R. Suleiman and I. Crosman. Princeton, NJ: Princeton University Press.

Jacobs, R. 2000. *Race, Media, and the Crisis of Civil Society.* Cambridge: Cambridge University Press.

Jaeger, W. 1945. *Paideia: The Ideals of Greek Culture*, vol. I. Oxford: Oxford University Press.

Jakobson, R. 1987. "Linguistics and Poetics," pp. 62–94 in *Language and Literature*, ed. R. Jakobson. Cambridge, Mass.: Harvard University Press.

    1990. "My Favorite Topics," pp. 61–66 in *On Language*, ed. R. Jakobson. Cambridge, Mass.: Harvard University Press.

Kane, A. 1991. "Cultural Analysis in Historical Sociology: The Analytic and Concrete Forms of the Autonomy of Culture." *Sociological Theory* 9: 53–69.

Kemp, B. J. 1989. *Ancient Egypt.* London: Routledge.

Ku, A. 1999. *Narrative, Politics, and the Public Sphere.* Aldershot: Ashgate.

Labaree, B. W. 1979. *The Boston Tea Party.* Boston, Mass.: Northeastern University Press.

Landes, J. 1988. *Women and the Public Sphere in the Age of the French Revolution.* Ithaca, NY: Cornell University Press.

Lang, G. E. and K. Lang. 1968. *Politics and Television.* Chicago: Quadrangle Books.

    1983. *The Battle for Public Opinion: The President, the Press, and the Polls During Watergate.* New York: Columbia University Press.

Leach, E. R. 1972. "Ritualization in Man in Relation to Conceptual and Social Development," pp. 333–7 in *Reader in Comparative Religion: An Anthropological Approach*, 3rd edn., ed. W. A. Lessa and E. Z. Vogt. New York: Harper & Row.

Leenhardt, J. 1980. "Toward a Sociology of Reading," pp. 205–24 in *The Reader in the Text: Essays on Audience Interpretation*, ed. S. R. Suleiman and I. Crosman. Princeton, NJ: Princeton University Press.

Lévi-Strauss, C. 1963. "The Sorcerer and His Magic," pp. 167–85 in C. Lévi-Strauss, *Structural Anthropology.* New York: Basic Books.

Lévy-Bruhl, L. 1923. *Primitive Mentality.* London: Macmillan.

Liebes, T. and E. Katz. 1990. *The Export of Meaning: Cross-Cultural Readings of "Dallas."* Oxford: Oxford University Press.

Luhmann, N. 1995. *Social Systems.* Stanford, CA: Stanford University Press.

Lukes, S. J. 1977. "Political Ritual and Social Integration," pp. 52–73 in S. J. Lukes, *Essays in Social Theory.* New York: Columbia.

Mann, M. 1986. *The Sources of Social Power*, vol. I. New York: Cambridge University Press.

Margolick, D. 2000. *Strange Fruit: Billie Holiday, Café Society, and an Early Cry for Civil Rights.* Philadelphia, PA: Running Press.

Marx, K. [1852] 1962. "The Eighteenth Brumaire of Louis Bonaparte," pp. 246–360 in *Karl Marx and Frederick Engels: Selected Works*, vol. I. Moscow: Foreign Languages Publishing House.

Mast, J. 2003. "How to Do Things with Cultural Pragmatics: A Case Study in Brief."
    Theory (Spring): 8–10.
Mayhew, L. 1997. *The New Public: Professional Communication and the Means of
    Social Influence*. New York: Cambridge University Press.
McCarthy, M. 1974. *The Masks of State: Watergate Portraits*. New York: Harcourt,
    Brace, Jovanovich.
McConachie, B. A. 1992. "Historicizing the Relations of Theatrical Production,"
    pp. 168–78 in *Critical Theory and Performance*, ed. J. G. Reinelt and J. R. Roach.
    Ann Arbor: University of Michigan Press.
Micro-Robert Poche. 1992. *Dictionnaire d'apprentissage de la langue française*, ed. A.
    Reg. Paris: France.
Moore, S. F. and B. G. Myerhoff (eds.). 1975. *Symbols and Politics in Communal
    Ideology*. Ithaca, NY: Cornell University Press.
    1977. *Secular Ritual*. Amsterdam: Van Gorcum.
Moreno, J. L. 1975. "Spontaneity and Catharsis," pp. 39–59 in *The Essential Moreno:
    Writing on Psychodrama, Group Method, and Spontaneity*, ed. J. Fox. New York:
    Springer.
Morris, C. W. 1938. *Foundations of the Theory of Signs*. Chicago: University of Chicago
    Press.
Myerhoff, B. 1978. *Number Our Days*. New York: Dutton.
Nietzsche, F. [1872] 1956. "The Birth of Tragedy," pp. 1–146 in F. Nietzsche, *The Birth
    of Tragedy and the Genealogy of Morals*. New York: Anchor Books.
Nochlin, L. 1993. *Realism*. New York: Viking.
Nolan, P. and G. Lenski. 1995. *Human Societies: An Introduction to Macrosociology*.
    New York: McGraw-Hill.
Noonan, P. 1998. *On Speaking Well*. New York: Harper.
O'Keefe, G. J. and H. Mendelsohn. 1974. "Voter Selectivity, Partisanship, and the Chal-
    lenge of Watergate." *Communication Research* 1, 4: 345–67.
Osborne, J. W. 1970. *The Silent Revolution: The Industrial Revolution in England as a
    Source of Cultural Change*. New York: Scribners.
Pavis, P. 1988. "From Text to Performance," pp. 86–100 in *Performing Texts*, ed. M.
    Issacharoff and R. F. Jones. Philadelphia: University of Pennsylvania Press.
Plato. 1980. *Gorgias*. London: Penguin.
Rappaport, R. 1968. *Pigs for the Ancestors*. New Haven, CT: Yale University Press.
Reiss, T. J. 1971. *Toward Dramatic Illusion: Theatrical Technique and Meaning from
    Hardy to Horace*. New Haven, CT: Yale University Press.
Ringmar, E. 1996. *Identity, Interest, and Action: A Cultural Explanation of Sweden's
    Intervention in the Thirty Years War*. New York: Cambridge University Press.
Roach, J. R. 1993. *The Player's Passion: Studies in the Science of Acting*. Ann Arbor:
    University of Michigan Press.
Roth, G. 1963. *The Social Democrats in Imperial Germany*. New York: Bedminster
    Press.
Rouse, J. 1992. "Textuality and Authority in Theater and Drama: Some Contemporary
    Possibilities," pp. 146–58 in *Critical Theory and Performance*, ed. J. G. Reinelt
    and J. R. Roach. Ann Arbor: University of Michigan Press.

Sahlins, M. 1972. *Stone Age Economics*. New York: Aldine de Gruyter.

Schachermeyr, F. [1953] 1971. "The Genesis of the Greek Polis," pp. 195–202 in *Political Sociology*, ed. S. N. Eisenstadt. New York: Basic Books.

Schechner, R. 1976. "From Ritual to Theatre and Back," pp. 196–230 in *Ritual, Play, and Performance: Readings in the Social Sciences/Theatre*, ed. R. Schechner and M. Schuman. New York: Seabury Press.

1977. *Ritual, Play, and Social Drama*. New York: Seabury Press.

1981. "Performers and Spectators Transported and Transformed." *Kenyon Review* 3: 83–113.

1987. "Victor Turner's Last Adventure," pp. 7–20 in V. Turner, *The Anthropology of Performance*. New York: PAJ.

2002. *Performance Studies: An Introduction*. New York: Routledge.

Schudson, M. 1981. *Discovering the News*. New York: Basic Books.

1992a. "Was There Ever a Public Sphere: If So, When? Reflections on the American Case," pp. 143–64 in *Habermas and the Public Sphere*, ed. C. Calhoun. Cambridge, Mass.: MIT Press.

1992b. *Watergate in American Memory*. New York: Basic Books.

Scott, M. B. and S. M. Lyman. 1968. "Accounts." *American Sociological Review* 33 (Feb.): 46–62.

Service, E. R. 1962. *Primitive Social Organization: An Evolutionary Perspective*. New York: Random House.

1979. *The Hunters*, 2nd edn. Englewood Cliffs, NJ: Prentice-Hall.

Sewell, W., Jr. 1980. *Work and Revolution in France: The Language of Labor from the Old Regime to 1848*. New York: Cambridge University Press.

1992. "A Theory of Structure: Duality, Agency, and Transformation." *American Journal of Sociology* 98, 1: 1–29.

Simmel, G. 1968. "The Dramatic Actor and Reality," pp. 91–8 in G. Simmel, *The Conflict in Modern Culture and Other Essays*. New York: Teacher's College Press.

Slater, P. 1966. *Microcosm*. New York: John Wiley.

Smelser, N. J. 1959. *Social Change in the Industrial Revolution*. New York: Free Press.

Smith, P. 1993. "Codes and Conflict: Toward a Theory of War as Ritual." *Theory and Society* 20: 103–38.

Smith, P. and J. C. Alexander. Forthcoming. "Introduction: The New Durkheim," in *The Cambridge Companion to Durkheim*, ed. J. C. Alexander and P. Smith. Cambridge: Cambridge University Press.

Snow, D., E. B. Rochford, S. Worden, and R. D. Benford. 1986. "Frame Alignment Processes, Micromobilization and Movement Participation." *American Sociological Review* 51: 464–81.

Spencer, W. B. and F. J. Gillen. 1927. *The Arunta*, 2 vols. London: Macmillan.

Spillman, L. 1997. *Nation and Commemoration: Creating National Identities in the United States and Australia*. New York: Cambridge University Press.

Stanislavski, C. [1934] 1989. *An Actor Prepares*. New York: Theatre Arts Books.

Stanner, W. E. H. 1972. "The Dreaming," pp. 269–77 in *Reader in Comparative Religion*, ed. W. Lessa and E. Vogt. Evanston, IL: Row, Peterson.

Swidler, A. 1986. "Culture in Action: Symbols and Strategies." *American Sociological Review* 51, 3: 273–86.

Sztompka, P. 1999. *Trust: A Sociological Theory*. New York: Cambridge University Press.

Taylor, C. 1989. *Sources of the Self: The Making of Modern Identity*. Cambridge, Mass.: Harvard University Press.

Thrift, N. 1999. "The Place of Complexity." *Theory, Culture and Society* 16, 3: 31–70.

Trinh, T. M.-H. 1989. *Woman, Native, Other: Writing Postcoloniality and Feminism*. Bloomington: Indiana University Press.

Turner, J. H. 2002. *Face to Face: Toward a Sociological Theory of Interpersonal Behavior*. Stanford, CA: Stanford University Press.

Turner, V. 1969. *The Ritual Process*. Chicago: Aldine.

    1974. *Dramas, Fields, and Metaphors: Symbolic Action in Human Society*. Ithaca, NY: Cornell University Press.

    1977. "Symbols in African Ritual," pp. 183–94 in *Symbolic Anthropology: A Reader in the Study of Symbols and Meanings*, ed. J. L. Dolgin et al. New York: Columbia University Press.

    1982. *From Ritual to Theatre: The Human Seriousness of Play*. Baltimore, MD: PAJ Press.

    1987. *The Anthropology of Performance*. New York: PAJ.

Veltrusky, J. 1964. "Man and Object in the Theater," pp. 83–91 in *A Prague School Reader on Esthetics, Literary Structure, and Style*, ed. P. L. Garvin. Washington, DC: Georgetown University Press.

Verdery, K. 1991. *National Ideology under Socialism*. Berkeley: University of California Press.

Von Hoffman, N. 1978. *Make-Believe Presidents: Illusions of Power from McKinley to Carter*. New York: Pantheon.

Wagner-Pacifici, R. 1986. *The Moro Morality Play: Terrorism as Social Drama*. Chicago: University of Chicago Press.

    1994. *Discourse and Destruction: The City of Philadelphia versus MOVE*. Chicago: University of Chicago Press.

    2000. *Theorizing the Standoff: Contingency in Action*. Cambridge: Cambridge University Press.

Woodward, B. 2004. *Plan of Attack*. New York: Simon & Schuster.

Zelizer, B. 1998. *Remembering to Forget: Holocaust Memory Through the Camera's Eye*. Chicago: University of Chicago Press.

2

From the depths of despair: performance, counterperformance, and "September 11"

Jeffrey C. Alexander

Introduction

After introducing a perspective on terrorism as post-political and after establishing the criteria for success that are immanent in this form of anti-political action, this essay interprets September 11, 2001 and its aftermath inside a cultural-sociological perspective. After introducing a macro-model of social performance that combines structural and semiotic with pragmatic and power-oriented dimensions, I show how the terrorist attack on New York City and the counterattacks that immediately occurred in response can be viewed as an iteration of the performance/counterperformance dialectic that began decades, indeed centuries, ago in terms of the relation of Western expansion and Arab-Muslim reaction. I pay careful attention to the manner in which the counterperformance of New Yorkers and Americans develops an idealized, liminal alternative that inspired self-defense and outrage, leading to exactly the opposite performance results from those the al-Qaeda terrorists had intended.

To understand the sociological processes that created "September 11" (hereafter also referred to as "9/11") and what transpired politically, morally, and humanly during that tragic time and its aftermath, and also to understand how to prevent a tragic eternal return, we must reflect on the theoretical presuppositions that underlie our empirical perceptions. We need to theorize terrorism differently, thinking of its violence less in physical and instrumental terms than as a particularly gruesome kind of symbolic action in a complex performative field. If we do, we will understand, as well, how the American response to that terror thwarted its nihilistic intention and established a counterperformance that continues to structure the cultural pragmatics of national and international politics today.

Terrorism as (post)political

Terrorism can be understood as a form of political action, one of a very specific type. It is distinguished first by the sustained violence of its principal methods, in contrast to a politics that relies on organization and communication or one that rests, like those of most nation-states in their foreign relations, on the periodic but discrete application of coercion and force. Terrorism is distinguished, second, by the isolation of its practitioners, in contrast not only to the communal character of mass organizations but also even to the vanguard politics of Leninism, which seeks to establish thick network relations with groups whose ideology it can mold and whose solidarity it can claim.

Finally, terrorism is distinguished by the relative diffuseness of its ideology. Drunk on grandiose delusions of the millennium and on visions that make worldly success impossible in realistic terms, terrorist ideology cannot spell out the political steps to achieve its ideological aims. Because of this yawning gap between ideals and realities, the working ideology of terrorism focuses almost exclusively on tactics and rather little on broader strategy. Another way of putting this is to say that terrorism focuses on deeds more than words.

These disjunctions reflect the institutional failures that breed a politics of terror, which flourishes only in social situations where *politics*, in the classical sense of the term, has not been allowed free play (Crick 1962). In much of the contemporary Arab-Islamic world, national and regional institutions have flattened drastically and have narrowed the dynamics of political will-formation. Discursive, democratic, and humane forms of political expression have become impossible.

Hobsbawm (1959) once called banditry and peasant riots *pre-political* – to differentiate them from the militant and sometimes violent revolutionary politics that characterized what he took to be the normal, class-war politics of his day. Contemporary terrorism might be called *post-political*. It reflects the end of political possibility. In this sense, 9/11 expresses, and displaces, the bitterness of an Arab nationalism whose promises of state-building, economic development, and full citizenship lay in tatters throughout the North African and Middle Eastern world. Terrorism is post- rather than pre-political in another sense as well. Its profound experience of political impotence is expressed not merely in cultural or metaphysical terms but in a hungry will to power and a manifest ambition to rebuild a great Arab-Muslim state.

Rather than defeating its opponents through political struggle, terrorism seeks to draw blood. Its tactics deliver maiming and death; they serve a strategy of inflicting humiliation, chaos, and reciprocal despair. Beyond these primordial ambitions lie three destabilizing aims. These flow in increasingly powerful ripples from the initial drawing of blood:

- to create *political* instability by murdering key leaders and overwhelming the immediate political process;
- to achieve *social* instability by disrupting networks of exchange and by sowing such fear that distrust becomes normal and chaos ensues; and
- to create *moral* instability by inducing authorities to respond to these political and social threats with repressive actions that will delegitimate key institutions in their own society. Such repression may be domestic or foreign, and it is less a matter of actual engagement in violent and suppressive actions than of how these actions are framed.

The post-political and the civil

Does terrorist action typically succeed in these aims? This depends on context. Success is a direct function of the authoritarian nature of the regime against which terrorism takes aim. Post-political tactics are much less likely to succeed in societies that allow politics to mediate power, and this is particularly the case in legitimate, deeply rooted democratic regimes. Post-political action certainly does produce significant, sometimes world-historical, and almost always existentially horrendous effects. In societies that have more developed civil spheres, however, such effects are not nearly as transformative as their initiators had hoped.

The seemingly demonic ferocity of terrorists, their ruthless willingness to sacrifice the lives of others and their own, indeed does draw blood and does create social and political chaos and instability. The slaughterhouse of World War One began with terrorist assassination. Anarchist and syndicalist violence in late nineteenth-century America marked new phases of anti-capitalist agitation. The activities of the Red Brigades, the Baader-Meinhof gang, and the Weathermen in the late 1960s and early 1970s sent shockwaves of terror throughout significant parts of the Italian, German, and American populations. White militia groups wreaked terrible havoc in Oklahoma City and elsewhere in the 1990s.

Still, none of these terrorist waves, so effective in narrowly post-political terms, succeeded in translating their immediate tactical "achievements" into the broader strategic aims of moral delegitimation and regime change. The reason is clear: in civil societies, to eschew the tactic of politics is to be blinded in broader strategic terms. In democratic societies, in order to achieve broad effects political actors must orient their tactics to address the moral frameworks that compel the larger population. This is exactly what terrorism cannot do. It is hardly surprising then that on September 11, the terrorists who attacked the Twin Towers produced exactly the opposite effect than the one they had in mind.

This broad sociological claim about the ineffectiveness of terrorism in a civil society might be countered by pointing to earlier terrorist movements, from the Irish and South African to the Zionist and Palestinian, which seemingly did achieve institutional success. It would take a different and much more comparative essay to respond fully to such counterclaims. Here I focus only on one terrorist act. Yet we might consider the Palestinian Liberation Organization (PLO) as one brief case in point. While it first came to world attention through acts of terror, the PLO began to achieve its aims of territory and quasi-statehood only later, during the years of *Intifadeh* (uprising).

This youth-centered, stone-throwing protest movement against Israeli occupation engaged not in murderous, post-political terrorism but in highly effective political dramaturgy (Liebes 1992a, 1992b). The young Palestinian "Davids" created sympathy, not only outside Israel but also within it, for their struggle against the Israeli military "Goliaths." What eventually followed was an occasionally enthusiastic but more often resigned acceptance of the Palestinians' national ambition among influential segments of the Israeli public that had been steadfast in their opposition to the PLO during its terrorist days.

A dramaturgical framework of politics

Despite the critical importance of politics, the difficulty that terrorism has in gaining success cannot be explained in purely instrumental terms. Success and failure in politics is not a game. It neither responds simply to available resources nor is guided exclusively by rational choice. Terrorism has a moral reference, and its understanding demands a cultural-sociological frame.

We must consider terrorism as a form not only of political but also of symbolic action. Terrorism is a particular kind of political performance. It draws blood – literally and figuratively – making use of its victims' vital fluids to throw a striking and awful painting upon the canvas of social life. It aims not only to kill but in and through killing aims also to gesture in a dramatic way. In Austinian (1957) terms, terrorism is an illocutionary force that aims for perlocutionary effect.

Performative actions have both a manifest and latent symbolic reference.[1] Their explicit messages take shape against background structures of immanent meaning. In other words, social performances, like theatrical ones, symbolize particular meanings only because they can assume more general, taken-for-granted meaning structures within which their performances are staged. Performances select among, reorganize, and make present themes that are implicit in the immediate surround of social life – though these are absent in a literal sense. Reconfiguring the signifieds of background signifiers, performances evoke a new set of more action-specific signifiers in turn.

It is these signifiers that compose a performance's *script*. Social performance cannot be reduced to background culture. Performance is initiated because actors have particular, contingent goals. Scripts are cultural, but the reverse is not equally true: background cultures are not themselves scripts. It is not "culture" that creates scripts, but pragmatic efforts to project particular cultural meanings in pursuit of practical goals.

Scripts narrate and choreograph conflicts among the sacred, profane, and mundane. An effectively scripted narrative defines compelling protagonists and frightening antagonists and pushes them through a series of emotionally laden encounters. Such agonistic action constitutes a *plot*. Through plotted encounters, social dramas create emotional and moral effects. Their audiences may experience excitement and joy if the plots are romances or comedies, or pity and suffering if they are melodramas or tragedies. If the scripted narrative is effective and if the performance of the plot is powerful, the audience experiences catharsis, which allows new moral judgments to form and new lines of social action to be undertaken in turn.

The scripts of social dramas initially are imagined by would-be authors and agents (Turner 1982). These scripts actually might be written before a performance begins, but they also may be emergent, crystallizing only as the drama unfolds. Here, the dramas that scripts are meant to inspire aim at *audiences* composed of the publics of complex civil societies. The *actors* in these social dramas may be institutional authorities or rebels, activists or couch potatoes, political leaders or foot soldiers in social movements, or the imagined publics of engaged citizens themselves. The motivations and patterns of such actors are affected deeply, though are not controlled, by *directors*. In social dramas, these are the organizers, ideologists, and leaders of collective action (Eyerman and Jameson 1991).

Social-dramatic action can be understood, in these terms, by the theatrical concept of the *mise-en-scène*, literally, putting into the scene. Such dramatic enactment requires control over the *means of symbolic production*, which suggests a stage, a setting, and certain elementary theatrical props. For social dramas, control over such means points to the need to create platforms for performance in the public imagination and, eventually, to create access to such media of transmission as television, cinema, newspapers, radio, and the Internet.

The elements of performative success and failure

When theatrical dramas are successful, there emerges a kind of "fusion" between these diverse elements of performance, a coming together of background meaning, actors, props, scripts, direction, and audience. Actors seem really to "be" their role. Their performances are experienced as convincing, as authentic.

Audiences, sometimes literally but always figuratively, forget for the moment that they are in a theatre or movie house. The performance has achieved verisimilitude, the aesthetic quality of seeming to be real.

If such triumphant fusion is not easy to produce in theatre, in social performance it is that much more difficult to effect. In small societies with more simplified and integrated social organization, the social-dramatic task is less challenging than in more complex and less integrated ones. Indeed, the frequency with which performative fusion is achieved marks the centrality and effectiveness of ritual in earlier societies. Even in complex societies, however, fusion is still possible, and it frequently is achieved in settings where the elements of performances can be controlled carefully: between the faithful and their priest, rabbi, or mullah; between children and their mothers and fathers; between patients and their doctors and therapists; between motivated employees and inspiring managers; between partisan audiences and artful orators.

The more complex the society, however, the more often social performances fail to come together in convincing, seemingly authentic ways. The more that institutional and cultural resources become differentiated from one another – the more political and ideological pluralism allows conflict – the more common performative failure becomes. In complex societies, real social rituals are few and far between.

Long before postmodern philosophers declared the end of metanarratives, the metaphysical logic that established the *telos* of performances in traditional societies began to disappear. As societies become more complex and cultures less metaphysical, the elements of social performance become contingent and more difficult to coordinate and control. Action becomes open-ended, and everything can go awry. Rather than being sympathetically infused with teleological prejudice, social dramas become endemically unconvincing. Actors often seem inauthentic and manipulated, as if they are puppets and not autonomous individuals. Modern audiences tend to see power at work and not to see meaning. They attribute to would-be actors instrumental, not idealistic, motivations.

Performances may fail if any of the elements that compose them are insufficiently realized, or if the relation among these elements is not articulated in a coherent or forceful way. If there is not access to the means of symbolic production, for example, the effectiveness of the other elements goes for naught. Such failure to gain access to contemporary media might be the product of social distance, powerlessness, poverty, or of the unconvincing and unpopular dramatic content of the performance itself.

Even if productions are projected fully onto the public stage, they will fail if the roles and institutions mediating audience interpretation do so in a critical manner. Such interpretive criticism has the effect of separating dramatic intention from dramatic reception. It alienates actors from audience, de-fusing rather than re-fusing the elements of performance. In complex societies, critics, intellectuals, social authorities, and peer groups continuously comment upon the social-dramatic stream, as do the professional journalists who wish to appear merely to report upon it. But even if access is gained and if performances are interpreted positively, the thoroughgoing success of a performance can be thwarted if audiences are fragmented. Cultural antagonisms and/or social cleavages can create polarized and conflicting interpretive communities. A drama that is utterly convincing for one audience-public might seem artificial to another. Insofar as group understandings of critical performances diverge, their existential and moral realities become irreconcilable.

Performative failures allow the law of unintended consequences to enter into the cultural sphere. Social dramas produce unintended interpretations; they become performative contradictions in the philosophical sense. Ambiguity replaces clarity. There is a doubleness of text. For the social dramas of complex societies, there seems always to be an absent audience alongside the putative visible one that performers themselves have in mind. The absent audience is likely to understand the performance in a manner that belies its script and the actors' and director's intentions. In this way, the total meaning of a performance is delayed. It is deferred beyond a drama's immediate reception to the audiences waiting "off stage." In complex societies, then, interpretation is marked by *différence* (Derrida 1978).

The performative contradictions of East versus West

In the face of conservative claims about the clash of civilizations, it seems important to begin by emphasizing that, while there are distinctive differences between the great monotheistic religions of the East and West, in broad comparative terms they share the same general symbolic order to a remarkable degree (cf. Lapidus 1987; Udovitch 1987; Mirsepassi 2000; Alexander 2001).

Both the Judeo-Christian and the Islamic religious traditions, which in some significant part have formed the backdrop for their inter-civilizational dynamics, are dualistic and Manichean. They are relatively "this-worldly" and "ascetic" in Weber's (1978) terms, and they contain powerful egalitarian strains. Both have legitimated not only heterodox but also revolutionary movements. Finally, and most tellingly for the present case, each has developed powerful religious legitimation for just, or holy, wars. Drawing from sacred narratives of judgment, each tradition has produced ethical prophecies that legitimate violent means for holy ends, prophecies that culminate in apocalyptic visions of the pathway to paradise.[2] The dichotomies informing the complementary Eastern and Western narratives of salvation and damnation can be sketched out in a very rough way (Table 2.1).

Table 2.1 *The structure of Eastern and Western narratives of salvation and damnation*

Sacred/Friend	Profane/Enemy
Peaceful	Violent
Cooperative	Antagonistic
Honest	Deceitful
Equal	Dominating
Rational	Irrational
Solidaristic	Fractious
Ethical	Instrumental
Honorable	Corrupt
Faithful	Cynical

If the same semiotic code supplies the signifiers for the sacred political actions in both religious and civilizational traditions, why do groups representing these civilizations stand today in such dangerous conflict? The reason is that mediated through a series of historical developments, the signifieds of these signifiers have become strikingly, even fatefully, different. The Christian Crusades, the geopolitics of the Mogul and Ottoman Empires, the military triumphs of European empire – through such historical developments as these, the shared signifiers of the great monotheistic religions became connected with concrete signifieds that conveyed not their mutual understanding of the sacred and profane but extraordinary cultural difference and social antagonism. Over the long course of historical time, and with tragic and sometimes terrifying consequences, there gradually emerged the pronounced tendency for the Islamic and Judeo-Christian religio-political civilizations to embody evil for each other. What has developed is a self-reinforcing system of cultural-cum-social polarization, in which the sacralizing social dramas of one side have been the polluting dramas of the other.

From the mid-twentieth century, this system of performative contradiction has been fueled by such proximate social and political developments as Israeli statehood; the failure of pan-Arabism and economic modernization in the regions of the Islamic crest; the increasing relative and often absolute impoverishment of what once was called the Third World; the globalization of capital markets and the undermining of national sovereignty; the rise of feminist movements; American displacement of France and Britain as the pre-eminent capitalist and military power; and the end of the bipolar world and the emergence of America's asymmetrical military, cultural, and economic position.

At every point, these economic and political developments were mediated, channeled, and crystallized by the background codes and narratives that polarized the East and West as cultural-political regions. The religious orientations that East and West share in the most general comparative terms were so refracted by social history that mutual misunderstanding became the norm. Indeed, what has remained constant through the twists and turns of contingent events is the polarizing cultural logic that forms a background to them. The social performances on one side are misperceived by audiences on the other. Even when Western actors are scripted and are played as sincere protagonists, they pass fluidly, artfully, and authentically into the position of antagonists in the scripts that emerge from the perceptions of the "Eastern" side. At the same time, when Islamic scripts portray Eastern actors as protagonists in leading roles, they are easily reinterpreted as antagonistic "others" in the eyes of Western audiences.

There is no better illustration of this performative contradiction than the *jihad*. Created as a violent means for religious-cum-political purification within medieval Islam (Black 2001), the *jihad* was applied to Western occupiers in a later historical time (Kepel 2002). For its Islamic practitioners and key sections of Islamic audiences, this modern *jihad* is viewed as a sacred and highly demanding performance of holy war. For its non-Islamic victims and audience, the performance of *jihad* is interpreted in precisely the opposite manner, as an authentic demonstration of the polluted and demonic qualities of Islam itself.

The most recent and most highly consequential emplotments on this tragic contrapuntal culture structure resulted from American performances in Afghanistan in the 1980s and the Gulf War in the 1990s. The Afghan war, despite its apparent triumph for the West, marked a failed performance, for it unintentionally produced an anti-Western understanding in a significant segment of its audience. Having helped Islamic insurgents dislodge the Soviet occupation of Afghanistan, a defeat that significantly contributed to the larger project of destabilizing the Communist "evil empire," the United States declared victory and withdrew. This triumphal exit was interpreted as typical Western indifference by the national and religious formations that framed the anti-Soviet war from their own, radically different point of view. This construction of Jewish–Christian–American infidelity is what generated the first wave of organized anti-American *jihad*, a vicious and determined counterperformance.

The interpretation of the Gulf War and its aftermath followed a similar pattern. Presented to Western audiences as a virtuous war of liberation, it merely served to confirm Western deceit and aggression to groups of radical Islamic nationalists. The post-war United Nations (UN) treaty, which allowed Iraq continued sovereignty while sharply curtailing its economic and military freedom,

was regarded widely at the time of the war's conclusion as reasonably motivated and humane in its concerns. During the course of the 1990s, however,
the treaty provisions – and the treaty's steadfast and aggressive American and
British guarantors – came to be regarded, first by radical Islamic groups in
the region and subsequently by many humanitarian agencies and critical intellectuals around the world, as selfish, militaristic, and even orientalist. Once
again, the unintended consequences of performative action had intensified the
polarizing understandings of earlier misinterpretations. These audience reactions inspired Islamic radicals to engage in new and even more destructive
counterperformances in turn.

These tragic misperformances recall another war-ending misinterpretation
that became, equally unwittingly, a war-starting one. When the triumphant
Allies wrote the Treaty of Versailles after World War One their strategic aim was
to secure a long-term international peace. But the treaty negotiations, and the
final document, were also scripts that allowed leaders to project performances
to their French, American, and British audiences back home. Not surprisingly,
German audiences read these performances in a very different manner. Eventually, a talented but malevolent Austrian political actor wrote a new script for
holy war and directed Germany's tragic performance in it. The Western world
has come to rue that day.

Initial success: bin Laden assembles the performative elements of terror

Osama bin Laden was another world-historical actor who would lead another
"people" in counterperformance against the West in another time. Like that other
infamous but highly effective demagogue before him, bin Laden responded to
the social despair and the moldering anger that marked significant segments
of his home audience – in this case an Arab-Islamic, not a German, one.[3]
Activist in the anti-Soviet holy war and embittered, impotent observer of the
Western occupation of Saudi Arabia during and after the Gulf War, bin Laden
proved himself to be enormously effective in staging the next phase of the
contrapuntal performance cycle of East versus West. He imagined how a new
kind of performance could be staged in the conditions of today. His innovation
was to turn terrorism into mass murder and to place this counterperformance
on the world stage. Bin Laden not only imagined himself as the protagonist of
a massively organized and globally televised *jihad*, but he also had the awful
artfulness and the personal resources to actually place himself in the center of
the real thing.

Because bin Laden was rich and well connected, he possessed the resources
to hire "actors" for a vastly larger terrorist organization than ever had been put

together before, and he also had the networks to find possible actors and to interview them before allowing them to join his production teams. But more than resources were involved. Bin Laden was charismatic and creative. He had a real feeling for the story line, the traditional Islamic agonistic that plotted virtuous al-Qaeda heroes fighting for their sacred honor against villainous Americans with money in their hearts and blood on their hands. This cunning director established secret training camps that allowed backstage rehearsals for the public performances to come. In these protected spaces, fresh recruits were coached on how they could assume the parts assigned to them faithfully and convincingly in the al-Qaeda script. When the new "method" could be assumed with utter authenticity, the actor-terrorists were released into "performance teams," which secretly prepared for the full-dress production of martyrdom in Western lands.[4]

But perhaps what most distinguished bin Laden was his ability to command the means of symbolic production. He needed a worldwide stage and means for murder on a scale far larger, and more dramaturgically compelling, than he ever before had been able to acquire. His demonic genius was to teach his would-be martyrs yet another role – that of student-visitors to America who were eager to learn to fly the big planes. Once the actor-terrorists possessed this skill, they could commandeer passenger jets that already were inside the American staging area. With these props, the martyr-terrorists could attack and could try to destroy the symbols of polluted power that were central to the emotional dynamics of their script. If they were fortunate, they also could kill thousands of Americans, and other Westerns, who were outside the passenger plane. If this occurred, then the bin Laden performance of *jihad* would possess the widest possible public stage.

As the world learned at 9:03 a.m. on September 11, 2001, bin Laden's performance of mass terror unfolded with barely a hitch. It created a shocking narrative of gothic horror that unfolded, in agonizing and simultaneous detail, before an audience of hundreds of millions. The terrorist-martyr-actors succeeded in destroying polluted icons of modern American capitalism, the Twin Towers, which evocatively symbolized their atheistic Western enemy. The terrorist performances created not only unprecedented physical destruction and loss of life but also moral humiliation and emotional despair, and they captured the world's media attention for days on end.

In purely sociological terms – which for the sake of analysis must bracket normative considerations – this performance surely marked an extraordinary achievement. So many personnel and so much materiel had to be organized and directed. The scripts had to be refined so continuously. The terrorists' method acting had to be sustained so continuously. So many failures were possible, yet in the end, the play went on.

The audience responds: joy and despair as interpretations of the terror-performance

Yes, the play went on, but with what result? Did the performance have its intended effect? Was the plot, when enacted, perceived as martyrdom for a just cause? Did the physical destruction lead beyond immediate social instability and chaos to political imbalance and moral delegitimation? Destabilization is both objective and subjective. Emotions are coded and regulated symbolically; the objects of cathexis simply are not felt but simultaneously are understood. Because traumas are subject to interpretation, different background understandings led to different reactions and, eventually, to different paths for recovery.

Such considerations point to the fragmentation that marks contemporary societies. If the elements of artful staging are defused, and are difficult to bring successfully together, so indeed is the audience. In most public events, in fact, there are many different audiences, and their reactions to the same event often are framed by fiercely incompatible scripts. It was the failure to understand the separation of audience from performance – and the fragmentation of these separated audiences into different and often hermetically sealed interpretive spaces – that made the initial success of the terrorist *jihad* so short-lived and the response to it at most only a partial success.

The events on that morning of September 11 played before profoundly different viewing groups. Many Arab-Islamic audiences hailed the performances with great applause. The Arab streets, it was reported authoritatively, sometimes danced with joy. Among Arab elites, emails of satisfaction and triumph were passed quietly. Among these groups, real performative fusion was obtained in the destruction's immediate wake. Terrorists were perceived as martyrs who had gone on to their heavenly reward. The infidels had been punished, and Allah would treat them, too, in an appropriate way. As the producer and director of this world-historical drama, and indeed as its protagonist-at-a-distance, Osama bin Laden became an object of extraordinarily intense identification. He was lionized as a hero, mythologized in an instant. His likeness was emblazed on T-shirts that were displayed like totemic images on human bodies. Recordings of his triumphant words were reproduced and continuously replayed on video and compact disc. The fusion among script, performance, actors, and audience was indeed impressively achieved.[5] But what about the other audience?

When *jihad* emerged in medieval Islamic society, its success did not depend on wide audience response. Success required only the performance assassination itself. Because social structure and culture were simpler and more integrated, the *jihad* message was readable, clearly and directly, from the act. In complex global society, nothing can be further from the truth.

At first, however, it appeared that the American audience might react in a manner consistent with al-Qaeda's script. As the drama unfolded, Western viewers witnessed objective destruction and experienced fears of personal annihilation and of the center giving way. The unimaginable destruction of giant buildings and the vicarious experience of mutilation and violent death were palpable, shocking, and psychologically debilitating. Because Western viewers identified with those who were attacked, they experienced the injuries as if they were attacks on their own buildings, bodies, and minds.

That the jaws of destruction had opened and the final days were at hand were powerful experiences in the immediate aftermath of the terror. Images of just punishment, of hell and damnation, are deep and recurrent themes in the Western imagination, and images of the New York City crash site were framed by aesthetic archetypes of apocalypse that recalled the late medieval paintings of Hieronymus Bosch. Dust blotted out the sun. Day turned to night. People caught on fire, suffocated, and jumped to their death. Hysteria and wild screaming were recorded and were transmitted worldwide. Strong men cried; firefighters and guards and policemen were brought to their knees, and they died in abject confusion, gasping for air. In the towers above, rich and powerful men and women waited helplessly, their sophisticated machines useless, and they died in even greater numbers. Unable to evoke an explicitly religious framework, commentators and observers evoked metaphors of the long-feared nightmare of nuclear holocaust to describe the scene, and they soon named the crash site "Ground Zero."

Not only physical but also ontological security was threatened, and there was a specifically American dimension as well. For in the country's collective imagination, America remained a virgin land (Smith 1950), a shining beacon on a protected hill. It also was imagined as a fortress that foreigners would forever be unable to breach. Indeed, the nation's sacred soil had not been stained with American blood since the middle of the second century before.

The innocent honor of this mythical America stood in grave danger of being polluted on this day. Fear stalked the land. Americans were reluctant to project themselves into their environments. There was a real and immediate deflation of generalized social trust. People stopped driving, stayed away from public transportation, and failed to show up for work. The stock market dipped sharply, and deposits were withdrawn from banks. Tourism evaporated, and pleasure traveling disappeared.

These early American reactions, projected worldwide as denouement to the initial performative act, provided some Arab-Islamic audiences with evidence that the terrorist activity had succeeded not only in its immediate but also in its ultimate aims. These initial impressions were justifiable, but they eventually proved incorrect. The structural conditions for fusion proved impossible to overcome, and bin Laden's terrorist performance would be as subject to mis-interpretation as those actions that America once had initiated on its own. The fragmentation of media and critics was a social fact; so were the polarized background meanings that structured the audiences for the terrorist performance on a global scale. The contrapuntal logic of East–West confrontation continued, and there emerged counterreadings that eventually generated counterperformances.

Bin Laden misperforms: American counterreading and idealization

What was heroism for one audience was terrorism for the other. In fact, the terrorist pollution and destruction of American core symbols produced, within large segments of the American audience, a one-sided idealization in turn of everything American. This idealization began almost immediately, became stronger in the hours and days after the event, and worked itself out at many different levels of social structure and cultural life. It marked the beginnings of a counterreading that provided the script for the counterperformance that continues today.

This counterreading allowed the nightmare story of terrorist destruction to be retold – by critics, commentators, and reporters; by victims, helpers, and sideline observers; and by political, social, and intellectual leaders who were the once and future directors of American action on the world stage. For themselves and for their audiences of listeners, viewers, and readers, these groups recast the humbling and fearful destruction of America as an ennobling narrative, one that revealed the strength of an ideal American core.[6] The existence of this inner, spiritual core was asserted in a matter-of-fact way, as if it had to do neither with metaphysics nor metaphor but was a matter of self-evident, natural truth. "The fire is still burning, but from it has emerged a stronger spirit," remarked New York Mayor Rudy Giuliani when he led a memorial service at the site one month later. Following upon a series of deeply structured symbolic antitheses – ideal and material, soul and body, light and dark, truth and falsehood – Americans described the terrorist destruction as having an effect only on external, physical forms. The ideal inner core of America was still intact; indeed, as a result of the effort at destruction, this core actually had grown stronger than ever before. Rather than being threatened or destroyed, the social center was being reconstituted as an ideal and not as a material thing. Because the center of society existed in the imagination, in the nation's soul, it certainly would be rematerialized in the days ahead.

This counterreading of the terrorist performance took leave from the mundane vagaries of time and place, from the dust, grime, and blood that marked the physical terrorist site. It constituted a new imaginary that created an alternative, a liminal time and space, an existential zone located in the collective consciousness, not in the material world. The new time was symbolized as a new calendrical date, 9/11, a numerical sequence referring literally to an emergency call but whose pragmatic meaning was transformed into an iconic marker of time. After September 11, it was remarked continuously, "Nothing has ever been the same." The new beginning, in other words, marked the beginning of a new world.[7] Transcendent rather than geographic, this new world would fill in and would smooth over the crater that threatened the center of American life.

Before 9/11, America had been fractured by social cleavages, by the normal incivilities attendant on social complexity, and even, on occasion, by unspeakable hostilities. After 9/11, the national community experienced and interpreted itself as united by feeling, marked by the loving kindness displayed among persons who once only had been friends, and by the civility and solicitude among those who once merely had been strangers. There was an intense generalization of social attention, which shifted away from specificity, concreteness, and idiosyncrasy to abstraction, idealization, and universality.[8] This idealizing emotional and moral framework spread from the physical to the social world, from the individual to the collectivity, from the family to the business community, from the city of New York to the American nation, and from the fate of the American nation to (Western) civilization itself.

Before September 11, the giant Twin Towers that struck upward from the bottom of Manhattan were perceived routinely, were taken for granted as mundane physical objects. If they were noticed at all, it was for their ugliness and vulgarity and for the intrusive and almost aggressive manner in which they towered over lower Manhattan life, overshadowing, it was sometimes said, the light of "Lady Liberty" herself. By the very act of their destruction, however, the towers moved from the mundane and profane to the sacred of symbolic life. They were re-presented as having embodied not capitalism but enterprise; not the bourgeois but the cosmopolitan; not private property but public democracy. They were reconstructed retrospectively as their architects once idealistically had envisioned them, as cool icons of aesthetic modernism, symbols of economic energy that were deemed now to have been compatible fully with the famous statue that represented political freedom in the harbor beyond.

If these physical containers were transformed in the American imagination, so much more so were the maimed and murdered people whom these buildings once contained. Before 9/11, the merchants and traders of Wall Street often had been the objects of envy and resentment, maligned as selfish and indulgent, as a new and unattractively yuppified social class. In America's fiercely fought, even if largely symbolic, class war, no group launched such critical salvos more fiercely than the often resentful remnants of America's skilled working class, largely white, ethnic, and male. Yet they themselves also were frequent objects of popular disdain, ridiculed as macho and racist, as unlettered, beer-drinking, red-necked conservatives too quick to wrap themselves in the American flag. It was this class who composed the larger part of the firefighters and police officers who entered the Twin Towers in the ill-fated efforts to help the elites who worked in the floors above.

As they perished, the members of both groups were transformed symbolically. They were made innocent and good, were portrayed in a mythical manner that abstracted from their particular qualities of gender, class, race, or ethnicity.

The first-place level of transfiguration focused on the victims and participants as archetypal individuals *tout court*. In the magazine, television, and newspaper elegies that were composed about them, which indeed amounted to commemorations, in the weeks and months after the tragic event, the traders and firemen, secretaries and police became the heroic subjects in sentimental, often heart-wrenching stories about their pluck and their determination. Their highly genred (Bakhtin 1986) biographies revealed that the strength, dedication, and kindness of the innocents murdered on September 11 allowed each one to build a meaningful and coherent life.

The second level of idealized reconstruction focused on the family. Whatever sociological statistics might have to say about divorce and loneliness, absent fathers and latch-key children, abandoned wives and extramarital affairs, the now mythically reconstructed individuals who perished on 9/11 were represented as members of warm and loving families. They were devoted husbands and wives, attentive mothers and fathers, loyal children and grandparents. Their familial love was always constant, vivid, and pure.

The third level of transfiguration concerned the economic elite itself. The highly profitable, often cutthroat, and relentlessly competitive business enterprises who rented space in the Twin Towers were represented as decent, entirely human enterprises. They made an honest living, and their industry contributed to the bounty of American life. Their employees often had risen from rags to riches, and they were, by ethnicity, taste, and personal life, no different in any important way than any other participant in American life. On the day after 9/11, Cable News Network (CNN) interviewed the president of the investment firm Cantor Fitzgerald, all of whose employees in the World Trade Center had died. In the course of recounting his company's tragedy, this powerful businessman broke down and wept in a pitiable way. This scene was remarked upon throughout the world. It was the human face of 9/11's American side: it was a sign that the terrorists had targeted human life, not the West or some abstraction of modernity and capitalism. It was also a demonstration that the humanity the terrorists had tried to destroy somehow had managed to survive.

From this transformation of degraded and antagonistic economic classes into idealized images of individual, family, and enterprise, the generalization of solidary feelings expanded like a ripple from a stone that had been thrown into the middle of a tranquil pond. New York City often had been portrayed as a dirty, angry, and competitive place, the epicenter of the cutthroat, impersonal cosmopolitanism that conservative Americans loved to hate. After 9/11, it was presented as a prototypically human place. It was a living organism attacked by virulent foreign bodies, and it was fighting for its life. Residents of small towns sent messages not just of condolence but also of identification. "Arkansas Prays for You" and "Southwest Airlines Loves NYC" were messages scrawled at the wreckage site. One Midwestern town raised money for a replacement fire engine, and others for new earth-moving machines.[9] Hundreds of Americans swiftly traveled to the city and joined volunteer brigades to clean up and to purify the damaged area and to help those who had been traumatized by the events. Europeans publicly pronounced their love and affection for this quintessentially American city and expressed alarm over its injury. New York City became the center of the ideal core, concentrating within itself the spirit, energy, and openness to difference that made America the "land of the free and the home of the brave."

These gestures of identification towards the center from the peripheries had the reciprocal effect of strengthening national and supra-national solidarity in turn. While it was only one part of New York City that was injured, and only 2,813 particular persons who perished within it, the news headlined an attack on "America," and ordinary citizens everywhere expressed themselves with the plural first-person pronoun "we." In the long aftermath of 9/11, during the period of the new beginning, it was not uncommon for this identification to expand outside of the American nation as well. In the first year of the Bush Administration, there had been increasing hostility and separateness between America and Europe. After 9/11, the German prime minister proclaimed, "We are all Americans now." The reciprocal bonds that connect Europe and the United States were reasserted idealistically, and the moral debt from World War Two was repaid symbolically. The North Atlantic Treaty Organization (NATO) declared its determination to defend America, as if to underscore the bond of extra-national, shared civilization itself. Once again Europeans and Americans were united under a great cause to fight for the common good, but this time the unity was wider, for it extended to Germany and Russia and Japan.

From counterscript to counterperformance: the "war against terrorism" and beyond

Osama bin Laden's terrorist performance had achieved physical destruction and social instability, and it briefly threatened to disrupt the nation's political life. But it did not achieve terrorism's most significant goal, which has to do with the moral delegitimation of the regime itself. This performative turn seemed to have taken the director, bin Laden, by surprise, and certainly it must have disappointed him deeply. According to the binaries of his background script, if al-Qaeda was strong and pure, then Americans were soft and corrupt, their regime democratic only in the formal sense. Convinced of their weak motives, devious relations, and corrupt institutions, bin Laden believed that neither Americans nor their government would be able to respond politically, socially, or morally to his perfectly executed script.[10] In fact, however, the effect of al-Qaeda's performance was the very opposite from the one it had hoped to achieve. Rather than moral destabilization, there was revivification. Osama bin Laden's terrorism was performed before a fragmented and polarized audience, and it produced a reading counter to those intended by the terrorist-actors themselves.

This counterreading led to a new militarization of America, and later to a new war that would destroy al-Qaeda's national-territorial base. The cultural-sociological processes described here were causes to these more material effects. The new solidarity that developed in reaction to 9/11 deepened the divisions that had produced it. The idealization of America and the West was constructed in relation to an equally powerful stigmatization of everything not it. The new national unity produced a new global polarity at the same time. The counterreading had created an idealized and powerful protagonist, and it demanded an equally threatening antagonist in turn. Without it, there would be no tension to the plot, and the redemption of the moral actors would not be allowed to unfold realistically. Purification demanded pollution, and salvation required revenge. The discourse of friends and enemies was ready at hand. The terrorists were constructed as bitter and frustrated, as marginal, as weak and cowardly human beings. They were monsters, not men, and their actions had no principled rationale.

Against such sinister creatures the only appropriate response was force, for they could not be reasoned with but only suppressed. "None of us will forget this day," President Bush told the nation on the evening of September 11, "yet we go forward to defend freedom and all that is good and just in the world" (quoted in Woodward 2002: 30). There must be a war against terror. The terrorists were evildoers. "We haven't seen this kind of barbarism in a long period of time," the President later remarked (Woodward 2002: 94). He added, "This crusade, this war on terrorism is going to take a while." But it was not only a matter of recalling from the fog of memory the Christian campaigns against the Muslim usurpers of earlier times. Fiercely virtuous military campaigns had defended Republican regimes against "despotic" invaders from Athens to Florence to the beaches at Normandy (Hanson 2001).

Will the war against terrorism succeed? Will it not produce inevitably another counterperformance in turn? Even the most successful of the Crusades failed to roll back Islam's energetic expansion, much less its theological-political self-regard. Terrorism produces wars against it, and crusades produce *jihads* in turn. Contingent actions taken in freedom reaffirm the binding structures of contrapuntal plot. Perhaps this logic of performance and counterperformance has not been appreciated fully yet by the leaders of either side.

With the arrival of the "Age of Terror" (Talbot and Chanda 2002), the power to initiate the newest phase in the contrapuntal cycle has moved from West to East. But the *mis en scène* has not been altered. Islamic terrorism is a dramatic gesture, the Western response to it a dramatic misunderstanding. These Islamic and Western scripts fuel iterative sequences of misperformance.[11] Unless the cycle is broken, it will undermine the prospects for social stability and international understanding and, for many unfortunate persons, the very right to life.

Notes

The first draft of this essay was presented in late September 2001 at the Sociology Institute of the University of Konstanz and in CADIS at the École des Hautes Études en Sciences Sociales in Paris. I am grateful to Professors Bernhard Giesen and Michel Wieviorcka for making those occasions possible.

1. Here I draw from, "Cultural pragmatics: social performance between ritual and strat-egy" (ch. 1, this volume), in which I try to synthesize the pragmatic and textual dimensions of cultural action. I develop a model of the different elements of social performance and discuss how these elements are fused, de-fused, and re-fused in different social situations.

2. "Prophetic religion . . . assumes the exclusiveness of a universal god and the moral depravity of unbelievers who are his adversaries and whose untroubled existence arouses his righteous indignation . . . The precursor and probable model for this was the promise of the Hebrew god to his people, as understood and reinterpreted by Muhammad . . . The ancient wars of the Israelite confederacy, waged under the leadership of various saviors operating under the authority Yahweh, were regarded by the tradition as holy wars. This concept of a holy war, i.e., a war in the name of a god, for the special purpose of avenging a sacrilege, which entailed putting the enemy under the ban and destroying him and all his belongings completely, is not unknown in Antiquity, particularly among the Greeks. But what was distinctive about the Hebraic concept is that the people of Yahweh, as his special community, demonstrated and exemplified their god's prestige against their foes. Consequently, when Yahweh became a universal god, Hebrew prophecy and the religion of the Psalmists created a new religious interpretation. The possession of the Promised Land, previously foretold, was supplanted by the farther-reaching promise of the elevation of Israel, as the people of Yahweh, above other nations. In the future all nations would be compelled to serve Yahweh and to lie at the feet of Israel. On this model Muhammad constructed the commandment of the holy war involving the subjugation of the unbelievers to political authority and economic domination

of the faithful . . . The religion of the medieval Christian orders of celibate knights, particularly the Templars . . . were first called into being during the Crusades against Islam and . . . corresponded to the Islamic warrior orders" (Weber 1978: 473–5).

3. "We – with God's help – call on every Muslim who believes in God and wishes to be rewarded to comply with God's order to kill the Americans and plunder their money wherever and whenever they find it. We also call on Muslim *ulema*, leaders, youths, and soldiers to launch the raid on Satan's U.S. troops and the devil's supporters allying with them, and to displace those who are behind them so that they may learn a lesson. The ruling to kill the Americans and their allies – civilians and military – is an individual duty for every Muslim who can do it in any country in which it is possible to do it, in order to liberate the al Aqsa Mosque [in Jerusalem] and the Holy Mosque [in Mecca] from their grip, and in order for their armies to move out of all the lands of Islam, defeated and unable to threaten any Muslim" (1997 CNN interview, excerpts taken from "*Osama bin Laden v. the U.S.*: Edicts and Statements," www.pbs.org/frontline, quoted in Bernstein 2002: 90).

4. "Bin Laden organized a network of about a dozen different training camps . . . Each *mujahid*, or holy warrior, was given a code name so that even his fellow recruits generally did not know his real name . . . The training . . . was accompanied by steady infusions of Islamic fervor, in the form of Koran study, movies, lectures, and pamphlets. There was great stress on the glory of giving one's life for Allah, and the two greatest prohibitions [were] called 'love of the world' and 'hatred of death.' A key slogan was 'In time of war there is no death'" (Bernstein 2002: 86). "One of the pieces missing in the reconstruction of the September 11 plot," Bernstein later comments (2002: 145), "is the training in hijackings while they were in the United States." Did the terror-performers have "at their disposal mock-ups of passenger aircraft interiors where they could have gone through dress rehearsals"? While "it is possible," of course, "that they dispensed with such rehearsals, and simply made their plans on the basis of what they knew of the interiors of Boeing 767s from having been passengers on them," Bernstein suggests it "would seem more likely that the hijackers would have preferred to do some serious practice." The terrorists did have a sheet of final instructions, evidently prepared by Mohammed Atta, about how to prepare themselves just before the performance began. The night before, they were to shave their bodies of excess hair and to read *Al Tawba* and *Anfal*, the war chapters in the Koran. The goal was to control the inner self so that it would not interfere with their performative role.

> Remind your soul to listen and obey . . . purify it, convince it, make it understand, and incite it . . . and do not fight among yourselves or else you will fail. And be patient, for God is with the patient. When the confrontation begins, srike like champions who do not want to go back to this world. Shout "*Allah'u Akbar*" because this strikes fear in the hearts of the nonbelievers. (Bernstein 2002: 173)

5. A videotape discovered by American forces in Afghanistan in the months after 9/1 allowed Western audiences to become privy to bin Laden's own response to the 9/1

terrorist performance and to his close associates' comments about the broadcast of other Arab-Islamic reactions as well. It constituted, in this sense, the genre of a "play within a play."

> A few weeks after the attacks, bin Laden was with some of his close aides and a visitor from Saudi Arabia, and, sitting on a rug, relaxing with their backs leaning against the wall behind them, they expressed joy at the extent of the destruction, and they made jokes . . . about the events of September 11.
>
> "The TV broadcast the big event," said Sulaiman Abou-Ghaith, a radical Kuwaiti cleric who served as a close adviser to bin Laden. "The scene was showing an Egyptian family sitting in their living room. They exploded with joy. Do you know when there is a soccer game and your team wins? It was the same expression of joy."
>
> "A plane crashing into a tall building was out of anyone's imagination," the visitor from Saudi Arabia put in. "This was a great job" . . . He was Khaled al-Harbi, a veteran of the wars in Afghanistan, Bosnia, and Chechnya who had lost his legs in combat.
>
> "It was 5:30 p.m. our time," bin Laden said. "Immediately, we heard the news that a plane had hit the World Trade Center. We turned the radio station to the news from Washington. The news continued and there was no mention of the attack until the end. At the end of the newscast, they reported that a plane just hit the World Trade Center."
>
> The visiting sheik interrupted to give a kind of religious sanction to the happy news. "Allah be praised," he intoned . . .
>
> Bin Laden continued his account of how he experienced September 11. "After a little while," he said, "they announced that another plane had hit the World Trade Center. The brothers who heard the news were overjoyed by it." (Bernstein 2002: 9–10)

6. These recastings were not reported as constructions but were presented as actual accounts, as objective descriptions, and objective rememberings. This ambiguity, how the implicit social role of journalism in such liminal situations contradicts its explicit professional ethics, is revealed nicely in the Foreword written by the executive editor of the *New York Times*, Howell Raines, to *Out of the Blue: The Story of September 11, 2001: From Jihad to Ground Zero*, authored by a *Times* journalist and based on the staff's reporting of the previous year.

> As daily journalists, of course, we do not set about our work with the idea of being teachers or moral historians. We are engaged in an intellectual enterprise built around bringing quality information to an engaged and demanding readership. Sometimes that means writing what some have called the first rough draft of history. Sometimes it also means constructing a memorial to those whose courage and sacrifice we have recorded or – to speak more precisely – erecting a foundation of information upon which our readers can construct their own historical overviews, their own memorials to those who are lost and to the struggle to preserve democratic values. (Bernstein 2002: x)

7. For a discussion of "new beginning" as a metaphorical construction that allows consensual commitment and social reform, see Edles' (1998) reconstruction of this image as one of the core representations that allowed the Spanish transition to democracy in post-Franco Spain.

8. Thousands of examples of such generalization and abstraction can be culled from the communicative media in the days, weeks, and months that followed 9/11. The nuanced ways in which this idealization functioned as a medium for identification and solidary-extension would be well worth the effort at hermeneutic reconstruction. A single quotation, merely as illustration, will have to suffice here. As the one-year anniversary of the tragedy approached, a flood of books appeared, written by some of the same journalists who initially had reported the events in the daily news media. The generalization and memorialization that formed the contents of these books then were condensed further and were broadcast to a much larger audience by the short book reviews published in the daily media in turn. Under the headline "On a Hijacked Airliner, Moments of Moral Clarity," the following paragraph appeared in a review of a book-length account of the passengers on United Flight 98, who evidently were able to overwhelm the hijackers and to prevent a fourth terrorist conflagration.

> Heroism is rarely the province of kings. This certainly emerged as a lesson in the many acts of courage we saw on Sept. 11, and it is a sustaining message within the story of the men and women who helped bring down United Flight 98 in the woods of Pennsylvania that day, on the one hijacking mission that failed to strike an intended target. The passengers and crew members were "ordinary" men and women who remind us again that no one, in fact, is ordinary; they saved innumerable other lives and contributed to our sense in the midst of that tragedy that as capable as we humans are of destruction, we are even more reliably capable of love, dedication, and sacrifice. (*New York Times*, August 29, 2002: E5)

9. "In Normal, Illinois, three local radio stations set up a tent in front of Schnucks Supermarket on Veterans' Parkway to collect donations in five-gallon water bottles – and the money came in at the rate of $5,000 per hour" (Bernstein 2002: 247–8).

10. In one of his commentary videotapes released after September 11 by the Arabic television station Al-Jazeera, bin Laden prematurely equated the physical destruction of American buildings and the horror Americans experienced with the destruction of the heart of the American social organism, that is, with "America" in a social and moral sense:

> Here is America struck by Almighty God in one of its vital organs so that its greatest buildings are destroyed . . . America has been filled with horror from north to south and east to west, and thanks be to God . . . God has used a group of vanguard Muslims, the forefront of Islam, to destroy America." (quoted in Bernstein 2002: 252–3)

11. The Iraq war demonstrates the continuation of this cycle in a particularly dramatic and unfortunate way. From its very inception, the principal actors talked past one another

with little understanding or appreciation of the manner in which their actions would be perceived by some appreciable segment of the audience on the other side. On record for insisting that "events aren't moved by blind chance" but by "the hand of a just and faithful God," US President George W. Bush justified the American-led invasion of Iraq in his January 2003 State of the Union address: "We do not claim to know all the ways of Providence, yet we can trust in them . . . This call of history has come to the right country" (quoted in Lears 2003). Two weeks later, the spiritual leader of the Palestinian group Hamas, which initiated the strategy of suicide terrorism in Israel and the West Bank, instructed Muslims around the world to retaliate in the event of an American attack. Describing the imminent invasion as "a crusader's war" against Islam by "the envious West and the U.S. first among them," he insisted that, "as they fight us, we have to fight them" (quoted in Benet 2003). The day before the actual conflict began, Iraqi president Saddam Hussein described war with the United States as "the decisive battle between the army of faith, right and justice, and the forces of tyranny and American-Zionist savagery on the other." Declaring himself a "*jihad*ist," he called for a "holy war" that would "wipe out the ranks" of the invading American troops (quoted in Tyler 2003).

References

Alexander, K. 2001. "Was it Inevitable? Islam Through History," pp. 53–70 in *How Did This Happen? Terrorism and the New War*, ed. J. F. Hoge, Jr. and G. Rose. New York: Public Affairs.

Austin, J. L. 1957. *How to Do Things with Words*. Cambridge, Mass.: Harvard University Press.

Bakhtin, M. 1986. *Speech Genres and Other Late Essays*. Austin: University of Texas Press.

Bennet, J. 2003. "Hamas Leader Tells Muslims to Retaliate if U.S. Attacks," *New York Times*, February 8, p. 9.

Bernstein, R. 2002. *Out of the Blue: The Story of September 11, 2001, from Jihad to Ground Zero*. New York: Times Books.

Black, A. 2001. *The History of Islamic Political Thought*. New York: Routledge.

Crick, B. 1962. *In Defense of Politics*. London: Penguin Books.

Derrida, J. 1978. "Force and Signification," pp. 3–30 in *Writing and Difference*, ed. J. Derrida. Chicago: University of Chicago Press.

Edles, L. D. 1998. *Symbol and Ritual in the New Spain: The Transition to Democracy after Franco*. Cambridge: Cambridge University Press.

Eyerman, R., and A. Jameson. 1991. *Social Movements: A Cognitive Approach*. Cambridge, Mass.: Polity Press.

Hanson, V. D. 2001. *Carnage and Culture: Landmark Battles in the Rise of Western Power*. New York: Doubleday.

Hobsbawm, E. J. 1959. *Social Bandits and Primitive Rebels*. Glencoe: Free Press.

Kepel, G. 2002. *Jihad: The Trail of Political Islam*. Cambridge Mass.: Harvard University Press.

Lapidus, I. M. 1987. "Islam and Modernity," pp. 65–88 in *Patterns of Modernity,* vol. II: *Beyond the West,* ed. S. N. Eisenstadt. London: Francis Pinter.

Lears, J. 2003. "How a War Became a Crusade." *New York Times,* March 11, p. 25.

Liebes, T. 1992a. "Decoding TV News: The Political Discourse of Israeli Hawks and Doves." *Theory and Society* 21: 357–81.

    1992b. "Our War/Their War: Comparing the *Intifadeh* and the Gulf War on U.S. and Israeli Television." *Critical Studies in Mass Communication* 9: 44–55.

Mirsepassi, A. 2000. *Intellectual Discourse and the Politics of Modernization: Negotiating Modernity in Iran.* Cambridge: Cambridge University Press.

Smith, H. N. 1950. *Virgin Land: The American West as Symbol and Myth.* Cambridge, Mass.: Harvard University Press.

Talbot, S. and N. Chanda, eds. 2002. *The Age of Terror: America and the World after September 11.* New York: Basic Books.

Turner, V. 1982. *From Ritual to Theatre: The Human Seriousness of Play.* New York: PAJ Publications.

Tyler, P. 2003. "War Imminent as Hussein Rejects Ultimatum," *New York Times,* March 19, pp. 1, 9.

Udovitch, A. L. 1987. "The Constitution of the Traditional Islamic Marketplace: Islamic Law and the Social Context of Exchange," pp. 150–71 in *Patterns of Modernity,* vol. II: *Beyond the West,* ed. S. N. Eisentstadt. London: Francis Pinter.

Weber, M. 1978. *Economy and Society.* Berkeley: University of California Press.

Woodward, B. 2002. *Bush at War.* New York: Simon.

3

The cultural pragmatics of event-ness: the Clinton/Lewinsky Affair

Jason L. Mast

Introduction

Imagined communities generate events that compel community-wide attention, regardless of size or degree of social and cultural differentiation. Early in the twentieth century Durkheim famously argued there "can be no society that does not experience the need at regular intervals to maintain and strengthen the collective feelings and ideas that provide its coherence and its distinct individuality" ([1912] 1995: 429). Rituals, he specified, represent the processes through which solidarity and collective identity are rejuvenated. While social and cultural differentiation has made ritual-like processes in twenty-first-century America more difficult to sustain, this imagined community (Anderson 1983) continues to produce events that draw issues of collective identity and solidarity to the fore of its individuals' consciences (cf. Larson and Wagner-Pacifici 2001).

Contemporary ritual-like events, however, differ markedly from the processes Durkheim described. They are subject to much higher degrees of conflict, dis-consensus, and contingency. Victor Turner (1969, 1974, 1982) responded to this critical fact when he pushed his ritual framework towards the theory of social dramas. Social dramas represent events in the making that compel community-wide attention, generating narratives, oftentimes conflicting, that define and explain what has occurred and its seriousness. The Clinton/Lewinsky Affair, which dominated the national spotlight in 1998, was just such a drama. It appeared to erupt from an initial occurrence for which the vast majority of the country's citizens wanted, if not demanded, an explanation and some form of redressive action. The resulting fourteen-month-long social drama was structured by the thrusts and parries of multiple publics competing to control the meaning of the event *in media res*.

Explaining Monicagate, however, requires that we analyze the particular cultural and political context out of which the social drama erupted. Early in

Clinton's first term, Congressional Republicans, with the support of an exuber-
ant, solid quarter of the nation's citizens, began to construct Clinton's assumption of power as representing a national "fall from grace" drama. After meeting
with some narrative success that enabled significant political victories, the persuasive power of the Republicans' dramatic narratives began to erode. Towards
the end of its first term, the Clinton Administration became increasingly effective at controlling social dramas. The Administration's new-found social dramatic acumen enabled it to weather the right's relentless symbolic and political
onslaughts. The Administration's narratives shored up support from its Democratic base, and increasingly secured the sympathy of the silent, swayable,
middle majority of American citizens. In this chapter I will analyze the cultural
pragmatics, or structure and action dialectics, that produced Monicagate's fre-
netic beginning and shaped the contours of the event's unfolding. In so doing
I will show how the cultural pragmatic framework explains the apparent paradox of how Clinton, though impeached by the House Republicans, remained in
office to finish out his second term with high approval ratings, and the sympathy
and support of a majority of American publics.

The theoretical roots of cultural pragmatics

Cultural pragmatics addresses a range of social phenomena that are variously
referred to in sociological literature as degradation ceremonies (Garfinkel 1956),
secular rituals (Douglas 1966), moments out of time (Turner 1969, 1974,
1982), media events (Dayan and Katz 1992), and, of course, collective rituals (Durkheim [1912] 1995; Shils and Young 1953; Lukes 1975; Alexander
1988; Smith 1991; Edles 1998). These sociological conceptualizations describe
highly orchestrated collective processes that produce a "break" from mundane,
routine social life, and for this reason are central to the maintenance of social
order and the formation and extension of collective identity. These processes
emerge in response to initiating occurrences that appear to demand attention
interpretation, and remedial action. It was such *apparent* occurrences that precipitated events like Watergate (1972), the hostage crisis in Iran (1979), the
Iran-Contra Affair (1987), Rodney King's videotaped arrest (1991) and the
acquittal of his police subduers (1992), the bombing of the Alfred P. Murral
Federal Building in Oklahoma City (1995), and the death of Diana, Princes
of Wales (1997), as well as Monicagate and the Clinton impeachment tria
(1998). In each case, these event-processes demonstrate ceremonial qualities
On the one hand, as non-routine events, such processes conform to historically grounded, routine structures with more or less agreed upon beginning
middles, and ends. On the other, they are adorned with overt aesthetic dimer
sions in the form of intentionally exaggerated symbolic performances. Suc

event-processes concern themselves with attributing meaning to an initializing occurrence in order to bring about a change in the social status of an individual or group, simultaneously creating and resolving conflict between segments of a collectivity.

From mundane to extraordinary experiences, social life is inextricably infused with meaning. An "occurrence" is any cognized happening (Molotch and Lester 1974: 102), and cognition suggests some degree of interpretation. Yet, while meaningful, occurrences exist only temporarily and relatively discretely in a social actor's awareness; they neither transcend their originating contexts nor take root in a larger public's consciousness. An "event," by contrast, is a set of narratively interconnected occurrences that achieves "generalization," drawing a public's attention away from the specificity of everyday life (Alexander 1988; Smelser 1963). As unusually significant meaning constellations, events become lasting points of demarcation in the flow of collective time and retain the potential to inform ongoing social experience. Structurally, events take shape from stark clashes of meaning structures within a broad cultural system of shared sign relations. At the same time, such clashes are both orchestrated and reactively mediated by purposeful, creative human agents who narrate the interconnections between occurrences.

What explains event-ness's natural feel, the sensed rightness of its status, and the passions it can generate, a naturalness that belies the self-conscious quality of an event's orchestration? Durkheim's late work ([1912] 1995) explains one absolutely critical piece of this puzzle.[1] As anchoring nodes in the cultural fabric, Durkheim explains, the sacred and the profane stand in diametrical opposition to one another as "hostile and jealous rivals" ([1912] 1995: 37). It follows that "the mind experiences deep repugnance about mingling, even simple contact, between the corresponding things, because the notion of the sacred is always and everywhere separate from the notion of the profane in man's mind, and because we imagine a kind of logical void between them" ([1912] 1995: 37). Durkheim concludes that rites and ritual ceremonies function to maintain this logical void, re-establishing and reaffirming individuals' understandings of their community's symbolic boundaries between good and evil and right and wrong. Individual actions are shaped by the way actors understand their situations vis-à-vis these meaning structures. By focusing on the processes that establish the foundations for social understanding, Durkheim laid the groundwork for a cultural sociology. Such cosmological mechanisms must play a central role in any explanation of social order or variations thereof. By retaining the theoretical centrality of meaning, Turner 1969, 1974, 1982), Alexander (1988), and others (e.g. Smith 1991; Edles 1998) have demonstrated that the basic processes Durkheim illuminated explain the structure and outcome of even the most conflict-laden, chaotic, or violent contemporary events. Collectivities, whether wracked by violent expressions of difference or seemingly seduced into sleepy indifference, are ontologically tethered to the world via cultural systems that render social interactions sensible by structuring lived experiences into coded discourses, myths, genres, and narratives.

The "natural" repugnance or shock many Americans demonstrated during the Clinton/Lewinsky Affair's inception, which contributed to the precipitation of full-fledged event-ness, exemplifies this symbolic dynamic of a perceived profanation of a sacred space, for instance, counter-democratic actions being found in a democracy's sacred center (see Alexander 1988; Alexander and Smith 1993; Douglas 1966). Degrees of exasperation point to the interconnectedness of affect and meaning structures. The logic of structuralism – the culture system's relative stability, its constitution of consciousness – suggests particular actions, like taking another human's life, are culturally predetermined to provoke purifying, restorative rituals: the sacred's status seems natural to us and the "logical void" between it and the profane is not negotiated or reflectively considered during everyday, mundane experience. Rather, this cultural structure informs our worldly interpretations even though it is socially constructed and its idiosyncratic contents are essentially arbitrary.

Despite the natural feel of such breaching events, turning an "occurrence" into an "event" in postmodern, highly differentiated, late capitalist America – gaining control over its meaning by persuading countless anonymous others to share one's interpretation and recommendation for remedial action – is an exceedingly contingent and combative process. Social actors and parties work to create events, to define occurrences as such, often in the face of considerable opposition from actors who would rather let this occurrence pass by unnoticed. When an eventworthy occurrence develops, and widespread public attention does shift towards investigating and making sense of it, multiple and motivated parties emerge to impose on this eruption a "master narrative" (Wagner-Pacifici 1986). Their goal is to control its ultimate interpretation and effects. Controlling the event's outcome points beyond meaning to such "material" effects as determining the meting out of punishments, redistributing resources such as money and positions of power, and restructuring institutions.

A theoretical caution: the cynical tendency towards reduction

Normative and political orientations may tempt us to reduce Monicagate to partisan politics, prurient titillation, and "mere scandal." This interpretive urge is strong enough for some scholars to "wonder if the events themselves were not imaged, or imaginary" (Larson and Wagner-Pacifici 2001: 736). They point to polls that showed "only a minority of Americans followed the impeachment hearings closely" and to the fact that the Affair appeared "discontinuous, [and] unsupported by any 'plot'" (Larson and Wagner-Pacifici 2001: 737). Yet this is precisely *not* to understand what makes an occurrence into an event, and what differentiates contemporary social dramas from earlier rituals.[2] As will be shown, it is the competition between groups of producers, actors, and partial audiences that characterizes *any* contemporary "affair," and multiple plots are the rule. It will require introducing a much more elaborate theory of social performance to allow me to further explain these points.

The ritual and social dramatic analytical frameworks that have dominated earlier sociological interpretations of such events have contributed significant insights. For instance, demonstrating a prescient cultural pragmatic sensibility, Alexander's (1988) analysis of Watergate offers a thickly described hermeneutics of the event's primary phases and explains its outcome in terms of "non-rational ritualization" becoming the order of the day.[3] Yet, at the same time Alexander was demonstrating culture must figure robustly in sociological explanations, others were arguing that late-capitalist, postmodern societies' meaning systems are too fragmented and commodified, their audiences too jaded and skeptical, for ritual-like productions to actively engage members of an imagined community (Wagner-Pacifici 1986; Jameson 1982: 84–5). This latter line of theoretical speculation performs a kind of contorted dance: simultaneously attributing central explanatory importance to culture while arguing capitalism has reduced culture's contents to commodities and instruments of power, forces some interesting theoretical contradictions.[4]

In her analysis of the kidnapping and murder of Italian Prime Minister Aldo Moro, for instance, Wagner-Pacifici (1986) argues the cultural realm has been fully colonized by postmodern capitalism and symbols reduced to commodities and weapons. In a nutshell, culture is determined by the mode of production and infused with power. While her analysis is rich with conceptual insights into the pragmatics of social-dramatic productions, Wagner-Pacifici's theoretical presuppositions of postmodern society undercut her analytical gains. On the one hand, she makes culture structures important to the event's outcome. The event's self-appointed interpreters make use of socially pre-structured meanings to influence their audiences, and audiences rely on these frames to make sense of Moro's situation and fate. Yet, at the same time, Wagner-Pacifici also argues that, once capitalism has commodified symbols, their effectiveness gets diminished, that, as commodities, symbols are ubiquitous, degraded, and cheapened through repetitive use. Consumer-savvy moderns are thus uninterested and too apathetic and disenchanted to be taken in by elite narratives about Moro's predicament. Within this ontology about culture's relation to human life, in which symbols are reduced to superficial, empty vessels, how can meaning and interpretation be central to the event's dynamics (cf. Alexander and Smith 1998)?

Goffman drew our attention to the "problem of misrepresentation" (1951: 298), that people have the ability to present persuasively false meanings, and it is certainly true that political and normative predilections pull on epistemology (Said 1978; Clifford 1988). Still, it is vital that sociology resist subsuming meaning to collective power and individual practice. Yes, culture is in part a "tool kit" (Swidler 1986), and studies such as Wagner-Pacifici's demonstrate this in a powerful way. We use words intentionally to try to communicate particular ideas for particular reasons. Yet culture's relevance to social life depends on its relative autonomy from the social structure, in its structural form, or *langue* (language) (see Kane 1991). While culture is made present through *parole* (speech), or through an actor's use of a particular "tool," it is made meaningful and comprehensible, and therefore socially influential, because of the "tool's" analogical and antipathetic relations to other tools in the "kit" that are not explicitly in play, but which, nonetheless, exercise power in the experienced social situation (Barthes [1968] 1977a; Eco 1976; Saussure 1985). Action is always citational (Derrida 1988). Each instantiation of meaning draws forth unseen signs and symbols, rooted in the cultural fabric, into momentary if non-conscious presence.

There is also the matter of temporality. A "tool's" meaning in social life is the product of its relation to other tools that are made present by actors in a temporal flow of successive instantiations. Flows of signs demonstrate structures; they are discourses, narratives, myths, and genres. Understanding a tool's particular meaning at a particular time requires locating its presence in relation to the overall structural flow. Just as the meaning of a word is determined by its location in the structure of a sentence, so the sociologist must account for where a particular tool stands in relation to the more general cultural-structure in which it is invoked. These are the structures of social life, and must be the center-pieces of sociological explanations. Limiting our sociological understanding of action to "what gets done," and seeking to get beyond the problem of meaning (Wuthnow 1987) inevitably attributes inordinate degrees of instrumentality to social practice. The meaning of action is thus shaped more by the structure of the sociologist's explanatory narrative (for instance, see Larson and Wagner-Pacifici 2001), than by the experiences and understandings of the social actor actually engaged in an event.

However, sociology that simply debunks and elucidates is insufficient and partial. Sociology must aim to understand and explain. Cultural pragmatics is an analytic solution to the philosophical conundrum of how theory and practice interact in the production of everyday life. It provides a conceptual frame work for mapping, and thickly describing, the incongruities between words and deeds. It enables us to explain events in terms of their meaningful contents for participants, the power relations brought to bear in the event, and the influenc of material factors on event production and reception, without negating the background culture's continuing structural effects (Derrida 1988).

The Clinton/Lewinsky Affair

Monicagate's dramatic prelude

Monicagate was a coded, narratively structured social drama, given form through the interactions of political and social elites, critics and interpretive entrepreneurs, and multiple American publics. At different times throughout the event, each of these three clusters of agents assumed the lead role in focusing the production's spotlight, while the other two groups assumed the role of audience, as though inhabiting the seats in a darkened theatre, celebrating or booing the production along. Each cluster of agents simultaneously enacted a role and interpreted the others' performances. The form and outcome of Monicagate was the product of these interactions.

Yet the event's interactions were themselves structured by participants' reliance on shared, collective representations. Adopting the cultural pragmatic perspective, it becomes clear that the symbols and discourses mobilized during the political battles that preceded the scandal, and were continually invoked throughout Monicagate, combined to form identifiable narrative structures. Agents' invocations of particular symbols during the event, such as regular recourse to the symbol "Slick Willie" to villainize Clinton, suggest dynamics sociologically more profound than the fact that particular agents used symbols instrumentally as tools or weapons. Cultural pragmatics acknowledges social actors orient towards meaning with intent, but it analytically probes deeper by asking, for instance, why a particular symbol is meaningful, what makes it damaging like a weapon, and why does its invocation produce positive reactions in some audience members and adverse reactions in others?

Monicagate's main protagonists drew on dramatic structures from two popular film genres, the bank robber and gangster films of the late 1920s and early 1930s, and the bad cop films and television news narratives of the 1990s. Rooted in America's political and social history, these popular culture structures are latently present in civil society members' understandings of citizenship. While these cops and robbers genres shape American participants' understandings of routine flows and hiccups in the everyday meting out of justice (Christensen 1987; Gibson 1994; King 1999),[5] it is during political scandals and social crises that their dramatic tropes are most forcefully deployed and their social, interpretive power made explicit. Monicagate's three clusters of agents routinely drew upon these culture structures' tropes to describe themselves as victims or as agents of justice on the one hand, and to frame the other clusters in the social drama as villains and perpetrators of injustice on the other.

Elements from the bank robber and gangster genres began to permeate civil discourse during Clinton's bid for the Democratic nomination in 1992, most notably in the mushrooming use of the name "Slick Willie" to capture the candidate's charisma, charm, and sharp intellect, on the one hand, and the suspicion that within him lurked a penchant for mischief and a talent for deceit, on the other. The use and force of the symbol increased its hold over American imaginations from early 1992 until late in 1995, when tropes from the bad cop genre forcefully emerged in the discourse of civil society to describe Republicans investigating the president and accusing him of criminal wrongdoing. While American publics – whether composed of Clinton enthusiasts, ambivalent moderates, or unwavering conservatives – were exposed to and invoked these genre idioms with increasing frequency during these time periods, the way any particular public oriented towards these symbol-complexes remained contingent. In effect, the idioms came to serve as lexicons for, and sites of, symbolic contestation between publics.

Clinton entered office in January 1993, having won the election with the smallest portion of the popular vote (43 percent) since Richard Nixon's 1968 victory.[6] Exit polls indicated Clinton, Bush, and Independent Party candidate Ross Perot, all drew remarkably high unfavorable ratings, and the *New York Times* editorial page framed Clinton's victory as a "fragile mandate . . . of tenuous proportion."[7]

It was Clinton's impressive biography that helped the candidate win the trust of the Democratic base and a decisive portion of the nation's undecided moderate middle. The facts of Clinton's rise to the national stage resonated with the American myth that any boy with talent and pluck, no matter how humble his origins, could become the president of the United States. Clinton's campaign overcame its candidate's "character issues" and assuaged voter suspicion by emphasizing his rise from a broken home in rural Arkansas to becoming a Rhodes Scholar, Yale Law School graduate, and governor of his home state. Clinton's campaign combined these biographical facts with their candidate's youthful enthusiasm to construct the image of a natural populist.[8] Within the narrative context of a nation adrift in economic stagnation, the Clinton campaign's dramatic strategy was extraordinarily effective, particularly when the candidate was juxtaposed to Bush Sr.'s genteel aloofness.

The election drama carved the nation's citizenry into three distinct audiences. Both the Democratic and Republican Party bases, each comprising roughly a quarter of the voting public, reacted to Clinton's campaign and victory with strong feelings. Yet, despite the political passions stirred in both parties' bases, Clinton's five-percentage point victory over Bush Sr. indicates the nation's enormous third audience at the political center was decisive in the contest, and voted as much against Bush's poor handling of the nation's economic malaise as for Clinton himself.

Despite his compelling personal narrative and the hope he inspired in many, Clinton entered the presidency with a binary character as a result of the bruising symbolic battles of the Democratic primaries and general election contest. In addition to representing the best and brightest of a new generation of political leadership, Clinton entered the White House as "Slick Willie." An editor of Arkansas's most widely read newspaper, the *Democrat-Gazette*, initiated the symbolic linkage between Clinton and this gangster symbol in the late 1980s. The moniker was picked up by national media outlets[9] and fused to Clinton's national character early in 1992, as a tide of allegations of womanizing, dope smoking, and draft evasion threatened to overwhelm the frontrunner's campaign for his party's nomination. The allegations themselves cast a shadow of duplicity around Clinton, and ironically, this suspicion was only strengthened by the deftness with which Clinton rhetorically evaded and confounded his critics and questioners.

Was the symbol simply a nickname, a "tool" designed for practical effect? Quite the contrary, the symbol's invocation, spread most effectively by the *New York Times* liberal political commentator and satirist, Maureen Dowd, indicates the initial formation of a negative and polluting cultural structure. Though often used in jest, the symbol, rooted deeply in American popular and political culture, would play a large role in Clinton's later emplotment in Monicagate.

The prototypical gangster of this genre comes from an impoverished rural area to the big city, rises through the ranks of a criminal organization through hard work, ambition, quick wits, and a kind of business acumen, to become the head crime boss of an enormous profit-making enterprise, a role quite similar to the president of a legitimate corporation. Bold, charismatic, reckless, and vainglorious, a top gangster is an outgoing and expansive performer driven by an uncontrollable lust to show the world that he is *somebody*. His desires are boundless. While his rural roots have left him lacking in cultural knowledge and manners, he nonetheless remains a ladies' man. Not needing love in the traditional sense, the gangster associates with "loose women" because of their easy and eager availability. These associations ultimately come at a high price. Because he always wants more and must constantly conquer new territory, the gangster's ultimate defeat seems a natural product of his desires and demands of life (Sobchack and Sobchack 1987). Though a master of escape to his very end, the higher he rises the more others seek his demise, and the more isolated and paranoid he becomes.

Willie Sutton, the original "Slick Willie," was a bank robber in the early 1930s known for the gentlemanly and personable demeanor with which he handled his victims when plying his trade. Bank robbers like Slick Willie Sutton, and gangsters like Al Capone and Baby Face Nelson grew to mythic stature in Depression-era America, when American society was seen as failing average Americans, and lenders and wealthy capitalists were foreclosing on small businesses, farms, and homes. Though flawed in important respects, gangsters were interpreted as more similar to average Americans in life circumstances and moral sensibilities than were representatives of material wealth and institutional power.

In the American collective imagination the gangster symbol, in both its real person and filmic forms, came to represent a kind of romanticized outlaw, a good-bad guy, or a pragmatic Robin Hood. The intensity with which portions of the Depression-era public came to identify with these social renegades is perhaps best illustrated by people's reaction to John Dillinger's violent death by the guns of FBI agents outside the Biograph Theatre in 1934, Chicago. Immediately after his fall from the gunshots, hordes of onlookers descended on the scene and began mopping up the icon of romantic populism's blood with their clothes.[10] Just as Dillinger drew fire from the feds, the highly popular gangster film genre came under institutional fire as well. Drafted in 1930 and strictly instituted in 1934, the Hays Code represented a quasi-governmental, religious reaction to the gangster's increasingly beloved status in the American imagination. The product of collaboration between William Harrison Hays, who served in President Warren Harding's cabinet, a grab-bag of religious figures, and Hollywood moguls whose industry was plagued by scandals, the Hays Code was a self-regulatory code mandating that criminal acts should "never be presented in such a way as to throw sympathy with the crime as against law and justice or to inspire others with a desire for imitation." The simultaneity of these regulatory mechanisms' enactment, and the Hays Code's explicit reference to the connection between real gangsters and the cinema's version of these outlaws, suggests that the existences of real objects and representations of real objects mutually constitute one another through a feedback loop dynamic (Schechner 2002; Turner 1982).

While Clinton entered the White House tenuously as a good-bad guy, by July 17, 1995, the *Washington Times* was describing the Clinton White House as shrouded in a "Climate of Suspicion." *TIME Magazine*'s headline the following week was "Whitewater Tricks; New Hearings Prompt the Clintons to Make New Revelations – Only to Be Caught Short Again." What led to these constructions in which, for a sizeable portion of the nation's political center, Clinton was increasingly associated with the negative codes of gangsterism?

1993 saw the development of several Clinton White House scandals: "Travelgate," concerning charges of nepotism and the mismanagement of federal travel funds;[11] Vince Foster's suicide;[12] the failure of Arkansas' Madison Guaranty S&L run by the Clintons' friends and periodic business partners the McDougals.[13] The White House staff's resistant and evasive responses combined with the developments themselves to create the *Times*'s "climate of suspicion."[14] While Congressional Republicans' approval ratings began to rise, Clinton's approval ratings repeatedly set record lows, hovering between the mid-30s and 40s until spring 1995.

The single most significant political consequence of the climate of suspicion surrounding the Clinton White House was the Democratic Party's loss of control of both the House of Representatives and the Senate in 1994's November elections.[15] This transferred an enormous amount of institutional power to the Republicans who treated their sweeping victory as a mandate from the public and as an indictment of the Clinton White House.[16] Earlier that year, Attorney General Janet Reno had appointed Robert Fiske to head the investigation into the Whitewater land and S&L dealings and Vince Foster's suicide. November's shift in Congressional power enabled the Republican-controlled Senate to remove Fiske and appoint Ken Starr to the role of special prosecutor. Additionally, the House and Senate Banking Committees both began hearings on Whitewater. And Newt Gingrich, as the new Speaker of the House, became increasingly vocal in his criticisms of Clinton, announcing upwards of twenty new task forces and subcommittees to investigate him – a number he was later forced to reduce.

A shift in the dramatic landscape, in which new villains emerged, occurred after the Republicans won control of Congress. While the bank robber and gangster genres continued to shape civil discourse after 1995, polls indicate that a growing majority of citizens began to both orient towards their idioms with greater degrees of irony, and to emphasize the quasi-heroic dimensions of the gangster figure when describing Clinton. The declining significance of the gangster genre's *polluting* dimensions was due in part to the rising power in the discursive arena of the "bad cop" film genre (cf. Christensen 1987; King 1999), whose tropes were increasingly drawn upon to characterize the investigative authorities pursuing Clinton and working so hard to assassinate his character. These symbolic shifts facilitated one another, and as Clinton's political team became more successful at morphing the president's accusers into bad cops, Clinton's transformation into the quasi-heroic, quick-thinking, gangster escapist accelerated.

The bad cop picture represents a mutation of the rogue cop genre film popular in the mid- and late 1970s. Rising to prominence in the wake of Watergate, the rogue cop picture pits a stoic, everyman cop-figure fighting for justice against both street criminals and representatives of institutional authority. His departmental superiors and political authorities have become sources of corruption, and instead of representing authors and protectors of justice, they are portrayed as standing in the way of justice. Shifting the locus of corruption, the bad cop genre proliferates in the wake of 1991's widely and frequently televised home-videotape clip showing Los Angeles policemen violently subduing African American motorist Rodney King.

In the bad cop genre no character is left completely innocent or virtuous; rather, all characters are portrayed as struggling against social forces to maintain a civilized dignity. The bad cop is one of the few that gives up this struggle completely and exercises his power in frequently arbitrary, yet always self-interested ways. While the pervasiveness of corruption amongst the league of police foot-soldiers is left ambiguous, those with the power to investigate and physically subdue others are portrayed as the clearest representatives of potential evil. This genre's presence in the collective constitution of the real was powerfully demonstrated in 1995, when attorney Johnny Cochran represented OJ Simpson's official police investigators as bad cops. The investigators' exact motives for targeting Simpson remained rather ambiguous; they were simply sinister, if shaped by racism and desire for notoriety.[17] Actor Denzel Washington, the lead in this genre's quintessential filmic representation, *Training Day* (2001), received one of the film industry's highest honors for his portrayal of a bad cop whose "nihilistic magnificence" and "underhandedness" left onlookers – both in the film and in its audiences – rapt in a state of puzzlement.[18]

After successfully gaining control of Congress by running explicitly against the Clinton Administration during 1994's midterm elections, the Republicans' increase in institutional authority appeared to reflect a similarly impressive increase in symbolic authority and trust vis-à-vis American voters. However, as the number and severity of their attacks on Clinton increased, the Republicans' tactics and subjects of scrutiny began to alienate the moderate swing voters who had helped them gain their new-found power.

During this time the president and his staff grew increasingly adept at shaping the political arena's dramatic landscape, and moved to formalize their processes of meaning production with the development of a new scandal management team (Woodward 1999: 275). In 1994 and 1995 several convictions resulted from the Whitewater investigations. While initially quite damaging politically, the Clinton Administration grew increasingly skilled at framing such convictions as inconsequential prosecutorial successes against obscure land developers and speculators. The convictions drew only scant coverage by national newscasts, and received most of their attention in late-night talk show monologues, which mocked Gingrich and the Republicans' repeated promises that Clinton's undoing was nigh. To the contrary, Clinton's symbolic framework began to improve, a process that was catalyzed by his masterfully presidential reaction to the bombing of the Alfred P. Murrah Federal Building in April 1995.

Additionally, November and December of 1995 were dominated by narrative constructions of Clinton versus the Congressional Republicans in a battle over the federal government's budget. Clinton's handling of the stalemate led the Republicans to take the extraordinarily unpopular step of officially shutting down all government services, twice. The powerful and emotionally charged performances Clinton delivered throughout these battles over the budget solidified a shift in the political arena's symbolic landscape. By the end of the battle over the budget, talk of "scandal fatigue" began to emerge to describe the shifting mood amongst the nation's moderate middle. Whereas during the prior two years Clinton was effectively coded as evasive and worthy of suspicion to many, the Clinton versus Republicans show-down marked the dramatic recasting of the Republicans in the political sphere's role of the bad cop. The Republicans' various investigative efforts were increasingly interpreted as less motivated by democratic ideals and more driven by counterdemocratic forms of partisanship. During this shift in symbolic landscape a critical plot-point occurred: Clinton began his intimate relationship with Monica Lewinsky three days into the government shut-down.

Independent Council, Ken Starr's investigative reach was expanded in 1996 by Attorney General Reno to include "Filegate"[19] and allegations of Clinton officials lying to Congress. This increase in Republican investigative power fueled the symbolic expansion of their villain framework and catalyzed what could be called the "Gingrich-ification" of Ken Starr. Undaunted by, or unaware of this trend, the Republicans continued to insinuate that the investigative efforts would "reveal" mortally damaging facts about the Clinton White House. Despite the periodic unearthing of White House improprieties and questionable past dealings,[20] none of these instances was symbolically transformed into the damning evidence the Republicans had been promising. As a consequence, (1) the Republicans' continual promises of a mortal blow fueled "scandal fatigue," (2) Starr's investigative expansion resulted in the symbolic linkage of his political motives with Newt Gingrich's, and (3) the Republicans were increasingly framed as bad cops, driven by counterdemocratic motives and by a personal dislike for Clinton.

A critical plot development occurred in 1997. As the investigations continued, an anonymous call was placed to Paula Jones's attorneys alerting them to Clinton's relationship with Lewinsky (retrospectively presumed to have been made by Linda Tripp). An important series of additional plot points followed that led to the public revelation of Clinton's involvement with Lewinsky. Lewinsky was subpoenaed by Paula Jones's lawyers, for instance. She also met with Clinton to "practice" for her deposition, was offered a job at Revlon by Clinton's friend, Vernon Jordan, and she shared a copy of a document titled "Points to Make in an Affidavit," containing instructions for responding to questions about the Kathleen Willey case, with her then friend, Linda Tripp. Shortly later, Tripp contacted Starr and agreed to tape conversations with Lewinsky about her relationship with Clinton. Starr then requested and was allowed to expand his investigation to include possible perjury and obstruction of justice in the Jones case. FBI and US attorneys questioned Lewinsky and offered her immunity in exchange for testimony. And finally, on January 17, 1998, Clinton gave a deposition denying he had been in a sexual relationship with Lewinsky.

In the months to come, the Republican dramatic production worked to frame these events as part of a chain of discovery of facts about Clinton's true nature. They also sought to frame initial public reactions of shock and intense interest as constituting a natural response to what should be considered a clear transgression of sacred boundaries. The Clinton production team, on the other hand, and Democrats more generally, dramatically framed these events as part of a long-standing, secretive, villainously orchestrated plan to attack Clinton personally for political gain.

Monicagate's first phase

The social processes resulting from the news release of Clinton's possible relationship with Lewinsky appeared to take on a life of its own. The breach occurred on January 21, 1998, at 1:11 a.m. when Matt Drudge posted the headline "Blockbuster Report: 23-Year-Old, Former White House Intern, Sex Relationship With President" on his website. After learning of Drudge's web-posting, the *Washington Post* ran the story on the 21st as well with the headline "Clinton Accused of Urging Aide to Lie."

The news's rapid spread sparked massive, widespread shifts in attention among people working in political institutions and news media, and pulled citizens away from their mundane routines to center on a particular occurrence. One Administration official stated that an "air of unreality" had taken hold in Washington;[21] those in the Washington D.C. area were described as "flabbergasted" and "shocked beyond belief;"[22] and one commentator, reflecting on the qualitatively new tone in the nation's capital at the close of the event's first week, symbolically linked the event with Watergate, stating "Friday evening brought to close a week [not seen] since the darkest days of Watergate."[23]

Audiences actively engaged the emerging ritual-like process as well. Breaking from their routine affairs, people flooded Internet news websites, crashing many servers due to the heavy traffic, bought newspapers in record numbers, and tuned into cable news networks, which experienced dramatic increases in viewership.[24] E-civil spheres mushroomed online, as chatrooms filled with people seeking to discuss and debate the events.

Watergate continued to play a central role in the event's symbolic framing. Conservative critic William Safire invoked a piece of Watergate's naturalistic imagery, characterizing the atmosphere around Clinton as a "*firestorm* that [is] going to break out around him."[25] The metaphors Watergate and firestorm are images of uncontrollable, natural forces. Safire's use of firestorm symbolically links Clinton with Nixon, and characterizes the press and public reactions as natural, uncontrollable, and furious reactions to the assumed corruption.

Sam Donaldson's spontaneous, oft-repeated response to the breach indicates the event's fused, ritual-like feel of irresistible momentum: "If he's not telling the truth, I think his presidency is probably numbered in days. This isn't going to drag out. We're not going to be here in three months talking about this . . . I sat here during Watergate, we all did. I am amazed at the *speed with which this story is going.*"[26] Actively partaking in the telling of the story, Donaldson nonetheless describes the process as propelled by a momentum all its own.

Clinton was the central character in the initial stages of the incipient drama. In terms of *mis-en-scène*, the critics rendered him a lone figure at center stage. His physical performance in his initial interview with Jim Lehrer on *The News Hour* was described as "visibly shaken and unsteady in his responses;"[27] he appeared as though a "picture of isolation," and "withdrawn . . . secretive and evasive."[28] His verbal performance was framed critically as "legalistic and evasive," "carefully worded . . . cryptic, partial, and insufficient," and "dependent . . . so heavily on omission and factual elision."[29] Clinton was quickly framed a "counter-democratic" (Alexander and Smith 1993) character. He was cast in the image of a guilty man who was once thought of as heroic if flawed but had been revealed as an impulsive fraud.

Within the first couple of days after the news's release, polls registered dramatic changes in public opinion, indicating a substantive expansion of a ritual-like process and the fusion of audiences with the Republican drama.[30] The number of Americans who disbelieved both of Clinton's denials – of having an affair with Lewinsky and suborning her to perjure herself – rose substantially, from 28 percent disbelieving Clinton on January 21 to 62 percent disbelieving him on January 23. Desires for Clinton's resignation were on the rise as well, with 67 percent wanting his departure from office if the allegations were true, and 56 percent favoring impeachment if he refused to step down voluntarily (ABC News).

Actors in an incipient social drama respond to a breach and mounting sense of crisis by working to control the meaning, and thus the consequences of the news. They invoke symbols with great metaphoric reach, and try to discursively construct and embody favorable symbols, codes, and literary archetypes in their actions. Actors' control over the means of symbolic and emotional production, their access to power, and their approaches to establishing the drama's *mise-en-scène* contribute to the formation of audiences' interpretations.

The Republicans' dramatic intentions included encouraging ritualization, liminality, and a collective sense of being "out of time." Narratively and dramatically this involved establishing and maintaining narrative clarity and simplicity, and a sense of narrative boundedness in which the beginning had just occurred with the "revelation" of the Lewinsky Affair. The subtext of their early efforts was that "we have discovered an evil in the social center, now we must expel it." Their narrative and dramatic efforts were also aimed at hiding the machinations that went into preparing and bringing the social drama into being. That is, they sought to hide their backstage efforts that went into bringing the drama to stage; or, put theatrically, to hide their multiple "investigative rehearsals" that contributed to the news's outing.

The Republicans sought to encourage spectators' "natural outrage" at the news. Durkheim's (1995) and Mary Douglas's (1966) work on the relation between the sacred and the profane suggests the public's shock was in some sense culturally predetermined. Both argue that the profane must be removed from a sacred center via ritual means. The US office of presidency is perhaps the most sacred symbol in the US's national cultural order. Clinton's actions of sexual indiscretion and alleged perjury, if judged by the broad consensus that followed the news, were initially interpreted as representing a profanation of that sacred center.[31] It must be reiterated, however, that in highly differentiated democratic societies the sense of flow that audiences experience when they are fused with a social dramatic production is never self-sustaining. It demands constant effort and performative style to maintain the representation of compelling substance. In this regard, the Republicans found themselves in a dramatic bind.

Despite signs of shock, outrage, titillation, and civic re-engagement across American publics, the breach could not sustain itself. Social dramas require that producers claiming interpretive authority and legitimacy engage in a continual process of narration. Yet producers are constrained by their emplotment in the developing social drama. Audiences interpret a producer's claims to non-partisanship, neutrality, and disinterestedness, for instance, vis-à-vis the claimant's character development in the drama thus far.

In January 1998, the Republicans were confronted with a social-dramatic paradox: to successfully pollute Clinton they needed to narrate the breach's meaning and dramatize Monicagate's consequences as representing a dire threat to the nation's political center. Yet, they were prevented from engaging the social dramatic battle for fear of further concretizing the bad cop image the Clinton team had so successfully attributed them to date. The genre posits that bad cops pretend to be heroes. They use their authority to manufacture crises so that they can benefit from appearing to resolve them. In more concrete terms, bad cops plant evidence only to claim to discover it. Once "discovered," the bad cop removes the social threat – the evidence and the framed criminal – and assumes the role of hero for having protected and restored what is sacred in society.

A memo sent to Congressional Republicans by party strategist Frank Luntz during the breach's first week indicates Luntz sensed he needed to warn Republican characters against playing into the bad cop genre's logic:

If you comment, you will take a non-partisan, non-political situation and make it both partisan and political. Do not speculate. Do not hypothesize. Too many Americans justify the President's behavior because they dislike his accusers. Please don't add to that justification.[32]

To have fully engaged the breach and dramatized it as representing a crisis of democracy, the Republicans would have run the risk of portraying themselves as bad cops who had manufactured the evidence against Clinton only to have "discovered" it in order to reap the rewards of a new-found heroic status. Such actions would have solidified the Clinton team's well-developed narrative: that "Monicagate" simply represented the latest installment of Republican machinations to delegitimize the president. Yet, simply acting as if they were neutral onlookers would not prevent the Clinton team from dramatically situating Monicagate's news within a narrative of a long, secretive, meticulously orchestrated Republican plot to frame the president. Dramatically checkmated, the Republicans were unable to engage in dramatic contestation over the news's meaning and consequently they quite quickly lost narrative control over the incipient event. Within two weeks they were effectively coded and dramatically defined as unfit carriers of the ritual project.

The Democratic production faced no such dramatic restrictions. As the only character *en-scène* in this early phase, Clinton used his vast power and means of symbolic production to contest the veracity, and therefore the meaning of the allegations. He had at his disposal the media's unwavering attention and the symbolic props of dignity and grandeur afforded by the White House setting, which he employed masterfully. For instance, in what was scheduled to be a press conference on education policy on January 26, 1998 Clinton stood dramatically below an image of Teddy Roosevelt, "The Rough Rider," on horseback, and forcefully denied the charges to the riveted media and nation. Wagging his finger in scorn at his viewers, he famously declared, "I did not have sexual relations with that woman, Miss Lewinsky. I never told anybody to lie. These allegations are false."

Most critics raved about the performance, suggesting it seemed to flow naturally from Clinton's knowledge of and comfort in the truth. With "his eyes narrowed and his finger stabbing in the air,"[33] Clinton appeared "strengthened and energetic."[34]

Clinton looked at the American people in the TV eye. He put on his most determined face and punched the air with his finger to drive his point home. There was none of the parsing of the facts that he used to cover his hindquarters in past scandals. No, these were direct, declarative sentences.[35]

Sympathetic and traditionally moderate critics reasoned the performance was too seamlessly compelling, its authenticity too perfectly embodied and delivered, to be the product of a consciously, intentionally deceptive actor. It would demand an unimaginable will to deceive and unto hitherto unforeseen performative skills for Clinton to achieve felicity through falsity under such extreme conditions, critics assumed. Deception, it was believed, would have left a revealing trace. On the other hand, convinced that Clinton always lied, the Republican base marveled at the performance, reading the president's assertiveness as indicative of a certain degree of pathology.

Clinton received aid from a skilled supporting cast as well. In a powerfully dramatic intervention the following morning, Hillary Clinton appeared on NBC's top-rated morning show, the *Today Show*, and synthesized all of the elements of the Administration's dramatic strategy into a succinct, coherent plot. Up to this time Mrs. Clinton had been a polarizing figure. The core of the left championed her as a representation of how capable women could serve and improve the public sphere. The core of the right distrusted her and saw her as inappropriately presumptuous and ambitious in her role as First Lady. Neither of these audiences would be swayed by her *Today Show* appearance. Her performance as a loyal wife who believed and would defend her husband under such embarrassing circumstances, however, won her the respect of the critically important political middle still reeling from the just-released allegations.

During the interview the First Lady assumed the authoritative tone and demeanor of a drama's narrator, a role whose interpretive authority stems from its critical distance from, and narrative omniscience of, the action on center stage. Successfully taking on this role would allow Mrs. Clinton to appear as though she were capable of perspicaciously overseeing the event's overall plot, and would thus cast her as a neutral expositor in the eyes of the drama's followers.

She stated the plot simply and matter-of-factly:

This is the great story here, for anybody willing to find it and write about it and explain it, is this *vast right-wing conspiracy* that *has been conspiring against my husband since the day he announced for president*. A few journalists have kind of caught on to it and explained it, but it has not yet been fully revealed to the American public. And, actually, you know, in a bizarre sort of way, this may do it.[36]

The First Lady's unproblematic access to the US's highest rated morning news show placed her face in the living rooms and kitchens of millions of people across the nation.[37] The timing was impeccable, though it was emphasized very early in the interview that her appearance had been scheduled weeks in advance and was to address a different subject. In contrast to her husband's performance the night prior, Mrs. Clinton entered people's lives unofficially, during their familiar routines, and she treated her audience as if she were a friend dropping in to discuss a personal problem. Her role and title of First Lady brought her added deference from the interviewer, and allowed her to enact her script without interruption, oppositional retorts, or the elaboration of counternarratives. Of course, it would be either bold or stupid dramatic practice to be interviewed by a hostile critic.

During her performance, the First Lady worked to shift the drama's *mise-en-scène* by emphasizing what her tone and demeanor suggested should be obvious to all witnesses, that "the great story here" was not about her husband but about his accusers. In this manner Mrs. Clinton helped shift the social-dramatic focus from Bill Clinton to his accusers while simultaneously drawing on systems of representation that framed the investigators as counterdemocratic villains.

The phrase "right-wing conspiracy" invoked imagery of a secretive, coordinated orchestration to oust her husband from office. Her wording, "against my husband," conjured imagery of the private sphere, thus emphasizing the sexual dimension of the accusations as opposed to the issues more directly related to Clinton's office. "Husband" instead of "the president" suggested that the accusers were taking aim at an unfair target, the family, which is perhaps the very hub of the private sphere.

Finally, Mrs. Clinton's use of the phrase "since the day he announced for president" framed the current events in the context of an ongoing, long-lasting historical effort. The First Lady's phrase countered the Republicans' dramatic intentions by pointing out that the allegations and "the real story" did not begin *that week*. Rather, her dramatic framing of the plot, suggesting that the story actually started long ago, functioned to erode the audience's sense of dramatic boundedness; to deflate spectators' senses of being "out of time" and in a "bracketed" moment. It further encouraged the audience to detach from the production to study it for signs of orchestration or manipulation. It suggested that if the audience members looked closely they would be able to see the elaborate history of backstage machinations and rehearsal efforts the accusers had engaged in. Mrs. Clinton's performance was orchestrated to play as an impassioned though reasoned request of audiences and media to interpret her husband's initial "evasions" as instances of restrained frustration. She asked onlookers to identify with and understand the hero's careful patience in the face of such personalized, counterdemocratic efforts. Her account invoked a romantic narrative of a reluctant hero, a kind of Robin Hood, a generally merry, peace-loving man, being forced to fight villainous conspirators seeking to harm him and his family.

Roughly twelve hours after his wife's performance, Clinton-the-accused entered one of the nation's most sacred physical spaces and delivered his State of the Union Address. Clinton's performance during this highly symbolic event capped Monicagate's first phase, and sealed his dramatic production's dominant, if tenuous narrative control over the event.[38] As *New York Times* columnist John Broder framed the evening's performance: "Few other politicians of his generation – or any other – could have pulled off a performance like that of Mr. Clinton tonight . . . Mr. Clinton sailed forward into the stiff wind of adversity."[39] In one of the most watched Addresses in the late twentieth century, Clinton made no mention of the scandal or of Lewinsky. His words and physical demeanor evoked the script "I am going back to doing the work of the nation."[40] Counter to the Republicans', Clinton's script emphasized a return to the routine and mundane, and strove to further defuse the once ritualized atmosphere.

In addition to these performances, many of the Democratic production's lesser characters and sympathetic critics worked vigorously to discursively frame Clinton's accusers in a counterdemocratic light. Ken Starr, the Office of Independent Council, Linda Tripp, and Monica Lewinsky were all placed *en-scène* through this supporting cast's efforts.

The loose symbolic framework of bad cop that had dogged Independent Council Ken Starr began to crystallize under the pressure of repeated portrayals of him as an abusive investigator relying on strong-arm tactics. For instance, Harvard Law Professor Alan Dershowitz's direct linkage of Starr's tactics to those of overly aggressive police officers practically cast Starr in the lead role of a "good cop, bad cop" routine, in which the good cop leaves the interrogation room to allow Starr to "work the suspect over":

Perhaps [Starr's actions] will get [public officials] – and the public – to think about the broad implications of arming prosecutors and the police with untrammeled authority to conduct stings, to record conversations and to coerce cooperation by threatening prosecution. No citizen should be targeted by a sting without a "sting warrant" based on probable cause. Nor should any citizen be subjected to the abusive tactics used against the President by Kenneth Starr.[41]

By the end of Monicagate's first phase Starr was coded as an extension of the Republican Party, enacting a conspiratorial plot to destroy the president politically and personally. Seeking to satisfy his personal and political interests, Starr was understood as relentlessly persecuting the president, stretching the law, and exceeding his mandate.

To paraphrase Derrida, nothing exists outside the coding. The Democratic production worked hard to dramatically frame the Office of Independent Council as a counterdemocratic institution that endangered the democratic ideals of the nation by granting a kind of ambiguous legal protection to the investigator's expansive use of his position's power. Anthony Lewis's Op-ed column in the *New York Times* stated this sentiment succinctly:

I am sure of one thing. The Constitution was not meant to give us – and we should not want – a system of government in which a roving inspector general with *unaccountable power* oversees the President of the United States . . . Altogether, what we see in these events is the picture of an *exceptionally zealous prosecutor*. And we see one operating with *no meaningful restraints on his power*.[42]

As the first phase of Monicagate drew to an end, Democratic opinion-makers had largely succeeded at portraying the OIC as an unconstitutional character in the drama. Polls indicate that Clinton supporters and sizeable portions of the swayable political middle were beginning to consider the OIC a counterdemocratic institution that granted unlimited power and resources to an investigator that could assert his authority arbitrarily.

Once in place, the symbolic frameworks of Monicagate's breach and crisis phases remained remarkably steady over the subsequent months. The majority of skeptical, swayable publics that constituted the political center had settled into understanding Monicagate through the Clinton team's dramatic framework. Due to the Democratic production's dramatic and discursive efforts, the Republicans were not perceived as legitimate carriers of the ritual project to this sizeable majority. The machinations of their dramatic production had been rendered highly visible, their back-stage effectively brought to the fore, and their script rendered overly artificial and contrived. On the other hand, though now in the minority, the conservative base remained passionately anti-Clinton, insisted the president was lying, and interpreted the Clinton team's response as a farce that threatened the very foundations of American democracy.

Monicagate's middle phase

Public opinion trends steadied after the State of the Union Address and a polarization between two publics solidified. By the end of July a majority (57 percent) opposed Clinton leaving office under *any* conditions while a small but devout 35 percent supported continuing efforts to investigate and expel him. There were two downward shifts in anti-Clinton public opinion after January: pro-resignation sentiments decreased 20 percentage points, and pro-impeachment sentiments decreased 16 percentage points (ABC News poll, July 31, 1998). Yet, alongside these trends, at the end of July, 68 percent of the social drama's audience believed Clinton had an affair with Lewinsky and lied about it, an increase of 18 percentage points over the same time. These contrasting poll trends indicate an interesting dramatic dynamic took place between February and early August. A sizeable portion of the general public resisted identifying with the Republican dramatic production *despite* believing Clinton had lied about his relationship with Lewinsky, on the one hand, and that he had repeatedly, assertively lied about not lying, on the other. Starr's late July disapproval ratings hovered around 60 percent. These trends indicate the Clinton dramatic production's efforts succeeded during the previous six months, effectively vilifying Starr and further delegitimating the investigative process. As mentioned above, the Republicans were unable to engage in any vigorous dramatic dueling because the Clinton team had successfully sculpted the dramatic landscape such that vigorous Republican action would be read through the idioms of the bad cop genre. By keeping the past six years of relentless symbolic attacks on the president by Republicans in Monicagate's script, the Administration's production essentially neutered the Republicans of any symbolic power and cast in doubt their right to perform and narrate.

Within this context, two micro-events in the drama's middle phase nonetheless functioned to bring publics back to considering the Republicans' discursive and dramatic offerings, and reinvigorated the event's initially ritually charged atmosphere. In particular, Starr's investigative pressure eventually led the Clinton production to have its star publicly admit to an "inappropriate relationship" with Lewinsky (performed on August 17). This dramatic confession placed Clinton back *en-scène* and infused the Republican drama with new energy. The confession reinvigorated the right's base, and caused those at the political center, who had decided to back Clinton because they did not trust his inquisitors, to reconsider their loyalty to a guy that had lied to them. Once powerfully deflationary, Clinton's "finger stabbing in the air" performance became his "wagging his finger in shame" performance, and was used forcefully by Republicans to parody Clinton's initial performative enthusiasm and to reiterate his "slickness," the strength of his skills at deception.

Less than a month later the Starr Report's release on the Internet and in book form revitalized the event's prior, substantively charged atmosphere as well. The Report's Internet debut on September 11 triggered another break from the mundane in people's everyday lives.[43] "Americans across the country tried to participate in this unprecedented kind of electronic town hall meeting," a reporter described, but "were shut out because of the overload on the computer network."[44]

The *New York Times* editorial page's reaction to the Report's contents framed Clinton in terms that could be found in any film textbook's discussion of the gangster genre's anti-hero:

No citizen – indeed, perhaps no member of his own family – could have grasped the completeness of President Clinton's mendacity or the magnitude of his *recklessness*. Whatever the outcome of the resignation and impeachment debates, the independent counsel report by Mr. Starr is devastating in one respect, and its historic mark will be permanent. A *President who had hoped to be remembered for the grandeur* of his social legislation will instead be remembered for the *tawdriness of his tastes and conduct* and for the disrespect with which he treated a dwelling that is a revered symbol of Presidential dignity.[45]

Both of these micro-events reversed previous poll trends. Clinton's *job approval* rating dropped to 57 percent, tying its lowest mark set just after the scandal broke. Public calls to "just drop the matter" lessened substantially: down 17 percentage points from the prior month's poll, 47 percent of the public favored ending the investigation with the Report's publication. On the other hand, 51 percent favored further investigations and congressional hearings on impeachment (ABC News, September 14, 1998).

At the culmination of Monicagate's first phase, three audiences had merged into two when the majority of publics in the political center came to understand the event largely through the Clinton team's dramatic narrative. Polls indicate that Clinton's admission to having lied combined with the release of the Starr Report to encourage the audience of Clinton sympathizers to split into two audiences. Once again the public was constituted by three audiences, each with a different interpretation of what was taking place in the political arena. Polls also indicate that some of the skeptical centrists who had come to sympathize with the Clinton team's narrative disassociated from both parties' dramas, indicating there was a likely chance this drama would end without heroes of any sort.

Later in Monicagate's second, middle phase, on August 21, Clinton's taped testimony before the Grand Jury was aired on national and cable television. The tape's release ultimately backfired on its creators. Seeking a successful degradation ritual, the Republicans intended the tape to shame Clinton in front of the nation. The cinematography framed Clinton like a criminal before a tribunal. He was taped only from the waist up, similar in style to a classic "mug shot" of gangster film imagery. While reporting on the event varied across the political spectrum, the tape's airing was largely framed as an extreme, unjust attempt to publicly degrade Clinton. Though multiple publics witnessed the event, the tape's airing appeared to further delegitimate all parties involved and to fracture any ritual resubstantivization processes that followed Clinton's confession and the Starr Report's publication.[46] The footage and its ironic consequences for the Republican dramatic effort again illustrate the contingency of such events and the dramatic producers' limited ability to estimate how their production efforts will be received by various publics.

In the November midterm elections the Republicans not only failed to increase their 55-to-45 margin in the Senate, but the Democrats picked up five seats in the House. This Democratic gain represents the first time since 1934 that the president's party gained seats in a midterm election.

Monicagate's third and final phase

The House hearings and impeachment proceedings contained some of the most dramatic settings and formally ritualized proceedings of the entire event, yet the Republicans were still unable to get a broader audience to cathect with their production. From the outset Republican Representative Henry Hyde tried to infuse the proceedings with an atmosphere of grave solemnity, invoking

Roman law, the Magna Carta, the Constitutional Convention, and referencing the Civil War's battles of Bunker Hill, Lexington, and Concord.

Democratic Representatives Barney Frank (Mass.) and Charles Schumer (NY) resisted accepting the Republicans' impeachment script that called for solemnity, reverence, and gravity, by performing comedy. In opposition, Frank and Schumer turned the hearings into a farce by repeatedly cracking jokes and making disruptions that frequently had the House Democrats rolling with laughter:

Franke: "Now, by the way, on that subject, my colleague from Arkansas challenged Mr. Craig before and said that the president never admitted to 'sexual contact' with Ms. Lewinsky; he used the phrase 'inappropriate intimate contact.' And I suppose they might have been having an inappropriate intimate conversation about which country they'd like to bomb together. (Laughter)."[47]

Though the hearings provided the Republicans the opportunity to intervene in Americans' lives more directly and forcefully than before, only a small portion of the American public tuned in the television to watch their production. The television-ratings story of the weekend was CBS's decision to break away from coverage of the impeachment vote to televise a football game between the New York Jets and the Buffalo Bills. When CBS cut away to the game, its ratings quadrupled to 12 million viewers, more than doubling CNN's highest spiked rating of the day at 5.3 million for Clinton's address to the nation.[48]

Conclusion

Political power is constrained by and must operate through symbolic, dramatic power. This is an analytic distinction; it does not necessarily follow that the two exist separately in the empirical world in any strong sense. Yet Monicagate demonstrates we must certainly not reduce symbolic power to political power, as the Republicans were unable to establish the event's master narrative despite the vast means of symbolic production at their disposal and their superior numbers in both Houses of Congress.

In this chapter I have demonstrated how cultural pragmatics contributes a theoretical explanation for how events enter into social existence. The theoretical framework offers a set of concepts for analyzing the processes through which highly differentiated, imagined communities constitute an event's reality. These processes take the form of agonistic competitions undertaken to mobilize solidarity and consensus around scripted narratives.

Cultural pragmatics accounts for how meaning, in the form of background collective representations, shapes social actors and audiences' interpretations in a deeply structural way. Yet it allows for contingency by reconciling culture's deeply constitutive power with social actors' abilities to creatively and agentically situate and strategize vis-à-vis the symbolic structures in which they are embedded.

Some earlier sociological analysts of Monicagate have argued that, "because no collective actions followed" Clinton's impeachment, "this symbolically most significant of events in our commonwealth *failed to occur* with the solemnity that would have allowed it to take its place alongside Watergate in the American political unconscious. It failed to induce despair, as it failed to induce shared indignation and togetherness" (emphasis in the original; Larson and Wagner-Pacifici 2001: 738).

My argument in this chapter, based not only on an alternative theory but on discursive and statistical data, contradicts these claims. Indignation and despair were felt, and togetherness was experienced, though perhaps not solely in the way that liberal sociologists might sympathize with or respect. But the theoretical lesson here is vital. Action is not the sole indicator of meaning. Because multiple audiences experienced Monicagate's events in several identifiable ways, analysts must be very careful not to conflate their own common-sense understandings of the event with those of the audience. Geertz (1983: 75) cautioned to be mindful of the taken-for-grantedness of common sense.

There are a number of reasons why treating common sense as a relatively organized body of considered thought, rather than just what anyone clothed and in his right mind knows, should lead on to some useful conclusions; but perhaps the most important is that it is an inherent characteristic of common-sense thought precisely to deny this and to affirm that its tenets are immediate deliverances of experience, not deliberate reflections upon it.

Indeed, hermeneutics begins where common sense ends. In this abridged analysis of the Clinton era I have argued that political actors and audiences alike understood Monicagate through the sense-making structures of the codes of civil society (Alexander and Smith 1993), and through the tropes of popular film genres that historically have dramatized the social relations and practices of justice. While each cluster of agents experienced these cultural structures as commonsensical, they were culturally constructed and contingent.

It was through these collective representations that America's imagined community dramatically reaffirmed itself as real. Monicagate's clusters of agents expressed disbelief, anger, resentment, and even hatred for one another. Between the competing parties and skeptical audiences, however, a common code of civil discourse, and shared popular cultural tropes about cops and their prey, sustained the energizing moral fabric of democratic life.

Notes

1. Giesen's work on *epiphany* (ch. 11, this volume) establishes a theoretical framework for examining how social actors experience the sacred. In his empirical application

of the concept epiphany (ch. 8, this volume), Rauer examines how Brandt's kneefall before the Warsaw Memorial literally performed an interaction with the sacred, and initiated profound shifts in German collective identity as a result.

2. The normative tendency to reduce the significance of Monicagate is particularly strong after September 11, 2001. But this interpretive urge represents and reaffirms an important cultural sociological point. Understanding turn-of-the-century American life and collective identity requires us to treat this impulse as indicative of an important plot point in a narrative Americans tell themselves about themselves: contemporary civil discourse makes sense of an America before and after 9/11, which was not but now is serious, which was naïve but has been forced into a state of knowledge. Contemporary discourse indicates America believes it has been forced out of the Garden and made aware of the reality of evil. Post-9/11, many people look back on Monicagate and ask incredulously, "we were concerned about *that*?" This interpretive trend testifies to the fact that yes, we *were* concerned about *that*, and passionately enough to battle fiercely over defining what exactly *that* was, its seriousness, and what should be done about it. Far from being imagined or in some sense "not real," Monicagate continues, and will continue, to exercise influence over American collective sense making. Sociologically, representations diminishing Monicagate's seriousness (while empirically erroneous in their own right, in my opinion), must figure prominently in investigations of contemporary intra- and inter-national affairs.

   Most significant are two sociological facts. First, in many ways Monicagate infiltrated people's everyday lives to the extent that the event assumed constitutive status, effectively defining the year 1998. Vast amounts of data demonstrate the event became the preferred communal reference point for Americans in their everyday interactions: from quantitative data such as polls, cable-TV news' ratings, Internet website and chatroom traffic indicators, and newspaper space allotted to covering the event, to such qualitative forms as the content of late-night talk show monologues, newpapers' letters to the editor, and frequently overheard heated discussions amongst friends and strangers about "what Clinton was thinking" and what should constitute an impeachable offence. Second, from the cataclysmic quality of the event's inception to its tepid finale, it was meaningful, and is explicable because it was dramatically and narratively structured and lived.

3. See Schudson (1992: 155), and Schwartz (1998), on the persuasiveness of Alexander's account.

4. The combination of meaning's centrality with the reduction of symbols to commodities and instruments of power encourages the reduction of culture to practice. Social actors are represented as instrumentally orienting towards symbols as material tools to be used to dupe others in one's pursuit of desired ends. The theoretical contortion stems from trying to reconcile the centrality and persuasiveness of meaning with the need to reduce social actors to uber-agentic, savvy consumers of culture who are too jaded by culture's commodification to engage any symbolic performance of collective identity in the first place. Social actors are thus portrayed as influenced by the instrumental manipulation of symbols on the one hand, and maintained as too savvy and suspicious to buy into any symbolic production, on the other.

5. See Barthes (1977b), Schechner (1977, 2002), and Mukerji and Schudson (1991), for theoretical arguments that establish the need to examine popular cultural structures' influence in the creation of everyday understandings. See Christensen (1987), Gibson (1994), and King (1999), for empirical applications of this theoretical turn that demonstrate the interactive relationship between film and social life.

6. *Washington Post*, November 4, 1992. Clinton won 43% of the vote; Bush garnered 38%.

7. *New York Times*, November 4, 1992.

8. The authenticity of Clinton's populist image stemmed from an elegant symmetry between his campaign's selected means of symbolic production and a script that emphasized how the candidate's biography naturally demanded that he empathize with a public far removed from the world of Washington insiders. For instance, to highlight Clinton's differences from Bush Sr., – a distanced figure who seemed to personify the buttoned-down Washington establishment, who flew over the people's heads in Air Force 1, the archetypical symbol of governmental power – the Clinton campaign boarded a bus and headed into "America's heartland" (*Washington Post* July 18, 1992). During scheduled stops, the candidate who could "feel your pain" (*New York Times*, March 28, 1992) would toss a football with his running mate, and pledge to "give the country back" to ordinary citizens, who had been organized to appear as spontaneous audiences (*New York Times*, July 19, 1992).

9. The metaphor traveled from the Arkansas *Democrat-Gazette* across the Atlantic to the London *Times*, only to be picked back up in the United States by the *New York Times* shortly thereafter.

10. David Grann, *The New Yorker*, January 27, 2003.

11. In early July, 1993, the White House's report from its internal investigation was released.

12. Found dead on July 20, 1993 in Fort Marcy Park. Foster was the White House deputy counsel and longtime friend and business partner of the Clintons.

13. The *Washington Post* reported the Justice Department's investigative intentions in a front-page story on October 31, 1993, entitled "U.S. Is Asked to Probe Failed Arkansas S&L."

14. In terms of the "discourse of civil society," by 1995 the Clinton team recognized the need to change their scandal management techniques. Bob Woodward quotes Mark Fabiani, the publicity agent for Clinton's "Scandal Management Team" (a.k.a. "the rapid response team") stating, "look, we've got to build our reputation for openness" with the American public to both reduce the climate of suspicion and consequently to become more politically effective in terms of policy.

15. The *New York Times* reported that though the White House denied the election was a referendum on Clinton, many of the Republican victors had placed Clinton at the center of their campaigns for office (Berke, *New York Times*, November 10, 1994, A/1/6). "Morphing," a new advertising technique of slowly blending televised images together to form a new image, figured prominently in this election cycle. "In the Congressional races there'll be over 30 campaigns using some form of the morph and almost all exclusively using Clinton as the bad guy," said Dan Leonard, director

of communications for the National Republican Congressional Committee (quoted in *New York Times*, October 29, 1994, 1/9/1). See Sobchack's (2002) analysis of the effects of televisual montage on historical consciousness for an examination of the relationship between televised performances (and other forms of televisual symbolic manipulation) and audiences' understandings of the event's progression.

16. Bob Dole became Senate Majority Leader in the Senate and Newt Gingrich became House Speaker.

17. In this instance, even science's discursive hegemony was contained and controlled, as DNA evidence placing Simpson at the scene of the crime was narrated away through invocations of the bad cop genre's tropes. It was argued that Simpson's DNA was placed at the crime scene by bad cops investigating the double murder.

18. Elvis Mitchell, *New York Times*, October 5, 2001.

19. "Filegate" is the label given to the White House's improper procurement of hundreds of FBI files on Congressional Republicans and past presidential administrations' workers and advisers.

20. The Government Reform Oversight Committee released its "Travelgate" report criticizing the employees' firing and the Clintons' evasiveness in the investigation, for instance.

21. *New York Times*, January 22, 1998, A/25/1.

22. *New York Times*, Clines and Gerth, January 22, 1998, A/1/6.

23. *New York Times*, Broder, January 24, 1998, A/1/6.

24. MSNBC and FOX News posted 100% increases, and CNN recorded a 60% increase (*Boston Globe*, January 25, 1998, A/10; *Washington Post*, January 27, 1998, D/1).

25. *New York Times*, January 22, 1998, A/29/5.

26. ABC's *This Week*, January 25, 1998; emphasis added.

27. *New York Times*, Broder, January 23, 1998, A/1/6.

28. *New York Times*, Berke and Bennet, January 23, 1998, A/1/23.

29. *New York Times*, January 23, 1998, A/20/1.

30. The number of people believing Clinton had an affair with Lewinsky rose 20% in the first three days, and the number believing he had encouraged her to lie about the relationship rose 14% (ABC News, January 24, 1998). For the first time in his tenure, less than half the public (49%) believed Clinton had the "honesty and integrity required to serve effectively" as President (ABC News, January 29, 1998).

31. Given more space, I would argue that Clinton's symbolic framework is in part a product of the political and cultural battles of the late 1960s on the one hand, and more currently a product of the 1980s and 1990s culture wars on the other. It should be clear that I am not arguing that Clinton's actions in themselves, of necessity, compelled a particular public response.

32. Seelye in *New York Times*, January 24, 1998, A/8/3.

33. *New York Times*, Bennet.

34. *New York Times*, Broder.

35. *New York Daily News*, January 27, 1998, p. 28.

36. NBC News Transcripts, January 27, 1998; emphasis added.

37. NBC's *Today* show registered a 7.2 rating (percentage of the nation's 98 million homes with televisions) and a 29 share (percentage of sets in use) on January 27th, 1998, the day of Hillary Clinton's interview with Lauer. This was the show's second highest single-day rating since 1987. The previous high was set in 1989, the day after the San Francisco earthquake (*New York Daily News*, January 29, 1998, p. 4).

38. A nuanced distinction began to emerge in a majority of Americans' understandings of Clinton's self in late January, shortly after the Address. Clinton's *public self* became understood as autonomous enough from his *private self* to allow him to adequately perform the duties necessary to be President. Additionally, late January polls began to indicate the majority of Americans were willing and able to maintain a subjective distinction between these two selves, and that they were more concerned with Clinton's political than personal actions. After the event's first week approximately 66% of Americans favored Clinton's resignation if he committed either perjury or suborning of perjury, a full 25 percentage points greater than the 41% that supported his ousting if he had simply engaged in the affair (ABC News). It is my argument that this distinction may not have occurred or remained sustainable had Clinton continued to appear "visibly shaken," nervous, and evasive before his intently curious audiences and critics.

39. *New York Times*, January 28, 1998, A/1/6.

40. In addition to focusing on his Administration's accomplishments and plans, Clinton tried to cultivate the theme of the American people *getting back to work together* for the good of the nation. For instance: "This is the America we have begun to build. This is the America we can leave to our children – *if we join together to finish the work at hand*" or "we must work together, learn together, live together, serve together" (*Washington Post* online).

41. *New York Times*, January 28, 1998, A/25/2.

42. *New York Times*, January 26, 1998, A/19/5, emphasis added.

43. For instance, MSNBC's website more than doubled its previous web traffic record with more than two million people searching for the report before the web-managers could even get it fully posted.

44. *New York Times*, September 12, 1998, A/11/3.

45. *New York Times*, September 12, 1998, A/18/1, emphasis added.

46. The tape's airing invigorated the Republican base, with 63% of registered Republicans voicing a "strong desire" to see Clinton removed from office (ABC News, September 22, 1998). However, the tape inspired sympathy for Clinton from a majority of viewers with 63% of the public agreeing Clinton was justified in his anger towards his interrogators, 61% feeling it was wrong for Congress to release the tape, and 62% disapproving of the way Republicans were handling the Lewinsky issue (ABC News, September 23, 1998).

47. Federal Information Systems Corporation, Federal News Service, August 12, 1998.

48. *New York Times*, December 23, 1998, A/24/2. The many channels from which the ritual's would-be audiences had to choose contributed to reducing the potential for liminality that characterized Watergate's Hearings. The limited channels during

Watergate contributed to the sense that everyone was involved in and witnessing history as it was unfolding.

References

Alexander, Jeffrey C. 1988. "Culture and Political Crisis: 'Watergate' and Durkheimian Sociology," pp. 187–224 in *Durkheimian Sociology: Cultural Studies*. New York: Cambridge University Press.
Alexander, Jeffrey C. and Phillip Smith. 1993. "The Discourse of American Civil Society: A New Proposal for Cultural Studies." *Theory and Society* 22: 151–207.
1998. "Cultural Sociology or Sociology of Culture? Towards a Strong Program for Sociology's Second Wind." *Sociologie et Société* 30, 1: 107–16.
Anderson, Benedict. 1983. *Imagined Communities*. New York: Verso.
Barthes, Roland. [1968] 1977a. *Elements of Semiology*. New York: Hill and Wang.
1977b. *Image, Music, Text*. New York: Hill & Wang.
Christensen, Terry. 1987. *Reel Politics: American Political Movies from "Birth of the Nation" to "Platoon."* New York: Basil Blackwell.
Clifford, James. 1988. *The Predicament of Culture: Twentieth-Century Ethnography, Literature, and Art*. Cambridge, Mass.: Harvard University Press.
Dayan, Daniel and Elihu Katz. 1992. *Media Events: The Live Broadcasting of History*. Cambridge, Mass: Harvard University Press.
Derrida, Jacques. 1988. *Limited Inc*. Evanston: Northwestern University Press.
Douglas, Mary. 1966. *Purity and Danger: An Analysis of the Concepts of Pollution and Taboo*. New York: Routledge.
Durkheim, Emile. [1912] 1995. *The Elementary Forms of Religious Life*. New York: Free Press.
Eco, Umberto. 1976. *A Theory of Semiotics*. Bloomington: Indiana University Press.
Edles, Laura. 1998. *Symbol and Ritual in the New Spain: The Transition to Democracy After Franco*. New York: Cambridge University Press.
Garfinkel, Harold. 1956. "Conditions of Successful Degradation Ceremonies." *American Journal of Sociology* 61: 420–4.
Geertz, Clifford. 1983. "Common Sense as a Cultural System," pp. 73–93 in *Local Knowledge: Further Essays in Interpretive Anthropology*. New York: Basic Books.
Gibson, James William. 1994. *Warrior Dreams: Paramilitary Culture in Post-Vietnam America*. New York: Hill and Wang.
Goffman, Erving. 1951. "Symbols of Class Status." *British Journal of Sociology* 2, 4: 294–304.
Jameson, Frederic. 1982. "The Symbolic Inference; or, Kenneth Burke and Ideological Analysis," pp. 68–91 in *Representing Kenneth Burke*, ed. Hayden White and Margaret Brose. Baltimore: Johns Hopkins University Press.
Kane, Anne. 1991. "Cultural Analysis in Historical Sociology: The Analytic and Concrete Forms of the Autonomy of Culture." *Sociological Theory* 9: 53–69.
King, Neal. 1999. *Heroes in Hard Times: Cop Action Movies in the U.S.* Philadelphia: Temple University Press.

Larson, Magali Sarfatti and Robin Wagner-Pacifici. 2001. "The Dubious Place of Virtue: Reflections on the Impeachment of William Jefferson Clinton and the Death of the Political Event in America." *Theory and Society* 30: 735–74.

Lukes, Steven. 1975. "Political Ritual and Social Integration." *Sociology* 2: 289–308.

Molotch, Harvey and Marilyn Lester. 1974. "News as Purposive Behavior: On the Strategic Use of Routine Events, Accidents, and Scandals." *American Sociological Review* 39: 101–12.

Mukerji, Chandra and Michael Schudson. 1991. *Rethinking Popular Culture: Contemporary Perspectives in Cultural Studies*. Berkeley: University of California Press.

Said, Edward. 1978. *Orientalism*. New York: Pantheon Books.

Saussure, Ferdinand de. 1985. "The Linguistic Sign," pp. 28–46 in *Semiotics: An Introductory Anthology*, ed. Robert E. Innis. Bloomington: Indiana University Press.

Schechner, Richard. 1977. *Essays on Performance Theory 1970–1976*. New York: Drama Book Specialists.

   2002. *Performance Studies: An Introduction*. New York: Routledge.

Schudson, Michael. 1992. *Watergate in American Memory: How We Remember, Forget, and Reconstruct the Past*. New York: Basic Books.

Schwartz, Barry and Lori Holyfield. 1998. "Nixon Postmodern. (Richard Nixon)." *Annals of the American Academy of Political and Social Science* 560: 96–111.

Shils, Edward and Michael Young. 1953. "The Meaning of the Coronation." *Sociological Review* 1: 63–81.

Smelser, Neil J. 1963. *Theory of Collective Behavior*. New York: Free Press.

Smith, Philip. 1991. "Codes and Conflict: Toward a Theory of War as Ritual." *Theory and Society* 20: 103–38.

Sobchack, Thomas and Vivian Sobchack. 1987. *An Introduction to Film*. Boston: Little, Brown, and Company.

Swidler, Ann. 1986. "Culture in Action: Symbols and Strategies." *American Sociological Review* 51: 273–86.

Turner, Victor. 1969. *The Ritual Process: Structure and Anti-structure*. New York: Aldine De Gruyter.

   1974. *Dramas, Fields, and Metaphors*. Ithaca: Cornell University Press.

   1982. *From Ritual to Theater: The Human Seriousness of Play*. New York: PAJ Publications.

Wagner-Pacifici, Robin E. 1986. *The Moro Morality Play: Terrorism as Social Drama*. Chicago: University of Chicago Press.

Woodward, Robert. 1999. *Shadow: Five Presidencies and the Legacy of Watergate*. New York: Simon & Schuster.

Wuthnow, Robert. 1987. *Meaning and Moral Order: Explorations in Cultural Analysis*. Berkeley: University of California Press.

4

Social dramas, shipwrecks, and cockfights: conflict and complicity in social performance

Isaac Reed

Introduction

Since its post-positivist intersection with culture in the 1960s, sociological theory has taken myriad forms. Longstanding concerns have returned in new form, as a deeper and more detailed understanding of the symbolic has reorganized attempts to theorize social action and social structure. After the structuralist moment, sociological theorists have returned to praxis in its various forms: habitus, structuration, communicative action. The overarching narrative has been: "after the text, practices," as if by returning to praxis we can return to the real, the political, and the individual.

This move to pragmatics has, often covertly, undercut the attempt to take culture seriously, to analyze the thickness and depth of symbolic structures. Against this tide, the strong program in cultural sociology has continued to emphasize the autonomy of culture and the usefulness of the textual metaphor for understanding it, and remained unwilling to commit to a crude version of the meaning-as-use theorem. Now, however, cultural sociology has turned to the questions of contingency, agency, and creativity; in other words, it has taken up "cultural pragmatics," thus answering the call to theorize action without reducing meaning.

Part of this project has been the delineation of a general analytic schema of social performance, which, drawing upon theatre studies, analytic philosophy, and dramaturgical sociology, provides a framework for interpreting events in terms of what it takes to make meaning walk and talk. It is a theory of how structure, and in particular, structures of meaning, relate to action, and one whose general analytic outlook is connected to specific research concerns, including the analysis of political scandals and media events, and the development of a broad historical understanding of the differentiation of these elements such that one can explain failed performance and the contingency of audience interpretation in contemporary societies.

However, there are certain questions and concerns that Alexander's general theoretical schema does not address. In particular, there has remained the problem of theatre "proper": to what extent and in what way is "performance" or "dramaturgy" a metaphor for "real action"? From the perspective of a general performance theory, both a performance of *Hamlet* and a public trial have actors and audiences, scripts and a *mise-en-scène*. Yet these performances have quite different consequences and seem to sit inside different contexts of interpretation. Secondly, there is the problem of the conflict of interpretations. That there can be multiple audiences for any performance is an oft-repeated slogan. But how can we begin to differentiate empirically between the different ways audiences can be split? It seems empirically inadequate to say, from the perspective of general performance theory, that both the impeachment of Nixon in front of a nationally televised audience in the United States, something that, it could be argued, achieved almost ritual transcendence (Alexander 1988), and the prosecution of the recent war on Iraq by the United States on the global stage, both exhibited "multiple audiences."

I believe these problems can be addressed within the framework offered by Alexander's theory, through a specification of certain ideal types of social performance. As I mentioned before, the six elements of a social performance make up an analytic theory, in the sense that any performance can be said to contain these elements. However, the ways in which the elements come together, their relationship to each other, remains deliberately unspecified. By specifying the nature of the relations between elements, we can begin to differentiate types of social performance with an eye to empirical research questions. In particular, as will become clear below, I will be interested in the way in which motivated action and its interpretation by audiences vary in the way they relate to the set of collective representations and scripts that are the symbolic background for performance.

My method for the construction of these ideal types is a bit unusual, but I think has a special advantage, given the history and intellectual context of cultural sociology. I want to construct three ideal types of social performance by considering three classic accounts of culture-in-action from symbolic and structural anthropology: Victor Turner on the Henry II–Thomas Becket social drama, Marshall Sahlins on the arrival of Captain Cook to the Hawaiian Islands, and Clifford Geertz on the Balinese Cockfight. By construing a dialogue between the empirical events themselves, the anthropologists' accounts of them, and performance theory in the form of "cultural pragmatics," I hope to accomplish two tasks: to specify the elements of performance theory into identifiable idealtypical formations that will be useful for further research, and to relativize and systematize these famous anthropological accounts of culture-in-action. The latter purpose requires some words of explication.

The works of Turner, Sahlins, and Geertz on their respective cases are often interpreted as giving, in each case, a paradigmatic account of how culture and action relate, as specifying *the* model by which social researchers can comprehend how societies and their self-symbolizations work. As such, they have all drawn heavy criticism: analytic-theoretical, empirical, and normative. I want to argue, here, that in fact each account specifies a model of one type of cultural action, or performance, which can be seen as manifesting specific and empirically differentiable relations between the six elements of performance theory. As such, they should not be taken as paradigmatic accounts of action and history and their relationship to symbolic formations. This relativization should dampen many of the critiques brought against these various theories, for reasons which should become clear.

Beyond ritual

The use of the concept of ritual to analyze cultural action dates at least as far back as Durkheim's belief/ritual distinction in the *Elementary Forms of Religious Life*. Since then, the term has had a quite varied history within anthropology, sociology, and common parlance. For the purposes of this chapter, we can pick this history back up at the moment of Victor Turner's anthropology, and post-Parsonian Durkheimian sociology. It was Turner's insight that social processes that he observed in urbanized Western (and supposedly "secular") societies bore deep affinities with the "ritual process" as he observed it in his fieldwork among small African tribes. He extended this insight in several publications, and in particular he and Richard Schechner engaged with it to better grasp certain forms of theatre that were developing among the American avant-garde. But Turner also developed the concept of social drama to describe more contingent processes of cultural enactment, and he eventually differentiated liminoid activities in modern industrial societies from liminal moments in traditional rites of passage. The concepts of "social drama" and "liminoid" point beyond ritual as the central concept for the analysis of culture-in-action.

Likewise, within the post-Parsonian tradition of sociology, Shils's and Young's (1953) essay on the English coronation is a classic example of an analysis of a ritual in contemporary society that exhibits the nostalgia for more fused societies that Alexander and Mast identify in this tradition of social thought (see Introduction). It is the need to avoid these simplifications of the understanding of the role of the symbolic and the religious in contemporary Western societies combined with an impetus to increased theoretical sophistication and subtlety that, I believe, drives Alexander and Mast to give up on "ritual" as a central analytical concept for the analysis of performance. I agree with this approach, though I do think that, first, it may be possible to specify "ritual" as a type of performance, and that, second, the understanding of ritual as a relatively closed, limited, and determined performance (for better or worse) among sociological theorists may be a (useful) elaboration of a distinction *inherent and specific to Western societies.* That is, the relative unimportance of "ritual" for understanding key processes of differentiation, democratization, and political conflict may be the result of an emic distinction – other modernities may incorporate "ritual" and its strong connection to religion in a way that involves many of the contingencies of performance.

However, this chapter attempts the development of concepts directly tied to the immediate research concerns of the cultural pragmatics group, paramount amongst which are the conflict of interpretations and the role of liminoid culture, neither of which is easily comprehensible from the viewpoint of "ritual" as it has been generally conceived. Rather, I wish to leave ritual, and perhaps some of the cases that it does describe (for example, coronations and inaugurations), as a residual category for the moment, and instead try to advance the framework of performance theory through ideal-type specification of different kinds of social action.

For this purpose, these classic anthropological accounts can do a great deal of theoretical work, if interpreted properly. For they engage the problems of conflict of interpretations, and the role of popular and "fictional" culture in acute and identifiable ways. The Henry–Becket drama exemplifies complicity-in-conflict: all of the actors and audiences, though offering quite conflicting narratives and characterizations, work from within the same deeply felt set of collective representations. The notions of divine kingship, Christian martyrdom, and nascent English nationalism, to name just a few of the meaning configurations that make up the background culture-structure of the drama, are felt by and available to everyone, though who has both the skills and the social power to enact them is of course the key question. The case of Captain Cook exemplifies the opposite extreme, where the cognitive dissonance is so great, the separation of audience interpretations so wide, that one can only claim that the "same" drama was taking place by speaking very literally. And indeed, the (dramatically) ironic "working misunderstanding," which allowed the show to go on for some time, unraveled with both symbolic and literal violence. Finally, Geertz's account of the cockfight is, I think, the classic essay showing the deeply metaphorical, rather than merely reflective or functional, role of popular culture in differentiated societies. Though not all culture is "a reading of a reading" or "stories people tell themselves about themselves," the culture that is such a story – the games people play, the fictions they tell themselves – has deep and important, and at the same time *indirect*, social effects. How this differs from the more "serious" side of life found in social dramas and shipwrecks is a question I hope to begin to answer by further specifying the nature of this metaphorical relationship.

In what follows, then, I will briefly reconstruct the empirical outlines of each case as presented, respectively, by Turner, Sahlins, and Geertz. I will then consider their explanatory and interpretive efforts from the perspective of performance theory. This will enable me to suggest that while the Henry–Becket social drama, Captain Cook's shipwreck, and the Balinese Cockfight are all social performances, each, in its respective reconstruction by these anthropologists, signifies a specific type of social performance, whose empirical properties are generalizable in a way useful for further research.

Serious social drama: Henry II and Thomas Becket at Northampton

In his essay, "Religious Paradigms and Political Action" (Turner 1974) Victor Turner is most concerned to show how, when, and why Becket came to attach himself to the "root paradigm" of Christian Martyr, and then to delineate how this scripting of his role in social drama of the Council of Northampton explains the eventual outcome of the larger drama: that is, Becket's murder six years later. Turner also shows how the adoption of the martyr script takes the form of an initiation, with Henry II as initiator. But Turner's account is unorganized and confusing, for it is not entirely clear how the social drama model works itself out, nor where it really applies or what it really explains, so caught up is Turner in specifying the moment and nature of Thomas Becket's individual, psychological transformation (hence Turner's corresponding tendency to narrate the entire event from Thomas's point of view). Undoubtedly such an exploration of subjectivity is useful, but I want to adopt here a perspective that is both more analytical and more governed by the trope of dramatic irony, so as to reveal the working out, in the Henry–Becket performance, the specific nature of the ideal type I will call "serious social drama." In other words, I want to construe a dialogue between Turner's account and Alexander's analytic social theory of performance, whereby we might both come up with a clearer explanation of the event itself, and begin to delineate the empirically generalizable features of this type of event.

A stripped-down narrative of the central events in the Henry–Becket social drama might run as follows. Henry appoints his longtime friend and chancellor Thomas Becket to the see of Canterbury, with the probable intent of bringing the Church further under the Crown's control. Becket strikes a first blow for the Church by resigning his chancellorship, citing conflict of interest

Becket then proceeds to give up his former ways of sumptuous living, becomes highly religious and ascetic, demands that land that he asserts belongs to the Church be given back by the Crown, and insists that clergy who commit crimes should be tried by ecclesiastical courts. A now hostile Henry attempts to impose his will on Thomas through the counsels of Westminster and Clarendon, and at Clarendon Thomas agrees to many of Henry's demands verbally and thus betrays and angers the bishops. Upon realizing that the Constitution of Clarendon – which gives the power of trial to kings and nobles and makes officers of the King immune to excommunication, as well as stating that clergy cannot leave the country without the King's permission – is to be written down, however, Thomas refuses to sign the roll, and then goes into repentance for his "sin," writing to the pope to confess. The pope condemns ten of the Clarendon clauses. Thomas tries to leave England to confess in person to the pope, but fails. When he tries one last time to reconcile with Henry at Woodstock, Henry dismisses him with reference to his attempts to leave illegally.

At the Council of Northampton, Henry accuses Thomas of breaking the law, the pretense being that John the Marshal was owed some land from the Church, which Thomas had delayed in giving him. Henry arrives late, refuses to greet Thomas with a kiss, and then demands 500 pounds as payment. Thomas retorts ironically, but the bishops act as his guarantors and urge him not to upset the King. Henry continues to demand more and more money from Thomas, for various reasons, until the sum becomes astronomical. Thomas asks to consult with his clergy, thus alienating the barons who favored him. The clergy is divided as to whether Thomas should give in and resign. But after they try to give an initial sum for security and Henry turns it down, it becomes clear that Henry wants to ruin and perhaps imprison Thomas, and that ecclesiastical freedom is at stake. On a Monday, October 12, Thomas falls ill and retreats to St. Andrew's monastery. On Tuesday, October 13, he says the mass of St. Stephen, a martyr whose mass normally comes the day after Christmas, in St. Stephen's church outside of Northampton. Throngs of supportive commoners surround Thomas, who is dressed in his most holy garments, on the way to the church, and then again as he leaves the church to go to court. At court, with Henry upstairs, Thomas communicates his defiance of the King, and the King bullies the bishops into lodging an appeal to the pope against Thomas. The bishops return and pronounce this to Thomas, blaming him for the Clarendon Constitution. Thomas refuses this characterization, and Henry excuses the bishops from further participation. The barons then condemn Thomas as a traitor against the King, and Thomas pronounces that none of them has the right to judge him, and heads for the door, pursued by angry barons. He rides off into the night and into exile, and the rest "is history."

The Henry–Becket social drama might be reconstructed as follows. The primary actors of the drama are Henry, Becket, the barons, and the bishops, the audiences are all of the above, and "the people" (and perhaps "posterity"). There is also the pope, who plays a supporting role and serves as a quite important critical audience. The networks of social power that are important are Henry's connections to the means of force, by which, if he convinces enough of his barons, he can have Thomas imprisoned, and Thomas's high office of archbishop of Canturbury – he must at least be heard by the bishops, King, and barons. Furthermore, we have the more general political economy as a background power-struggle between church and state, and, of course the parallel legal systems, both of which have a good amount of legitimacy. It is in the nature of social drama, however, that all of these will be, to a certain extent, put up for grabs during the course of events. When this takes place, both the King and Thomas have good access to means of symbolic performance – Henry has his entourage, his castles, and his literal crown (and his hunting equipment), Thomas has his holy garments and his cross, and access to abbeys and churches.

The collective representations that provide the background meanings in which this drama is immersed include both the specific representations of events between Henry and Becket leading up to this split, and the more general Christian and feudal understandings of sacrality, the divine right of kings, and the infallibility of the pope and the Church, as well as some protonationalist notions of England as realm separate from that of Europe and the world. The specific scripts that will be put into scene are, then, that of a moral king accusing a corrupt churchman, and that of a holy martyr defying a raging tyrant. This conflict of interpretations, within the complicity of a Christian-feudal symbol system, is the key dynamic of cultural action that defines the Henry–Becket case as a serious social drama.

Turner's explanation of the events, beyond the implicit explanation involved in even the "bare" narrative above, is that the root paradigm of Christian martyrdom provided the narrative mechanism by which a cornered Thomas could win by losing. The key factor explaining the course of events at Northampton is the *mise-en-scène*, in acts and words, of the narrative of the defiant martyr confronting unjust power with holy truth. This is the posited mechanism which parsimoniously explains why (1) Becket defies the King's personal attacks on him and retreats to consult with his clergy, (2) Becket says St. Stephen's mass and draws the love and adoration of the crowds, (3) Becket enters the court defiantly carrying his own cross, (4) Henry stays upstairs and avoids confrontation with Becket, (5) Becket defies his own bishops' pleas and bullying, and (6) Becket interrupts and denies the barons any right to judge him, bringing them to make a violent attack on him. It also, of course, explains (7) why Henry' knights murder Thomas six years later, but since Turner does not provide the thick description for that aspect of the long social drama, I will leave it to the side at the moment, and retain merely the flee to exile as the end of the chain of events.

There are three key aspects of the serious social drama performative mechanism. First, Turner demarcates an "existential" aspect of root paradigms that extends beyond the more commonly elucidated aspects of culture structure, the cognitive and moral. This connects Turner's text to Alexander's meditations on authenticity as a product of social process – one performs not only the good and the true, but also the real. Furthermore, although we all certainly perform the real everyday, it is in the heightened times of social drama, the "times outside of time,"[1] that the real is not just mundanely reproduced, but at stake and subject to abrupt change. This also explains the raging debates, through the years, about Thomas's *authenticity* – was he really a dedicated martyr, or a proud man who "did the right deed for the wrong reason" (Turner 1974: 66)?[2] In serious social drama, for reasons that will become clear, the authenticity of actors is quite often a key issue open for contention – and in a way broader than (though still including) the attribution of subjective intentions.

Second, Turner points out that, despite the usefulness of his "situational" approach, it is not just the immediate actors in this drama that make up the world in which it takes place and which it transforms. For,

Within [the meeting at Northampton] coiled the tensions of the changing structure of Europe, and the form and content of its discourse were drawn from many centuries of literate debate. Although the actors were few, their interactions lend themselves only superficially to small group analysis, for each man there was the representative of many persons, relationships, corporate interests, and institutional aims. (Turner 1974: 71)

Thus the relationship of actions to the larger culture is, in this case, *metonymical*. The notion of metonymy captures the reality effect of serious social dramas, whereby the abstract categories of social good and bad, the general narrative structures of triumph or trauma, are made concrete and particular via walking and talking performers. Metonymical action takes place in an arena of cultural representations shared collectively, and the question becomes who and what is the (authentic) avatar of which trope or truth. When, in *la vie sérieuse*, reality is on the line, we still need concrete actors to actualize the abstract themes of generalized consciousness. When and if their performance succeeds, their specific actions come to be seen as *contiguous* with the general metaphysical categories that define the social field of interpretation (here I am following Jakobson and Halle 1956: 91–6). It is tempting to specify this form of action down to *synecdoche*, the substitution of part for whole or species for genus, but, given the varied nature of social universes of meaning, it's important to be more flexible.

Metonymical action is that of avatars: Henry represents English nationalism not by virtue of his *likeness* to a nationalist, but because he is its embodiment. A successful performance of metonymical action results in a social interpretation that closes the gap, in interpretive space, between the generalized signifier and its increasingly specified signified. Thus its incredible pragmatic power: the signifier Englishness (or "American presidency," or "justice") is presented as if attached directly to a person or thing in the immediate situation, hiding its reliance on a set of abstract, trans-contextual interpretive structures.

The notion of metonymy, and the way in which actors and acts come to embody wider cultural themes and socio-political configurations, brings us directly to the third of Turner's insights into serious social drama. The contested nature of interpretation takes place, in social dramas, within a more general complicity of opposing actors, interpretive camps, and social fissures. Everyone is arguing using more or less the same set of collective representations. Will Thomas Becket emerge as a true martyr or a corrupt monk? Is Bill Clinton a victim of conspiracy or a profaner of sacred office? It depends on whose interpretation carries the day, but all interpretations take place within a shared discursive field in which all of the social actors are immersed. Turner recognizes this, though he tends to slip towards discussion of it as a complicity between the two central subjectivities of the Henry–Becket drama:

> It should be stressed, however, that every sacrifice requires not only a victim – in this case a self-chosen victim – but also a sacrificer. That is, we are always dealing not with solitary individuals but with systems of social relations – we have drama, not merely soliloquy. In the case considered the sacrificer was Henry, who . . . in certain crucial moments almost egged Thomas on to commit himself to the martyr's path. There is constantly a curious complicity between the two, with Henry daring Thomas to make good his asseverations about the honor of the church. (Turner 1974: 69)

The more opposing actors share the same discursive frameworks and value-orientations, the more intense this complicity-in-conflict is. Clearly, not only a certain English proto-nationalism, a quasi-feudal understanding of kingship and violence, but ultimately (and perhaps to Becket's advantage and then to his ultimate "triumph"), the framework of Christianity is what defines the complicity in this case, and thus enables the conflict. Specifically, of crucial importance was the trope of the Christian martyr, on the one hand, and of the divine king, on the other. Indeed, in this drama the sacred of the Judeo-Christian was split in two in its empirical manifestation: King Henry – intimidating, loud, jealous, in direct control of the means of violence – came to represent all that inspires fear and awe in the Judeo-Christian sacred. Thomas – sickly "browbeaten," and yet steadily defiant – fit the Christian inversion which gives sacred status to the meek and the powerless, who, so deeply connected to the transcendent sacred of the other world, are not long for this one. That both men found and latched on to these "root paradigms," and intuitively understood the possible narrative interactions between them, is what Turner brings to the forefront in his explanation.

From this, we can draw some conclusions about the type of serious social dramas more generally, characteristics that will become clearer when compared to the two other types of social performance that follow. The actors in a serious social drama, who are usually important – that is powerful and/or sacred people – stand in for more general themes and issues in the society and culture at large. Furthermore, the audiences, which often include some of the prime actors themselves, can be split as to their interpretations of events, and it is the contestation of interpretations that is the key conflict in this "time outside of time," when the mundane workings of everyday power and legality are suspended so that they can be existentially thematized. The collective representations are, for all the actors, more or less "the same," which means that it is the act of specification and embodiment, in the *mise-en-scène*, that is the key site of interpretation. And thus, when the time comes for social drama, actors "cash in" their various political, economic, and social-structural advantages to enable symbolic production and control over interpretation.

Shipwreck in Hawaii

Marshall Sahlins has researched and written extensively on Captain Cook's arrival, departure, rearrival, and subsequent murder in Hawaii in 1798 (Sahlins 1981, 1982, 1985, 1989, 1995). He is most concerned to explain not only why Cook was killed by the Hawaiians, but more generally, the way in which Hawaiian culture was transformed by the arrival of the British, by way of its reproduction. This enables him to reintegrate history and diachrony into structuralist anthropology, and thus to develop an explanatory paradigm more appropriate to his cultural relativism and his historical interest.

His accounts have produced not only discussion but controversy. In a series of exchanges, he and Gananath Obeyesekere have battled over whether Sahlins is himself caught up in the "European imagination" of Hawaiians (and other colonized peoples) as "savages" (Obeyesekere 1992). I cannot go into the complexities of this debate here. Two comments will have to suffice. First, though Sahlins does focus mostly on the cultural framings of the Hawaiians, and is most concerned to explain the Hawaiians' action, and thus perhaps at times *assumes* an understanding of why the Europeans act the way they do, at several key points he relativizes the European frameworks of action: their mythological belief in the'sacrality of property, their strange Christian understandings of life after death, etc. (Sahlins also might point out ruefully that his focus on the Hawaiian chiefs' frameworks of action is justified by the fact that they killed Cook, not the other way around). Thus, within the cultural-sociological orientation, which insists on "different cultures, different rationalities," Sahlins does not exhibit European bias. In other words, the Sahlins–Obeyesekere debate can be understood in terms of competing and conflicting paradigms of scientific thought – culturalism vs. pragmatism. Second, the theoretical work I ask Sahlins' account to do for performance theory below – to show the dissonance that results when different orientations to action are brought to the "same" drama – should not be taken as implying an essential and unbridgeable distance between Western societies and their others. Rather, as I will go on to show later, "shipwrecks" can occur anywhere and anytime, and do not represent some essential narrative of history, but rather one of many mechanisms by which it proceeds. Thus the importance of relativizing Sahlins' account: history is not only made through shipwrecks.

A brief narrative of the main events of the Cook case might run as follows. Captain James Cook arrives at the Hawaiian Islands and is greeted as something of a chief/divinity.[3] A year later, he returns, appearing off Maui on November 26, 1778, but does not drop anchor and come ashore to Kealakekua bay until January 17, 1779, after having circumnavigated the island of Hawaii. There he is greeted with cries of "O Lono!" and escorted by priests to the principal temple, where he is made to imitate the wooden image of Lono, and worshipped with chants, anointed with coconut oil, and fed by hand. This ceremony is repeated on later days in different temples. On January 25, King Kalaniopuu arrives. On February 1 a British seaman dies, and is buried in the great temple by Cook and the Hawaiian priests. Also, on that day, with the permission of the priests, the British carry off the wooden fence and images of the temple, though not the main image of the god Ku, to use for firewood. On February 2 the chiefs begin to ask when the British will be leaving. Cook assures them he will be leaving soon, but promises to come back next year. The British push off.

A few days out, however, one of Cook's ships springs its foremast. The British return to Kealakekua bay on February 11. The Hawaiins are unfriendly, in direct contrast to the adoration expressed previously, and start stealing from the British to a degree not seen before. On February 13 an unarmed British party is beaten up. Cook blockades the bay, and heads ashore with marines to take King Kalaniopuu hostage. The King seems ready to let Cook take him aboard until his wife and some other Hawaiians intervene with some words to the King, at which point he sits down and refuses to go on. The Hawaiian crowd surrounding the scene learns that a chief has just been killed trying to leave the bay. Cook fires his gun at a man threatening him with an iron dagger. Nearly a hundred Hawaiians pounce on Cook, and one of them kills him with another iron dagger.

Within forty-eight hours of Cook's death, two priests of the god of Lono sneak out to the British ships (at the risk of reprisal from either the British or the Hawaiians), bringing with them 10 pounds of Cook's hindquarters. Upon presenting it to the British, they ask when he will return. Over the next few days, extensive "negotiations" take place about the possession of Cook's bones. Eventually, on February 20 and 21 the Hawaiian chiefs give up what the British take to be Cook's bones – mostly defleshed and burnt, but with the hands intact. It remains ambiguous as to what they actually were; into the nineteenth century both the British and the Hawaiians claim to possess Cook's remains. Further interactions between the British and Hawaiians take on a different nature than that between Hawaiians and Americans; despite the superiority of American economic influence, in the first twenty years of the nineteenth century many Hawaiian chiefs make political claims on the basis of relationships with the English, and several name their children "King George." Ensuing English travelers are not, however, treated worshipfully as Cook's men were.

In *Historical Metaphors and Mythical Realities* (1981), Sahlins begins his explanation, which generally interweaves the events referred to above in with the ritual and mythological structures that explain them, by detailing the mythico-historical situation in Hawaii at the time Cook arrived. Fundamental was the myth of the arrival of the priest Paao, whose relevance is assured by its reoc-currence in stories that attest to be accounts of contemporary events. In this myth, Paao comes over the sea from lands invisible, and installs a new chief as well as a sacrificial cult and image worship. The current (in 1778) King traces his line to Paao's chief, Pilikaaiea, who deposed the indigenous chief, Kapawa. Furthermore, the myth of Paao contains another usurpation story, encoded in the story of Paao's exit from his former island. This is the annual alternation of the gods of war and peace, Ku and Lono. Paao avoided the wrath of his brother (who had called up storms) by calling on mackerel and bonito to settle the seas; it is the transition from fishing one to fishing the other that marks the end of the four-month festival of Lono, and the re-emergence of those rituals that are associated with Ku, including sacrifice.

Now, it is important to realize that myth, in Hawaiian society, is directly connected to political intrigue and maneuvering, whereby real chiefs and kings come to real power by really killing other real chiefs and kings. It is this rela-tionship between "religion" and "politics" that cements Sahlins' explanation of the Hawaiians' action, for the relationship between gods and chiefs is one of genus to species – certain chiefs are personifications of gods. Thus gods come to earth in the form of chiefs or wooden idols, and "recur" in various histor-ical situations, the acting out of which is simultaneously the reproduction of the myths and the reproduction of society, neither without significant change. Many other chiefs had been taken as personifications of Lono, and when Cook was so taken, he was received as such, after he circled the island, encompassing, in space and time, the ritual circling of the wooden idol of Lono around the island that constitutes the Makahiki festival. Cook then left right on schedule, when the time of Lono was over, and that of Ku beginning – whose instantiation was the reigning chief Kalaniopuu. But his return rendered him *hors categorie*, and a direct threat to the King's power, which was supposed to be reinstalled upon Cook/Lono's exit. Thus the immediate breakdown of friendly relations between the British and Hawaiians (in particular the King and his chiefs), and the culmination of these hostilities in the murder of Cook.

Furthermore, though the British, in ensuing visits, slowly and surely shed their divine status by eating with women, the Hawaiian mythical structure, via the historical act of sacrificing Cook as an act of usurpation and reclaiming of power by the chief who instantiated Ku, incorporated Britishness into their conception of divinity. As Sahlins puts it, "Mediated by the sacrifice of Cook, the mana of the Hawaiian paramount had become British – hence the role of the British in Hawaiian politics in the decades that followed, despite their supercession in Hawaiian economics" (Sahlins 1981: 26).

But while Sahlins, in his many different accounts of the Cook fiasco, is mainly concerned with explaining the action of the Hawaiians and the ensuing history of those islands, it is clear from several of his accounts that a full explanation of the event at hand relies on the construction of a two-sided model of the "structure of the conjuncture." For what took place relied, of course, on the action of the British as well, and insofar as each side played certain roles in the other side's drama, a "working misunderstanding" took place (Sahlins 1982: 81). Thus if Kalaniopuu was the personification of Ku and enacted the myth of the usurpation of chiefly power, Cook was, for the British, the high priest of Imperialism, a mythological structure combining elements of Christianity, the white man's burden, and bourgeois notions of private property and the pursuit of economic gain. This explains why Cook let himself be received in the way he was, as well as explaining why he refused the women who were offered to him:

Cook in fact was not about to yield to temptations of the flesh, though quite prepared, when there was no danger of introducing "the venereal," to allow his "people" to so make display of their mortal weaknesses. According to Zimmerman . . . Cook never spoke of religion, would tolerate no priest on his ship, seldom observed the Sabbath . . . It appears there could be only one Authority on board a vessel of His Majesty's Navy. Hence if Hawaiians really did present their sacred chiefess to Captain Cook because he was a god . . . we can be sure that he refused her – for something like the same reason. (Sahlins 1981: 12)

The ironies of the encounter aside, it is important to see the extent of the working misunderstanding, and thus the two-sided nature of the drama that was the Cook encounter. On the one side, the Hawaiians receive Cook as Lono, because he arrives, like chiefs-as-personifications-of-gods have done before, from far away. They proceed to act out their own history, including his adoration by priests, his resentment and murder by a "rival" chief, and the ensuing shift in Hawaiian mythical notions of kingship and sacrality. On the other, the British, led by their sacred hero Captain Cook, arrive and interact with the Hawaiians as "savages," who since they are not Christianized and are superstitious, are likely to make the mistake of treating white men like "gods" (note, of course, that the meaning of this term depends on who is using it and who it refers to: in this case it is the British misunderstanding the nature of Hawaiian religion, and attributing to savages a "nonsense" belief, whereas in fact, within the quite coherent and believable myth-system of Hawaiians, Cook-as-personification-of-Lono makes a good deal of sense). The British interact primarily with economic ends in mind, and thus are happy to be so treated.

The real shipwreck that is the object of understanding here, then, is not the springing of the *Resolution*'s mast or even the murder of Cook, but the cognitive unraveling of the working misunderstanding. The play's the thing, and in this case, one misused prop set the entire drama off course. This is evidenced by the manifest confusions that ensue: the British think the Hawaiians are really crazy when they ask when Cook will be coming back, the Hawaiians are miffed as to why on earth the British want Cook's bones. For "everyone knows" that, on the one hand, there is no reincarnation, and, on the other, that it's the conqueror who keeps the spoils of the slaughter – as well as the mana they represent. The sheer cognitive dissonance here reveals the absorbing power of drama, and proves Sahlins' structuralist point that *"plus c'est la même chose, plus ça change"* (Sahlins 1981: 7)

Importantly, though, it is the cognitive dissonance that really constitutes the shipwreck-as-encounter, that makes this a model of cultural change initiated from the outside. A quick counterfactual will reveal this. If Cook's ship had not sprung its mast, and he was not murdered, would we still have a "shipwreck"? The answer is clearly yes. For Cook's actions had already entered the mythological structure of Hawaiian history, such that Lono's priests had gained in power, and a certain "Britishness" had been lent to certain sacred Hawaiian symbols – the semiotic network had shifted slightly, and contained the seeds for further shifts. We also must imagine that the working misunderstanding still would have unraveled at some point, perhaps with a similar result. Thus the ideal type of the performance of an "encounter" would capture this episode, whether it resulted in this specific murder or not. The specific historical events to be explained could be different, the "structure of the conjuncture" that explains them would be the same.

As we start to relativize this thesis in a comparative way, we can point to three particular features of Sahlins' explanation. The first I alluded to above: the way in which this history is a history of action based on achieving understanding (on each side) and misunderstanding (between sides). The explanation of action in the case of a shipwreck is achieved mostly by understanding how actors *comprehended* the events that occurred, and comprehended their interactions with and reactions to those events.

Thus while in the case of the serious social drama the authenticity of the actions, and the actors, as they re-enact the mythological structure, is at issue, in a shipwreck the comprehensibility of action and actors is at issue. Thus if social dramatic action is primarily metonymical, then shipwreck action is primarily *categorical*, exemplifying the structuralist model of the cultural categories groping to encompass and define the world, even when it does not quite seem to "fit." If social dramatic actors act to *make real*, shipwreck actors act to *make sense*. Of course, this does not mean that shipwreck action is "cognitive" in some restricted sense of the word. As Garfinkel (1967) showed long ago, the actions of making sense can be quite morally and emotionally loaded.

Finally, in the case of a working misunderstanding, we have the opposite of the complicity that so exemplified the Becket–Henry case, and can be taken as a central feature of serious social dramas in general. In shipwrecks, there is *conflict without complicity*. And thus they are the ideal case of an *encounter*, wherein a set of social actors are confronted by a set of acts or events in which the intersubjectivity between them and the authors of the acts they confront is minimal. In this case we can speak coherently of the application of cultural categories to an obdurate and obstinate "reality," or rather, as good structuralists, show that there was never really an option, for if the world is infinite, it only comes to mind within a finite set of categories. The results can, of course, be disastrous.

Cockfighting in Bali: sports as metatheatre

Geertz's account of the Balinese Cockfight (Geertz 1973a) is not offered as an explanation but as a reading of a reading. He, the ethnographer, is reading the cockfight as a text, one produced by the Balinese as a comment upon themselves and their own existential dilemmas: "The culture of a people is an ensemble of texts, themselves ensembles, which the anthropologist strains to read over the shoulders of those to whom they properly belong" (Geertz 1973a: 452–3). Geertz marches his talent for interpretation of the specific content of other cultures – his ability for thick description – before the reader with such skill that we are inclined to believe him when he claims that "the essential vocation of interpretive anthropology is not to answer our deepest questions, but to make available to us answers that others, guarding other sheep in other valleys, have given, and thus to include them in the consultable record of what man has said" (Geertz 1973b: 30). The tension here between existential humanism and dialogic anthropology has rearticulated itself in the post-modern challenge to interpretive ethnography, whereby Geertz is taken to task for the false universalizations of Western philosophy that underlie his claims to really know the natives. But Geertz should be read as much more, and much less, than an existential interpreter; the existentialist reading represses the scientific moment in Geertz, where he uses theories to guide his interpretations, and develops models that are generalizable. In particular, in "Deep Play: Notes on the Balinese Cockfight," Geertz develops an explanation of the cockfight that can be taken as exemplifying liminoid social performance.

To develop this idea, we have to simultaneously relativize and generalize Geertz's account of the cockfight. It should be taken neither, as many of his critics have taken it, as a paradigm account of culture in action,[4] nor, as Geertz would sometimes have it, as a "message in a bottle," a small fragment of cultural content, from which one can only draw conclusions about the idiosyncratic ways different cultures solve the same existential quandaries. Rather, noticing the extensive reconstruction of Balinese culture, social structure, and personality structure that precede and accompany Geertz's description of the cockfight (not to mention his extensive work on Bali contained in other essays), the "Deep Play" essay should be seen as developing an interpretive explanation of why the Balinese hold cockfights. This explanation can be reconceived in terms of the theory of performance.

The social behavior of cockfighting in Bali might be briefly described as follows. Balinese men spend a great amount of time grooming, feeding, bathing, and otherwise caring for their cocks, which are the only animals that are treated so well in Balinese society. When the time and space can be arranged, they bring these cocks to cockfights, which take place in a ring approximately fifty feet square. Through a rather ad hoc process, matches are made between two cocks, by their two owners. The cocks have spurs attached to them, and, at the sound of a gong, released in the ring, at which point, they "fly almost immediately at each other in a wing-beating, head-thrusting, leg-kicking explosion of animal fury so pure, so absolute, and in its own way so beautiful, as to be almost abstract, a Platonic concept of hate" (Geertz 1973a: 422). When a wound is inflicted, the round ends, and further rounds continue in this manner until one cock is killed by the other.

Before the fight begins, however, betting within an elaborate and strictly defined system takes place. The center bet, settled quietly between the two parties represented by the two cocks, is usually for a large sum, and is always even money. Between any two men on the side of the ring, however, individual bets can take place, and these are usually for smaller sums, and always takes uneven odds: from 10–9 all the way down to 2–1. These are arrived at by frantic jostling, yelling, and negotiating, and depend very much on the perception of the evenness of the upcoming fight. The biggest fights are those that are evenly matched and have heavy center bets, and also then high side betting at the 10–9 end of the spectrum. Those considered "true cockfighters" are mainly interested in such "deep" fights, and, since the odds are relatively even, their fortunes do not change much in the long run. Those who are interested in making gain on smaller fights, in gambling for money, and who thus tend to risk losing money as a result, are disparaged as missing the point of cockfighting.

Men who lose deep cockfights become immediately depressed, while those who win become joyous. Furthermore, one is expected to support and bet along family or village lines when cockfights oppose cocks belonging to different groups. And generally, cockfighting serves as a reference point in conversation for the pronouncement of judgment and the production of understanding:

the word for cock . . . is used metaphorically to mean "hero," "warrior," "champion," "man of parts," "political cadidate," "bachelor," "dandy," "lady killer," or "tough guy." A pompous man whose behavior presumes above his station is compared to a tailless cock who struts about as if he had a large, spectacular one. A desperate man who makes a last, irrational effort to extricate himself from an impossible situation is likened to a dying cock who makes one final lunge at his tormentor to drag him along to a common destruction. (Geertz 1973a: 418)

Now, Geertz's explanation of cockfighting can be grasped by considering the cockfight as a social performance. First and foremost, it engages certain key background collective representations, which Geertz reconstructs prior to, and along with, his description of cockfighting. He identifies three central binaries that run through Balinese culture: human/animal, good/evil, and control/loss of control. In particular, notions of animality and uncontrolled behavior tend to line up with socially defined evil behavior:

The Balinese revulsion against any behavior regarded as animal-like can hardly be over-stressed. Babies are not allowed to crawl for that reason. Incest, though hardly approved, is a much less horrifying crime than bestiality . . . Most demons are represented – in sculpture, dance, ritual, myth – in some real or fantastic animal form. The main puberty right consists in filing the child's teeth so they will not look like animal fangs. Not only defecation but eating is regarded as a disgusting, almost obscene activity, to be conducted hurriedly and privately, because of its association with animality . . . In identifying with his cock, the Balinese man identifying not just with his ideal self, or even his penis, but also, and at the same time, with what he most fears, hates, and ambivalence being what it is, is fascinated by – "The Powers of Darkness". (Geertz 1973a: 419–20)

Next, the script that condenses some of these meanings is well-defined, it is an inversion inside the ring: "For it is only apparently cocks that are fighting there. Actually, it is men" (Geertz 1973a: 417). There are specific prescriptions (stage directions, scripts) to create a deep match, which are or are not met depending on the *mise-en-scène*. As Geertz writes:

THE MORE THE MATCH IS . . .

1. Between near status equals (and/or personal enemies)
2. Between high status individuals

THE DEEPER THE MATCH

THE DEEPER THE MATCH . . .

1. The closer the identification of cock and man (or, more properly, the deeper the match the more the man will advance his best, most closely identified cock).
2. The finer the cocks involved and the more exactly they will be matched.
3. The greater the emotion that will be involved and the more the general absorption in the match.
4. The higher the individual bets center and outside, the shorter the outside bet odds will tend to be, and the more betting there will be overall.
5. The less an "economic" and the more a "status" view of gambling will be involved, the "solider" the citizens who will be gaming. (Geertz 1973a: 441)

The social power involved is made clear by this script: high status men are the ones who control and lead this activity, and who bring weight and meaning to it. Furthermore, the status system, as known by everyone, is taken for granted as a condition of play, and to this degree sits as a collective representation also enacted by cockfighting.

When the fights take place, the *mise-en-scène* is a hectic combination of gestures and shouts for betting, careful caretaking and preparation of the cocks by the men they will represent, and rulings and time-keeping by the umpire. Thus the actors are the cocks, the men they represent, and the umpires, playing to an active, participatory audience that crowds around the stage. Geertz characterizes the cockfight as one of Goffman's "focused gatherings" which, "take their form from the situation that evokes them, the floor on which they are placed, as Goffman puts it; but it is a form, and an articulate one, nonetheless. For the situation, the floor is itself created . . . by the cultural presuppositions which not only specify the focus but, assembling actors and arranging scenery, bring it actually into being" (Geertz 1973a: 424).

Thus cockfighting can be analyzed in the terms of Alexander's performance theory. But our explanation as such is incomplete, for we need to account for the role of cockfighting in Balinese society, and specify what it is, in particular, that makes this type of performance different from serious social drama (remember, in a cockfight "no one's status really changes" (Geertz 1973a: 443)) and from encounters with other cultural formations. For the cockfight is full of complicity, but does not act out Balinese socio-historical reality in the same direct way as, say, the Council of Northampton redirected the course of the Church's role in England. Rather, the cockfight, as a liminoid activity,[5] relates *metaphorically* to Balinese society.

These performances in the liminoid sphere are *metatheatre*, by which I mean to indicate that while all action is citational in that it references scripts and background sets of collective representations, action in the liminoid sphere, which has its own set of signifier–signified relations, or semiotic practices (within the sphere of, say, cockfighting), also makes a second reference, more hidden but no less deep, to the general troubling questions and problems of action in real life. Metatheatre presents imaginary solutions to real problems.[6] When a "deep" fight is achieved, the flow that takes place as a result of a successful cockfight, while merging signified and signifier within the liminoid sphere, continues to have a separate referent outside of the fight itself – certain themes and tensions in Balinese culture. This is the key insight of Geertz about cockfighting: that it is "a story they tell themselves about themselves" (1973a: 448). But this needs to be taken as a meditation on the role of popular culture in differentiated societies, not an analytic definition of all cultural action.

The cockfight achieves this by a resignification process, whereby a system of economic rationality (the betting) becomes the means to a different, meaningful end, the acting out of a story about the Balinese social order:

What sets the cockfight apart from the ordinary course of life, lifts it from the realm of everyday practical affairs, and surrounds it with an aura of enlarged importance is not, as functionalist sociology would have it, that it reinforces status distinctions (such reinforcement is hardly necessary in a society where every act proclaims them), but that it provides a metasocial commentary upon the whole matter of assorting human beings into fixed hierarchical ranks and then organizing the major part of collective existence around that assortment. Its function, if you want to call it that, is interpretive: it is a Balinese reading of Balinese experience, a story they tell themselves about themselves. (Geertz 1973a: 448)

I think this understanding of the cockfight as social performance can give us a more cultural, meaning-centered, vision of the "relatively autonomous fields" that Bourdieu is so concerned with. Indeed art – and for that matter, football – has its own set of rules. But performing within these constraints, fleshing out these scripts (defensive strategy to contain an "explosive" football offense, how to dunk a basketball) simultaneously refer to other spheres of meaning that sit at the center of *la vie sérieuse* (war and victory culture, codes of honor and cool in the ghetto). In essence, the work of sublimation is a complex cultural and social interaction that is not so much a rechanneling of drives as a repetitive, active, working out of meaning structures in a realm protected from the exigencies of politics and economics, so that the very culture structures upon which those activities depend in part for their constitution can be realized as pure aesthetic form.

Now, of course, theatre, sports, and all the rest of our liminoid activities are of course also social practices in their own right, and as such also respond to the exigencies of power and money, but I insist that there is something to the common reference to these things as "culture" in everyday parlance. This obviously is an enormous issue for social science, one which I cannot hope to adequately address here. But I think that understanding the cockfight as a certain type of social performance – as liminoid metatheatre – can help us begin to specify the indirect, metaphorical, and incredibly powerful role of popular culture in constituting the collective representations in a given society.

The fundamental aspects of this type of performance have been laid out in the course of my discussion of Geertz's essay, but it will be useful to summarize them here. Liminoid metatheatre is, first of all, *play*; it is separated from *la vie sérieuse*, and therefore its influence on the social system and the culture that frames it is indirect. Secondly, liminoid action is fundamentally metaphorical in relation to the larger society. The cockfight is *like* status competition, football is *like* war and combat. Thus if metonymical action *makes real*, categorical action *makes sense*, metaphorical action *rereads* and *re-presents*.

In this light, we can see why the standard sociological critiques of Geertz's essay miss the point. Instead of arguing over whether Geertz excludes the exigencies of real life, real power, and real actors' solutions to real problems, we should insist that life is not only a football game, and, if we want to critique Geertz's essay for missing some aspect of Balinese society, we can only ask Geertz to explain why it was not thematized *in this instance of metatheatre*, and in what instance of popular culture it *is* thematized.

Conclusion: notes for further research

Having specified, and summarized, the essential features of these types of social performance, I would like to offer here some brief reflections on their significance for the research paradigm of cultural sociology which is advancing through the construction of a "cultural pragmatics."

First, as I adumbrated earlier, the focus on social drama within cultural sociology, and the corresponding move away from ritual, has significance along many dimensions of social theory, including the normative. While sociological engagement with and critique of democratic theory, and in particular the theories of Jürgen Habermas, has taken many turns and directions, the cultural-sociological line has most often been to emphasize the content-specific nature of democratic culture. Formal mechanisms of publicness, cultural sociologists argue, are not enough, one needs the "discourse of civil society," understood in terms of binary codes of rational/irrational, and romantic and ironic narratives, to enable the thematization of lifeworld issues in the public sphere in a democratic way. In this context, the move from ritual to social drama is important because it places positive value on conflict and contention in interpretation. Against earlier Durkheimians, cultural sociologists minimize the normative importance of ritual in constituting a democratic society; in fact, we have become increasingly suspicious of the way in which ritual, by assuming understanding *and* agreement, can risk the exclusion of alternative voices and ethical concerns (Mouffe 2000).

Second, as debates about culture and politics heat up the public sphere, the issue of cultural "shipwrecks," which have long been a key subject for post-colonial studies, communitarian political theory, and postmodern anthropology, becomes increasingly urgent. Jeffrey Alexander's chapter on the different interpretations given to the events of September 11, 2001 attempts to gain sociological traction without enacting the reification that is characteristic of Huntington-inspired accounts of "civilizations" and is so normatively problematic. The model offered here of shipwrecks is specifically intended to be generalizable beyond clashes between the "West" and its others. Though it is *not* an analytic theory, the ideal type of "shipwreck" reoccurs, I suspect, across the board and from macro to micro (think again of Garfinkel's breaching experiments).

Finally, much needs to be done, empirico-analytically and normatively, to account for the metaphorical and indirect role of popular culture, and in particular, in the contemporary West, of those quasi-religious experiences of collective effervescence: watching sports live, and going to the movies. If the late Durkheim lives, it is on the silver screen, and in college basketball arenas. I am unconvinced that such social texts, or their collective experiencing, can be reduced to either "hegemony" or "resistance." Rather, their extensive spirals of signification constitute a performative field whose empirical effects have yet to be specified.

Notes

1. See Alexander's analysis of the Watergate crisis, which, while still operating within the ritual framework, articulates well the meaning of Turner's apt phrase (Alexander 1988).
2. Turner is referencing T. S. Eliot's *Murder in the Cathedral* (New York: Harcourt Brace, 1935).
3. Here it becomes especially clear how even the most bare narratives are "interpretations" and thus raise theoretical and epistemological issues, not to mention political hackles. For the purposes of the ideal types to be constructed here, however, I am

taking this "fact" as part of a first-order interpretation, to be accounted for by the second-order interpretation of Hawaiian mythology.

4. Cf. Ann Swidler (2001), *Talk of Love: How Culture Matters* (Chicago: University of Chicago Press), and Michael Burawoy (1991), "Reconstructing Social Theories," pp. 8–28 in Michael Burawoy et al., *Ethnography Unbound: Power and Resistance in the Modern Metropolis* (Berkeley: University of California Press).

5. Cf. Victor Turner (1982) *From Ritual to Theater: The Human Seriousness of Play* (Performing Arts Journal Publications). Turner adopts the term "liminoid" to describe the leisure activities that, in "industrial societies," have, from his perspective, similarities to the "liminal" qualities of the ritual process as he observed it in small-scale African societies. I use the term loosely the same way here, though I do not accept the sharp distinction between industrial and pre-industrial societies. Rather, any society with a sufficient amount of differentiation such that it can self-define some of its activities as "play" or "theatre" or "sport," can have "liminoid metatheatre."

6. Though the phrase comes from George Lipsitz, the reference is to Lévi-Strauss' account of the Oedipus story in "The Structural Study of Myth": "The myth has to do with the inability, for a culture which holds the belief that mankind is autochthonous . . . to find a satisfactory transition between this theory and the knowledge that human beings are actually born from the union of man and woman . . . Although experience contradicts theory, social life validates cosmology by its similarity in structure. Hence cosmology is true" (Lévi-Strauss 2002: 216).

References

Alexander, Jeffrey C. 1988. "Culture and Political Crisis: Watergate and Durkheimian Sociology," pp. 187–224 in Jeffrey C. Alexander, ed. *Durkheimian Sociology: Cultural Studies*. New York: Cambridge University Press.

Garfinkel, Harold. 1967. *Studies in Ethnomethodology*. Englewood Cliffs, NJ: Prentice-Hall.

Geertz, Clifford. 1973a. "Deep Play: Notes on the Balinese Cockfight," pp. 412–53 in Clifford Geertz, *The Interpretation of Cultures*. New York: Basic Books.

1973b. "Thick Description: Toward an Interpretive Theory of Culture," pp. 3–30 in Clifford Geertz, *The Interpretation of Cultures*. New York: Basic Books.

Jakobson, Roman and Morris Halle. 1956. *Fundamentals of Language*. The Hague: Mouton.

Lévi-Strauss, Claude. 2002. "The Structural Study of Myth," pp. 206–31 in Claude Lévi-Strauss, *Structural Anthropology*. New York: Basic Books.

Mouffe, Chantal. 2000. *The Democratic Paradox*. New York: Verso.

Obeyesekere, Ganath. 1992. *The Apotheosis of Captain Cook: European Mythmaking in the Pacific*. Princeton, NJ: Princeton University Press.

Sahlins, Marshall. 1981. *Historical Metaphors and Mythical Realities: Structure in the Early History of the Sandwich Islands Kingdom*. Ann Arbor: University of Michigan Press.

1982. "The Apotheosis of Captain Cook," pp. 73–103 in Michael Izard and Pierre Smith, eds. *Between Belief and Transgression*. Chicago: University of Chicago Press.

1985. *Islands of History*. Chicago: University of Chicago Press.

1989. "Captain Cook at Hawaii," *Journal of the Polynesian Society* 98: 371–425.

1995. *How "Natives" Think: About Captain Cook, For Example*. Chicago: University of Chicago Press.

Shils, Edward and Michael Young. 1953. "The Meaning of the Coronation," *Sociological Review* 1: 68–81.

Turner, Victor. 1974. "Religious Paradigms and Political Action," pp. 60–97 in Victor Turner, *Dramas, Fields and Metaphors: Symbolic Action in Human Society*. Ithaca: Cornell University Press.

5

Performing a "new" nation: the role of the TRC in South Africa

Tanya Goodman

Introduction

This chapter examines the case of the South African Truth and Reconciliation Commission (TRC) as an example of a modern ritual of performance that has played a critical role in the transition from Apartheid to democracy. While many observers have characterized the TRC as a legal tool to facilitate political transformation and some have criticized it for failing to provide adequate forms of justice, such approaches miss a significant aspect of the TRC and its impact on South African society. Rather, if we apply a model of social drama, this theoretical perspective allows us to focus on how the TRC testimonies helped to frame Apartheid as a "cultural trauma" (Alexander 2002, 2004; Eyerman 2001, 2004; Giesen 2004) that required acknowledgment and demanded repair. Moreover, the social drama model reveals the way in which the TRC opened a space for the creation of a new national identity, one which rested on a recognition of bonds of solidarity. In this chapter, I will show that the TRC is an unusual case of cultural performance because it is one that referred to and inspired universal rather than exclusive group affirming principles. And, I will argue that it was a successful performance in that it offered not only a catharsis, but also a pathway to new definitions of belonging and was therefore transformative.

In contrast to earlier theories of ritual and social drama (Durkheim 1912; Turner 1977), recent work has shown that cultural performances take place not only to remind us of what we already agree on, but also as a way of dealing with disaster, both natural and human, and during major social transitions. During such times of upheaval, cultural performances can either serve to rekindle and affirm, or to create and generate, fundamental values and beliefs. And they do so via the simplifying and sacralizing mechanism of ritual. Democratic founding moments are particularly open to such processes, in part because it is in these moments that a sense of integration and shared identity can be produced and people can see themselves as connected, in some situations for the very first time. While some sociological work has focused on the symbolic processes that mark the commemorative moments of democracies (Spillman 1997; Cerulo 1995), these cases are most often situated in a celebratory perspective. The South African case is an interesting departure because it did not hearken back to a golden age nor rely on symbols of pre-existing social cohesion; rather, the performance sparked by the TRC referred to a supra notion of solidarity and a universal moral community in order to forge a foundational myth for the new nation.

I begin this chapter with a brief outline of the role and structure of the TRC. I follow with an explanation for why the TRC should be considered as a modern form of ritual. Next, I take seriously the suggestion that the TRC be characterized as a social drama and highlight elements of the TRC which fit the model of cultural performance. In so doing, I show how particular aspects of the TRC contributed to its universalizing and transformative outcome. Here, I pay particular attention to the TRC's emphasis on testimony and the ways in which these stories, through various cycles of performance, were woven into a national narrative by third parties such as TRC Commissioners and the public media. I will argue that the TRC performance successfully engaged a somewhat initially disinterested (mainly white) audience and managed to persuade, at least some of them, that the Apartheid past was evil and that repair of the social fabric was required. In general, this chapter will show that even in a modern secular state where people have been divided and suffered enormously, it is possible for an institution like the TRC to evoke sacred qualities that engender identification, empathy, and shifts in meaning and action.

Background to role and structure of the TRC

On December 16, 1995, a newly renamed South African public holiday called the "Day of Reconciliation,"[1] Archbishop Desmond Tutu, Chairperson of the TRC, addressed the first meeting of the panel of TRC Commissioners:

We have seen a miracle unfold before our very eyes and the world has marvelled as South Africans, all South Africans, have won this spectacular victory over injustice, oppression and evil. The miracle must endure. Freedom and justice must become realities for all our people and we [the TRC] have the privilege of helping to heal the hurts of the past to transcend the alienations and the hostilities of that past so that we can close the door on that past and concentrate in the present and our glorious future. (TRC Press Release 1995)

Although many had feared that the end of Apartheid would come only as the product of a bloody revolution, the "miracle" of the relatively peaceful South African political transition rested on a negotiated compromise between the old National Party (NP) and representatives of the newly unbanned political parties such as the African National Congress (ANC). Part of the political compromise resulted in the formation of the TRC and it was positioned as the primary institutional solution for dealing with the challenge of what to do with a violent and racist history and how to structure a transition from a past of conflict to a future of peace. The metaphors of "bridge building" – as a way to move out of the past – and the "rainbow nation" – as a vision of harmony for the future – were used frequently by public intellectuals and politicians. And these images were also literally embedded into the founding documents which established the TRC – the 1993 Interim Constitution and Parliament's Act 34: Promotion of National Unity and Reconciliation 1995 (hereafter Act 34) – which set the stage for the "new" South Africa.

The TRC was composed of seventeen Commissioners and three Committees: a Committee on Amnesty, a Committee on Human Rights Violations (HRV), and a Committee on Reparations & Rehabilitation. The Amnesty Committee heard testimony from those who had committed gross violations of human rights under Apartheid. Such violations were defined narrowly in Act 34 as killing, torture, abduction, and grievous bodily harm. If amnesty applicants met certain criteria – providing full disclosure, demonstrating that their acts were committed with a political motive, and showing a measure of proportionality – then these individuals were granted amnesty from prosecution. The HRV Committee took statements and heard testimony from victims and survivors of such acts. And the Reparations & Rehabilitation Committee was responsible for crafting policies and payments for those who were named as victims.

In the end, the TRC took over 20,000 statements from victims, and received more than 7,000 amnesty applications from people who participated in Apartheid-era crimes (TRC Final Report 1998). The TRC started hearings in April 1996 and delivered a preliminary five-volume 2,500-page report and recommendations to then-President Mandela in October 1998.[2] In March 2003, the remaining two volumes of the report were delivered to Parliament and included the findings from the Amnesty Committee and a chapter devoted to victims' stories.

The TRC hearings as a ritual space

My explanation of the TRC as a cultural performance and its possibility for generating new definitions in social relations relies on a neo-Durkheimian framework that appreciates the form that rituals take in the modern world and the relationship between ritual, social drama, and solidarity. In this section, I will show how the hearings of the TRC were located in a liminal space and generated a sense of "collective effervescence" (Durkheim 1912) and "communitas" (Turner 1977). Focusing on these properties will highlight the tangible universalizing power that was produced through the hearings, and their telling.

Durkheim's study of ritual in *The Elementary Forms of Religious Life* (1912) alerted us to the dynamic that unfolds when people come together in groups and perform ceremonies that reinvigorate the sacred and remind the group of their social connectivity. One of Durkheim's great contributions therefore was to show how a study of ritual can help us understand solidarity in society. Although Durkheim's emphasis was on *pre-existing* bonds of solidarity, we can use his recognition of the significance of ritual to expose the ways in which such processes may create new social connections. Applying Victor Turner's (1977) work helps to expand this insight by identifying what he calls "communitas" – the spontaneous, immediate, yet fleeting recognition of a sense of universal human connection as either existing or possible – that is produced through ritual. For Turner, it is during the liminal phase of ritual processes where such a sense of communitas may be perceived among participants, and the effects can be transformative as they are then carried away by members of the group or society. As Alexander (this volume: p. 41) suggests, "rites not only mark transitions but also create them, such that participants become something or somebody else as a result. Ritual performance not only symbolizes a social relationship or change; it also actualizes it."

For a number of reasons, the TRC can be shown to have occurred in a liminal space; a space that was, as Turner describes, "betwixt and between" (1977: 95); something that occurred both in and out of normal trajectories of cultural space and time. The founding legislation for the TRC was itself part of a document that occupied a liminal space – a postscript to the Interim Constitution (1993) which was drafted during an explicitly transitional political period. The TRC was also mandated to complete its operations within two years, thereby setting its work apart in time. And metaphorically, it was set up to straddle the past and future, as an "historic" and "tender bridge" to facilitate a transition, as Archbishop Tutu (2000) would later claim, "from repression, from evil, from ghastliness to democracy and freedom."

The TRC was perched in a unique position since it not only operated in a liminal space but was also set against the backdrop of great effervescence that characterized the largely peaceful political transition. Nelson Mandela's early speeches (1990 in Deegan 2001) after his release from prison gave hints that notions of forgiveness and provisions of a "home for all" might prevail

And South Africans of all races had a sense that the "world was watching." For whites, this was a time to finally throw off the mantle of pariah and be included in the global community. For blacks, this was a chance to prove their capability in power. Mandela's personal charisma and expressed lack of bitterness combined with Tutu's vision of the "rainbow nation" contributed to the general optimism and a willingness to engage in a particular kind of nation-building exercise. The notion of a "rainbow nation" became part of popular political discourse, and although it may have glossed over the serious economic disparities that were (and still are) a legacy of Apartheid, it was a "necessary myth" that held the country together during the period of transition (Jacobs 2001). Economic claims and hardships were temporarily put on hold while the business of building a new nation, socially and culturally, was put into play.[3] What later emerged in this space was the compelling power of the TRC testimonies and an emotional energy that surprised almost everyone.

Setting the stage for the TRC

Public hearings for the TRC were held across the country in small towns and large cities between 1996 and 1998. It was a tremendously, and deliberately, public process with an immediate audience present in the hearing room and a recognition by all those who participated in the hearings that an audience in the rest of the community, the country, and the world stood the chance of being confronted by the testimonies. Those who testified were able to speak in their home language with simultaneous direct translation, and every person in the room was provided with access to a headset. The TRC received considerable local, national and international media coverage. Newspapers carried front-page stories, radio stations reported live, and television news often opened with a headline from the TRC. The South African national television broadcasting company (SABC) commissioned a weekly summary report, the "TRC Special Report," that played during prime-time, and replayed during the week.

The setting for the TRC was also rich in ceremony and symbolism. As the TRC traveled to different areas in the country, it chose different venues in which to stage the hearings, ranging from old Apartheid civic halls to anti-Apartheid sites of resistance in churches and schools. The forum for hearings consisted of a blend of religious and secular practices. Often directed by Archbishop Tutu dressed in flowing red religious robes, many sessions began with a prayer and ended with a press conference. A solitary "peace" candle would be lit and a banner reading "May the Truth Reconcile Our Nation" or "Truth: The Road to Reconciliation" hung behind the chairs of the Commissioners who sat at white linen-draped tables. When witnesses were sworn in, they were offered the choice of a religious or secular oath as they promised to tell the truth. In many settings, songs became a part of the process. Depending on the location of the hearings, the nature of the abuse being discussed, and sometimes to help quell tensions, Commissioners invited those present at the hearing to sing a religious hymn, the new national anthem,[4] or traditional lullabies.

The proceedings were open to all – a factor in itself which reversed many of the old Apartheid laws that had instituted spatial racial segregation. Many of the survivors who came to testify bore visible scars of the Apartheid regime and were physically crippled, tortured, and disabled. Many others recalled the ways in which they or their loved ones had suffered, and frequently broke down in tears as the memory was spoken out loud. One of the earliest sessions in the hearings of the HRV Committee that received major media coverage involved highly charged testimony by victims and family members of those who had disappeared, been tortured, or brutally killed. Late in the day after the testimony of Mr. Malgas, a quiet and dignified old man sitting in his wheelchair who described the torture he suffered at the hands of the security police, Archbishop Tutu, apparently overwhelmed by emotion, broke down in tears and laid his head on the table. This scene was captured and replayed by local and international media. As an example, Robert Block, a reporter for *The Independent* recounted the atmosphere:

[Tutu] was not the only one to cry. Witnesses, onlookers, commission gophers, journalists all broke down at one time or another as the widows and mothers of apartheid activists laid bare their personal pain and loss to the world . . . Sometimes the tears seemed to be contagious. A witness would sob and then a member of the audience would begin to cry. Soon the tears would spread like a bush fire . . . One foreign observer was overheard to remark: "This country is so traumatized. If one person is hurt then so is everybody." (Block 1996)

Block's account is indicative of the kind of emotion – and the interpretation thereof – that much of the testimony at the TRC provoked. His account also shows the degree to which multiple participants – individuals, immediate audience, reporters, observers, Commissioners – were involved in and affected by these hearings. Moreover, Block's description hints at a sense of the universalizing power evoked through such testimonies as people engaged in listening to and accepting such narratives. This type of observation was repeated by many other journalists reporting on the TRC.

Besides the religious and secular symbols that served as a legitimizing frame certain ways in which the TRC operated endowed its proceedings with a sacred and liminal character. As the TRC process unfolded, the structure of the hearings often transgressed the old hierarchical relations of dominance and oppression replacing traditional forms of exclusion with acts of inclusion. It was here that many victims, for the first time, received official recognition and acknowledgment. In the eyes of the previous Apartheid regime, these people would have been considered as less than human, their suffering made silent, and the violations to which they had been subjected kept secret. At the HRV hearings, however, the audience was always asked to rise out of respect for the victims as they entered the hall, and rise again once the person completed their testimony. On those occasions when victims were allowed to confront their perpetrators in amnesty hearings, the power dynamic also shifted for the first time and an upside-down quality pervaded the space as victims (or their lawyers) interrogated those who had tortured or murdered their loved ones.

Such shifts occurred not only in the dramatic repositioning of participants, but also in the vocabulary used in the narratives and the definitions attributed to the characters they described. Those who had been called "terrorists" in the past by the Apartheid state security forces, now became "freedom fighters," and victims were renamed as heroes. Those who had been on different sides of the political spectrum now shared the same place inside the TRC as well as the same page of the newspapers being read across the country or the same space on radio or television broadcasts. And they shared the same moral space of judgment and evaluation. In this reversal of positions of villains and victims, evil and good, a blurry space emerged into which the TRC process injected a notion that "all had suffered."[5]

As Turner suggests, in these moments of liminality which transgress everyday structures and relationships "it is as though [the participants] are being reduced or ground down to a uniform condition to be fashioned anew and endowed with additional powers to enable them to cope with their new station in life" (1977: 95). The degree to which the TRC instigated a sense of leveling and how this space provoked an awakening to a shared bond was often highlighted in the media. For Antjie Krog, a white Afrikaans poet and journalist who reported weekly on the proceedings of the TRC, the intensity of the hearings clearly generated a new sense of human connection:

It's not about skin color, culture, language, but about people. The personal pain puts an end to all stereotypes. Where we connect now has nothing to do with group or color, we connect with our humanity. (Krog 1998: 45)

Krog's comment suggests that for a ritual like the TRC to be successful in producing a sense of "communitas," it is not necessary to have pre-existing agreement (Alexander, this volume; see also Lukes 1977). In fact, engaging in such a process can break down prior categories of exclusion. In the case of South Africa, before the TRC process took place there was no collective understanding of Apartheid that was common across the categories of those who suffered, those who perpetrated, and those who stood by acts of violence. The cultural performance of the TRC was significant because it expanded beyond group boundaries to an even more generalized background culture – that of social solidarity and an imagined moral community. Rather than reinforcing or privileging particular racial groups' view of the past, the TRC process sought to create a shared understanding of history, as well as a shared vision of the future.

By providing a space in which individual testimonies about the trauma of Apartheid could be heard, the TRC facilitated the recognition of particular individuals' suffering. At the same time, the way in which people responded to and reported on this suffering – by placing it within a broader narrative framework – effectively universalized the trauma and began to redefine the boundaries of inclusion and exclusion. To understand what I mean by this dynamic, we must next explore the performance of testimony.

Foundations of the TRC

While the TRC may seem like a novel device for reckoning with the past (in part because of the enormous international attention devoted by institutions and the media), its form and function rested on a number of global and local precedents. In terms of commissions, the TRC followed in the wake of at least fourteen similar commissions which took place between 1974 and 1995 in a variety of locations across the world, including war crimes tribunals and truth commissions most notably in Chile, Guatemala, Argentina, and East Germany (Hayner 1994). In the rest of Africa, commissions of inquiry into human rights violations had already been held in Uganda, Ghana, Zimbabwe, Niger, and Togo, with varying degrees of success and failure. South Africans themselves had witnessed a set of investigative commissions leading up to the dismantling of Apartheid in the late 1980s and early 1990s – the remarkable 1992 and 1993 ANC Commissions of Inquiry examined complaints about human rights violations by prisoners and detainees in their training camps; the somewhat ineffectual and oft-derided 1989–90 Harms Commission investigated the existence of government-sponsored assassination squads; and the well-respected 1991 Goldstone Commission examined political violence and intimidation issuing reports in 1992, 1993, and 1994. The TRC, however, was unique because it privileged the testimony of victims and survivors through its HRV hearings; a choice which decisively shaped its performance, interpretation, and impact.

In South Africa, there is also a strong tradition of using theatre for consciousness-raising and to solve social problems. During the most restrictive

periods of Apartheid censorship, community theatre was often used by political activists to communicate and mobilize around specific issues. Much of
this theatre was participatory in that the play was workshopped so that actors'
own experiences were integrated into the text (see, for example, Athol Fugard's
plays, the history of the Market Theatre, and the tradition of workshop theatre in
the labor movement). The anti-Apartheid movement was also well aware of the
compelling spectacle that could be produced at the funerals of political activists.
Steve Biko's lover at the time of his murder, Mamphela Ramphele (1997), for
example, describes mass funerals during the struggle years where the wishes of
widows and family members were often subjugated and molded according to
the movement's needs. Speaking of a service conducted in English where it was
unlikely that the family or community understood what was being said, Ramphele suggests "the political theater of mass funerals was not primarily intended
for the audience in physical attendance, but for national and international audiences. The latter audience assumed greater importance in the message being
communicated because of the potential action that could mobilize in support of
the cause" (1997: 107).

Once South Africa entered its post-Apartheid phase, the conditions underpin-
ning the establishment of a new democracy no longer generated an appropriate
space for the protest theatre of the old days; yet the TRC arguably played a role
of problem-solving and civic education that resonated with this older cultural
form. Similarly, like the social movement actors of the anti-Apartheid struggle,
the TRC kept its multiple audiences in mind. While the TRC's work was mainly
targeted at a South African audience and its primary goals were to help "heal
the nation," it too was conscious of its global audience. Frequent references to a
recognition that "the world is watching" were made not only by the organizers
of the TRC, but also by ordinary people who gave testimony or reflected on the
hearings.

Finally, while the notions of talk therapy and catharsis have a long Western legacy in the work of Freud and other psychoanalysts (and can certainly
be found in South African Western systems of thought), the legitimacy of a
forum such as the TRC which privileges the power of public testimony and
the promise of healing through talk can also be traced to indigenous cultural
forms. Of course, ritual and an oral tradition are strongly associated with certain African cultures. Looking specifically at South Africa, Nancy Scheper-
Hughes (1998) draws parallels between the dynamic of the TRC and not only
the notion of healing through confession and purging found in the interaction
between sangomas[6] and witches, but also the significance of public shaming
found in the popular courts[7] of justice. In the case of sangomas, Scheper-
Hughes cites the work of Berglund (1989) and Ngubane (1977) to describe
how sangomas encourage "witches" to confess and purge themselves of harmful

feelings which are seen as potentially "congeal[ing] into sickness, misfortune, and death in the community." From their side, "witches" claim that "speaking out" offers them "a means of 'emptying themselves' of the burden of evil and restoring feelings of lightness and emptiness that signify balance, health, and good relations." (Scheper-Hughes 1998). Such notions are similar to the claims made by the TRC about the power of giving testimony and its therapeutic effects.

But my analysis rests not on the lay interpretation of talk as therapy but rather on telling (and hearing) as a performance where an audience is persuaded that a particular representation of the past is authentic and where this audience is convinced of the concomitant necessity for remedy. However, before delving into the front stage of TRC testimony and their translations and interpretations via various cycles of performance, we need to consider the back stage of the TRC to understand what the conditions of possibility for such testimony were.

Behind the scenes

Launching the TRC took great organization and resources and it is important to note the ways in which different decisions both informed and shaped the work of the TRC. While I have already considered aspects of the *mise-en-scène* and choreography of the hearings in the section above describing the ritual space of the TRC, this section further outlines the ways in which the structure and function of the TRC were invested with different power dynamics.

Here again, appreciating the TRC as the product of a political compromise is important. As part of the amnesty deal offered to the exiting National Party, the definition of "gross human rights violations" was narrow and limited, effectively excluding the more "mundane" aspects of Apartheid brutality such as forced removals from land, the humiliation of pass laws, and the effect of unequal education. As a consequence, this limitation restricted not only who could apply to the TRC but also what kind of story they could tell or the degree to which their story would be "made to fit" (see, for example, Grunebaum-Ralph 2001: 201; Wilson 1999). Moreover, as some have argued, this narrow definition permitted those who had been beneficiaries of Apartheid to avoid taking responsibility for their complicity (Mamdani 1997; Statman 2000).

To ensure that those who wanted to submit testimony to the TRC qualified according to Act 34, a statement-taking process was put in play which resulted in a peculiar form of rehearsal as witnesses were prepared during the first round of telling their story. Although victims were provided the space to offer a personal narrative, the standard statement form also contained boxes to check off and conditions to match in order to qualify. Buur (2001) describes how "stories about violations became coded right from the outset and underwent changes so that they fitted the vocabulary" of the Information Management System database – a system into which all violations had to be entered. Because there were only a delimited set of categories, the IMS vocabulary "retrospectively re-framed and re-ordered past experiences."[8]

The public hearings of the HRV were also stage-managed to some degree because of the sheer number of cases (approximately 20,000 statements were received) and the exigencies of time and space. As a consequence, not all those who made statements could appear before the TRC (approximately 2,000 public testimonies were heard). To decide which cases would be heard in public, the TRC claims to have used criteria of representativeness and breadth so that victims testifying reflected not only the spectrum of types of abuses suffered in the area but also the different groups who had been targeted. Within these categories, victims were also chosen to reflect different gender, race, age, and geographical demographics in the region (TRC Final Report, Vol. 1, ch. 6). When it came to perpetrators of violence, the TRC adopted what they called an "even-handed" approach as they sought to treat everyone fairly while, at the same time, striving not to morally equate the actions of different parties. Although they were still criticized by some politicians for failing to draw distinctions in terms of a "just war" philosophy (see Asmal et al. 1997; ANC Statement 1996; ANC Further Submissions 1997; Buur 2001), the TRC counted as one of its positive outcomes, and proof of their commitment to fairness, the fact that both the ANC and the former leader of the NP, F. W. de Klerk, criticized the Final Report in the days leading up to its release. The stand taken by the TRC Commissioners, many of whom had fought alongside the ANC representatives who took them to court, was covered avidly by the national and international media. Reports on the Final Report's official release carried such headlines as "None Escape TRC Wrath" (Cohen 1998) and "Apartheid Indictment Finds Fault on all Sides" (CNN World 1998).

While some observers have criticized the selection of cases made by the TRC (see, for example, Chapman 1999; Wilson 1999; Motsemme and Ratele 2000; Bozzoli 1998; Ross 1997), I believe these choices based on principles of representivity, inclusion, and fairness are significant not only because they mimic the democratic legal principles expressed in the new South African Constitution and Bill of Rights, but also because on a more symbolic level they can be seen as techniques of drawing expansive boundaries around notions of who might qualify as being worthy of belonging to the national community. By making space for a vast range of victims, including those who were subjected to abuse by the South African security forces *and* those who were victims of actions by liberation movements, the TRC essentially cast as wide a net as possible of (potential) inclusion around all those who had been subject to the violence engendered by the Apartheid regime. In hearings as well as in the Final Report, the TRC effectively went so far as to include those who had been bystanders, and even many perpetrators, into this universal embrace.

To understand how the testimonies given to the TRC were deployed and inserted into a narrative for the new nation, we have to look not only at the stories that were told inside the TRC but also at how these stories were interpreted through various cycles of performance. To do this, we need to capture how these stories moved through space and time.

The TRC cycles of performance

The hearings were the public face of the TRC and provided the stage for the first cycle in the performance of coding Apartheid as evil and constructing new notions of who belongs and what such a community should look like. Despite the organized criteria for kinds of testimony and frames within which claims could be made, the TRC hearing space also enabled a degree of freedom for unexpected and transformative moments. Although statements had been taken and prepared in advance, once the opportunity was opened for victims and perpetrators to offer their testimonies in the form of a public narrative, the significance of performing for an audience came to the fore.

The TRC process involved multiple audiences: the immediate audience of victims, perpetrators, and observers who were in attendance at the hearings; the Commissioners who represented the state; the intermediate audience of the media who reported the hearings; the broader audience of the South African nation; and the global audience of the world at large. The testimonies that were given inside the TRC by victims and survivors of human rights violations were first told by these witnesses, then recounted by the Commissioners, and then further articulated by journalists as each story was placed within a larger narrative frame and performed for an expanding audience. Once the testimonies moved outside the walls of the TRC, they reverberated through public space in news stories, televised reports, radio broadcasts, art, and academia. But this is only one part of how the stories moved through space – in the *telling*. A second significant aspect of performance rests in the *hearing* – or how such stories and the grander narrative were heard by a broader audience. And what navigates between these two parts of the performance of the TRC is the role played by third parties – the TRC Commissioners and the media.

Commissioners as empathic interlocutors

The Commissioners took seriously what they saw as their job of listening to testimony. In the Final Report, they write:

> The Commission tried to listen, really to listen – not passively but actively – to the voices that for so long had been stilled. And as it listened to stories of horror, of pathos and of tragic proportion, it became aware of the high cost that has been paid by so many for freedom. (TRC Final Report, Vol. 5, ch. 8: 2)

Even before we consider the flow of the narrative between witnesses, Commissioners, the media, and the audience, one can already see from this short excerpt how the trauma of Apartheid was framed by the TRC. In brief, the story of the "new" South Africa was painted as a terrible yet triumphant tragedy. Stories of suffering were coded as sacrifice and brave heroes were constructed as emerging from the horror. Because they defined their listening role as an active one, Commissioners often took the liberty of inserting themselves into the proceedings and became facilitators in the telling of the tale. In many cases, Commissioners seized these moments to bring together disparate threads in the story and to place a broader frame over the events. In fact, those witnesses who told stories which did not "fit" this overarching pattern were often cut short or persuaded to rephrase their testimony so that it made sense in the larger narrative (see, for example, Motsemme and Ratele 2000; Grunebaum-Ralph 2001).

Throughout much of the HRV testimony at the TRC, the Commissioners served as an interlocutor between the witness and the idealized new state. In such a position, they acted as both an impartial judge and as an empathic listener with the capacity to offer apology and acknowledgment – a role I call "empathic interlocutor." Part of the almost formulaic rhythm of the HRV hearings involved some type of official recognition by the Commissioners of the pain suffered by those testifying. But this recognition was not merely directed to the individual; rather, it involved a simultaneous designation of such suffering as a sacrifice on both an individual and a collective level and, once coded as a sacrifice, Commissioners framed such suffering as a step on the path towards the creation of a democratic society.

Thus, whether witnesses were white or black, activist or bystander, their individual experiences of trauma were woven into the overall drama of the nation as moving from oppression to freedom. And the new nation was now seen not only as the result of great pain but also as a new vantage point from which this pain could be explained and justified. Moreover, the experience of pain was now deployed as a binding mechanism across divisions of race and ideology so that whereas people may have suffered differently, the trauma itself was recast as both a leveling and transcendent experience across such differences. At the end of one full day of testimony from a vast spectrum of people at the HRV hearings, for example, the Chairman wrapped up the proceedings by codifying the lessons learned and wrapping a disparate number of witnesses into a universal embrace by claiming:

The overwhelming majority of people who have suffered in this country and who have borne the brunt of the resistance are black South Africans. Some times it is not a bad thing to remember that here and there were white people, Indian people, coloured people, who dared to pay the price as well in putting this together. And I think the fact that we had an African woman, a white woman, Indian woman, [and a] white man, tell a very *similar* story, means that in the struggle *we were together*. Let's hope, *as we build the future, we will be together as well*. (Durban HRV Hearings 1996; emphasis added)

Although this particular example was directed towards the many witnesses who had testified, the pattern was similar after each testimony where Commissioners would validate certain experiences as suffering and perform this drama not only for those immediately present but also for those in the broader collective. As an empathic interlocutor, Commissioners would recognize individual experiences, designate them as brave and/or sacrificial, and then insert these experiences into the story of the new nation. In many cases, the movement through these phases of coding the narrative also involved references to a zone of common human dignity and moral regard. And it was these characterizations of a moral community that enabled the individual experience to be framed as worthy and the future of the collective to be painted as hopeful. This progressive narrative of the birth of the new nation relied on two processes – reckoning with the past and imagining the future. To accomplish this, a clear demarcation of the past from the future was made by designating certain elements as profane and investing the future with sacred qualities. Commissioners framed stories that told of suffering in terms of an honorable sacrifice in anticipation of freedom from oppression. Through these tales, the horror of the past was now seen as the midwife of a new, sacred democracy.

Thus the TRC Commissioners played a critical role in the process as they facilitated the expression and interpretation of witness testimonies. As empathic interlocutors, they gave recognition to each story and then placed the individual narrative within a broader text of the "new" nation. The themes that emerged through this process of story telling and interpreting often involved translating the individual story of suffering into a narrative which made such suffering worthy of social attention (see Morris 1997). This dynamic usually moved through three phases: first, asserting the dignity of the individual; next, universalizing the suffering; and then, inserting the individual traumatic event(s into the national narrative (see also Wilson 2000). Looking at the transcripts from the hearings, it becomes clear that such interpretations were performed not only as an acknowledgment of an individual's testimony, but also for the immediate audience and for a local and global audience with whom the media would engage in a next cycle. The media, in turn, would add their own layer of interpretation.

Media as sympathetic interpreters

It is not enough to seek the dimensions and impact of the TRC within the walls of the official hearings. We must also consider the broader audience for whom the TRC played and the means through which the TRC performance was conveyed. The mass media – radio, television, and print – played a significant role in how the testimonies heard inside the TRC were both amplified and focused on a national scale. Just as the Commissioners took a particularly active stance when it came to hearing and interpreting the testimony given to the TRC, so too did many journalists who reported on the proceedings. Rather than assuming the role of objective observer or passive reporter, many journalists saw the TRC hearings as an opportunity to engage in a form of civic education. For the first time, as Anthea Garman (1998) has described, many journalists covering the TRC began to work in the first person. They became visible actors in the drama of telling tales of the old South Africa and the stage hands for the construction of the story of the new South Africa. As a result, stories heard inside the TRC were actively framed and reframed through the media and, like the Commissioners, journalists inserted these stories into the larger progressive narrative of the traumatized but triumphant emerging democracy. And it was through these stories that many people in the extended audience of South African society were able to access and engage in the TRC process.[9]

Just as the liminal quality of the hearings enabled a reversal of roles, terminology, and designations of good and evil, media reports also contributed to the leveling of categories and dismantling of hierarchies. Once again, participants in the drama of the Apartheid past were recast in the public sphere so that those who had previously been named as terrorists became brave heroes, and those who had been valiant guardians of the Apartheid state became villains. Security force operatives whose testimony in the TRC revealed their role in assassinations and torture were now dubbed with nicknames like Prime Evil (Eugene de Kok) and Dr. Death (Wouter Basson). Through these recategorizations, the media took the stories of pain and murder and painted such incidents as representative of a breach caused by Apartheid violence that would be healed by democracy.

What is remarkable here is that although the independence of the media is a cherished principle in an established democracy, ironically in the transition to democracy phase which the TRC occupied, many actors in the South African media saw themselves as "contributing to the new South Africa"[10] by playing a role in translating the stories that were heard. In this third cycle of performance, therefore, one can see how the media keyed in on specific stories and replayed the claims to trauma, denoted heroes and villains, and participated in the demarcating of the sacred and the profane.

Audience reception and response

A discussion of the TRC as a performance is incomplete without some understanding of how the audience received and interpreted this performance. As with all performances, it is important to recognize that audience reception is contingent and audiences are not homogeneous in terms of race, class, gender, etc. Moreover, audiences are at a distance from the actors who populate the performance, and achieving authenticity and flow are therefore major accomplishments. In particular, for a performance such as the TRC to be successful in its local context with the message it strived to communicate, members of the audience who did not share a common history would have to come to agree on a new version of the past as well as a new vision of the future.

As I have mentioned earlier in this chapter, the TRC testimonies were performed for multiple audiences – immediate, extended, and imagined audiences at a local, national and global scale, as well as disparate groups spread across race and ideology – and a full exploration of these different audiences must be reserved for another essay. In general terms regarding the South African audience, however, it is clear that the TRC had an impact. Even for those who were skeptical or critical of the process, the TRC was so avidly covered by the media that it became impossible for South Africans not to contend with the stories emerging from the hearings. As many observers reported, after the TRC it was no longer possible for whites to claim that they did not know what had happened in the past. But even more interesting were those occasions when a sense of fellowship and solidarity was invoked.

To gain some idea of the degree to which the broader South African public engaged with the performance of the TRC, two sources should prove informative. One source is national surveys of the South African population. Although there have been varying responses to the question of whether the TRC has helped race relations, South Africans have been shown to now share a common understanding of the past. In a survey reported by James Gibson (2002), South Africans were asked to rate whether the statement: "Apartheid was a crime against humanity" is true or false. An overwhelming majority of all racial groups (86 percent of total; 73 percent of whites) believed the statement to be true. As Gibson suggests, the fact "[t]hat only a relatively small minority of South Africans reject this statement surely constitutes an important element of a collective South African memory shared by all racial groups" (Gibson 2002: 30).

A second source of interest is a collection of messages posted to a special part of the official TRC website that was called a "Register of Reconciliation" (ROR). The ROR was both a physical and virtual document to which people were invited to contribute personal messages in response to what they heard from the TRC. The ROR is populated mainly by white writers from South Africa as well as abroad. My analysis of these messages shows that a large majority of the people writing in the ROR voice their agreement with the claims made at the TRC, acknowledge the suffering that resulted from the Apartheid system, and conclude with an expression of remorse and a sense of moral responsibility. Many writers seem to suggest by virtue of their explanations of having been betrayed by those in authority, that in some way they too "suffered" or were "damaged" by the Apartheid government. While many observers of the TRC would decry the drawing of any sort of parallel between the lives that most white people led compared to black people and/or anti-Apartheid activists, what is compelling here from a theoretical point of view is how this inscribing of a common boundary around black and white potentially defines a new, shared collectivity.

Just as the stories told at the TRC were framed as traumatic, so too do those writing messages to the ROR describe the past as tragic. Descriptions are often phrased in the passive tense, especially when dealing with victims or bystanders. The images and recollections are filled with pain and anguish. For the contributors to the ROR, there is a clear distinction in the past between "us" and "them"; where "they" are black people who were treated as less than human. In pictures painted of the future, however, the tone is heroic or celebratory and is most often described in the active tense. Whereas people were seen as suffering in the past, now they are seen as contributors and co-creators in the future. Instead of dichotomies between "us" and "them," it is now "we." This "we-ness" forms the basis of descriptions that people offer of themselves as "fellow" South Africans and underpins a sense of pride in the new nation, both as a triumph for the South African people and as a beacon for the rest of the world.

Conclusion

In post-Apartheid South Africa, the TRC was established as one mechanism for dealing with the question of how to transition from a divisive history. Rather than being a legal structure which heard adversarial testimonies and dispensed punishment, the TRC became a public space of story telling and witnessing to which the nation, and the world, were invited. As a modern ritual of performance, the TRC set the stage for a new national narrative and the stories which were heard inside its walls became threads in the drama of trauma and triumph. To understand how the testimonies given to the TRC were deployed and inserted into a narrative for the new nation, I have tried to capture how these stories moved through space and time. I have shown that through a series of performance cycles, and with the aid of empathic interlocutors and sympathetic interpreters, the TRC process helped to designate the events of the Apartheid past as evil and the future of the new democracy as sacred. I believe the TRC operated during a particularly ripe moment in the trajectory of the emerging new nation. This "window of opportunity" was deeply connected to the "founding moment" of a new democracy and the euphoria and effervescence that surrounded that moment.

Lastly, one other way to gauge how the TRC message was adopted is to see the way in which it was adapted and extended into the different layers of society in general. The TRC exercise was indeed one that touched the nation at large. Once the testimonies moved outside the walls of the TRC, they reverberated again in public discussions,[11] theatre,[12] art exhibitions,[13] novels,[14] and documentary films.[15] The model itself was adapted by local-level organizations and communities[16] who saw themselves as struggling with internal tensions fueled by the vestiges of Apartheid. These examples provide evidence of how the TRC was taken as an authentic and legitimate way of dealing with the past. The narratives of tragedy and triumph can be heard in the public space, and metaphors of bridge-building and rainbow nation have become part of everyday discourse.

On a global scale, these echoes resound again as TRC-type processes are instituted in a number of cases where countries are seeking to deal with a violent past.[17] And iterations are heard again in a slightly different form in the United States where calls have been made for a TRC-type process to deal with issues such as slavery and race relations.[18] These echoes suggest that there is something very compelling about the form and outcome of a process such as the TRC, and that even in our modern world, people are hungry for rituals that offer repair and recognition.

Notes

1. The (re)designation of the date (December 16) for this particular national holiday is a significant symbol and story in itself since it re-presented a prior Apartheid era national holiday called "Day of the Covenant" which had been used to commemorate the Battle of Blood River – a defeat of the Zulus by the Afrikaner Voortrekkers (the Boer pioneers). In the "new" South Africa, this date now stands for reconciliation.

2. According to the drafting legislation, the TRC was only supposed to last two years. An amendment was made to increase the time span an additional nine months for the completion of the Human Rights Violations hearings and the drafting of the preliminary final report. The Amnesty hearings were extended until mid-2001.

3. Since Thabo Mbeki replaced Mandela as President of South Africa in 1999, Mbeki has ardently promoted a notion of "Two Nations" – one rich, one poor; one white, one black – that takes more seriously the economic ramifications of Apartheid. Although lately Mbeki has somewhat softened his original delivery of this idea, many of his public speeches continue to privilege economic reconstruction over social reconciliation. While the "rainbow nation" myth still circulates more than ten years later, such a vision is indeed vulnerable until the vast socio-economic gaps are closed.

4. The structure of the new national anthem is demonstrative of the hybrid symbolism that is being embraced in the "new" South Africa. In the first half, the new official anthem is composed of an African language section of "Nkosi Sikelele Africa" – the anthem that was sung by the resistance movements. The second section is a portion of the old English language anthem – the "Call of South Africa." And the third section is a piece of the old national anthem sung in Afrikaans – "Die Stem."

5. Of course, this assumption is somewhat problematic from an advocacy point of view. See, for example, Jeremy Cronin's writing (1999 quoted in Statman 2000) where he argues that by universally positioning all South Africans as both victims and perpetrators – what the Report terms the "'little perpetrator' in each one of us" (TRC Report Vol. 1, ch. 5: 108) – the TRC Report distorts South Africa's history of racial domination and exploitation.

6. Sangomas are the traditional healers in South Africa, sometimes colloquially known as "witchdoctors."

7. Popular courts, also called "kangaroo courts," "community courts," "people's courts," or "street justice courts" were those held within the communities to deal with actions deemed to violate the individual or the collective.

8. For more details on the structure and format of the statement taking process as well as other behind-the-scenes action at the TRC, see Buur 2000, 2001. The IMS is a database developed by the American Association for the Advancement of Science (AAAS) for use in tracking human rights violations and was provided to the TRC. The IMS has been used in other countries such as El Salvador and Haiti as well.

9. Of course, not all South Africans and not all journalists were supportive of the TRC; however, the performance itself was so compelling that people had to confront it regardless of whether they were positively or negatively disposed towards it.

10. Journalists and editors Max du Preez (1997), Stephen Laufer (1997), and John van Zyl (1997), among others, have expressed such a sentiment.

11. See, for example, letters to the editor in national newspapers, the SABC *TRC Special Report*, the workshops run by CSRV and other NGOs, the Healing of Memories Workshops, and the emergence of Khulumani (a victims support and lobbying organization).

12. See, for example, the plays *Ubu and the Truth Commission*, *The Story I am About to Tell*, and Pieter Dirk Uys' *Truth (O)missions*.

13. See, for example, the exhibitions "Miscast" and "Fault lines," and artwork by Sue Williamson, Judith Mason, and Nan Hamilton.
14. See, for example, novels by Gilliam Slovo, Nadine Gordimer, J. M. Coetzee, Breyten Breytenbach, and Antjie Krog.
15. See, for example, the documentaries by Frances Reid and Deborah Hoffmann *Long Night's Journey Into Day* (2000), Bill Moyers' *Facing the Truth* (1999), Mark Kaplan's *Where Truth Lies* (1999), Sturla Gunnarsson's *Gerrie and Louise* (1996) and the SABC's five-part CD-Rom documentary *South Africa's Human Spirit* (1999).
16. See, for example, the Wits Health Sciences Faculty, Dorbyl Corporation, United Cricket Board, UCT Health Sciences Faculty, and in issue areas such as the media and HIV/AIDS.
17. For a summary and brief description of all truth commissions to date, see the United States Institute for Peace special internet library (http://www.usip.org/library/truth.html, accessed November 18, 2003).
18. Examples include the Reparations for Slavery debate, the Tulsa Riots, Rosewood, and the Greensboro, North Carolina, Truth and Reconciliation Commission.

References

Act 34: Promotion of National Unity and Reconciliation. 1995. Available from Government of South Africa website at http://www.polity.org.za/govdocs/legislation/1995/act95-034.html (retrieved January 9, 2002).

African National Congress. August 1996. Statement to the Truth and Reconciliation Commission. Available from ANC website at http://www.anc.org.za/ancdocs/misc/trcall.html (retrieved September 3, 2005).

    May 12, 1997. Submissions and Responses by the ANC to Questions Raised by the Commission for Truth and Reconciliation. Available from ANC website at http://www.anc.org.za/ancdocs/misc/trc2.html (retrieved September 3, 2005).

Alexander, Jeffrey C. 2002. "On the Social Construction of Moral Universals: The 'Holocaust' from War Crime to Trauma Drama." *European Journal of Social Theory* 5: 5–85.

    2004. "Toward a Theory of Cultural Trauma." In *Cultural Trauma and Collective Identity*, ed. Jeffrey C. Alexander, Ron Eyerman, Bernhard Giesen, Neil J. Smelser, and Piotr Sztompka. Berkeley: University of California Press.

Asmal Kader, Louise Asmal, and Ronald Suresh Roberts. 1997. *Reconciliation Through Truth. A Reckoning of Apartheid's Criminal Governance*. Cape Town, South Africa: David Phillips.

Ball, Patrick. 1996. "Who Did What to Whom?" American Association for the Advancement of Science. Washington: AAAS. Available on AAAS website at http://shr.aaas.org/www/contents.html (retrieved June 8, 2002).

Berglund, Axel-Ivar. [1976] 1989. *Zulu Thought-Patterns and Symbolism*. London, Cape Town and Johannesburg: Hurst David Philip.

Block, Robert. 1996. "When the Truth is Too Hard to Bear." *The Independent*, April 17.

Bozzoli, Belinda. 1998. "Public Ritual and Private Transition: The Truth and Reconciliation Commission in Alexandra Township, South Africa 1996." *African Studies* 57: 167–96.

Buur, Lars. 2000. "Institutionalising Truth. Victims, Perpetrators and Professionals in the Everyday Work of the South African Truth and Reconciliation Commission." PhD Dissertation, Aarhus University, Denmark.

    2001. "Making Findings for the Future: Representational Order and Redemption in the Work of the TRC." *South African Journal of Philosophy* 20: 42–68.

Cerulo, Karen. 1995. *Identity Designs: The Sights and Sounds of a Nation.* New Jersey: Rutgers University Press.

Chapman, Audrey. 1999. "Truth Commissions and Truth Finding." Presented at the TRC: Commissioning the Past Conference, June 7–9, University of the Witwatersrand, Johannesburg, South Africa.

CNN World. 1998. "Apartheid Indictment Finds Fault on all Sides." October 29. Available from CNN at http://www.cnn.com/WORLD/africa/9810/29/truth.commission.03/ (retrieved June 8, 2002).

Cohen, Mike. 1998. "None Escape TRC Wrath," *Daily Dispatch,* South Africa. October 30. Available at http://www.dispatch.co.za/1998/10/30/southafrica/AATRC.HTM (retrieved June 8, 2002).

Colvin, Chris. 2000. "'We Are Still Struggling': Storytelling, Reparations and Reconciliation after the TRC." Research report written for the Centre for the Study of Violence and Reconciliation in collaboration with Khulumani (Western Cape) Victims Support Group and the Cape Town Trauma Centre for Survivors of Violence and Torture, December. Available at http://www.csvr.org.za/papers/papcolv.htm (retrieved November 10, 2003).

Constitution of South Africa. 1996. Available from Government of South Africa website at http://www.gov.za/constitution/1996/96cons.htm (retrieved June 16, 2004).

Deegan, Heather. 2001. *The Politics of the New South Africa: Apartheid and After.* Harlow, and New York: Longman.

du Preez, Max. 1997. "When Cowboys Cry." *Rhodes Journalism On-line Review* 14, *Special Edition.* Available at http://journ.ru.ac.za/review/14/cowboys.html (retrieved May 15, 2002).

Durban HRV Hearings. October 24, 1996. Available on South African Department of Justice TRC website at http://www.doj.gov.za/trc/hrvtrans/HRVDURB3/day1.htm (retrieved January 12, 2005).

Durkheim, Émile. [1912] 1995. *The Elementary Forms of Religious Life,* trans. Karen E. Fields. New York: Free Press.

Eyerman, Ron. 2001. *Cultural Trauma: Slavery and the Formation of African American Identity.* Cambridge: Cambridge University Press.

    2004. "Cultural Trauma: Slavery and the formation of African American Identity." In *Cultural Trauma and Collective identity,* ed. Jeffrey C. Alexander, Ron Eyerman, Bernhard Giesen, Neil J. Smelser, and Piotr Sztompka. Berkeley: University of California Press.

Garman, Anthea. 1998. "What Did Covering the TRC do to the Media?" Presentation at the Media Dealing with the Past Seminar organized by the Heinrich Boll Foundation, November 29, Berlin.

Gibson, James L. 2002. "Does Truth Lead to Reconciliation? Testing the Causal Assumptions of the South African Truth and Reconciliation Process." Revised version of a paper presented at the Annual Meeting of the American Political Science Association, August 30–September 2, 2001, San Francisco, CA.

Giesen, Bernhard. 2004. "Triumph and Trauma," in *Cultural Trauma and Collective Identity*, ed. Jeffrey C. Alexander, Ron Eyerman, Bernhard Giesen, Neil J. Smelser, and Piotr Sztompka. Berkeley: University of California Press.

Grunebaum-Ralph, Heidi. 2001. "Re-Placing Pasts, Forgetting Presents: Narrative, Place, and Memory in the Time of the Truth and Reconciliation Commission." *Research in African Literatures* 32: 198–212. Also available online at http://muse.jhu.edu/journals/research_in_african_literatures/v032/32.3grunebaum-ralph.html (retrieved April 19, 2003).

Hayner, Priscilla B. 1994. "Fifteen Truth Commissions – 1974 to 1994: A Comparative Study." *Human Rights Quarterly* 16: 597–655.

    1998. "Truth Commissions: Exhuming the Past." *North American Congress on Latin America (NACLA) Report on the Americas* 32, 2: 30–2.

Interim Constitution of South Africa. 1993. Available from South African government website at http://www.polity.org.za/govdocs/legislation/1993/constit0.html (retrieved July 15, 2004).

Jacobs, Sean. 2001. "The State of (Building) the Nation." *Epolitics*, 32 (June 1). Institute for a Democratic South Africa (IDASA). Available from IDASA at http://www.idasa.org.za/m_main.php?view=2&art_id=161 (retrieved April 19, 2002).

Kleinman, Arthur, Veena Das, and Margaret Lock (eds.). 1997. *Social Suffering*. Berkeley: University of California Press.

Krog, Antjie. 1998. *Country of My Skull: Guilt, Sorrow, and the Limits of Forgiveness in the New South Africa*. Johannesburg: Random House.

Laufer, Stephen. 1997. Excerpts from the Media, Truth and Reconciliation workshop in Cape Town quoted in *Rhodes Journalism On-line Review* 14, *Special Edition*. Available at http://journ.ru.ac.za/review/14/extracts.html (retrieved May 15, 2002).

Lukes, Steven. 1977. "Political Ritual and Social Integration," pp. 52–73 in *Essays in Social Theory*. New York. Columbia University Press.

Mamdami, Mahmood. 1997. "Reconciliation Without Justice." *Southern African Political and Economic Monthly* 10: 22–5.

Morris, David B. 1997. "About Suffering: Voice, Genre, and Moral Community." In *Social Suffering*, ed. Arthur Kleinman, Veena Das, and Margaret Lock. Berkeley: University of California Press. Essays originally published in *Daedalus: A Journal of the American Academy of Arts and Sciences*, Winter 1996, 125: 25–46.

Motsemme, Nthabiseng and Kopano Ratele. 2000. "Losing Life and Re-Making Nation at the Truth and Reconciliation Commission." Presented at Discourses on Difference and Oppression Conference, July 19–22, University of Venda, South Africa.

Available at http://www.geocities.com/culdif/motsem.htm (retrieved November 23, 2003).

Ngubane, Harriet. 1977. *Body and Mind in Zulu Medicine : An Ethnography of Health and Disease in Nyuswa-Zulu Thought and Practice*. London, New York and San Francisco: Academic Press.

Ramphele, Mamphela. 1997. "Political Widowhood in South Africa: The Embodiment of Ambiguity." In *Social Suffering*, ed. Arthur Kleinman, Veena Das, and Margaret Lock. Berkeley: University of California Press. Essays originally published in *Daedalus: A Journal of the American Academy of Arts and Sciences*, Winter 1996, 125: 99–118.

Ross, Fiona. 1997. "Blood Feuds and Childbirth: The TRC as Ritual." *Track Two, Special Issue on Truth, Reconciliation and Justice* 6, 3 & 4. Available from the Centre for Conflict Resolution at http://ccrweb.ccr.uct.ac.za/two/6_34/p07_blood_feuds.html (retrieved November 11, 2003).

Scheper-Hughes, Nancy. 1998. "Undoing: Social Suffering and the Politics of Remorse in the New South Africa." *Social Justice Special Issue: Beyond the Neoliberal Peace: From Conflict Resolution to Social Reconciliation* 25: 114.

Smelser, Neil J. 2004. "Psychological Trauma and Cultural Trauma," in *Cultural Trauma and Collective Identity*, ed. Jeffrey C. Alexander, Ron Eyerman, Bernhard Giesen, Neil J. Smelser, and Piotr Sztomplca. Berkeley: University of California Press.

Spillman, Lyn. 1997. *Nation and Commemoration: Creating National Identities in the United States and Australia*. Cambridge: Cambridge University Press.

Statman, James M. 2000. "Performing the Truth: the Social-Psychological Context of TRC Narratives." *South African Journal of Psychology* 30: 23–33.

TRC Final Report, 5 vols. 1998. Cape Town: Juta & Co. Available at http://www.polity.org.za/govdocs/commissions/1998/trc/1chap5.htm or from http://www.news24.com/Content_Display/TRC_Report/1chap5.htm (retrieved January 23, 2003).

TRC Press Release. December 16, 1995. Available from TRC Official website section on press releases at http://www.doj.gov.za/trc/media/prindex.htm (retrieved December 14, 2001).

TRC Register of Reconciliation. n.d. South Africa Truth and Reconciliation Commission. Available from TRC Official website at http://www.doj.gov.za/trc/ror/index.htm (retrieved April 17, 2003).

Turner, Victor. [1996] 1977. *The Ritual Process: Structures and Anti-structures*. Ithaca, NY: Cornell University Press.

1980. "Social Dramas and Stories About Them." *Critical Inquiry* 7: 141–68.

Tutu, Desmond. 2000. Commenting in SABC Special Series on CD-Rom "South Africa's Human Spirit: An Oral Memoir of the Truth and Reconciliation Commission," launched in Johannesburg on April 13, 2000. South African Broadcasting Company. Available at http://www.sabctruth.co.za/index.htm (retrieved January 15, 2004).

van Zyl, John. 1997. "Human Rights and Wrongs." *Rhodes Journalism On-line Review*, 14, *Special Edition*. Available at http://journ.ru.ac.za/review/14/vanzyl.html (retrieved July 20, 2002).

Wilson, Richard A.1999. "Reconciliation and Revenge in Post-Apartheid South Africa: Rethinking Pluralism and Human Rights." Presented at the TRC: Commissioning the Past Conference, June 7–9, University of Witwatersrand, Johannesburg, South Africa.
  2000. "Reconciliation and Revenge in Post-Apartheid South Africa. Rethinking Legal Pluralism and Human Rights." *Current Anthropology* 41: 75–98.

6

Performing opposition or, how social movements move

Ron Eyerman

Introduction

The concept of social movement is a well-established term in the sociological lexicon. The aim of this chapter is not so much to once again attempt to define a social movement or to offer criteria for determining when forms of collective action qualify as genuine movements. In fact, some of the examples I use to illustrate my argument are not taken from "social movements" properly defined.[1] Rather, the aim is to explore what "movement" means, and to ask what is or can be said to be "moved" in the performance of opposition or extended protest. Social movement is a form of acting in public, a political performance which involves representation in dramatic form, as movements engage emotions inside and outside their bounds attempting to communicate their message. Such performance is always public, as it requires an audience which is addressed and must be moved. Following Goffman (1971) and others (for example, Schechner 1985; Hetherington 1998; Apter, chapter 7, this volume; Alexander, chapter 1, this volume), the application of a theory of performance calls attention to the place and space of movement, as well as how opposition is performed. Performance theory focuses on corporality, presence, and the pre-discursive, while at the same time including it. This allows us to better address questions concerning what happens when people enter a movement, how this affects their actions and the actions of others, and to ask how social movements move.

In analyzing how opposition is performed and what movement means, it is necessary to distinguish at least three distinct, yet interrelated, arenas or social spaces in which opposition is performed: an emerging social movement, its opponents, and, finally, the general public. A social movement emerges when groups of disparate and ever-changing individuals sense they are united and moving in the same direction. People and organizations move in and out of social movements but this sense of collective movement, continuous over time and place, is what makes a movement what it is. To achieve this, collective identity and solidarity must be forged, a process which necessarily involves marking off those inside from those outside, the Other against which the movement moves. Who we are defines and distinguishes who we are not, at the same time as it identifies what we are against. This Other must also be forged, providing a force to move against. Thirdly, movements address and attempt to influence, move, the general public, thus affecting public opinion, a more distant, invisible, and diffuse audience composed of potential supporters and opponents.[2]

While social movements may create an "us" and "them," they do so as a form of symbolic interaction, with mutual expectations involved, and they do so in front of an audience of potential supporters, who must also be addressed and moved, not least of which includes taking a political stance regarding the movement itself. To do this a movement must express and communicate, express common grievance and communicate discontent, to protest and in the best case to effect changes in attitudes and practices of those inside and outside the "movement." When the latter occurs, society itself may be said to have "moved." Social movement, in other words, involves many levels and dimensions of movement, mobilizing and affecting opinions, engaging emotions, changing laws, preventing some actions while encouraging others.[3]

The various levels of movement include the bodies, minds, and emotions of those inside and outside what has come to be identified as "the movement," the physical, geographical aspects of staging and managing collective actions, the decisions and practices which are incorporated in the process of changing established societal practice, the norms, rules, and laws which form the basis of society. All of these involve different aspects and sorts of moving and being moved. In analyzing and studying what social movements move means several established theoretical perspectives may be brought into play, from the now standard collective behavior, resource mobilization, political process, and cognitive approaches of the social sciences to the more unusual performance theory developed in the humanities. The former have been much discussed and there is no need to repeat them here (for recent overviews see Jasper 1997; Della Porta and Diani 1999). Performance theory will be discussed in more detail in the following sections.

Movement as mobilization of identity and emotion

Inside the movement

Social movements move by transforming identities and emotions, by focusing attention, and by directing and coordinating actions. Movements are often spurred into existence by cognitively framed emotions, anger, frustration shame, guilt, which move individuals and groups to protest, to publicly express and display discontent, engaging in what McAdam et al. (2001) call "contentious" actions. If sufficient numbers turn out, one may call this a "protest event." Such an occurrence may contain and collect enough energy and coherence to generate similar events in the future, as well as recall the memory of those in the past. This sequence of events can set in motion a process of collective will formation whereby individual identities and biographies are fused into a collective characterized by feelings of group belongingness, solidarity, common purpose, and shared memory, a "movement" in other words. Once in motion, this process has both situational (manifest) and long-lasting (latent) effects, a sense of moving together, of changing and being changed through participating in a large social force. This sense can emerge in context, through participation in collective actions. However, this feeling of movement may move beyond the situational, becoming incorporated into individual biography as significant experience and memory, as well as objectified in representational form in cultural artifacts or more structurally in networks and organizations, "free spaces" (Polletta 1999), which can preserve and transmit this feeling of "movement" between "protest events." One can be "moved," in other words, before, during, and after the fact, as one recalls a situation through hearing a piece of music or viewing a film or a photograph, which represents an event, as well as the movement itself becoming objectified in organizations and networks, which one may be "moved" to join or support. In this case, "movement" has moved from interactive experience to a narrative connected with individual and collective memory, from event to metaphor (Amin 1995).[4] With this, symbolic gestures and performative action are an added value in both the practice and the understanding of collective action, in that, as Alexander (this volume) puts it, "explicit messages take shape against *background structures of immanent meaning*." It is here that performance theory, with its focus on drama, staging, and scripts, as well as actual performing, is a valuable analytical frame.

Movement is here used as both verb and noun, but most of all movement refers to an experience of moving and of being moved by forces greater than one's self, individual will, or rational choices, an experience that is filtered through metaphor. In this sense, the metaphor becomes the thing, the noun. Randall Collins (2001) links this experiential process to Durkheim's notion of collective effervescence, where individual identities are temporarily transformed as groups form. In this sense, an emotional transference occurs, which produces a charged, collective emotional energy, a sense of belonging to some force greater than oneself. An empowering can take place, especially as cognitive shifts occur, and clarity of vision and purpose give direction to the sense of movement. How does this occur? Cognitive framing and ritual performances are important mechanisms. Cognitive frames, in the form of narratives structure, focus and direct emotion/energy and actions in particular directions. Within social movements this means in collective, political directions. Narratives are stories containing rhetorical devices, story lines, which link a particular occurrence/experience to others, broadening their meaning beyond the situational, imposing a higher order of significance, thus orchestrating and amplifying both the emotional experience and the meaning of the event, as individuals fused into a collective, with a purposive future and a meaningful past.

From inside, social movement involves the move to protest, from framed emotion to action, and the transformation of an individually based, diffuse experience into a focused, collective one. A central mechanism here is a set of ritual practices which are performed as part of collective protest. Public displays of commitment and solidarity, often build around collective voicing and parading, ritual practices which are also transformative in that they help blur the boundaries between individual and collective, between the private and public, and help fuse a group through creating strong emotional bonds between participants. The repeated experience of ritual participation produces a feeling of solidarity – "we *are* all here together, we *must* share something"; and lastly, it produces collective memory – "we *were* all there together" (Berezin 2001: 93). A collective story emerges, linking places and events together and a metaphor, the movement, is applied. We are here now, we were there then, and we will be together in the future. We are a movement.

This is not to say that the original "move" is necessarily individually based, for the framed emotion which led to protest may well have been aroused and supported through dialogue and interaction with others, in friendship networks for example (Diani 1995; Polletta 1999). The point is that even such networks move up a step in and through the ritual practices of collective protest. Here, the movement is both the setting, the space, the practices, and the outcome.

Outside the movement

Social movements address and interact with others, opponents, as well as that broad mass we call "the public." These others must be "moved." Charles Tilly (2003: 45) has pointed out that in making their contentious claims "political actors follow rough scripts to uncertain outcomes as they negotiate demonstrations, humble petitions, electoral campaigns." In these actions, which Tilly calls their "repertoire of contention," collective actors must find ways to express that they are "worthy, united, numerous and committed." A social convention which we know as the "demonstration" was invented for just this purpose. On Tilly's (2003: 203ff.) account, the term "demonstration" was first heard in the 1830s and had become a recurrent phenomenon in Britain and the US by the 1850s. As social process, the demonstration merged two established forms o:

public display: (1) the procession, where groups would collectively march to a common meeting place, and (2) the presentation of a collective petition to some authority. The size of a demonstration, the number of participants, has often been thought to speak for itself, thus making reporting the numbers involved a constant source of conflict and controversy. Important as well in this reporting were the appearance and behavior of those involved, as the "numerous" also had to reveal themselves as "worthy," yet at the same time "committed" and determined, at least to the extent they sought acceptance and inclusion into the larger political community. Other demonstrative performances may seek different ways to express protest and opposition, which do not include being worthy, but still committed, something which can be a cause of tension between the various coalitions which make up a demonstration, and which points to a limitation in the contentious politics approach.[5]

Demonstrations are now accepted forms of political action and in demo-cratic societies are protected by law and even encouraged as important forms of political socialization and societal renewal.[6] However, demonstrations do not speak for themselves, they are performances which must be rehearsed and put in play, as well as seen and interpreted. A demonstration, following Tilly, involves (1) gathering deliberately in a public space – preferably one which combines visibility with symbolic significance, (2) displaying both member-ship in a politically relevant population and support for some position by means of voice, print, or symbolic objects, (3) communicating collective determina-tion by acting in disciplined fashion in one space and or moving through a series of spaces. Demonstrations became a more or less conventional means of "drawing forbidden or divisive issues, demands, grievances, and actors into public politics" (Tilly 2003: 204). It became, in other words, both an expression and an extension of democratic principles, the right to free assembly and to free speech.

While many studies have focused on the successes or failures of collective action, as measured in traditional views on power and influence, demonstrations and other forms of mobilization can be studied as performance, as the perfor-mance of opposition. As an example of the former, in the early 1950s Claude Bourdet, an important French intellectual, argued (in a series of articles in newly established left-liberal journals like *L'Observateur* and *Les temps modernes*) that one of the main blockages to reforming the French colonial system in a more progressive direction was the power of the "colonial lobby," made up primarily of business, farming and landowning interests. It was private inter-ests, in other words, that directed action and moved actors, while the general public could be moved in the same cause on the basis of "infantile emotions," presumably of a nationalist sort (see the discussion in Sorum 1977: 65ff.). The notion of shared interests has been basic to the analysis of social movements.

As correct and useful as this argument might be, it leaves out significant aspects of what Charles-André Julien, a contemporary of Bourdet, called "the North African drama" (Sorum 1977: 66), which performance theory, by calling attention to the role of meaning and emotion, can help illuminate. This "drama", giving a particular case universal significance, can perhaps be illustrated through a quotation. In the midst of the French and Algerian war, a central actor on the French side, one Colonel Antoine Argoud explained what his military forces were doing with these words: "We want to halt the decadence of the West and the march of Communism. That is our duty, the real duty of the army. That is why we must win in Algeria. Indo-China taught us to see the truth" (cited in Horne 2002: 165). The good colonel added drama on a grand scale as he lifted the ferocious battle between opposing sides in a contentious struggle to a world historical plane. Similarly, on the other side, Marxist-inspired Jean Paul Sartre and his colleagues argued that colonialism was "condemned by history" and thus the actions of the French settlers in Algeria and of the French army, no matter how rational, were retrograde and, in the long run, meaningless.[7]

The notion of "framing" (Snow and Benford 1988), an important concept in recent social movement theory, is a middle step here.[8] Framing calls attention to the cognitive processes of making sense and the often contentious struggle to define a situation, but it can also involve dramatization, placing an event, a demonstration for example, within a narrative which lifts it from being a single occurrence and gives it wider significance through connecting it to others. In a sense, framing flows into ideology (Jasper 1997: 157). Social movements artic- ulate frames as much as they may make use of them as resources in mobilization, in that activists make sense of their own protests through already existing nar- rative frames (Eyerman 2002a). Performance, on the other hand, is what gives this story life, adds drama and activates emotion, through *mise-en-scène*. If social movements articulate frames of understanding, the performance of protest actualizes them. As mentioned earlier, performance focuses on corporality and presence; performance is what makes a movement move and helps it move others. The performance of opposition dramatizes and forcefully expresses a movement through designed and stylized acts, communicating protest beyond the movement itself.

Alexander (this volume, ch. 1) defines cultural performance as the social processes through which actors display for others the meaning of their social situation. He cites the definition of performance provided by John MacAloon (Alexander, this volume) as an "occasion in which as a culture or society we reflect upon our selves, dramatize our collective myths and history, present our selves with alternatives, and eventually change in some ways while remaining the same in others." Performances are at once part of everyday life and marked off from it. A demonstration, for example, is arranged within the everyday, yet as an event it breaks routines and opens a space in which the elements of performance, such as the rearranging of time and breaking of rules, occur (Schechner 1985). In this sense it is a form of collective exemplary action (Eyerman and Jamison 1998), which can be distinguished from the repertoires of strategic action which are the normal focus of social movement analysis. From performance theory one can highlight the following: a system of representation, which contains chronological narration and collective representations which provide a background to performance, aspects of which are drawn upon and articulated (Alexander, this volume, chapter 1; Apter, this volume, chapter 7). These narratives can be a resource from which "scripts" can be drawn, as in a theatre performance. However, as McAdam et al. (2001: 138) point out:

Performances within repertoires do not usually follow precise scripts to the letter; they resemble conversation in conforming to implicit interaction rules, but engage in incessant improvisation on the part of all participants. Thus today's demonstration unfolds differently from yesterday's as a function of who shows up, whether it rains, how the police manage today's crowds, what participants learned yesterday, and how authorities responded to yesterday's claims.

Scripts, which can also be called "traditions," guide actions but are modified as interactions, something which also influences reception. An audience familiar with the conventions of performance are predisposed in their interpretations of their meaning; in viewing the performance of opposition, much depends on how the action unfolds. Here one might distinguish between conventional and emergent performance. Audiences, however, or parts of them, can be sympathetic or not and read what they see accordingly, that is, within their already existing frames. This means that the gap between performance, the messages which movements wish to convey, and its reception is a problematic which both activists and sociologists must ponder.[9]

As in a theatre performance actors and roles are important. Movement actors perform and convey; they also dramatize, adding powerful emotions to their actions which re-present known narratives through the use of symbols. Performance necessarily involves a *mise-en-scène*, a vision, a setting, and a physical environment, which may itself be laden with symbolic meaning, thus influencing both performance and reception. The ritual performance of a May Day parade/demonstration may offer an example. Here there are actors and directors, symbols and scripts. There are also designated places, which may have symbolic value themselves, a certain city square and parade route may have historical reference. The event is also staged and choreographed, placards are printed in advance and laid out in designated places in the staging area, so that demonstrators can fall in line behind them as they prepare to march. Time-tested slogans may be called out and responded to during the march, as it follows its designated route. After moving to the final destination, a historical square, for example, speakers and speeches make use also of formats and phrases which represent the traditions of the group, recalling its history and linking the present event to those of the past. Depending on the context, May Day can represent, perform, power or protest, and opposition. Apart from the ritual performance of a May Day parade, ritual aspects of contemporary demonstrations have come to resemble carnival-like progressions, "occasions" (Hetherington 1998: esp. chapter 7) or "happenings" where the display and performance of identity and the more traditional politics of protest flow easily into one another. Such occasions provide a space where opposition can be performed, a "scene of protest" (Cockburn et al. 2000: 71), at the same time as lifestyles are expressed and reproduced. Performances here are ritualized, but less routinized and controlled by tradition and party politics than May Day parades, as disparate subcultural networks gather in the same place to represent themselves, and their lifestyle politics, in public. Of course, as Schechner (1985) and others have shown, even more traditionally political demonstrations contain their relatively spontaneous aesthetic aspects. Here the control of tradition and party discipline is less constraining and outcomes are less predictable.[10]

Moral performance

One may also speak of moral performance in relation to social movements and the performance of opposition. The notion and practice of civil disobedience have a long tradition in political protest. From Henry David Thoreau's withdrawal to Walden Pond to Gandhi's classic formulation of *satyagraha* (truth force), opposition has had a performative tradition to draw upon.[11] One aspect of social movement practice is the attempt to extend the bounds of solidarity, of moral empathy, by placing items and objects on the political agenda which do not naturally appear there. This involves cognitive movement and a *mise-en-scène*. Morality is usually conceived as a form of evaluative judgment and a following of principled praxis. According to Arne Johan Vetlesen (1994), moral performance runs through a (dialectical not unidirectional) sequence made up of three distinctive levels: perception, judgment, action. One must perceive another, an object or person, as part of the moral domain, which means an object of respect and concern. This creates a relationship, an emotional bond, an in-between, with the other, and its situation, just treatment and dignity are thus matters of central concern. The perception of another as an object of our concern is the basis of judgment, we take a stand in relation to their condition, by deeming it worthy of our concern and are in a position to evaluate that condition. From this action may follow. As a basic human capacity empathy allows one to develop an appreciation of how the other experiences her situation.

Empathy requires the ability, and the possibility, to see and to hear, to listen and to feel with another, it allows an openness and receptivity to another, by whose condition one feels "addressed." One is emotionally and cognitively "moved" and this may lead to physical movement, to speak out, to protest, and to speak of and for another.

If the first step in dehumanization is to reduce an other to a simple phrase, an enemy, a parasite, or a terrorist, the first step in moral performance or empathy is attentiveness to the complexity of another's status and situation, something which can be viewed as an attribution of subjectivity.[12] This may involve seeing the other as an agent or victim of historical or natural forces and "forced" to act in certain ways. Depending on the narrative frame through which this is interpreted one may find the actions sympathetic or reprehensible, certain acts of "terror" may be viewed as an acceptable weapon of the weak, for example, the other may be viewed as an unfortunate victim of famine, drought, or war beyond his control. There may also be variations in the sense that how one views the other may involve different responses and actions. For example, for the French opposition during the war with Algeria (1954–62) there were at least two views of the Algerian rebels: reformists associated with the *L'Express*, viewed them as potential partners in a dialogue to renegotiate the relationship between France and a relatively independent Algeria. Marxists and other anti-colonialists associated with *Les temps modernes*, on the other hand, saw them as a historical agent of world historical dimension ushering a new stage of development, a view which accepted violence as a necessary means. This, of course, lent itself to a more morally tolerant view of the other. In his preface to a central text of the French opposition, Franz Fanon's *The Wretched of the Earth*, Jean Paul Sartre (1968: 22) wrote "the rebel's weapon is proof of his humanity." While both sides could find common moral ground in opposing the use of torture against the rebels and be moved to protest against the actions of their government and its army, they disagreed in their perception of the other and what means he could apply in rebellion.

Franz Fanon was an important actor in this particular conflict and struggle for representation, and analysis of his role and writings provides some useful cautionary reflections on this process. In his view, the colonial other is always "overdetermined from without" (quoted by Homi Bhabha [1986: xiii]). In other words, even when empathetic, the attribution of subjectivity occurs through an already existing interpretive frame where, as Bhabha puts it, "the colonial subject who is historicized as it comes to be heterogeneously inscribed in the texts of history, literature, science, myth" (1986: xiii). Even for the sympathetic Westerner, the attribution of agency and subjectivity begins within an existing discourse, while for the colonized subjectivity begins and occurs through acts and practices, which may lend themselves to various interpretations. How the two are mediated, the discursive practices of the viewer and those of the actions of the other (in becoming a subject/object for the viewer), is an interesting process to study in context. It is the acts and actions of the colonized, the acts of becoming a subject, which make him/her visible in the first place. This collective movement moves the Western viewer. It forces, if nothing else, emotional and cognitive reinterpretation. The case of the non-political "victim" is something different. Here the other must be discovered, made visible through other means than his or her own acts, except perhaps for the act of suffering. But even this must be made available and then framed in an already existing narrative of victimhood.

Viewing the other as an object of moral concern also reflects back upon the viewer. As a former French army officer wrote concerning the use of torture in Algeria, "the frightful danger there would be for us to lose sight, under the fallacious pretext of immediate effectiveness, the moral values that alone have up to now made for the greatness of our civilization and our army" (cited in Talbott 1980: 103–4). Thus while some might view terror as an acceptable weapon of the weak, few in the oppositional movement were willing to view torture as an acceptable weapon of the strong. Viewing the other, even an enemy, as an object of moral concern reflects and thus affects the moral standing of the viewer. Social movements can make use of this reflection/representation in their own strategic performances. The use of non-violent tactics which characterized the early, religious-based, American civil rights movement built upon the assumption that they and their opponents shared a Christian world view. Activists assumed, in other words, that opponents would treat their acts of opposition as moral acts and respond accordingly, as an expression of their own morality. The violence which met their non-violent protests apparently shocked many of the ministers who composed the movement's leadership, just as many Catholic and left-wing intellectuals in France, especially those who had been active in the resistance against fascism, were shocked by the tactics of the French military in Algeria.[13]

In the same conflict, an extraordinary encounter between a French social scientist, herself a victim of Nazi torture during World War Two and the leader of the FLN's terror squads, reveals something of the morality and emotions involved in contentious politics. In the course of their secret and highly sensitive meeting in the midst of war in Algiers in 1957, the FLN leader claimed "We are neither criminals, nor assassins." Very sadly and very firmly, the social scientist, Germaine Tillion, replied: "'You *are* assassins.' He was so disconcerted, that for a moment he remained without speaking, as if suffocated. Then his eyes filled with tears and he said to me, in so many words: 'Yes, Madame Tillion we are assassins . . . It's the only way in which we can express ourselves'" (cited in Horne 2002: 213–14). Here, perhaps, we have a meeting of two moral subjects, as opposed to the streets of Algiers and the streets of the American

South, where other emotions prevailed and where another sort of framing of the other led to very different forms of contestation.[14]

There are strategic aspects of performance in social movement and in moving others. On the individual level, one way of moving others is through strategic performance. In his dealings with the complex situation in Vietnam at the end of World War Two when his fragile new government confronted an array of external occupying forces as well as internal opposition, Ho Chi Minh represented himself and his movement in various ways depending on the context and the audience. William Duiker (2000: 344) writes:

> By portraying the Vietminh Front as a broad-based movement armed with a program that could appeal to all progressive and patriotic forces . . . In portraying himself as the avuncular figure from the countryside, the "simple patriot" in the worn khaki suit and blue cloth sandals, Ho won not only the hearts of millions of Vietnamese, but also the admiration and respect of close observers.

Similarly, Gandhi's careful choice of clothing challenged Western images of masculinity and maturity, as well as proving effective in disarming his opponents (Young 2001: 326ff.).

In order to move others in calculated ways, key actors in social movements must develop what Duiker calls a "strategic arsenal" of representations and roles that move others in appropriate ways. During the Algerian war, the FLN used public relations techniques and the services of two of its "best-fitted talents" (Horne 2002: 245) to their advantage at the United Nations, an important arena in their contentious politics: "Both were extensively-travelled cosmopolitans, popular and at home in salons across the world . . . Both had married attractive foreign wives . . . who helped open many doors to the Algerians in the United States. Both seemed the very antithesis of the hard-eyed revolutionaries." These "movement representatives" appeared, in other words, the very opposite of expectations garnered through other representational sources, like the Western mass media, and also for that matter very different from the appearance favored by Ho with similar aims in mind. How one represents a "movement" in order to move outsiders is thus not only a factor of what one is representing, exemplifying movement ideals and identity, but also of what one wishes to communicate to a particular audience.[15] The most powerful movements combine exemplary and strategic aspects in their performances. Gandhi's innovative and distinct form of nationalism was powerful for just this reason, its non-violent civil disobedience claimed both the moral high ground and proved to be an effective weapon at the same time.[16]

Both strategic and exemplary performances can perhaps be contained within the broad category of self-presentation as understood in Goffman's dramatological perspective. However, social movements are collective actors and collective self-presentation is a central aspect of their performance. Performance here is also complicated by the multiple actors involved, their various intentions, as well as by the multifaceted, mixed, and often contradictory audiences who will interpret them.[17] One person's terrorist is another's liberation fighter. It might also be worth pointing out that the very term "movement" has or can have a legitimating and even tactical function in contentious politics. To be recognized as a movement, rather than a "terrorist" organization, for example, can confer a degree of legitimacy on a group and its actions in that they impute political and in that sense popular, rather than merely criminal, motivations. Part of a group's representational struggle may indeed be to achieve recognition as a movement, something which "moves". In their study of Hamas, a group many would identify as terrorist, the Israeli social scientists Mishal and Sela (2000) appear keen to convince their audience that this is the case with that organization.

On a collective level, social movements can be important forces in moving the bounds and borders of empathy. While it is common to think of collective identity in terms of demarcating those inside and outside, "us" and "them," social movements can also adjust and expand the borders in their representations of who is inside and who outside.[18] Michael Ignatieff (1999) writes that the most common feelings of empathy are for those nearby, family members and friends and when something happens to them, it affects us, but this can quite easily be expanded to include a community, especially in times of crisis, a catastrophic flood or fire or when an ethnic or religious group is threatened. The projections and representations of the imagined community of the nation have been a major mechanism in expanding feelings of empathy beyond the local, the regional, and the face-to-face. National crisis or traumas are occurrences which recall the collective and stretch the bounds of solidarity and empathy.

Social movements can themselves be mechanisms which "move" the bounds of empathic feelings in this way, by attempting to speak for and represent an unseen deserving other, who are not a "natural" or obvious part of a collective. They can stretch the limits of what is imagined beyond the "normal" bounds of political, social, and geographical community. Movements of solidarity, or expressions of solidarity within movements, are an example. The current "anti-globalization" movement can serve as an illustration. If the anti-colonial movements of pre- and post-World War Two can still be placed within the frame of the nation-state and the idea of the nation, as a "natural" political community, in that they were nation-based movements which opposed colonial policies carried out in their name, the current anti-globalization movement represents another sort of imagined community, than the nation. While there are, of course, national aspects to this emergent movement, such as nationally rooted opposition to the European Union, its bases are widely dispersed networks and its guiding images speak in the name of an "other," the victims o "global capitalism," in distant parts of the world. What moves activists, in other words, is not necessarily a local or national community, but feelings of solidarity for vaguely defined and widely dispersed vicitims of invisible social forces. These feelings are publicly expressed through protest events at the meetings of the "leaders of global capitalism," as they move around their transnational domain. It is this unseen and non-present other which the movement seeks to represent and make visible through its protest actions in front of a very visible and present other. This performance of opposition is made through forms of protest which are very cognizant of the presence of the mass media and the idea that through them "the whole world" is watching. It is an empathetic feeling for the condition of this unseen vicitim which, in part of course, "moves" the movement at the same time as the boundaries of community are expanded to include them.

How is this achieved, how does this new movement "move"? Firstly, one should not discount the importance of previous movements and their traditions of opposition and protest which remain alive and influence contemporary protest. One of the exemplars of the attempt to move the boundaries of identification and empathy is the labor movement, which sought to unite workers of all countries in common cause and understood itself and its aims as truly "international" (Wennerhag 2002). The current anti-globalization movement has inherited much from the labor movement and more recently from environmentalism. This includes some fundamental ideas about the forces "moving" world development, as well as the means towards opposing them and some of the ideological frames which give them meaning: anarchism, syndicalism, populism, deep ecology, and so on. The nascent movement has also inherited many of its constituent ritual practices, including the demonstration and all its repertoires and scripts, placards, collective singing and chanting from previous movements. There is also a long history of moral protest to draw upon, from Abolitionism to Third Worldism, as well as contemporary networks of opposition, especially a range of youth subcultures and scenes. For the latter especially, "movement" involves style-based and cultural expressions of opposition rather than the more explicitly political opposition that is usually associated with the concept, something which has produced its own tensions and dynamics within the movement. It also may confuse others. Naomi Klein (2001: 311) cites the following report from the Toronto police radio during a protest/happening: "This is not a protest. Repeat. This is not a protest. This is a kind of artistic expression. Over."[19] Unlike the labor movement, there is no overarching and dominant ideology, but rather a set of images and phrases expressing opposition, which serve as basis for moving the bounds of empathy to imagined others in distant parts of the globe. These images and phrases are necessarily very general and broad, even vague, providing an umbrella under which many diverse individuals and groups can gather: animal rights, new forms of taxation to aid underdeveloped regions, reclaiming the streets and other public places from the intrusion of big business, in the traditional populist struggle of the "people" against the "system" and its privileged representatives. New forms of technology, from cell phones to portable computers (Cockburn et al. 2000), as well as new forms of business and political associations, provide the forms through and against which the new movement takes form.

One unintended consequence of the globalization of protest has been that demonstrations require greater mobility and flexibility on the part of participants, a factor which contributes to their role as spaces of social learning. Movements move consciousness by opening up public spaces in which learning and experimentation can occur (Eyerman and Jamison 1991). Demonstrations have always been occasions for communicating ideas, as well as forming and displaying new identities. In part because of the distances involved and the crossing of national boundaries, with all this implies in terms of language, law, and traditions, demonstrations have lasted longer than usual, requiring that activists remain overnight in temporary collective dwellings. This has provided additional space for education and political and social interaction between activists and with the local community. Demonstrations, in other words, have become extended periods of intensive political socialization, which is now even more significant because of the young age of the majority of activists.

Demonstrations, especially in the current context, can also be occasions where the performance of identity, the expression and representation of self, appears as important to many participants as the attempt to move others. Anti-globalization demonstrations have taken on this character and created a tension between aims and the groups which represent them. They have also made outcomes, and, in turn, the reception on the part of the viewing public, more unpredictable. The creative tension between expressive and more instrumental aims of the demonstration is here intensified, making each demonstration a unique event or happening, yet still part of a chain of protest events, a movement, where the previous occasion provides a point of reference for the next. The participants may vary but there are apparent network connections and also identifiable incremental learning processes, even if different subgroupings may take away different lessons from each event, depending on the aims and intentions.

While the traditions of protest inherited from the past help explain the forms and repertoires of the new movement, older forms of technology, especially television and film, have been essential in providing, as well as spreading, its content, especially in regard to expanding the borders of empathy. The images conveyed through these media, moving images of suffering, provide the raw material that can then be framed and explained as caused by the agents of global capital. Such images are part of what has moved individuals and groups to protest in the first place. These mediated and coded images, visual messages, can move emotions and spur re-cognition, they can shock and stimulate re-evaluation. Through what Ignatieff (1999: 10) calls "a new kind of electronic internationalism" they help in the process of expanding, moving, the borders of empathy, creating the moral sensitivity and predispositions which may also stimulate protest and, eventually, social movements.[20] Once in motion, the latter may generate their own images as means of maintaining momentum and also recruiting others, and as forms for expressing the movement's identity and purpose.

Conclusion: social movements and collective performance

Social movements move individuals, their emotions and cognition, as they forge individuals into collectives and empower groups. They move as they effect change in consciousness and social practice and they move institutions by changing their practices. Movements do this by fusing individuals into collectives and collectives into focused and directed social forces. This is accomplished through social conventions like public demonstrations and their constitutive ritual practices. Such practices help "frame" understanding by linking present events and practices to those of the past and the future. This is accomplished through narratives which, at the same time, widen and amplify their significance. Once in motion, this emergent social force can move others, opponents and potential supporters, through its actions and displays. In this process, cognitive changes can occur, new knowledge formed and acquired, new or altered forms of consciousness and social practice can emerge or be prevented from emerging. On the more mundane level of routine politics, social movements empower organizations and actors to engage in "moving" institutions, through altering established social practices.

Performance theory adds a new dimension to the study of social movements in linking cognitive framing, narration, and discourse with the practice of mobilization. Performance theory calls attention to corporality and presence, to acting and acting out, to the role of drama and the symbolic in movement activity. It turns our attention to the performance of opposition and the aesthetics of movement, to the choreography of protest, as well as to the moral and emotional in mobilization. Looking through the lens of performance also brings forth the tension between the expressive and the strategic which I believe to be characteristic of contemporary social movements.

On a collective level, strategic performance is part of a social movement's representation of itself, a collective self-presentation. Leaders and activists in the various phases of the American civil rights movement, for example, chose different symbolic means to express and exemplify their "movement." In the early 1950s, when movement aims focused on acceptance and integration and a progressive narrative framed self-understanding, the ideal of the "good Negro" was adopted as a form of collective self-presentation. Exemplary representatives like Martin Luther King, Jr. and Ralph Abernathy often appeared at the head of marches and demonstrations in newly bought or pressed bib-overalls and work shirts, when they were not wearing the more traditional suit and tie of the minister-community leader and "race man."[21] In the later, Black Power phase the black leather jacket and beret became prominent and expressive of a younger, urban generation's striving for autonomy and distinction. An entirely different type of verbality and gesture accompanied this performance of opposition, which sought to demonstrate both an opposition to the dominant white society and, at the same time, to the "integrationist" mode and practice of other movement leaders. These forms of symbolic expression were guided by scripts and narratives, those of an earlier black nationalism and a "redemptive narrative" (Eyerman 2002a), which give them wider meaning by connecting them to a collective past, as well as the present situation. The latter is especially conditioned by strategic aspects, since performance is aimed at moving others by presenting consciously chosen evocative images. Strategic performance is designed with affect in mind. It must also be effective, and there is always an element of chance and risk involved. The aim, after all, is to move, emotionally and cognitively, in a particular direction, but how a performance will affect others cannot be entirely predicted, and this uncertainty regarding reception is only amplified through the intervention of mass media.

Collective self-presentation is part of the process of collective identity formation. As Goodwin et al. (2001: 8–9) point out, the notion of collective identity is often used to point to a cognitive process of boundary drawing, demarcating "them and us," leaving out the emotional side of this process. The inclusion of performance theory, which focuses on bodily presence, on moving, the emotive and evocative, is an important corrective in this regard. However, performance can also be interpreted as non-emotional or strategic role playing, a doing without feeling or real engagement. While tactics and strategic actions are central to all forms of collective political action, social movements move because they engage emotion and values. Group solidarity is an emotional as well as cognitive experience. Movements must contain, therefore, non-strategic performances which motivate, move, actors because they believe in what they are doing, that what they are doing is the right (moral) thing to do. How is this effected? What is it that in the midst of a demonstration, for example, creates a sense of belongingness that would move one demonstrator to come to the aid of another under attack from the police or opponent? Creating an emotional bond is part of what is meant by collective identity and social movement must bond disparate individuals, even those who may already form some sort of "network," together in an emotional way. The demonstration is one form which creates the possibility for such bonding. In the space opened through a demonstration, making visible and real the boundaries between them and us, these processes can be set in motion. Collective acts, such as singing, shouting slogans, and so on, are means employed. But it is not simply or merely *in situ* that this occurs, for art and music can carry the strong emotional content which makes such bonding possible even between protest events such as demonstrations. Demonstrations, after all, are only one form of collective protest and while visible and dramatic, not the most common.[22]

Creating and evoking moral empathy is part of what makes a "movement." It is part of demarcating "we" and marking off "them." Demonstrators will rush to aid a fallen comrade, but it is unusual and requires a widening of the zone of empathy when they do the same for a fallen policeman in the same situation. Empathy is first of all created through presence, through being there, when participation is an expression of side-taking and thus belonging. "We" are all together on this occasion against "them." Empathy, as well as belonging, can also be represented and reinforced through markers and symbols, buttons, pieces of clothing, flags, placards, and so on, infused with symbolic value. These represent "us," to participants, as well as marking off this group for and against "others." In this sense, demonstrations are processes of identity and empathy formation re-enacting narrative dramas, as public practices, a form of ritual street theatre. This relates both to the demonstration as a collective practice in itself and to the more consciously arranged and performed plays and pieces which occur within them. In this expressive dramatization, the values, images, and desires of the movement are revealed and membership solidified.

This articulation and objectification of the movement can occur through speeches as well as through scripted and costumed performance, death masks representing the bodies of people or animals killed by "greedy capitalists," who are themselves represented as "fat cats with cigars," and so on. Through such performances a movement not only expresses what it stands for and what it stands against (representing and demarcating itself), binding participants together, but also creates an emotional bridge, a widening of the zone of empathy, to those non-present others who are represented as the victims of the forces that should be stopped. This is a process of emotional movement, a widening of "us" beyond the bounds of the present situation, as it represents those "not here, yet still with us," if only symbolically. Part of a "movement" its representation and expression of something transcendent, greater than "I" and the "here and now" of the current event. The "movement" thus moves itself and its participants to another level of experience, the experience of solidarity with unseen, unknown others, and at the same time adding an emotional charge through moving (expanding) the range of moral empathy. The expressive performance that is a demonstration aims at evoking and representing this in visible form. These acts of representation are amplified and diffused to much wider and broader audiences when they occur on camera, broadcast through mass media, exposing the movement to non-present viewers. This enlarges the audience of potential supporters and opponents, who also may be "moved" by what they see and hear.

Opposition is performed in public spaces, some of which are chosen for their particular symbolic significance and their media accessibility, with the "whole world watching," as the popular movement chant would have it. This *mise-en-scène* is central to how social movements move. There is a setting, a stage and a script, performers, and audience. Movements as coordinated series of protest events become scenes upon which opposition is performed and attention, both inside and outside, is focused on a particular problematic, "globalization" say, or "women's rights," "the environment," "family values", and so on. This focus intensifies and highlights, dramatizes, an issue or a cause, making it visible and multiplying its emotional intensity. But it does not determine its reception. Viewing a televised pro-(Vietnam) war demonstration while working at JFK airport in the 1960s, one of my workmates was moved to tears by "all the Americans" he saw in the flags carried by demonstrators. Even though I was myself moved in an opposite direction, the issue of national identity was brought clearly into focus for both of us by this event. As in a dramatic theatrical performance, the protest event, and the movement making it happen, highlighted an issue and focused our attention. The audience was moved, just as those on stage were moved to action. Social movements move even those who view them from afar, but whom they move and in which direction is not something easy to control or predict. The world that is watching is multifaceted and the media which mediates the message adds its own refraction. Movements move, but in differing directions.[23]

Notes

1. This chapter reflects the beginning stages of forthcoming research to be carried ou at the Center for Cultural Sociology, which will build upon four case studies i analyzing, among other things, the role of social movements in expanding the border of moral empathy and in creating a global public sphere. These case studies wil include the French-Algerian War, Gandhi's cultural nationalism, the Vietnam Wa and the current anti-globalization movement.

2. Much of the existing literature on social movements concerns not so much ho movements move, but who they move. This calls attention to processes of mobiliz tion, to the potential for and success of recruitment (Klandermans and Tarrow 198 McAdam et al. 1988). The processual transformation where "mobilization potentia

(Klandermans 1988), individuals and groups predisposed to protest, becomes social movement has been designated as a causal chain and studied at the micro and macro levels. Other research has called attention to meso level interactions (Gould 1991; Gerhards and Rucht 1992), to framing (Snow et al. 1986) and the role of movement intellectuals (Eyerman and Jamison 1991).

3. In accomplishing this, a movement might also claim to represent an other, as opposed to confronting one. In their protest, movements may speak for and call upon the plight of an other, another group, or Nature, for example, as being victimized and unable to speak for themselves.

4. Richard Brown (1977) distinguishes types of metaphors. That which he calls iconic, where metaphor creates the object or image as a unique entity (85), fits well here. Paul Ricoeur (1978) links metaphor and narratives, something which Hayden White (1978) also develops.

5. Habermas' (1989) notion of the modern public sphere, public opinion, and forms of representation are relevant here. Social movements are a modern phenomenon dependent upon the existence of a legally sanctioned public sphere where public opinion can be influenced. Movements represent themselves within this sphere, as a constituent element in its articulation.

6. Some countries even have laws specifying the right not only to protest and demonstrate, but also to be seen and heard by the Other to whom the protest is addressed. This has meant that complex negotiations in planning demonstrations are often necessary, between those responsible for civic order and representatives of protesting groups.

7. Ashis Nandy (1983: 1) offers a cogent argument for expanding our interpretations of the motivations for colonialism. Against the dominant notion that colonialism is about economic gain and political power, he writes, "in Manchuria, Japan consistently lost money, and for many years colonial Indochina, Algeria and Angola, instead of increasing the political power of France and Portugal, sapped it." In his view, colonialism is a state of mind, a consciousness, and a culture.

8. According to Snow and Benford (1988) framing has three functions: punctuation, modes of attribution, and modes of articulation. The first emphasizes a perceived injustice and defines corrective action. The second is diagnostic and prognostic, attributing blame and offering alternative futures. The third relates to the mobilization potential of a "frame," its resonance and empirical credibility and narrative fidelity.

9. There is no handbook of performance for movements. Activists make use of conventions and traditions, which are rooted in various national and international traditions. There is no general theory of social movement performance, at least none that I am aware of, as there is for theatrical performance. The question of what makes for a good performance and whether or not this can be formalized and then generalized is something which might be possible to better address in a globalizing world. However, glocalization, the mixing of the global and the local, is still the rule.

10. Demonstrations, especially contemporary ones, are often directed and coordinated by various network coalitions, which means that they may unfold differently even

immediately

where the overall aim may be the same. For example, the current "anti-globalization" movement stages protest events around the globe and the coalitions which organize these protests are composed of local, national, and international groups. This mix, along with local political cultural traditions, affects how the event will be staged. The best account of this process I know of is that provided by Norman Mailer (1968, esp. book two). In this account of the October 1967 anti-war demonstration in Washington, DC, Mailer reveals not only the problems of internal coalition-building and the compromises forged in negotiations with the other side, but also the centrality of drama and aesthetics in preparing and mounting a demonstration. He notes, for example, the importance of selecting a route which allows the lines of demonstrators a clear view of their symbolic target, in this case the Pentagon, as well as how the promise of dramatic confrontation and civil disobedience was an important mobilizing factor, especially amongst the young.

11. According to Young (2001: 323) Gandhi "adapted from Irish nationalists and the British suffragettes."
12. In recounting the transformation of his consciousness from "cold warrior" to anti-war activist, Daniel Ellsberg (2002: 213ff.) recalls his first encounter with the moral tactics of civil disobedience. The rational choice model and the strategic decision-making which had defined Ellsberg's world view, as well as his career up to that point was fundamentally challenged. He writes, "I found myself hearing a surprisingly coherent doctrine and a relevant body of experience supporting it, all new to me. It was intellectually challenging, plausible, a new way of understanding problems and possibilities. Apparently there was an arithmetic of power you could do without a zero, at least without the starting point familiar to me. Yet if it did without an 'enemy' and the threat of violence, it didn't forgo the notions of adversarial conflict, opposition, struggle, resistance, and moral judgement." Prior to this encounter, the concept of "enemy" had defined Ellsberg's life and work.
13. Young (2001: 294) discusses the issue of subjectivity and subjection with examples from Albert Camus' novels.
14. The Algerian in this dialogue was none other than Saadi Yacef, the FLN leader responsible for its bomb squads. Yacef became famous to Western audiences when he played himself in Gillo Pontecorvo's extremely powerful and successful film *The Battle of Algiers* (1965), a film which he also co-produced. This film, which won many prizes and was banned in France for years after the war, was an important medium in creating empathy for the Algerian side in this struggle. It moved audiences throughout Western Europe and the United States, especially during the years of activism around 1968. It makes interesting viewing even today.
15. While this audience may be diverse and multiple, there may be some more general underlying codes. Ashis Nandy (1983: 72) explores the interplay between "western" and "eastern" cultures, which colonialism brought about. He writes "colonialism replaced the normal ethnocentric stereotype of the inscrutable Oriental by the pathological stereotype of the strange, primal but predictable Oriental – religious but superstitious, clever but devious, chaotically violent but effeminately cowardly

Simultaneously, colonialism created a domain of discourse where the standard mode of transgressing such stereotypes was to reverse them: superstitious but spiritual, uneducated but wise, womanly but pacific." This helps explain the specific content of the "strategic arsenal" used by leaders in anti-colonial movements and the tactics of the movements as a whole. They played on these stereotypes. It also helps us understand the so-called counter-images promoted by sympathetic movements in the home countries. Ho Chi Minh was a poster figure in the American anti-war movement. The images portrayed were just those of this "spiritual, uneducated but wise" Oriental, who had turned militant in a non-chaotic, non-(Western) masculine, way. The noble savage became the noble warrior, fitting the needs of Western radicals for an alternative cultural model. The same can be said in relation to Africa and the appeal of its national liberation movements. Reception of *The Battle of Algiers*, mentioned earlier, would prove an interesting study in this regard. While the intention may well have been to criticize colonialism and especially the French military, the film is ambiguous in its portrayal of the central "para" officer, whose hard, military logic leads to victory in that particular battle, even as the rebels eventually win the war.

16. Young (2001: 323) finds the roots of Gandhi's innovation in the Chartists' combination of physical and moral force. His discussion (2001: 325ff.) of Gandhi's conscious use of fashion to challenge and resist colonial cultural forms is illuminating. He writes, "this performative, hybrid mode was the secret of his popularity, of how he achieved the active and enthusiastic support not only of the Indian Hindu bourgeois elite, but also of the vast majority of the Hindu peasantry with whom he publicly identified – a peasantry whom no other politician or political party had succeeded in mobilizing effectively at a national level" (2001: 346). On the role of performance in Gandhi's tactics there is no better example than his famous Salt March. Through a series of quotations from various sources, Nandy (1983: 105–6) offers this compilation: "the Salt March makes its point through richly tragi-comic incidents . . . Gandhi marches for twenty-four days from his *ashram* in Ahmedabad to Dandi, 241 miles distant on the seashore, there to pick up salt in defiance of the Salt Laws imposed with crushing effect on the Indian peasant by the British Raj . . . The image of Gandhi marching in a loin-cloth to the seashore with a motley band of seventy-eight workers set on picking up a pinch of salt is deceptively anachronistic, even in 1930. The march was to last sufficient time for the eyes of India and the world to be riveted on the frail old man of sixty-one plodding on under a merciless March sun . . ." "On the Salt March he fully entered the world of the newsreel and documentary. Henceforth we have many glimpses of him flickering in black and white, a brisk, mobile figure, with odd but illuminating moments of likeness to Charlie Chaplin" (Ashe). As Gandhi marched, behind him "the administration was silently crumbling as three hundred and ninety village headmen resigned their posts" (Ashe). "When they reached Dandi they camped for seven days . . . On 6 April Gandhi rose at dawn, took his bath in the sea, and then walked over to the natural salt deposits. Photographers at the ready, he picked up a treasonable pinch

of salt and handed it to a person standing at his side. Sarojini Naidu cried out, 'Hail deliverer!' and then he went back to his work. The news flashed round the world and within days India was in turmoil; millions were preparing salt in every corner of the land . . . Like automata, the British administration responded with blind and incoherent action of extreme violence . . . Between 60,000 and 100,000 non-violent resistors went to jail" (Nandy 1983: 106).

17. The issue of intention versus reception is vital here. Emma Tarlo (1996: 62ff.) analyzes the difference in relation to Gandhi's choice of clothing as part of the performance of opposition. Gandhi was aware of the fact that he might be misunderstood and thus announced his intentions whenever he dramatically changed clothing styles. He understood clothing as a form of communication, whose meaning could be misinterpreted. In this understanding, clothes were exemplary, "an outward expression of the moral integrity of the wearer – an expression of truth" (Tarlo 1996: 82). Gandhi's choice of the *dhoti*, or loin-cloth as the media insisted on calling it, which Tarlo extensively analyzes, was meant to express the truth of the situation of the Indian poor, as well as his own integrity. This had to be explained, especially since the first reactions, both inside India and in Great Britain, were varied, but almost universally hostile. This conscious choice of clothing reflects also a tension between the expressive/exemplary and the strategic. While the former is not concerned with effects, the latter is. Gandhi's choice of clothing was meant to be both: to express moral integrity and to challenge British rule through offering an alternative mode of being. His invention of the so-called "Ghandi cap" is an example of the tension between intention and desired effect. After documenting Gandhi's own explanation of how he came upon the exact style of headgear for the new Indian man, Tarlo (1996: 83) writes, "although it is clear that Gandhi was deliberately searching for a suitable national cap, [his choice] suggests he was not fully aware of how important a symbol of opposition to the British his invention would become. His primary motive was to invent a form of pan-Indian headgear which anyone could afford and wear." The violent reaction of British authorities, however, increased the symbolic value of the cap. Gandhi was able to play on the ambiguity of a piece of clothing which now became a symbol of opposition. He could make the reactions of British authorities, to an "innocent piece of cloth," a "beautiful, light, inoffensive garment, valued for its practicality" (cited in Tarlo 1996: 85) seem ridiculous, at the same time as he promoted its political usage.

18. Here one might draw upon the phenomenological perspective as laid out by Alfred Schutz in distinguishing cosociates and contemporaries.

19. Klein (2001: 311ff.) offers a brief history of the origins of Reclaim the Streets, a central network actor in contemporary protest. On her account, the key event in the emergence of this network was a new British law, the Criminal Justice Act of 1994, which had the unintended effect of uniting political and non-political youth subcultures around the notion of defending public space. From the point of view of these groups, public thoroughfares were now "occupied territories" which needed to be reclaimed. Streets were thus made into contested spaces. In the Gothenburg protests, the network widened its scope to become "reclaim the city."

20. Ignatieff (1999: 11) points out the moral ambiguity of these televised images: "On the one hand television has contributed to the breakdown of the barriers of citizenship, religion, race, and geography that once divided our moral space into those we were responsible for and those who were beyond our ken. On the other hand, it made us voyeurs of the suffering of others, tourists amid their landscapes of anguish. It brings us face-to-face with their fate, while obscuring the distances – social, economic, moral – that lie between us." Susan Sontag (2003) offers another view of the role of televsion and of images generally in affecting emotion. In a critical reflection on her own work *On Photography* (1977), she writes "images shown on television are by definition images of which, sooner or later, one tires. What looks like callousness has its origin in the instability of attention that television is organized to arouse and to satiate by its surfeit of images. Image-glut keeps attention light, mobile, relatively indifferent to content. Image-flow precludes a privileged image" (2003: 105–6). In her view, the compassion which may be aroused by such images is fleeting and unstable. If this emotional response is to have more powerful effect it must be translated into action. Even when moved to compassion, "if one feels that there is nothing 'we' can do – but who is that 'we'? – and nothing 'they' can do either – and who are 'they'? – then one starts to get bored, cynical, apathetic" (2003: 101). It is here that a movement is essential. But what starts the movement?

21. Philip Smith (2000) perceptively analyzes Martin Luther King from the point of view of a theory of charisma. He points out the role of narrative reframing in explaining the success and failure of mobilization.

22. Demonstrations are usually collective public events, but they can also be individual and private, such as fasting and hunger strikes. Young (2002: 325) points out that one of the innovations of Gandhi's tactics was to transgress taken-for-granted borders, such as those between public and private domains.

23. The well-documented fragmentation of media audiences in contemporary society makes the reception of mediated performances all the more difficult to control and predict. As Tarlo (1996: 99ff.) reveals, even Gandhi had difficulty controlling the interpretations of his own activists regarding the politics of clothing in their movement. This also points to a central and as yet unresolved issue: what are the criteria for a successful movement performance? On the one hand, movements vary in their aims and their tactics and, especially regarding loose coalitions, may even have contradictory aims. Judging their "success" is thus a complex and complicated issue, which surely must be contextualized.

References

Alexander, Jeffrey. 2002. "The Social Construction of Moral Universals." *European Journal of Social Theory* 5, 1: 5–85.
    (2004). "From the Depths of Despair: Performance and Counter-Performance on September 11." *Sociological Theory* 21, 1: 88–105.
Amin, Shahid. 1995. *Event, Metaphor, Memory.* Berkeley: University of California Press.

Berezin, Mabel. 2001. "Emotions and Political Identity: Mobilizing Affection for the Polity," in Jeff Goodwin, James M. Jasper, and Francesca Polletta, eds., *Passionate Politics*. Chicago: University of Chicago Press.

Bhabha, Homi. 1986. "Foreword: Remembering Fanon," in Franz Fanon, *The Wretched of the Earth*. New York: Grove Press.

Brown, Richard. 1977. *A Poetic for Sociology*. Cambridge: Cambridge University Press.

Cockburn, Alexander, Jeffrey St. Clair, and Allan Sekula. 2000. *5 Days That Shook the World*. London: Verso.

Collins, Randall. 2001. "Social Movements and the Focus of Emotional Attention," in Jeff Goodwin, James M. Jasper, and Francesca Polletta, eds., *Passionate Politics*. Chicago: University of Chicago Press.

Della Porta, Donatella and Mario Diani. 1999. *Social Movements*. Oxford: Blackwell.

Diani, Mario. 1995. *Green Networks*. Edinburgh: Edinburgh University Press.

Duiker, William J. 2000. *Ho Chi Minh*. New York: Hyperion.

Ellsberg, Daniel. 2002. *Secrets: A Memoir of Vietnam and the Pentagon Papers*. New York: Viking.

Eyerman, Ron. 2002a. *Cultural Trauma*. New York: Cambridge University Press.

2002b. "Music in Movement: Cultural Politics and Old and New Social Movements," *Qualitative Sociology* 25, 3: 443–58.

Eyerman, Ron and Andrew Jamison. 1991. *Social Movements: A Cognitive Approach*. Cambridge: Polity Press.

1988. *Music and Social Movements*. Cambridge: Cambridge University Press.

Fanon, Franz. 1968. *The Wretched of the Earth*. New York: Grove Press.

1986. *Black Skin, White Masks*. London: Pluto Press.

Gerhards, Jurgen and Dieter Rucht. 1992. "Mesomobilization: Organizing and Framing in Two Protest Campaigns in West Germany," *American Journal of Sociology* 98: 555–95.

Goffman, Erving. 1971. *The Presentation of Self in Everyday Life*. New York: Doubleday.

Goodwin, Jeff, James M. Jasper and Francesca Polletta, eds. 2001. *Passionate Politics*. Chicago: University of Chicago Press.

Gould, Roger. 1991. "Multiple Networks and Mobilization in the Paris Commune, 1871," *American Sociological Review* 56: 716–29.

Habermas, Jürgen. 1989. *The Structural Transformation of the Public Sphere*. Cambridge: Polity Press.

Hetherington, Kevin. 1998. *Expressions of Identity*. London: Sage.

Horne, Allistair. 2002. *A Savage War of Peace*. London: Pan Books.

Ignatieff, Michael. 1999. *The Warrior's Honor*. London: Vintage.

Jasper, James M. 1997. *The Art of Moral Protest*. Chicago: University of Chicago Press.

Klandermans, Bert. 1988. "The Formation of Mobilization Consensus," in B. Klandermans, H. Kriesi, and S. Tarrow, eds., *From Structure to Action*. Greenwich: JA Press.

Klandermans, B. and S. Tarrow. 1988. "Mobilization into Social Movements," in B. Klandermans, H. Kriesi, and S. Tarrow, eds., *From Structure to Action*. Greenwich: JAI Press.

Klein, Naomi. 2001. *No Logo*. London: Flamingo.

Mailer, Norman. 1968. *The Armies of the Night*. Harmondsworth: Penguin.

McAdam, Doug, John McCarthy and Meyer Zald. 1988. "Social Movements," in N. Smelser, ed., *Handbook for Sociology*. Newbury Park: Sage.

McAdam, Doug, Sidney Tarrow, and Charles Tilly. 2001. *Contentious Politics*. New York: Cambridge University Press.

Mishal, Saul and Avraham Sela. 2000. *The Palestinian Hamas*. New York: Columbia University Press.

Nandy, Ashis. 1983. *The Intimate Enemy*. Delhi: Oxford University Press.

Polletta, Francesca. 1999. "Free Spaces in Collective Action," *Theory and Society* 28: 1–38.

Ricoeur, Paul. 1978. *The Rule of Metaphor: Multi-disciplinary Studies of the Creation of Meaning in Language*. London: Routledge.

Sartre, Jean Paul. 1968. "Preface," in Franz Fanon, *The Wretched of the Earth*. New York: Grove Press.

Schechner, Richard. 1985. *Between Theater and Anthropology*. Philadelphia: University of Pennsylvania Press.

Smith, Philip. 2000. "Culture and Charisma: Outline of a Theory," *Acta Sociologica* 43: 101–11.

Somers, Margaret. 1994. "The Narrative Constitution of Identity: A Relational and Network Approach," *Theory and Society* 23, 5: 605–49.

Sontag, Susan. 2003. *Regarding the Pain of Others*. New York: Farrar, Straus, and Giroux.

Snow, David and Robert Benford. 1988. "Ideology, Frame Resonance, and Participant Mobilization," pp. 197–218 in B. Klandermans, H. Kriesi, and S. Tarrow (eds.), *From Structure to Action*. Greenwich: Jai Press.

Sorum, Paul. 1977. *Intellectuals and Decolonialization in France*. Chapel Hill: University of North Carolina Press.

Talbott, John. 1980. *The War Without Name*. London: Faber and Faber.

Tarlo, Emma. 1996. *Clothing Matters*. London: Hurst and Company.

Tilly, Charles. 2003. *Collective Violence*. New York: Cambridge University Press.

Vetlesen, Arne Johan. 1994. *Perception, Empathy, and Judgement*. Pennsylvania: Pennsylvania State University Press.

Wennerhag, Magnus. 2002. "Globalism and National Sovereignty in the Globalization Movement," unpublished manuscript University of Lund.

White, Hayden. 1978. *Tropics of Discourse*. Baltimore: Johns Hopkins University Press.

Young, Robert. 2001. *Postcolonialism*. Oxford: Blackwell.

7

Politics as theatre: an alternative view of the rationalities of power

David E. Apter

And what is the aim of that stately and marvelous creature, tragic drama? Is it her endeavor and ambition, in your opinion, merely to gratify the spectators; or, if there be anything pleasant and charming, but evil, to struggle against uttering it, but to declaim and sing anything that is unwelcome but beneficial, whether they like it or not?   Plato, *The Gorgias*

Life is not determined by consciousness but consciousness by life.
                                                     Marx, *The German Ideology*

Locating the subject

Plato warned against the beguiling qualities of drama. If he was right then Marx was at least half wrong. Consciousness may be determined by life, but life is also determined by consciousness. This essay, a preliminary effort to analyze politics as theatre, emphasizes the second part of Marx's statement. The concern here is with the way theatrical aspects of politics shape consciousness. That is, how they become in effect lifelike, if not as pure representation then something else – display, mystique, mimetics, code, metaphor, symbolic condensation, manipulation – to suggest only a few of the attributes of all the world as a stage. This suggests a twofold purpose: to identify and examine significant aspects of the more general relationship between political discourse and political power, something not normally much dealt with within the framework of conventional political analysis. By the same token, we want to avoid some of the confusion associated with certain very commonly used concepts like political culture and ideology that, undeniably useful in the past, now have too many meanings (see for example, Eagleton 1991). However, the intent here is not as ambitious as this might appear. The present approach is intended to complement, not replace more conventional forms of political analysis. It is rather to add a dimension to the discussion of what remains at best a residual concern. Of particular interest is how and why public displays of drama, whether from above or below, generate power and particularly that form of power we can call consciousness. In pursuing this end it will be necessary to offer certain concepts here considered relevant for the empirical analysis of such matters.

For scholars who favor quantitative, institutional, and similar approaches in the name of science, this may go against the grain. Although political studies appear to have become more ecumenical in recent years, if anything the gulf between those who favor "science" over "discourse" has widened. Some, of course, would have it both ways (e.g. Laitin 2003).[1] But there is nothing unscientific in examining the significance of political theatre in terms of its potentiality for generating political power. We are not dealing with a rational kernel versus some mystical shell. In any case rationality may take on some strange guises.[2]

Although there is a large literature germane to the theatrical side of politics and the ways in which it produces political power, most of it is only indirectly related to political theatre as such. Moreover, what interest there is in such matters derives its inspiration from many fields and traditions, so much so that themes and emphases overlap and terms are used differently. Which makes for considerable analytical confusion. Also, very different cultural traditions are involved. French structuralist and post-structuralist theorists, for example, stress discourse, as in the work of such widely different figures as Barthes in literature, Foucault in social philosophy, or Ricoeur in philosophy. Americans tend to be more empirical even when the emphasis is interpretive. For example, an anthropologist like Clifford Geertz combines fieldwork on the "theatre state" with a more general concern with how events come to constitute a social text.[3] This, although a particularly useful point of departure, also raises as many questions as it answers. A construct like "social text," insofar as it emphasizes narrativized activities, can invoke ingredients from a virtual Who's Who of scholars from different disciplines all of whom differ strikingly from one another in their approaches although sharing as a common denominator a concern with interpretation as power.[4] For some, such power is constructed by means of tropes, metaphor, and metonymy, as in Kenneth Burke. For others, it involves territorialization, affiliation, and semiotic space, as in the work of Lefebvre. For still others, like Roland Barthes, it is the mythic dimension of narrative. As for political consequences, the more general concern is how textualization generates what Pierre Bourdieu refers to as symbolic capital, and particularly its subversive role as in Michel Foucault's inversionary discourse.[5]

All these thinkers, and many more, are in one fashion or another concerned with the interpretive dimension of power but few focus specifically on the role played by political theatre let alone the ways in which the latter links up to other and more recognized aspects of political structure and behavior. By focusing on political theatre, however, one can provide a particular emphasis to the more general question of how meanings form, and once formed how they register in some collective manner and result in interpretive action. Of course, to try and answer these and similar questions more fully would require far more space than is available. Here we can do no more than merely hint at some of the answers.

However arbitrary as it may appear, the way to begin is by placing "social text" at one end of a continuum and political power at the other end. Interpretive action is what connects the two. By interpretive action is meant that action deriving from the way people come to understand events and circumstances with a view to doing something about them. Which suggests that to relate these concerns to power itself, the need is to tighten the fit between structure, meaning, and consciousness; the self and the significance of reflexive knowledge; and the consequence of the latter for social action. On the face of it, these matters should certainly be of direct concern to political theorists,[6] and not just the occasional dialectician (Freitas 1986).

It is with these considerations in mind that we can turn to three levels of analysis incorporated in the present discussion. The first and most general is a pragmatic phenomenology that serves as a framework of how social life becomes consciousness by a process of interpretation – what textualization really means. "Pragmatic" as used here refers to the evocative power of events and activities seen from the point of view of the actors, including events that are recognized as politically significant not least of all as they are represented in gladiatorial combat between protagonists. Hence it is the intentionalities of action that result in interpretive repertoires relevant to the crafting of political power. Pragmatic phenomenology is more inclusive than what Jeffrey Alexander (2002) has called cultural pragmatics, the former engaging with "performance" at the level of discourse, language, narrative, text.[7]

The second level of analysis follows from the first. It is an emphasis on discourse. This requires the examination of interpretation itself, how meaning is created in the event. Political discourse becomes relevant as the means whereby interpretive "raw materials" are collectivized in the form of master narratives and transcribed as texts.

Finally, the two levels come together in a third, the politics of theatre, when actor-agents, producers, stage managers, corps de ballets, and conductors craft discourse as drama, transform public space into a stage, and unfold the script by intersecting the fanciful and the real, the first as story, the second as logic.[8] It is this last which is the central focus of the present discussion.

On political theatre

As for political theatre itself, it will have its greatest impact where these three levels are all at work in ways that invoke what used to be called "deep structures," i.e. those incorporating fundamental and mythic themes. It can express these in many different ways, mordant, sardonic, cynical, utopian, and simply entertaining. Sometimes theatrical strategies suggest theories such as Sorel's myth of the "general strike," surely a striking example of political theatre. Or it can involve sheer sentimentality, as in Pierre Nora's invocation of history as dramatistic metonymies and metaphoric moments, i.e. political memory as political drama that becomes iconographic for others. Crane Brinton, Mona Ozouf, François Furet, all in their separate ways, show how the French Revolution served as a theatrical revolutionary topos, the mother of all politically theatrical occasions (see, in particular, Ozouf 1976). As for parodic aspects – one thinks here of Brecht or Debord, but also street theatre, the theatre of the absurd, carnival, or happenings such as those put on by members of the Fluxus movement or the Situationist International (e.g. Ladurie 1979; Debord 1987; Knabb 1984; Semiotext 1982).

Political theatre, or better, politics as theatre is of course about performance in a public space. But the term public space is used differently from that of Habermas. His emphasizes its neutrality. With political theatre public space is anything but neutral. Rather it constitutes a semiotic ground that contributes to the authority, and on occasion the sanctity, of performance itself as, for example, on so many occasions in the case of the vast space, Tiananmen Square, or Red Square for that matter, or any of the other grandiose spaces (Albert Speer's great amphitheatre at Nuremberg where Hitler performed). But it can also be the Oval Office or 10 Downing Street. Size itself does not matter. For no matter how spectacular the event, or well woven the drama, political theatre also involves miniaturization, symbolic condensation and intensification, like the miniaturized versions of churches writ small in Renaissance paintings of the saints. Such symbolic condensation and intensification and the iconographic elements so incorporated, help to sacralize authority, even in its most secular forms.

Theatrical episodes may include demonology, witch-hunts, and staged trials (one thinks here of the Dreyfus case in Paris, the Reichstag trial, the Moscow trials, or the dunce cap victims of the Cultural Revolution), in which the state pursues acts of apostasy. Such trials, miscarriages of justice to be sure, contribute to building up the symbolic power of the state in legal-moral terms. Indeed, it is a demonstration that, however high the principle of rights, they depend on the grace of the state. And of course it is also the case that those on trial can turn tables and put the state on trial (as did Bukharin in the Moscow trials, or in court room antics of terrorists who accuse and judge the judges). Indeed, similarities between theatre and trials go back as far as Aeschylus' *Eumenides*.

Masters of political theatre abound. From the storming of the Bastille to the tumbrels of the Jacobin period, the French Revolution provided a model for all subsequent radical movements, its uses of political theatre not lost on the purveyors of dramatic monumentality in Nazi Germany, fascist Italy, the Soviet Union, not to speak of more liberal left theatrical events, demonstrations, marches for peace, strikes etc.[9] Today the world is witness to more ecclesiastical expressions, including a fundamentalism that involves terror, hooded night fighters, reminiscent of the Ku Klux Klan – a phenomenon that would have expressed itself in more secular fashion if only socialist and Marxist alternatives had not more or less disappeared. Indeed, in the space these ideas have left today's political theatre becomes the way in which racial, ethnic, religious, and ideological "plays" are expressed in more or less spectacular events.

So considered, political theatre is used for integrating, unifying, and establishing singular loyalties on affiliational parochial grounds that claim universalization by means of a single hegemonic national jurisdiction – as for example in Iran where the "revolution" was pure theatre. In which case it expresses solidarities as polarization – cleavage becoming a politics of insiders against outsiders, the pure against the pariahs.

Whatever the purpose, it should go without saying that there is nothing innocent about politics as theatre whether generative of power, expressive or representative of it as a form of pantomime. What it has is instrumental and indeed manipulative instrumental intents. While it uses many of the same properties as theatre itself, which can of course be very "political" as for example in Brecht, insofar as it is a property of real power rather than its imaginative counterpart, it has consequences of its own. But theatre qua theatre can instruct us about theatre as politics. Shakespeare certainly got it right with his Williams, Richards, and Henrys, their intrigues, hatreds, and passions, their panoplies and displays of power, and the inevitability of these matters in terms of what goes on behind the scenes in political life. So too did Charlie Chaplin with his great dictator. But it is one thing to use the drama of politics for dramatic theatre. It is another to use drama as politics itself.

Where they most resemble each other is in their tropes and mechanisms, plot, script, performance, staging, and rules for making visible the tensed relationships of roles. For both, success will depend on whether a performance possesses mimetic magic. But success for political theatre also depends on converting the audience into the play itself. Of course the theatrical event can be vacuous or deep, vicious or inspired. Some political actors are essentially sideshow barkers like Ronald Reagan or George W. Bush, both of whom came to occupy centre stage by means of the relentless celebration of American exceptionalism. For others, like the great dictators and their putative descendants, theatre is a form of public terrorism and displays of armed might, while for religious fanatics sacerdotal fulminations from the pulpit as stage endow the exercise of power with moral force and religious obligation. And there is always the occasional Learean tragedy – dramas of hanging on to power.

Political theatre can be divided into two dominant forms, from above and represented by the state and from below in oppositional social and political movements. Both can represent self, class, or functional interest. Or the play itself may embody millennial, revolutionary, and revivalist goals, drawing legitimacy from wellsprings of support, or discontent or moral outrage with expressions of good and evil as the ultimate political divide. Then the drama creates a heightened moral tension between what is legitimate and what is reprehensible. Politics as theatre in this sense takes the form of dramatic personas engaging in gladiatorial conflict, the chief actors on the political stage serving as surrogates for the political entities they represent, from political parties to chosen representatives. Or they may stand for violent and subterranean acts, in which terrorism creates its own virtue, murder invoking some higher cause (as in the "theatrical" events of September 11, 2001). Between them most political theatre consists of high jousting with more than an occasional murder in the cathedral. Whatever its ingredients, in the final analysis political theatre is performance and its general objects are more or less the same, the taking, keeping, and exercise of political power (Apter 1992).

Politics as theatre then is a free-standing element in the creation of political power. This is particularly the case where issues are directly confrontational, the script polarizing, its sequence of scenes and plot expressing a logic of events whose effect is to raise interests to the level of principle. It is this last condition that gives political theatre practical mobilizing effects; the more "revealing" of perceived "truths" the better (especially when such "truths" are depictions of economic, social, and political conditions). It is the dramatistic possibility which constitutes a standard against which to measure and compare situations, its outer limit that defining power which enables political theatre to play a crucial role in precipitating and promoting disjunctive moments – revolution, social transformation, the redemptive occasion. On such occasions, all life is on stage and all politics display – the drama becoming "meaning-*full*."

The more able to interrupt the rhythm of the quotidian, and to punctuate time with events as "history," and the more able to retrieve these for dramatic reuse, the more political theatre interrogates the taken for granted, and the normal. And the more effective it is in doing so the more it disturbs the petty pace of life from day to day, rendering the ordinary problematical. By combining the mythic with the logical what is created is an interior vision of rationality.

Political theatre, like its more general counterpart, can be variously tragedy, melodrama, farce, romance, and comedy with elements of each incorporated in a single dramatic instance. It can be further divided into subtypes according to style and language. Much of it involves telling fairy tales. Whatever the form there is about it an element of the fantastic. If its structure mirrors life, either as it is or as it should be, the cues are readily recognizable. And, *pace*

Marx, much that might pass for tragedy in its first instance, becomes farce in its second.

As for settings virtually any kind of space can be made to serve: a court room, a war crimes tribunal, political party conventions, ceremonial occasions, voting, acceptance speeches, revolutionary marches, bombings and murders in public spaces, etc. Venue only needs to be somehow appropriate to the kind of "show" so occasioned. Similarly, venue can be created by event, a spectacular political murder, a suicide bombing, or when terrorists or war criminals on trial take the offensive by turning the court room into a surrogate for the state, and the judicial process into a struggle between good and evil. Hence, in a context of struggle such venues become locations for the performance of miracle plays that exorcise the bad for the sake of the good.

And a good deal of political theatre is comedy. Indeed parliaments and congresses, and not so distantly the White House, offer great venues for political psychodrama, the revelation of sexual lapses, aberrations, and deviations of politicians and leaders, the kind of high comedy that brings careers low (something which seems to be more common in the Anglo-Saxon world than others).[10]

Structurally, what constitute typical occasions for political drama are beginnings, a founding of a state, its transformation, or, conversely, its rejection (especially if the denouement includes a redemptive *Aufheben*). In this sense and no matter the specific events and circumstances, one finds a fairly standard story. The structure will include a point of departure, a suggested trajectory, difficulties to be overcome, a moral setting that separates good and evil, an enabling prescriptive path which, if followed, will allow obstacles to be overcome. There will be a pause in the trajectory, the interruption of accomplishment, a crisis, an episode or act portraying failure, or catastrophic danger, followed by a recounting of the realization as triumph, or failure as tragedy. The content of the form then means a more or less standard and formulaic political story line.

As for content it will vary not only according to circumstances but also contexts – that is contextual meanings. As already suggested, a good political theatrical performance will allow for personalization – any personalization but within specified protocols that endow the relationships between roles, leaders, and subordinates, and their personas, with wider signifying attributes. So too situation, staging, setting, not to speak of costumes, music, and other elements load the plot with immediately referential and understood signifiers, the whole reconstituting the public experiences. The more widely understood the protocols, the more effective the signifiers, the more powerful the force of the play in providing its own consensual validation. A "play" dealing with political struggle will, typically, recount and memorialize selected events from mythic history preferably in terms of golden moment, an initial struggle, accomplishment through suffering and hard work, then a rupture, a fall from grace, and an ensuing tragic condition (such as loss of the patrimony, subservience to and domination by strangers or outsiders, portrayal as suffering victims) as structural specification of highs and lows of terrain, grace, insiders and outsiders, egos and alters, followed by an accomplishing struggle leading to a transcendental inversion – the last becoming first, the slave becoming the master. So too the prototypical main protagonist, hero or anti-hero, will suffer jail, exile, torture, etc., whereby survival accrues net gains in wisdom. Then Odysseus-like, redeeming the lost patrimony, or Socrates-like, redeeming truths from the dross, comes the triumphal accomplishment, with heroic acts serving instructive ends, the mobilization of supporters. So the play's the thing, a product of heroic inspiration – the hero, ostensibly at least, not for him or herself, but for party, state, or movement, etc. (Apter and Saich 1994). It is in the particularity of the script that the roles of the individual actors, the circumstances, and conditions of their relationships are laid down, but it is when the message so incorporated as plot establishes wider structural revelation that the events themselves are totalizing.

Whatever the form, if political theatre depends on the quality of its dramatic performances so too it requires an appropriately expressive narrative – narrative as plot as well as performance – framed within a semiotically endowed public space. Discourse, narrative, logic, performance, semiotic space – these are all essential ingredients for transforming bystanders into participants, spectators into audience, thereby incorporating the audience into the drama itself. By means of caricature, parody, or more tragic dramatic portrayals, political leaders are enabled to transform incipient alternatives into preferred modes of action, using political theatre to round up and collectivize individuals and groups by converting otherwise random or singular views into a more common understanding. Public space so defined condenses and intensifies the symbolic density of what is politically portrayed. It is not just in the acting out of a radical persuasion that political theatre serves as both a guide to action and an action itself.

This by no means suggests that political theatre is all of a piece. The characteristics described so far do not fall into clearly defined sets. In addition to these more sober considerations political theatre includes aspects of sheer entertainment and especially where governments try to keep the citizenry from dwelling on the negative aspects of their social life. The bulk of what passes for political theatre is not much different from advertising. And from below much of it can pass as more or less divertive street theatre as well as shocking and subversive spectaculars. If the first aims at passive support, the second requires a mobilization of the contrary, a proposed solidarity around rigoristic and more or less disciplined political goals.

Seen in this light, as artful expression, as a mode of narrative that constructs or reconstructs reality, political theatre is a ubiquitous feature of politics – any politics. It engages virtually all politicians, whatever their stripe and whatever their role, elected or hereditary, self-appointed or anointed. Virtually every political figure is acutely aware of being on stage. It is also the case that the socially discursive opportunity requires a latent political moment, an audience-in-waiting.

Performance

Even with a good script, one with tensile structure, a great deal will depend on the sheer quality of the performance by the actors. If the acting is poor, no matter how attractive the form or the subject matter, the "play" is not likely to accomplish its purpose. Here a good deal depends not only on the talents and abilities of the politician/actor, but an ability to mobilize the power of voice, gesture, as well as idea.

But not any idea – in politics ideas are the raw material drawn from the everyday experiences of social life. A good political actor will pick them up and transform what everyone knows into something he or she did not quite know in the same way before. Such an actor will create plots whose subject may be present events or the past and endow them with the prescience of the actor's own encounters. Sometimes, an event in a key actor's life will embody events that have taken place over many years, telescoping an entire social experience into one symbolic event giving it an exceptional degree of vitality as cultural representation – a way of reframing meaning itself. Stage in this sense may itself be part of the event.[11] The script may in effect write itself as the actors play their individual roles.[12]

This applies to a variety of political actors whether democratic, cosmocratic, "phallocratic," or charismatic. Whatever their role, they must possess some ability to expropriate other people's business, and make it their own. In this sense political actors are not simply actors but agents, "playwrights" who place themselves at the center of the play. They select the events to serve as dramatistic signifiers, mobilizing rhetoric in ways that radiate outward, embracing and capturing the audience. Under such circumstances if it is true that political theatre is only one factor in the formation of power, insofar as it helps to establish communities, that is discourse communities, it sets them apart from others. The most extreme versions of such communities privilege themselves in regard to truth. So the play itself embodies its own standards, its own culture, in which actor-agents serve as prosecutor, judge, and lord high executioner. Such a collective transcendence is both a form of individual therapy and a form of, *pace* Bourdieu, symbolic capital.

When we say that performance counts for a great deal what we mean is individual acting ability in terms of roles. Performance is measured by the quality of representation including expression, articulation, style, presence, and a sense of disciplined deployment of the spectacular. These help to make performance *performative*, the action-consequence counting for the audience (Austin 1980). In these terms performance endows even quite normal political acts with emotion and meaning. Of course other factors are at play, such as artistic and literary deftness. There is also the sheer power of the visual, the weight or weightlessness of words, written and spoken, in all of which the actor's creative impulses are manifested. It is performance that, when at its best, enables a politics as theatre to endow a particular space with a certain clarity, miniaturizing, focusing, concentrating and intensifying public attention, by magnifying a symbolic register. Political theatre then becomes a way of defining and communicating preferred and alternative political interpretations, a twofold process in which conventional knowledge may be emptied of content but ritually reinforced, and/or replaced by new referential and more gripping signs, symbols, and signals.

This suggests that there might be a premium on certain kinds of political theatre rather than others. It would exclude, for example, cheap drama of a kind hardly likely to generate symbolic capital. It would downplay the kind of political theatre that simply recites, recapitulates, regurgitates, and recycles accepted and ritualistic shibboleths. However, a good deal if not most contemporary political theatre is "theatrical" in just this sense, i.e. more spectacle and performance than substance – political "carnival." It allows tensions to explode harmlessly. One might even argue that most political elections are more a matter of cathartic mobilization than their ostensible purposes, to select among candidates for office. Political carnival makes a charade of participatory involvement, rendering public action celebratory and therefore harmless (Martin 2001). Political theatre in this sense is a commonplace of politics while the real business of politics goes on elsewhere, behind the scenes as it were. In this respect, staging, performance, presentation, script, spectacle, and sheer entertainment are everything, and substance virtually nothing, as perhaps in the now ritual requirement of so-called American presidential debates. Content is virtually nil. Performance is rated by commentators and the press in much the same manner as a figure skating competition (Clymer 2001).

However, where the rules of the game are called into question and confrontation takes center stage content comes to matter, both as truths and consequences. And it is here that one finds opportunities for cosmocratic agents, politicians who write their own scripts and play in their own plays. Indeed, the classic cosmocratic figures, secular or sacral, create texts blown up to virtually biblical proportions. Surrounded by cadres of "intellectuals," pored over by followers, the words appear ravishing, magical, offering a logic based on myth and a myth based on logic. In the past the most disjunctive and theatrical political events involved ideologies of nationalism, socialism, or other doctrinal alternatives.

Today the emphasis is on ethnic and religious or sectarian forms of nationalism and identity. Incorporated into narratives and texts, the language itself is revelatory. Reconstructed in the form of a drama engaging in mytho-logical exercises, political theatre in this sense can lay claim to embodied truths that become more true the more they transcend ordinary reason, to become at the extreme the justification for self-immolation and martyrdom. To be sure, sooner or later more bread and butter issues will return. But often it is tragically later rather than sooner. For when politics is subordinate to higher moral purposes the ensuing politics of extremism is likely to feed on itself in self-perpetuating ways.

To summarize the discussion so far, required are highly qualified performances in terms both of the acting and the character of the actors. Also necessary is deftness in emphasizing and selecting the content of the speaking lines. The play itself is text as action and expression – one might speak here of text-acts rather than speech-acts. Political theatre, as distinguished from theatre itself, is not mimetic of the world around it but an aspect of the world itself.

Agency

In political discourse generally the main way in which the text is narrated is by means of agents acting as interpreters, especially when they constitute chosen spokesmen endowed with a special insight or interpretive gifts – a quality that at the extreme might be called the oracular vision. As storytellers and mythmakers such oracular agents require appropriately theatrical sites, expressing themselves in a context publicly witnessed and staged with those participating being the recipients of now more formally formed dramatistic sequences, the effect of which is to endow events with symbolic significance.

Agents are those actors who on a stage take on larger-than-life proportions while at the same time condensing, miniaturizing, and personalizing both the role and the issues for which the role stands. As already indicated, quite often the script will include a recounting of their own lives, vicissitudes, and triumphs, these becoming metaphoric for those of others. Agency in this sense embodies "abstract personalism"; the more abstract the more connected to power, the more personal, the more the agent is insinuated in the interpretive lexicon of the community. It is on such actor-agents that the structure of the narrative depends. They "work" the play or script, and increase the effectiveness of leading and supporting roles. They stand for the relevant political coteries who, themselves both actors and manipulators of texts, can on necessary occasions serve as stand-ins and surrogates for the agent. They not only reinforce the text, plot, play itself, but by their actions and commentaries, they so interiorize that those who are in the audience not only become participants, but are drawn into a world that appears to be of their own making and with all their own conflicts, tensions, competition, jockeying for power. Hence politics as theatre is invariably a play within a play, in which the agent becomes the center of a kind of Tantric circle. We have already suggested that not any actor-agents will do but only those most effective as public performers exceptionally able in combining experiences and events using scripts and staging based on narrative interpretation, the whole susceptible to symbolic condensation. But also required for the effect to work is a certain aura or magic, players and audience forming a charmed circle. Not only will the identification between chief actors and their audiences become convincing, but, as one might see in a Peron, an Nkrumah, a Nelson Mandela (and although in a somewhat different way, an Arafat or a Bin Laden), the actor-agent seeks messianic power in the can(n)on's mouth. Playing the lead in their own plays, acting out their own political stories, they offer their own to the common experience and by doing so contribute a value-adding interpretive component. Such agents are in this sense scriptwriters as political leaders and political leaders as scriptwriters. Performer-storytellers, such agents position themselves on that "stage" that best represents the eye of history.

Especially in a populist age, it becomes easier rather than more difficult for agents to serve as protagonists in their own stories, becoming self-anointed representatives of a people, in whole or part as the case might be. In this context if politics is theatre, protagonists are in play, and agents are personas. The recounted life becomes the frame for a heroic reconstitution of the common experience, providing the agent with both authenticity and wisdom. So too it becomes possible to incorporate specific originating circumstances, birth and childhood, early trials and tribulations, which, when sufficiently rehearsed, show how everyone can recapitulate his or her own personal triumphs, rising above difficult occasions, beating the odds, overcoming obstacles, converting negative circumstances into transcending, and in some cases transcendental accomplishments. Thus the agent's journey, in defining larger goals, also provides a logic of accomplishment, transforming barriers and obstacles. So too the play itself invokes a hortatory impulse; what originates in suffering will produce determination while tribulation stiffens commitment. No matter how many failures or personal crises, or defining moral moments, successful resolution will lead to new possibilities and projects yet to be realized. Agency, as abstract personalism, includes an exilic form of the eternal return, the restored self as overcoming hero. Indeed, the "Odysseus factor" applies to a good many dramatistic political leaders – Lenin in Switzerland, Kwame Nkrumah in exile in hostile and strange lands, both coming back to take the patrimony, or Mao Zedong who suffered internal exile twice, once as a young man and once from the Communist Party.[13] Mandela was exiled to Robben Island. So too with so many others who, suffering downs, were never out, and who, by offering their own experiences as national sagas and bitterly learned wisdom, insisted that their doctrinal beliefs would serve as solutions that transcend circumstances. Indeed, a Lenin, a Mao, or a Mandela in their very different ways not only re-enacted the parable of Odysseus, returning to claim the expropriated patrimony, but also embodied a kind of Socratic power, a control of a higher logic from which could be derived insightful truths. Politics as theatre in this sense consists of miracle plays.

In many such instances the performers are renamed. That is, they change their names as they transform their personas, taking a *nom de guerre*, a *nom de plume*, or some underground designation. The change of name in a context of performance places the actor within the narrative of events. One thereby takes possession of venue itself, naming becoming self-regarding while standing for, variously, state or anti-state. Political figures so reconfigured become surrogates for bigger things. What such renaming accomplishes is a reciprocal conveyance of self by the actor to the audience and by the audience to the actor. Naming is particularly relevant in confrontational/theatrical events that take on the proportions of disjunctive moments. It is part of the same alchemy, whereby what otherwise might be singular events, when drawn from and endowed by memory, provide the materials for ready-made logical projections. Naming is in this sense a celebration of accomplishment in advance of the event; an amplification effect – a step-up function that increases the effect of the play itself.

And if the play's the thing, public theatre in this sense provides a certain spontaneity as well as mimetics, the renamed actor as improviser departing from the prepared script, the rehearsed role. Generally speaking, the more persuasive the performance, the more attractive the script, the more focused the role, the more the public stage affirms the realities for which it stands. Realities that are not so obvious but may represent, variously: alterity and difference, orthodoxy and heterodoxy, who to be for or against, a structure of polarities (Taussig 1993).

Spectacle

Which brings us to the significance of spectacle in and of itself. The spectacular is a form of captivation. It can be during a solemn occasion, a state funeral, surrender in a war, or some powerful and ritual occasion invoking the majesty, power, the authority of the state in a state funeral (as parodied in the description of the "great event" and the ludicrous planning of what was to be the defining moment of glory of the Austro-Hungarian Empire just as it was about to be destroyed, in Robert Musil's *The Man Without Qualities*).

Whatever the form, spectacle is the compelling aspect of political theatre in terms of aesthetics. It gives life to the narrative and textual aspects of political theatre. It is in itself a translation of words and symbols into performatives capable of triggering political actions. Spectacle includes settings. It calls upon such arts as location, finding pulpits on mountain tops, judges' chambers and oval offices, caves and squares. It provides secular landscapes with ecclesiastical endowments and ecclesiastical ones with secular functions (Geertz 1980). It makes possible visible coteries and enables chief actors and main political figures to place themselves at the center of a pantheon, to surround themselves with retainers and followers, not to speak of saints and sinners who play their roles in accord with some prior and understood choreography. So too with contributing paraphernalia, insignia, the wearing of a chasuble, parodic whiskers (as with Yasir Arafat) or a sash of high office, a crown, a funny hat, each bit converted each into an appropriate feature of a more overall ritual representation of power in the public realm. Spectacle recasts already familiar situations and episodes as display complete with appropriate setting, decor, staging, not to speak of relevant arts, paintings, drawings, insignia on walls of sanctuaries, sacred fabrics, music, drumming, etc. Parades, speeches, paraphernalia such as uniforms and medals, prancing horses, tanks and guns, public trials, humiliations, assassinations, all such presentations of self contribute to a "theatre of virility." Indeed, the last century has seen a bewildering array of supposed political saviors, men on horseback, imposing themselves as agents on a wildered citizenry pushed this way and that by the fanfare of dramatic openings and ending. Nor has sexual passion been lacking. There have been any number of thrusting, male, populist, cosmocrats cum political leaders who, drunk on presumed and past imperial glories, Roman Empires, Nordic tribes (or origins more generally), or casting themselves in the mold of crusaders, revolutionaries, seek the radical break, i.e. for one religion and against another, or for inversion, i.e. against colonialism, imperialism, capitalism. So agency can take form in set-piece theatrical roles, purifying redeemers, socialist, communist, or ayatollahs, or whatever, all of whom seek to establish their power by contriving a past and providing a logic and program for the future. The range is broad enough to include at one pole mystic political communion in a cause, and at the other the tinsel of an American political campaign, all show and little substance.

That sheer "show" counts for a lot is attested to by its universality. Take, for example, the surprising popularity even today of rituals redolent of the pomp and ceremony of late nineteenth- and twentieth-century imperialism, a form of theatre at which the British were particularly good. By using virtually any occasion to display power as civilization (such as durbars complete with charging "native horsemen" and bagpipes instead of the trumpets of Rome), "the Empire" represented itself as law and civilization spreading to all corners of the globe, manifested not least in the same massed shakos and gold braid of Queen Victoria's palace guard but on parade in New Delhi or Lagos, Canada or Australia, under the watchful gaze of the Viceroy, or Governor, or

Governor-General (and complete with sword, military whites, and raised dais). Within the Empire one could also invoke, to the larger advantage, the doleful circumstances of its particular parts, such as the incantations of an Ashanti priest recounting the death of a chief, the founding of its Confederacy, or in the intoning of blessings by priests and canons, the ritual sounds of an investiture of kings and emperors. By the same token imperial power could serve the funereal occasion, public sadness as display, invoked by muffled drums, empty caissons drawn by black horses (Cannadine 2001).

These are, of course, despite the solemnity of such occasions, more opera bouffe and caricature, but no less spectacular for all that. And there are occasions when there is little else to hold an empire or state together. For most of the hundred years of its existence one might say that what kept the component countries and territories of the Austro-Hungarian Empire from flying apart was precisely its spectacular political theatre, as Carl Shorske and others have described. And precisely because it was so ripe for caricature, power was particularly visible in censorship of theatre, that is, plays and their performances.

Textuality and narrativity

For spectacle to have such impact it first needs to represent something. It must embody that something in the narrativity of the spectacle itself. For if spectacle is not to wind up as mere opera bouffe, it will require substance, depth, logic, and an argument. In this sense, spectacle needs to contain and illustrate a deeper truth value, with or without objective foundation. In short, it needs somehow to be grounded. This grounding is basically textual. And here is where political discourse comes in. Texts purport to treat reality, historical or contemporary. In theatre, however, textuality is the narrated script – text as narrative and narrative as text. But at the same time, the script so devised cannot be composed of any text or any narrative. As indicated above, it needs to combine metaphors within the narrative with metonyms within the text, so that performance is not simply performance but a portrayed logic of interpretive outcomes. The most powerful of such scripts will contain deontological truths – that is, theoretically free-standing and self-grounded. The more ideologically elaborate the text, the more the events chosen as metonymies elevate the importance of the logic behind the enactment. Hence play, narrative, and text, as metaphors of equivalence, and metonymic for a logic, authorize political belief by means of the particular story, the selected episodes, the relationships of the roles and the quality of the performance itself. Indeed, the self-proclaimed superiority of a logic standing behind an ideology is, in political theatre, a product of its action.

Narrative, metaphor, text, and logic, then, go together as script, play, and recapitulated action, drawing spectators together, constituting followers out of audiences, mobilizing understanding to form a dramaturgy of power. The drama, when successfully played and re-enacted, builds up those continuities of language and performance that locate and anchor, by means of the events of the drama, the story line of retrieved history, and the logic of a projected future, a reconstitution of the body politic.

Which raises the question of how and when to treat the theatricality of a political act as a thing in itself. To answer that is to consider political theatre analytically, identifying its ingredients, i.e. the elements of theatre as they intertwine with normal politics. We need categories that locate some of the qualities inherent in the large view of the role of politics as theatre. But we also need to keep the inquiry in proportion, and to recognize that it can be used in a restricted way and a more general way. The more restricted is what Bagehot referred to as the dignified part of the constitution, in the British case, for example, the Crown. This emphasizes the sheer ceremonial pageantry of the state (the opening of Parliament, for example), and a wide variety of political rituals invoking spectacle and display. But it is restrictive in the sense that it would limit inquiry to largely ritualistic and ceremonial occasions that are a truly residual part of the complex business of the state. Nevertheless, even the restricted view suggests the important emotional role such occasions can play in terms of loyalty, jurisdictional affiliations, and citizenship, not to speak of the comradeship and sense of empowerment they provide. One only has to think of the choreography of offended propriety and ethical determinism in the role being played by President Bush in mobilizing and orchestrating a crusade, and the exploits of everyone from firemen and police to soldiers at the front, in a worldwide struggle with an otherwise rather shadowy enemy. Here the crucial ingredient is confrontation and the acts in the drama are constituted by military choreographies each with its own signifying pageantry not least of all knights in combat redolent of the Crusades.

Seen in this light, politics as theatre is a way of articulating tension between addressor and addressees, actors and audiences. It offers opportunities to recast dramatistically the stuff of public experience. In this sense, more than an ingredient of power it is an expression in and of itself especially where in the high drama growing out of public grievance and suspense prevailing jurisdictions, affiliations, and obligations are challenged. As for the play itself it establishes necessary relations; it reduces events to a manageable space while reaching for a kind of unification, integrity, and communion.

Some illustrative remarks

We might illustrate some of these remarks by considering the case of South Africa. There political theatre has played a crucial role in the transition from white to black rule. Most such acts centered around political violence in ethnic, racial, and not only class but caste terms, each event recapitulating previous ones to project alternative denouement, black revolution or virtual white dictatorship. Social polarization as political polarization was continuously reinforced by each successive incident of violence. These included not only "staged" confrontations between black and white but torture and trials, justice as fallibility. Inasmuch as Apartheid represented a caste-like form of polarization, its discourse based on a logic of separation, institutionally embodied in the political structure, it produced its counter discourse based on a logic of displacement, depatrimonialization, victimization, and dispossession. Virtually every legal political act was also illegal, a condition that endowed confrontation with theatrical propensities. Dramatic occasions included forcing people from their homes in the abolition of black townships and banishing them to Bantustans for example, or the trials and punishment of African political leaders, all contributing to political faultlines based on racial, religious, ethnic, linguistic, class, and similar factors, the stigmata of race serving as ground zero for the rest.

The context then was white wealth and power versus black poverty and powerlessness, a condition that not only offered up repertoires of violence but provided opportunities for folk heroes as actors with symbolic precedence. As scenes succeeded one another, each embodying the memory of previous battles, the symbolic measures of despair, glory, and loyalty as well as treachery, betrayal, torture, and death became more and more evident to the point that if ever an explosive denouement appeared over-determined, this was it.[14]

Yet the inevitable did not happen. There were, of course, many reasons why it did not. Institutional factors included the existence of a "democratic" state that if it denied access except to the few could be made open to the many, itself a last-shall-be-first revolution. As well, at the moment of transition, militant, radical, and Marxist alternatives to democracy began to lose their viability in keeping with a general decline of the left.

Another important factor was agency. And here we come to the exceptional role played by Nelson Mandela as actor-agent. The events of his life not only constituted a play but a play within all the other plays. It retrieved past events. It projected a future. Seized upon by all parties his role became a saving grace, a symbolic center. Mandela stood as a figure of both rationality and catharsis, the exceptional man, for some the militant, nationalist, political prisoner, for others the liberalistic lawyer. There was, too, a key dramatic occasion, the opening of the gates of his island prison, which also meant opening the gates of white political society to an imprisoned black community. It telescoped the acts of his own political life, hunted by the police, trial and imprisonment for eighteen years on Robben Island, his segregation from the segregated, his internal exile and triumphant return as the incarnation of the shining morality of black suffering and power. The events that took Mandela from radical militant, to chief, to moral redeemer and enabled him to dispense political balm to all sides while neutralizing the diehards, were theatrical to the extreme. The denouement was entirely unanticipated – Mandela as president of South Africa.

That *coup de théâtre* was to be followed by a second, this time under another exceptional actor-agent, Archbishop Desmond Tutu, the remarkable cleric who presided over the Truth and Reconciliation Commission. With himself as Narrator, dramas succeeded one another. As they unfolded in the public eye the worst secrets of both the regime and its opponents were revealed. The theatre was a court. The acts were the facts of one Apartheid horror story after another. Each in the telling, and by both victims and perpetrators, resulted in public mourning while opening up opportunities for redemption. The audience was in effect the "witness to the witnesses." In the end it offered a grudging embrace in a politics of reconciliation able, so far at any rate, to transcend and undermine quotidian racism and oppression.

History is replete with significant theatrical occasions – indeed that is what much of history consists of. How many of the grand events that qualify as "historical" revolutions, English, American, Russian, Chinese, were themselves the raw material for theatrical reworking as actual politics, each with its own iconography? Take, for example, some of the events leading to decolonization and the formation of new and independent nations with their emphasis on such themes as rebirths and foundings. In the Chinese case, revolution represented itself, that is in its communist moment, as a series of dramatistic events, each a scene like a station of the cross – appearing retrospectively in the official histories as virtually supernatural. Perhaps the most theatrical part of the Chinese Revolution is represented by Yan'an, the sanctuary and redoubt that became the moral epicenter of Maoist versions of primitive communism (Mao Zedong 1976). Not only was there performance, and a preoccupation with the symbolic side of power, but theatre became an expression of an interior discourse.[15] And what better stage than Tiananmen Square where the People's Republic was itself proclaimed and each succeeding political campaign, the Great Leap Forward, the summoning of the Red Guards to assault the headquarters, the funeral of Zhou En-Lai, and indeed, that extraordinary moment when democracy was proclaimed, the goddess of democracy herself wheeled into place when the students created a microcosm of the democracy they desired – to be killed or dispersed for their efforts. Each of these projects was duplicated elsewhere, all of China replicated such events thousands of times in centers all over the country and involving millions of people. One thinks here of the millions pressing forward, little Red Book in hand, in staged performances of unanimity and power. So much so that one might say that China's sequential revolution was one theatrical encounter after another.[16]

Hardly a day goes by without some kind of drama occurring, many in recurring and intensifying sequence. One has only to look at the Intifada. Similarly, in Northern Ireland. In Derry, for example, within the space of the inner city, acts of pure theatre occurred with elements of miracle plays, resonating with Catholic references despite secular means and ends. In all these, gaining supporters, and mobilizing and organizing depended on the generation of confrontational acts able to serve as the visual and "actualizing" evidence for what was being claimed. In each case successful performances were those that not only reached out to wider audiences but also by pulling them into the performance itself made them passionate actors, the audience transposed to the stage to become participants in the drama. In these terms concepts like ideology or belief system or culture cannot do justice to the complex series of acts, sustained by a narrative mode within the form of a sustained and suspenseful morality play.

To do research on such matters requires fieldwork in depth and with a phenomenological bias. My own work took me from work on case studies in Africa to research on terrorism in Latin America, to Japan, and the somewhat bizarre experience of living in fortresses built and manned by radical sects, a semi-underground in which militants opposing the construction of the New Narita International Airport fought pitched battles with police, in which in the acts themselves, or as interpreted, the "real" became unreal and the unreal constituted its own reality. A conflict as carefully choreographed and deliberately symbolically theatrical as one is likely to encounter, it showed how one could believe and believe passionately, while at some level not believing, or having doubts, at the same time. It is this quality which theatre more than any other mode of expression enables (Apter and Sawa 1984). While such power is by no means the exclusive consequence of political theatre, the latter is certainly one of its germane components.

How much is the play the thing?

The South African example is only one of innumerable instances where political theatre has played a direct role in politics. Among the ways that it generates power is by means of discourse theory, the latter in conjunction with political theatre helping us understand better how it is that people can talk themselves into doing the unimaginable and how politicians, priests, intellectuals, ascetics, martyrs, dictators, monarchs, anarchists, and thugs can become public actors whose discursive repertoires and rhetorical strategies make the symbolic performative and the performative symbolic.[17]

The whole needs to be larger than the sum of its parts, offering, in addition to structural understanding, moral resonance. In a sense the sound of language is as important as the meaning of its words, that is if the necessary chemistry between audience and actor, leaders and followers, states and citizens is to develop and before the members of the audience are to respond.

A really good theatrical performance in some appropriate agora and occasion will have a musical way with words, from sound bursts like machine-gun fire to the more sonorous tones of an orchestrated theory. This is especially the case where the actors, as living activists, give a reality to the words themselves – the actual living real of political action – the audience becoming followers in the degree they come to identify with, and recognize themselves in, the events of the drama and so share in common experiences with the leaders "on stage."

Similarly, with the specificity of the plot, the intensity of the interior narrative, intertwined as it must be with recognized issues, predicaments, and contradictions that are part of everyday life. So projected into public theatre politics provides a field for competition between different sets of actors provided by political movements, parties, factions, and other kinds of groups. The more each projects its own version of the same general plot, the more fine-tuned the judgments of a public according to its understanding of what is being portrayed, not least of all according to education, degree of cultural sophistication, the ability to contextualize situations and circumstances, etc. In these regards, good political leaders and successful manipulators of political theatre tend to be acute in gauging the best strategies and combinations of these and other factors. Almost all pay great attention to how they present themselves dramatistically, and many offer quite precise instructions about how political theatre is to be stage-managed.[18]

Whether directly representational or more abstract, these are among the more important features of drama employed by political leaders. So too with staging, venues, time and place, as well as manner. It should be obvious that with the right combination of such properties the dramatic occasion creates its own effects and with instrumental consequences, most particularly the formation of symbolic capital. Indeed, in this latter regard, as suggested above, the dramatistic encounter constitutes a step function in the formation of symbolic capital. This would indicate that politics as theatre is not merely any recounting or manipulation of events in a public space, or any speech, torchlight parade, or solemn pronouncement from on high, or a terrorist event.

If political theatre works best when it provides symbolic condensation in doing so, paradoxically enough, it needs to refract within its more limited compass a broader imagery. Politics as theatre is thus both much like ordinary theatre, acting out a plot within a composed, bounded, and limited space towards which all gaze is directed and individuals transported beyond themselves. But with politics as theatre such focused attention requires sufficient intensity to enable the play to serve both as a surrogate for what it represents and a microcosm, or better, a simulacrum, of the large truths so embodied. In politics as theatre what become central are terrains (each with power to define the other). Examples include the kind of murderous tit-for-tat dramas between Palestinians and Israelis, those small enclosed spaces becoming the focal points for larger ecclesiastical and territorial truths, the significance of which is heightened by retrieved memories of a mythic past, leading to redemptive and mutually exclusionary outcomes, and all or nothing convictions about rights and wrongs, grievances and vengeful rectification. Such drama, and the daily events and episodes of which it is composed, elevates affiliation, intensifies the conflict over jurisdiction, makes terrains sacrosanct, boundaries impermeable, and crossings and passings dangerous, occasions for ritual killings, martyrdom, and sacrifice. As political theatre the instrumental consequence of such symbolic intensification is to endow jurisdiction with a dimension of inviolate interiority, further separating the two, each of which interprets what is witnessed in totally different ways, projecting as well a different denouement. Today the most serious political theatre is confrontational.

The above and below – confrontational politics as state and opposition

Politics as theatre, then, is about portrayals of power and powerlessness in which the respective roles of rulers and ruled are privileged theatrical roles by means of which symbols, ideas, and beliefs become personified, transformed from categories to performances, comedic, tragic, opera bouffe or simply a theatre of the absurd. It is present in some degree in all public debates, elections, speeches from on high, as well as the barricades. A good deal of it derives from the gladiatorial as distinct from the competitive impulse in politics. It contains an element of dueling. Actors are combatants, their actions accompanied by appropriate displays of pageantry and ceremony. On stage is a potential panoply of chiefs, kings, presidents, and dictators, the occasions for performance including their installations and demise, their ritual celebrations of power, their overthrow, and the events associated with each. Relevant in the mobilization of massed support for particular agendas, actors include not only political leaders but their followers, movements, and political parties. Underlying them all is the threat of violence, whether for, against, or between states.

The "below," particularly extra-institutional protest, revolutionary insurrection, and terrorism, places the emphasis on virtue lapsed or betrayed, dramatizing prolonged failures by a state to "hear," listen, act, or otherwise accommodate to unrequited but justiciable grievances. When converted into demands and enabling alternatives, interests can be elevated to the level of principles offering moral urgency to confrontations with the state. Occasions for political theatre include choreographed actions against police, demonstrations, and the usual and attendant visuals – water cannon, police in moonscape uniforms, etc. By and large those orchestrating extra-institutional protest are extremely performance-minded and adept at mocking those in power, making power itself look ridiculous.[19] With revolutionary insurrection political theatre is both internal as well as external, with acts within a movement as much theatre as those against the state. Similarly, terrorism is virtually pure theatre, deeds as events enacted by small bands seeking to render the state helpless, confused, and immobilized. Shocking events aim at converting citizens into, if not supporters, then at least bystanders, while the state is portrayed as helpless, clumsy, awkward, suffocating in and by its own paraphernalia, swaddled by its bureaucracy. Terrains so identified become virtually holy lands while serving as staging areas for organization, mobilization, education, and violent activities. Here the object is not to get the state to listen to demands but to overthrow the state as it is, the acts pursuant to that end, themselves constituting the acts of the play (Apter and Saich 1994).

So, for example, the virtually pure theatre of Sendero Luminoso in Peru, or the Red Brigades in Italy (not least of all in putting Aldo Moro on "trial" and then, after his execution, dumping his body exactly half way between Communist and Christian Democratic Party headquarters – the ultimate gesture of contempt).[20]

Masters of political theatre have always been abundant. From the storming of the Bastille to the tumbrels of the Jacobin period, the French Revolution was perhaps a model for the radical uses of political theatre (Schama 1989; Nora 1992) not lost on the purveyors of dramatic monumentality in Nazi Germany, fascist Italy, and the Soviet Union. But the variety of examples of political theatre, especially of a kind that rendered retrievals of the past as ways to authenticate a presumed future, is virtually infinite.

We have suggested that today's political theatre includes ecclesiastical expressions of violence, not least of all that kind of fundamentalism that at one time would have taken more secular modes, socialist and Marxist. It bears repeating these latter, having more or less disappeared, have left a space on stage for racial, ethnic, religious, and ideological dramas. These sacralize terrain, making of residence or location not something on a map but a mosaic of moral jurisdictions endowed with drenched signifiers, a condition making crossings and passages dangerous. Such jurisdictions are occasions for ritual celebration, raised panoplies, accoutrements, and all manner of symbolic paraphernalia, not least insignia of war and violence.

But political theatre is of course far more from "above" than below, and part of normal politics. And as already suggested, every democratic society affords plenty of such occasions. Every election is in large measure a theatrical performance; so too with parliamentary debates. Nostalgia and the politics of retrieval, mythologized pasts as critique of present lapses, are punctuated by those that make of solemn occasions instances of spectacle employed as theatrical events. Indeed, democracy, for all its claims to the contrary, is a far cry from the reasoned expression of competing claims within a framework of Enlightenment ideals. It is rather a series of theatrical occasions that make appeals to the voter by dramatizing and exaggerating fears and prejudices dressed up as policy preferences. By so doing, more serious claims are emptied of reasoned content while serving to convince skeptical pluralities.

Thus even in well-entrenched democracies like the United States, political theatre as mobilization can be used to override constitutional niceties and undermine legal protections. This is so especially when the play is about transcending political evil and realizing the political good by exorcizing demons in some palpable way, even though a mythical harmonious state, an original harmony of the spheres, a universal rationality, is as illusory as the perfectly equilibrated.[21]

Politics from below deals with contingencies that have in a sense gotten out of hand. Not any contingencies, of course, but those that on closer inspection turn out to derive from systemic conditions not fully recognized politically. Discourse from above will always try to regularize and eliminate such contingencies. Politics from above abhors randomness and favors order. But some contingencies have a way of refusing to be so managed, most particularly when they are seen to represent structural contradictions, social cleavages that, if they harden into boundaries, turn jurisdiction itself into a matter of contention, a condition in which opportunities for contentious politics through resorting to theatrical means are enlarged. Virtually all of the subversive theatrical performances today are dramatistic interventions arising out of perceived economic and social gaps within countries as well as between them. Modern global tendencies offer propensities for dramatic violence, the reordering of events, made possible by the increasingly fractured and divided character of advanced modernity, the social fissures, cleavages, and faultlines of wealth and poverty. These, and the polarizing tendencies they represent, create both opportunities for semiotic and moral space within which can be enacted those rituals of combat which the play itself reworks in traditional themes, primordial chaos, casual injustice, and rectifying principles. When contingencies are such that events become randomized, those without authority begin to take matters into their own hands, using violence to express inversionary objects. It is then, too, that political theatre is likely to depend on spectacular acts. Which is why we said at the onset that politics as theatre is most significant in moments of confrontational disjunction, especially when the play is about self and/or collective overcoming, the transcending project. One might say that whatever the concrete form the space formed by the state and the opposition to it may take, together they constitute a theatre in the round.

This is not to suggest that the propensity towards inversionary political theatre correlates with some threshold of inequality. But it can provide the contingent events out of which such theatre is composed. To turn contingent events into theatrical performance requires involvement by those who themselves are far from the margins of social, economic, and political opportunity. The agents who engage in theatrical discourse, including those favoring extra-institutional modes of politics, are usually themselves among the more privileged. It is they who reach out for wider clienteles and followers, create theatrical episodes, seek confrontation by committing violent acts, spectacular events of which are designed to dramatize polarization as between inversionary and redemptive alternatives that reveal the hegemonic character of the state. To the degree that such proposals are intrinsically subversive of prevailing laws and orders, so the stage is set for the dramas to unfold.

Nor does the emphasis on politics from below suggest that this is some-how different in kind from ordinary politics. Every political campaign, every competition between candidates, each time politicians line up on one side or another in favor or against legislation, and especially when principles, real or illusory, appear to be involved, politics is as much drama as it is about some more ostensible object. But it is at the exceptional moment that the theatrical side of politics is critical insofar as it engages individuals in the larger pro-cess of interpreting their predicaments in terms of collective action. That is, inversionary discourses, radical in nature, seek to reveal in dramatic events, not least of all confrontations, terror, and protest, the justiciable insensibility of the state when seen from the standpoint of those most penalized – those who need the most and get the least from political institutions unable or unwilling to adequately respond appropriately. In which case theatrical spectacles can include deliberate atrocities designed to undermine the conventional practices and discourses of politics, the acts of the drama, the more transfiguring the better, serving as rhetorical and symbolic tropes. So events are reinvented as drama, an imaginary real more "real" than the events themselves especially when the ethical fine tuning of political equity refines prevailing notions of justice. Seeking the theatrical in the event, inversionary political theatre is a way of translating alternative interpretive meanings into transcending truths.[22]

By the same token, subversive political theatre serves up as signifiers events that are metonymies for alternative political ideologies, larger principles gener-ted out of violated rights and mobilized grievances. When political movements challenge the limits laid down by the state by acts and events of confrontation, subversive political theatre needs to demonstrate within the play itself how rea-son derives from ruptures, the more disjunctive the better. Political theatre in this sense contributes to building dissident and subversive discourse communities that thrive on conflict with the state. It is as discourse communities that these can establish their own boundaries, define their own territories, and use political theatre to reinforce their claims. The more transformational, foundational, or redemptive the objects, the more theatre devolves around confrontational and violent events.

From above, political theatre incorporates past foundings, transformations, redemptions, all of which serve as mythic foundations for continuous revalidation of the state and mobilize them for a purposeful intent, not least of all war. By this means the state celebrates its own legitimacy based on "deep myths of culture" (Turner 1974).

Between the "above" and "below," the range of theatrical alternatives and strategies varies. But no matter how performance, substance, plot, and focus alternate in style and mode of expression, the common denominator that makes political theatre a phenomenon in and of itself is the dynamics between audience and actor, drawing the two together, and where it succeeds, that is becomes intrinsically power, it constitutes a kind of transcendent reality. By framing the analysis as theatrical confrontations between hegemonic and inversionary discourses, it should be remembered that unlike theatre qua theatre, the events of each drama are grounded, concrete, empirical. They "represent" socially significant recognizable predicaments the particular circumstances, situations, and ingredients of which are restructured for, by, and as interpretive action. To the extent that this is so, the theatrical component is crucial in the exercise of political power. Where political theatre differs from just plain theatre, however, is in terms of a prior knowledge of power. Theatre is, after all, entertainment. Political theatre may indeed be entertaining. But it is in the end dangerous.

Dramatistic morphologies

All political theatre can be said to derive from a common ancestor, the dramatistic transcendence of chaos, the primordial condition of politics is one in which gods and other lords spiritual sported with the lords secular, to master the randomness of situation by the portrayal of fate. Nor has this primordial object disappeared today. Politics as theatre from above tends to center around ritualized spectacles whose deep structures are myths of the state. From below it involves "inversionary" events resulting from movements with revolutionary, terrorist, nationalist, or similar aims, where the emphasis is on those aggrieved for whom the benefits from society and state leave off. In this sense what becomes dramatized is the state of "social toxicity" as a consequence of state policy and institutional power. Insofar as the discourse then is directed not only to why and what institutions need to be changed but how, theatre become "real" insofar as it generates its own events.[23] Political theatre in this polarized sense is endgame politics. Violence, always a possibility, becomes endemic –

structural problem. Both sides create the drama. Each mobilizes principles by defining their violation by the other. Signifying events constitute moral codes that become visible on the ground, the fresh outrage of newly dead bodies, the savagery of the other, and each side tries to define the other as a primitive alter. In this sense violence as theatre creates its own objects, its own plots, it miniaturizes as sacred those theatrical venues which are scenes of violation – such places defining terrain, boundaries, jurisdictions, and establishing the rules and rituals of crossings and passings.

However, if the "play" should end, with one or the other side triumphant, then the problem is to keep the drama going without it becoming thin, repetitive, mimetic. Should an inversionary movement succeed and in fact come to power it will need to keep itself alive as acting out a moral drama the more it attempts to dominate or replace prevailing institutions. And the more ritualized and emptied of meaning the play becomes.

With political theatre from below scripts follow a generative morphology that specifies an original condition of grace, a fall (depatrimonialization, dispossession, dispersal, etc.), leading to a recitation of perceived grievances and suffering, from which the logic of a transcending accomplishment can be derived – rectifying claims, rights, and demands (particularly as these relate to the defined responsibilities of the state and how far such responsibilities should extend and apply) with narrative sequences condensed into acts.

Such depth is all the more necessary given drastic changes in the political landscape. Conventional boundaries, jurisdictions, and affiliations are undergoing alterations on the ground and as categories. So too with regional groupings and associations, not to speak of state and society. The European nation-state is eroding both as a functional unit and legal entity. Migrations, immigration, the ebb and flow of cultures and populations, require a more deliberate understanding of society which has become more intermediated in complex ethnic, religious, linguistic, as well as class, status, and other ways. Not only have jurisdictions and affiliations altered but also beliefs about them – and as subject to controversy, fratricidal, factional, sectarian, and ethnic. In turn these occur within national boundaries rather than between them.

Similarly, hitherto conventional lines of distinctions, such as between combatants and non-combatants, are becoming eroded, and the meanings of war and peace have blurred. Confrontations are increasingly "popular," drawing in and engaging most if not entire populations, the rationality of such action depending on which substrate of logic is preferred, such preference deriving less from "interests" than from selected memories and experiences – real and imagined. As for incorporated and recounted narratives, it is the mythic that provides the basis of a logic with facts a sort of "imaginary real" (Smith 1991). By this means state power becomes more forceful than its rationality claims, the common rules of the political game no longer applying. Instead of "order-ing," territorial, political, or social boundaries serve as potential theatres of war, constituting, when conflict occurs, their own kinds of theatres. Today's politics displays an ever-widening range of mobilizing social and political movements. Many of these are not content to pursue conventional interests, ends, and goals. Rather their purpose is to take aim at the principles on which these rest. In which case political life itself conjures new social texts that occur when people try to make sense out of what is happening to them. In seeking solutions they inquire into their own conditions of possibility. To the degree that that is so, what is needed in political analysis is more emphasis on the differences such differences make. That is, more emphasis on words, things, and agents, rather than coalitions, interests, institutions. Not to dispense with these latter – of course not. Rather these need to be encompassed with a framework that would indicate how each by taking on symbolic endowments reinforces or redefines meaning and instigates action accordingly.

Just as moral principles can be deliberately eroded and replaced with excep-tionalism, so boundaries in the mind can be altered by changing the balance between what is seen and what is imagined (see, for instance, Barthes 1972, in which an analogy is made with wrestling and indeed the wrestling match). That is what constitutes the narrative possibility. Such possibilities take the form of certain recognized themes, patrimonies lost or found, territoriality violated or preserved, and affiliation, loyalty, or treason as well defined. It takes potentially severe and stringent means to encode new boundaries or for that matter restore older ones. The narrative opportunity builds on the magnification of grievance, the transformation of loss into political yearning, and conversion of loss into political passion.

Which brings us back to events. We have said, repeatedly, that the place to start is with events. A quick glance at cultural problematics would lead us to select historically relevant benchmark events that also serve as analytical (and moral) punctuation marks. The range of possibilities is virtually infinite, from constitutional conventions to revolutions (or the other way around), each with a context based on its own specific cultural and historical profiles. Qualifying events, in appropriately signifying sites, magnify the effect of speeches, masse marches, torchlight parades, military displays. All manner of venues can do, the atrical spaces like squares, parks, palaces, amphitheatres, this redoubt, that put a mountain top, an altar, a podium. Whichever they are they need to be capable of confrontational costuming and pageantry, so that flags, fires, music, and the ges tures and words to those on stage, broadcast to both a narrow circle of initiate and a wider group of potential recruits susceptible to mythic renderings of dut

The danger lies in becoming ridiculous. From today's standpoint it seem ludicrous that Hitler, in his uniform, mustache, his arm wearing the swastil stuck out in front of him, could convert the enormous and grandios pseudo-classical amphitheatre at Nuremberg into a virtual church, thousands sharing the performance, waving a sea of Nazi banners, on signal massing the straight-arm salute, the uniforms, the black and the red exhorting the body to the state. Similarly with Red Square and Stalin and his henchmen standing in their points of vantage in Lenin's tomb before endless displays of armed might, tanks, guns, gymnasts, or other massed testimonials to the new soviet man. Or, again, Mao in Yan'an creating a mythical kingdom that realized itself in a Communist middle kingdom in 1949 in Tiananmen Square and to be undone exactly forty years later in the very same place.

The frequency of more and less memorable expressions of political theatre would suggest that as a phenomenon it is ubiquitous enough to be taken for granted as intrinsic to the public face of politics whatever form it may take. What matters is the script, what it contains, how it is coded and the quality of performance, and choreography and to the extent that what is being acted out in the general implication of more specific circumstances, a decline and fall from grace defining an overcoming project, a narrative trajectory beginning with a period of suffering and longing and ending with a description of accomplishment – that is the how as well as the what to be accomplished, the self realized for bigger purposes, movement, state, cause, as the case might be. What goes with these is demonization, victimization, redemption, and other important devices. One has only to think of De Gaulle in exile in London during World War Two and his triumphal return at the Place de la Concorde, echoed in its own way on the left when Mitterrand arrived at the Pantheon for his inaugural for his first term as President, thereby transforming a "red" but dead space into a living the-atre. Consider the utterly theatrical events of the "war" against terrorism, or the tit-for-tat negative choreography of violence between Israelis and Palestinians. Today, of course, it is the drama of political violence that is on the whole the most disturbing, and the way in which staged and organized protest can endow particular places with sacramental or sacral qualities (think Jerusalem), inver-sionary pathos, yearning, and the hope that through violent actions what will result is that transubstantiation of the negativized "other," that the damned will be saved – the ultimately redemptive political trope. In this context individual acts transmute, provoking evocative scenes, signifiers for pathos, transgres-sion, suffering, transcendence, and accomplishment. Politics as theatre is most successful when its effects are to renegotiate tensed fragments of experience, reordering in terms of sin, defilement, guilt, and purification the rules laid down by political figures as "script-writers," "agents" who are political leaders.

The interplay of ingredients – a preliminary assessment

In these terms political theatre is a way of constituting a referential wholeness. In this sense politics as performance, play or drama is both free-standing, with a beginning and an end, but incomplete insofar as its end feeds into the next round. It is thus closed and complete and open-ended. In this way it contributes to and is intrinsic to chains of meaning forming an ongoing narrative. Thus each political sequence is a play that is itself an element in a sequence of others, the whole being greater than the parts. So the dramatistic side of politics contributes to belief, ideology, not to speak of religious or political preferences which, by means of the alchemy of political theatre, harden into doctrines – this in turn to the degree that the ordinary is endowed with the exceptional.

Political theatre is one particular dimension of a more general process but tailored in the form of recognizable parallels to theatre *tout court*. Theatrical episodes are among the ways that interpretation uses references to experiences, its "real" theatre a reality of lived experiences. Its themes are basic: death and dying, loss of patrimony, exclusion, to name a few of those most likely to be preferred by militant movements. The more a politics of theatre is transgressive, the more it inverts the order of things, opting for transubstantiating truths. This is the accomplishment of every successful revolution. Mobilized movements, by engaging events of their own making, choreograph acts to order and in so doing define or redefine prevailing terms of power. In contrast, from above, political theatre represents the triumph of order over chaos, a normative order embodying a preferred notion of justice, providing institutional gravitas, a constitution of self-embodying virtue.

This suggests a somewhat somber dynamics. It would include a wide range of possible circumstances, the terrifying drama of the holocaust, itself a stage for any number of totalizing theatrical encounters involving trauma, genocide in Rwanda, the dramatic standoff between Arafat holed up in Ramallah and a beleaguering Israeli army. In these terms, behind the deed lies the trauma, with death the configuring element. Suffering, exclusionary neutering, the transmogrification of souls, real or imagined, to merchandise – all are consequences of politics as theatre (Alexander 2002).

It should be admitted that discourse theory and theatrical politics suffer from certain operational deficiencies, an apparent lack of appropriate scientific methodologies, an absence of quantitative techniques. Yet paradoxically enough, both are extremely empirical, requiring fieldwork in depth, sophisticated engagement with the subject, and genuine contextual knowledge of a kind, indeed, eschewed by others than area specialists.

In this sense the present concern is with occasions when the "theatrical" component of events looms large, disrupting not only the order of things, but the orders of mind – indeed, an exceptional sequence of exceptional events is interpreted by suitable agents, so serving as a means to alter conventional political meanings of political life. When such events are reinterpreted not simply as events but links in "causal" chains connecting such events to explosive potential consequences, especially those designed to bring down governments, tear apart social institutions, and alter prevailing conditions of possibilities, then the analysis of discourse theory generally, and political theatre more specifically, becomes a critical addition to the body of prevailing political theory used for the normal study of politics. So too with that most breathtaking *coup de théâtre*, the events of September 11, 2001, still embedded in our retinas, such theory will pose questions about equity, power, and domination. Moreover, it starts from the events themselves as a point of departure, and the rationale for acts against taste, convention, and political stability undertaken by those most offended by the way things are, and the most willing to sacrifice for the ways things, at least in their view, ought to be. If it is the power of discourse theory to show how interpretation of events, cast in a dramatic mode, restructures rationality, then the emphasis is on experienced events as they form first into a social text, as Geertz would have it, and then into a theatrical one.

If it is correct that politics as theatre has become a crucial element in politics today, should this be a cause for concern? Was Plato essentially correct in taking such a dim view of theatre? He was right to be suspicious. For (whether writ small or large) to the degree it takes on its own reality it becomes a form of magic realism, to use Jameson's (1986) term. The more successfully actor-politicians play to the crowds the less significant are more ordinary ways of doing the business of politics. The trouble with symbolic capital is that it subordinates the reality of common sense to the acting out of belief. If it can override obstacles, it can also lead to disastrous solutions. One has only to look at the consequences of religious revivalism in conjunction with the moral space left by failed radical and Marxist alternatives. In this sense, to the extent that theatrical space defines a moral space, it can be filled by any ideology, any fundamentalism, any true and truly overcoming belief. Any nonsense suddenly becomes plausible and logical, including sacral residues reworked into dominant themes.

Political theatre is intrinsic to politics. It is also dangerous. It involves the instrumental manipulation of symbolic expression. The danger is greatest when it becomes a method of conveying some form of mystical tuition based on revelatory insights. It offers opportunities to beguile, entice, or entrap an audience, a public, or a citizen. It is also a way of encouraging a preference for passion over reason (Brown and Merrill 1993). In short, it is, among other things, a method of instrumental gulling. In this sense, it is suspect – not so different from Plato's warnings against music and poetry. It can be simply fun, entertaining, but not when that prevents citizens from taking a more proper measure of truth.

Yet to argue that political theatre and truth are inversely proportional would be utterly misleading. For in a world in which reality is, if not "unreal," at least increasingly bizarre, it is political theatre that can reveal a great deal about politics. It can be used to puncture the pretensions of those in power with the cruelty of parody or the devastating effects of comedy. It can be used as well to glorify those in power, reinforce or denounce extant political figures, firm up orthodoxies or tear down beliefs, or even more subversively, expose political subterfuges, and reveal what otherwise might have remained hidden from public view.[24]

Some tentative conclusions

We have emphasized those occasions in which political theatre is politics and politics is political theatre. Where it works it builds up power by intermediating between citizens and state in the several ways suggested. It codes meanings and adds dimensionality. Its scripts are weighty with referrals to past grievances and events. Its narratives celebrate the sorrowful. Its texts claim not only truth in the act but require acts that demonstrate higher truths, locating the worthy by virtue of their loyalties, and sanctifying jurisdictions dramatically defined. By weaving a fabric of belief out of a tissue of interpretations political theatre, unlike theatre more generally, works best when it exerts a kind of conversionary pull on its audience such that favored political ideas become superior insights. Those sharing such insights become a kind of chosen people; chosen not least of all in the sense such insights take on the power of logical truths. So too throughout history, especially in those combinations of theocratic and ideological doctrines, political theatre has been used to define or drive home the distinction between what is orthodoxy and what is blasphemy, what is dissent and what is subversion.

One does not want to overstate the case. As suggested, a great deal of political theatre is just, well, theatre. That is, it neither tries nor could it rise to such heights. But that does not mean it is irrelevant. Even where it lacks defining power, it serves other purposes, mostly celebratory, and it performs ritual functions. For in sharing in such dramatic occasions and fêtes of power political theatre enables people to feel that they have a stake in society for or against and in favor or opposed to government and the state. It reminds them of their share in power, even if politically they have little voice. So too with the subversive nature of carnivals, fairs, and other circumstances where personalization allows greater toleration of inversionary roles, and by means of parody and *lèse majesté*, sets aside at least for a moment the conventions of respect and authority age, status, rank, and property in bursts of familiarity if not intimate exchange.

Moreover, if through expert manipulation of the magic of time and place staging and players, actors and performance, script and spectacle, timing an choreography, as well as necessary resonance, an actor-agent as addresser t addressees is able thereby to collectivize an audience so that as a collectiv body it takes on jurisdictional and affiliation characteristics, so we can regar this as foundational politics whether of the state or oppositional politics. W have seen how this works when political leaders as actor-agents establish out c singular events certain designated situations that become moral moments and by doing so exempt themselves from commonplace judgments and the ordinary constraints of common sense. In this sense the performance of the right kind of play in the right kind of setting serves an enabling function for political leaders seeking exemption from the ordinary rules of the game.

Seen from that perspective, political theatre provides a rationale for political exceptionalism, imposing a claim on citizen loyalties even against their better judgment. In this sense, political theatre, by means of symbolic condensation, enables what Roberto Unger has called transformative practice and intersubjectivity. It affords political actors who can get away with it opportunities to redefine appropriate objects through the artful use of rhetoric, the right occasion of ceremony, and a script in which citizens come to recognize themselves as players of many parts.

And then there are exceptional dramatic moments that all history seemed designed to produce, "narrativity codes" leading to moral teleologies, previous sacrifices recounted (and so kept alive) with martyrdoms a saving grace imposing its validity of claims and demands on others. One thinks here of radical millennial solutions embodied in confrontational theatrical events, or those involving revelation, even religious ecstasy. This kind of theatre can make catastrophes sublime by the projection of the transcendental accomplishment. Daily life is lifted out of its commonplaceness. People become aware or are made to feel privileged by playing their own roles in the public drama. Then, in their own eyes, and those of others within a public space, a community becomes an elect, to enjoy the exceptionalism of its own commonality.

Whether beguiled, gulled, or through more reasoned appreciation of spectacle, narrative, text, story, logic, retrievals, and projections, political theatre, insofar as it reconstitutes the public interpretation of private interpretations, and as it touches on themes that affect daily life, endows the ordinary with the exceptional. The more political theatre allows for such forms of political transubstantiation – that is the translation of private discretion to a public entity, whether a government leader or the head of a guerrilla movement – what is so enabled is what has been called a discourse community, an elect, a chosen people. It is in these situations that political theatre, by creating symbolic capital, creates not only power but authority. In the special occasion this is a result of a conveyance of private and individual wills to a collective one – producing what can be called collective individualism.

In this sense political theatre provides opportunities for political leaders to not only engage the ordinary loyalties of citizens, subjects, or members of particular political groups, but to induce them as individuals to convey their personal discretion to a collectivity. Insofar as this generates symbolic capital, the result will be a fund on which individuals can draw, the value of whose capital to the individual is that he or she feels empowered, with personal qualities enhanced. By drawing more from the collectivity than individuals conveyed in the first place one transcends one's own limitations, and the collectivity transcends the limitations that circumstances have imposed on it. (This notion of conveyance adds an interesting dimension to rational choice theory and its individual rationality assumptions.)

As has already been suggested, political theatre becomes most significant in politically rupturing moral moments. That is, when political theatre aims at far more than ritual exercise, when it seeks to capture and encapsulate in performance such solemn occasions as the founding of new societies and states, or moments of revolutionary transformation, or redemptive moments, it becomes most important, especially in establishing when it is that old orders transgress and purifying alternatives come into being.

To summarize: in the last analysis, whether as state pageantry or a politics of resistance, political theatre is significant in the degree that it reinforces or undermines the state. For if our analysis is correct, it can contribute to powers that be or powers that are becoming, by means that have, on the whole, been obscured by more general views. It contrasts with that preponderance of political business that takes place, as it were, behind the scenes where the day-to-day work of governing goes on, committees, back rooms, over drinks and dinners, and other private or semi-public occasions. While these may have their own theatrical aspects, generally speaking they follow their own rationality and their own purposes behind closed doors, and with only more occasional or periodic nods and calculations with respect to public preferences, especially where voting and candidate choice are involved. Relevant information is largely based on the testimony of those most directly concerned with particular issues especially when vested interests sense decisional closure – government by secrecy, as it were, although subject to disclosure. Despite, or perhaps because of many and diverse power venues, what happens at political party meetings, caucuses, or in planning and legislative strategy sessions, or the specific tabling, shelving, or pursuing motions, follows its own coalitional rules (Hardin 1995).[25]

Political theatre requires visibility. It follows rules of performance in "scene(s)," scenarios, employing suitable "scenery." It contrasts to politics *behind the scenes* where the rationality rules of the game are relatively fixed and well understood by the participants. With political theatre the rules as well as the ends of politics are themselves the subject. In the case of power from "above" the rules of political order and procedure are reinforced by means of ritual occasions, spectacles, fêtes, and the invocation in regularized pageantry and in a variety of magisterial and ceremonial occasions (tradition playing an important role) in occasions of pomp, ceremony, and pageantry reinforcing public loyalties and symbolic solidarities.

From "below," especially when antagonistic groups engage in efforts to reformat the rules of order and procedure by means of staged confrontational events most particularly events of violence, the role of political theatre is to redefine situations so that those who would regard the state with disfavor would be inspired to change it. In both cases, as we have tried to show, the theatrical deployment of symbolically loaded events serves as the raw material for commitment. Politics as theatre then works best in defining moral moments. It can determine obligation, and establish discipline and affiliational loyalty. This argues for the assumption that there are fundamental attributes of political power independent of institutions.

We conclude this much too long and rambling discussion with a plea for a more nuanced approach to political analysis. Political discourse and political theatre should not be taken lightly or regarded as frivolous concerns. Political drama is not only relevant to real politics. It is a method of understanding politics in its full range, and on a par with historical, institutional, structural, behavioral, or rational choice modes of analysis. It emphasizes what even the most shrewdly designed theories based on principles of rewards and punishments, pleasures and pains, costs and benefits, inputs and outputs, or structural principles and institutional mechanisms overlook.

Nor, despite the emphasis on the exceptional, are democratic systems aloof. Every election is in large measure a theatrical performance; so too with parliamentary debates. Indeed, democracy, for all its claims to the contrary, is a far cry from the reasoned expression of competing claims within a framework of Enlightenment ideals. It appeals to voters by dramatizing and exaggerating fears and prejudices dressed up as policy preferences. Even serious claims are emptied of reasoned content in order to convince skeptical pluralities.

The more passionate the play and the more moral its objects the more the subtext is about purity and danger, as Mary Douglas (1973) called it. The more it invokes the sacred and the profane, the more dangerous its activities. The manipulation of theatrical power in this sense is more similar to church rituals, religious rites, exorcism, mysticism, all of which create a space for specialists, professionals, experts in projecting images of violation, sacrifice, betrayal, redemption, and other such themes on to a public stage and in ways that make for audience participation. Indeed, the craft of political theatre as distinct from theatre more generally, is to provide a sense of vulnerability overcome. It is the overcoming project defined, that brings political theatre home (Ricoeur 1967). In this sense and in relation to political power, political theatre exorcizes political danger through the collectivization of individual wills, this last distinguishing political theatre from more ordinary entertainments. It works best when it becomes hyper real even in its most sublime moments of unreality.

We have examined theatrical politics as a thing in itself. We have also considered it within the broader framework of political discourse theory and pragmatic phenomenology. Political theatre is part about the way people interpret their circumstances, personal and social, individual and collective, and how they come to change them. Both occupy the strategic space at the intersection of the personal and the public, the latter as audience and actor. Political theatre can in this sense be considered a field of action, one that works a kind of performative alchemy that transforms experienced events into hortatory admonishments. Political theatre is in this sense the abiding abode of the political imagination.

Notes

An early version of this paper was presented at a conference on political theatre held at SOAS, University of London, January 2002. A modified version was presented to the Program in Comparative Research, Yale University, March 2002. I am particularly indebted to Donal Cruise O'Brien, Julia Strauss, Robert A. Dahl, Jeffrey Alexander, Alan Trachtenberg, Kai Erikson, Mitchell Cohen, and Judith Friedlander for comments and suggestions.

1. See also Flyvberg (2001), who in turn attacks science in terms of the "epistemic" versus "phronesis."
2. One thinks here of superstructure among Marxists, early debates between Parsons and Blumer, or the critical sociology of such putative phenomenologists as Goffman, ethnomethodologists like Garfinkel, "death of the author" structuralists like Barthes and Foucault, not to speak of the "structural phenomenology" of Bourdieu.
3. See, for instance, Negara (Geertz 1980). This is one of the most explicit studies connecting architecture, geography, spatialization and symbolization to political theory.
4. One can cite, for examples, Roman Jackobsen, Roland Barthes, Claude Lévi-Strauss, Paul Ricoeur, Guy Debord, Hayden White, Terry Eagleton, Mary Douglas, Victor Turner, and, albeit in very different terms, Adorno, Durkheim, Dilthey, Mead, Mannheim, Parsons, Benjamin, etc.
5. See Burke (1952a), especially where he discusses what he calls a "mystic moment," a "stage of revelation after which all is felt to be different" (1952a: 305). See also, Geertz (1973), Barthes (1966), and Bourdieu (1977).
6. See Skinner (1985). Interestingly enough a good deal of grand theory went out of fashion just as it was becoming more and more politically relevant. Hence, kicked out the front door it is returning through the back especially in fields like economics and political science, where generally speaking market theory and rational choice leave little space for such concerns.
7. The contrast is with more formalistic theories, inputs and outputs, integration, balance, or equilibrium in part to incorporate as theory what these others exclude as contingencies. In these terms the original connection between the two emphases was Pareto's distinctions between rational action and "non-rationalistic" aspects of politics, residues, and derivations. Where distributional rationalities left off these provided the equilibrating elements of which "optimalities" and "ophilimities" could be composed. They filled the space otherwise left to contingencies, serving as the conditions of possibility for equilibrium outcomes.

8. Included in the notion of performance is the tension that arises out of denoted events, the dramatic impact of a specific story line. One also needs to know how politics as theatre works at the level of structure, and in two ways, form independent of content and then in terms of content itself – the first representing what Hayden White has called "the content of the form."

9. "Jules Michelet's triumphal narrative made the Revolution a kind of spectacular performance, at once scripture, drama, and invocation" (Schama 1989: 5). See also Nora (1992).

10. A good mixture of such high and low comedy with tragic overtones was the impeachment proceedings against President Clinton.

11. Geertz's (1973) twin notions of "thick description" and "social text" are relevant. The characterization of culture as template, and social text as a system of signifiers, points in an ethnographic direction.

12. One can favor the structural side of Geertz and use certain phenomenological modes to decipher social texts, the accomplishments of Bourdieu (1977) with his emphasis on the relationships between events structured according to the time, space, and exchange meanings endowed by those engaged in them.

13. Nkrumah's Agora was Black Star Square (thereby retrieving within his own the historical script of Negro suffering and slavery by using Garvey's "black star" as the constituting reference point). Mao, whose first arena was in the hills and mountains of Yan'an, used the caves his followers lived in as the ground for an Agora, his dramatic recounting of events taking place against a backdrop of weapons, horses, the sounds of gunfire, while virtually every defeat, like the stations of the cross, served as a narrative of victory. Such theatre eventually wound up in the Tiananmen Square, which became his personal forum as well as mausoleum. Today that space carries with it a different drama, with its own spectacle, the memory of the events of June 4, 1989.

14. Dispersed through the different narratives were multiple themes of oppression, not only between black and white but within the latter, British colonialism, Boer victimization.

15. For Mao the emphasis was on ideological struggle, critique plus uplift (Zedong 1976).

16. Nothing could have outdone the political theatre created by Mao during the Cultural Revolution when, it has been estimated, some 12 million people were packed into Tiananmen Square for the grand mobilization against those who came to power and sidelined Mao himself. Also the mock "trials" of officials when children, students, and others organized as Red Guards charged people for crimes they did not commit, humiliating, beating, and destroying their property were replicated in virtually every organized setting, schools, factories, rural settings and urban. Mao was very conscious of politics as theatre. For earlier theatrical "occasions" during the revolution and Mao's comments on political theatre itself, see Apter and Saich (1994).

17. All this has been known in one form or another since ancients like Plato saw the "city" as a discourse community. Composed of one part rational and logical principles and the other mythic belief, the "dialogue" was both a performative and symbolic script.

Plato's dialogues are "plays" in which the performance is contained in the action and the action is contained in the script.

18. Mao Zedong for example, issued quite precise instructions to the many theatre groups which were part of the Chinese Red Army during the Chinese revolution, arguing in good socialist realism terms that a peasant audience was far more preoccupied with authenticity, particularly in details of dress, utensils, household accountrements, etc. than in some particular plot. He believed that without such attention to detail the power of the narrative and the ideological meaning of the play would be lost (Apter and Saich 1994).

19. For an analysis of extra-institutional protest as political theatre see Apter and Sawa (1984).

20. Wagner-Pacifici puts it as follows. "For just as generic choices in theater effect the internal complexity of the characters, their range of relationships with other characters, and their possible relationships with the audience, so do generic choices in the theater of politics condition the amount and quality of public participation and character richness and psychological complexity. Here, the two ends of the generic continuum will be represented by Tragedy and Melodrama – Tragedy allowing for an encouraging audience identification with the tragic victim and his or her decisions, dilemmas, weaknesses and fate; Melodrama excluding the audience both from such identification and from any engaged participation beyond that of the prescripted booking of the villain and cheering of the hero" (1986: 20–2). See also Moss (1997).

21. As already suggested, theatrical occasions can occur in virtually every kind of expropriated venue – a court room will do, or a legislative body. A stunning theatrical terrorist act, one with a global impact in terms of shock, anger, and uncertainty – witness the impact of September 11, 2001 – can create an instant venue, as occurred with the Twin Towers which themselves are in process of becoming memorialized in an appropriate architecture. Democratic societies are particularly vulnerable to such self-constituted theatres of terror; this is all the more significant because, for the most part, democracies use political theatre to celebrate one or other aspect of enlightenment, including the struggle to accomplish its higher purposes. So too, fundamental retrievals and projections, its deep myths, historical struggles, etc., give way to popular re-enactments of constitutional revalidation and confirmation, the constitution itself constituting the logical divine behind secular politics.

22. Of course there are many kinds of political theatre, not least of all the theatre of the absurd. It becomes anything but absurd when and where cleavage politics becomes central and where events lead to both tragic consequences as well as themes for discourse. In this latter context, if and when political figures appeal to transcending ethical principles as a form of ideological persuasion, then passion and principle become likely handmaidens. With what consequence will depend a good deal on the power of performative persuasion. Among the characteristic qualities of such persuasion is what is best described as general aura of ethical romanticism.

23. Indeed, what distinguishes the destruction of the World Trade Center as a theatrical event was the way it set off a chain of further events from which not only discourses

but scripts, scenes, and stock parts unfold, increasing uncertainty, public fear, a ballet of responses that called for a display of force. The play substantiates an enticing agenda for jihadists on the one hand and world police on the other.
24. "Aristotle had said that, particularly in the arousing of pity, the rhetorician is most effective if he can bring before the audience the actual evidence of hardship and injustice suffered" (Burke 1952b: 81).
25. Despite publicity, few politicians seriously engage the public. The politics of choice is for the most part a politics of manipulation according to well-understood rules of the game. Indeed, the prevalence of common rationality rules and a shared understanding is perhaps a corollary of democratic politics in particular. Disagreement over possible outcomes within the framework of behind-the-scenes politics, is what gives rational choice relevance as a mode of analysis.

References

Alexander, Jeffrey C. 2002. "On the Social Construction of Moral Universals: The 'Holocaust' from War Crime to Trauma Drama," *European Journal of Social Theory* 5, 1: 5–85.

Apter, David E. 1992. "Democracy and Emancipatory Movements: Notes for a Theory of Inversionary Discourse." *Development and Change* 23, 3: 139–73.

Apter, David E. and Tony Saich. 1994. *Revolutionary Discourse in Mao's Republic.* Cambridge, Mass.: Harvard University Press.

Apter, David E. and Nagayo Sawa. 1984. *Against the State.* Cambridge, Mass.: Harvard University Press.

Austin, John L. 1980. *How To Do Things With Words.* Oxford: Oxford University Press.

Barthes, Roland. 1966. "An Introduction to the Structural Analysis of Narrative." *Communications* 8.

1972. *Mythologies.* New York: Hill and Wang.

Bourdieu, Pierre. 1977. *Outline of a Theory of Practice.* Cambridge: Cambridge University Press.

Brown, David J. and Robert Merrill.1993. *Violent Persuasions: The Politics and Imagery of Terrorism.* Seattle, Washington: Bay Press.

Burke, Kenneth. 1952a. *A Grammar of Motives.* New York: Prentice-Hall.

1952b. *A Rhetoric of Motives.* New York: Prentice-Hall.

Cannadine, David. 2001. *Ornamentalism.* Oxford: Oxford University Press.

Clymer, Adam. 2001. "Better Campaign Reporting: A View from the Major Leagues." *Political Science and Politics* 34, 4: 779–84.

Debord, Guy. 1987. *La Société du Spectacle.* Paris: Éditions Gerard Lebovici.

Douglas, Mary. 1973. *Natural Symbols.* New York: Vintage Books.

Eagleton, Terry. 1991. *Ideology.* London: Verso.

Flyvbjerg, Bent. 2001. *Making Social Science Matter.* Cambridge: Cambridge University Press.

Freitas, Michel. 1986. *Dialectique et Société.* 2 vols. Lausanne: L'Âge d'Honneur.

Geertz, Clifford. 1973. *The Interpretation of Cultures.* New York: Basic Books.

1980. *Negara*. Princeton: Princeton University Press.

Hardin, Russell. 1995. *One for All: The Logic of Group Conflict*. Princeton: Princeton University Press.

Jameson, Frederic. 1986. "On Magic Realism in Film." *Critical Inquiry* 12, 2: 301–25.

Knabb, Ken. 1984. *Situationist International*. Berkeley, CA: Bureau of Public Secrets.

Ladurie, Le Roy. 1979. *Carnival in Romans*. New York: George Brazillier.

Laitin, David. 2003. "The Perestroikan Challenge to Social Science." *Politics and Society* 31, 1: 163–84.

Martin, Denis-Constant. 2001. "Politics Behind the Mask: Studying Contemporary Carnivals in Political Perspective, Theoretical and Methodological Suggestions." *Questions de Recherche, 2*. Paris: Centre d'Études et de Recherches Internationals (CERI), Sciences-po.

Moss, David. 1997. "Politics, Violence, Writing: The Rituals of 'Armed Struggle'" in Italy," in David E. Apter (ed.), *The Legitimization of Violence*. London: Macmillan.

Nora, Pierre. 1992. *Realms of Memory*, vol. I: *Conflicts and Divisions*. New York: Columbia University Press.

Ozouf, Mona. 1976. *La Fête Révolutionnaire 1789–1799*. Paris: Éditions Gallimard.

Ricoeur, Paul. 1967. *The Symbolism of Evil*. Boston: Beacon Press.

Schama, Simon. 1989. *Citizens: A Chronicle of the French Revolution*. New York: Random House.

Semiotext 1982. *The German Issue* 4, 2.

Skinner, Quentin (ed.). 1985. *The Return of Grand Theory in the Human Sciences*. Cambridge: Cambridge University Press.

Smith, Philip. 1991. "Codes and Conflict: Toward a Theory of War as Ritual." *Theory and Society* 20, 1: 103–38.

Taussig, Michael. 1993. *Mimesis and Alterity*. New York and London: Routledge.

Turner, Victor. 1974. *Dramas, Fields and Metaphors: Symbolic Action in Human Society*. Ithaca: Cornell University Press.

Wagner-Pacifici, Robin Erica. 1986. *The Moro Morality Plan: Terrorism as Social Drama*. Chicago: University of Chicago Press.

Zedong, Mao. 1976. "Yan'an Forum on Arts and Literature," in *Selected Works of Mao Zedong*. Peking: Foreign Languages Press.

8

Symbols in action: Willy Brandt's kneefall at the Warsaw Memorial

Valentin Rauer

"Through all former and later pictures, [. . . I] see a kneeling man in Warsaw. [. . .] there are people who can say more with their back than others with thousand words. It was obvious that every part of this body felt something that wanted to be expressed – about guilt, penance and an infinite pain."

Cees Nooteboom[1]

Introduction

On December 7, 1970, Willy Brandt, the Chancellor of the German Federal Republic, was to sign the Warsaw Treaty, one of the treaties between Germany and Warsaw Pact nations currently seen as the first diplomatic step to the break-through of the Iron Curtain. The official signing took place in Warsaw and, as expected in the international political arena, it was paralleled by several commemorative ceremonies. The agenda included a visit to the Warsaw Memorial, erected in honor of the Jewish heroes of the 1943 Ghetto Uprising. Surrounded by the official political entourage and several representatives of the international press, Mr. Brandt stepped out of his vehicle, slowly approached the Memorial, straightened out the ribbon of a previously laid flower wreath and took a step back. Then something unexpected happened: he suddenly sank on to his knees in front of the Memorial and remained still for a minute. The next day, the response to his gesture was enormous. The picture of Brandt kneeling made its mark in the international press. All major newspapers in Europe and the United States enthusiastically featured this "emotional moment" in international relations.

Based on a media analysis of the German Chancellor Willy Brandt's kneefall in Warsaw, I will demonstrate that this was not just another media-hyped *occurrence* in politics but in fact an extraordinary *event* that marked the beginning of a new stage of development in the trajectory of German identity and memory. This performative event has changed the way in which Germans attempt to come to terms with their Nazi past (Barkan 2000; Moeller 1996: 1035). In the twenty-year period following World War Two, Germans have perceived themselves as victims of Hitler and Stalin rather than as victimizers. Reminders that Germany represents a "country of perpetrators" were usually dismissed by the majority of Germans either out of ignorance or resentment. The kneefall was the first symbolic public representation of German guilt that did not face general imme-diate defensive opposition in Germany. Quite the opposite, this event opened up the way for new forms of collective remembrance of and responsibility for the German past.

This breakthrough raises an essential theoretical question: how can a spon-taneous gesture that lasted only one minute have such a powerful latent impact on West German self-representation? Why and how is the kneefall currently perceived in the German public sphere as the decisive turning point in the his-tory of German collective memory? To expand on these issues, I will first refer to the epistemological impact of a performed social reality (Austin 1957; Der-rida 1982 [1971]; Eco 1977). Second, I will refer to two paradigms of social performance that may at first glance seem incompatible: the cultural-pragmatic approach of performance (Alexander, in this volume; Turner 1986) and the concept of "event-ness" (Giesen, this volume; Mersch 2002). The cultural-pragmatic approach provides analytical concepts for common performative productions and receptions in their entireties, and highlights that any actual performative action is always embedded in a certain cultural context, in narra-tives and scripts, and in power relations. The concept of event-ness, in contrast, focuses on the construction of *occurrences* as extraordinary *events* (Mast, this volume). This transformative construction of occurrences into events is crucial in the case of the kneefall because it enables us to explain how rigid identities and collective memories can rupture and how they are rearranged. After an occurrence has been perceived as an "extraordinary event" we no longer see the world as before. The reconciliation of these two approaches will elucidate the question of why Brandt's kneefall as a performative act has had such a profound path-breaking effect on German collective memory; furthermore, it provides a theoretical contribution to performance theory, of how the relation between cultural stability and cultural change could be conceived of.

Performances between reproduction and event-ness

After Willy Brandt, the highest representative of the Federal Republic, had through his symbolic gesture acknowledged Germany's past as a perpetrator, former narratives of disclaimer and self-victimizing were not as acceptable as before. Brandt's acknowledgment was not a *formal* speech, but a symbol in action or a gestural performance. Such acts have much more power to construct a new social reality than formal contracts or agreements (Tambiah 1979; Turner 1986). The kneefall was a gestural "speech act" that expressed feelings of remorse and repentance. Performatives achieve their meaning by *doing* instead of *describing*; they do not *claim truth* in the Habermasian sense, but *create social reality* by doing something. Performatives are never true or false but "felicitous or infelicitous" (Austin 1957: 9f.). The "action part" of a speech act (e.g. "I am sorry," "I promise") creates a way of social "being" which did not exist before the utterance. The only epistemological doubt that can be raised concerns the pragmatic question of whether the act is infelicitous, inadequate, or fabricated; e.g. did the proper person make the apology, or was the apology performed authentically enough to enhance the moral status of the person or collective? Similarly, the weekly journal *Der Spiegel* featured the kneefall by asking the question: "Should Brandt have knelt?"[2] It may seem trivial at first glance, but Austin's epistemological distinction is crucial here: Brandt invented a new performative symbol to represent the German past, thus creating a new collective reality. The discussion that followed was able to react to this new reality only by questioning the *adequacy* of the symbol, not its *truth*. The reference of truth to identity was thus shifted from the "inner" world of consciousness into the "external" world of action, expression, and perception. The philosophical being was replaced by a social being. The Cartesian *cogito*, "I think, therefore I am," was transformed into "I perform, therefore I am." The internal world was superseded by its surface; the "true" inner self became irrelevant to the social meaning of the interaction communicated.[3]

However, all performative utterances depend on the *iteration* of certain textual models or scripts in order to be to be understood, which means that there is nothing like a *new* performance (Derrida 1982 [1971]: 307–30). In the media, Brandt's kneefall was equated to a mythical historical predecessor: medieval King Heinrich IV's kneefall in Canossa. Thirty years later, the kneefall became an object of iteration and mythification in its own right. It had been applied to various contexts (Yugoslavia, China/Japan, Italy, Chile etc.) as a symbol which one should take as a model to be followed while performing public acts of reconciliation. Derrida's concept of iteration explains that the effectiveness of performative acts lies in the fact that their activity is meant to be understood and shared.[4] However, what is missing from his perspective is an approach with which to study the social conditions within which such symbols in action occur. Textual iteration includes neither a notion of social power, nor of actors, nor of an audience passing judgments on or interpreting such acts. If there are only textual iterations of signs and scripts, performance theory is reduced to what Umberto Eco once called "pan-semiotical metaphysics." There is no latent context beyond the "world as text – the text as world" (Eco 1987: 15–17, my translation).

Therefore, from a sociological perspective, the more challenging question is how and why performances have the power to *transform* and *reproduce* social identities, hierarchies, or power-structures (Turner 1986). A person who has successfully apologized for his or her deeds no longer possesses the same "degraded" identity as before (Garfinkel 1956). In order to understand that "performative magic" (Bourdieu 1991) in a sociological sense, the audience perspective must be included. The Weberian charismatic leader does not *possess* a real extraordinary disposition, but performs before his or her audience in such a manner that everybody *believes* in his or her extraordinary-ness (". . . der Glaube an die Außeralltäglichkeit"). In the same sense, an extraordinary event is not extraordinary in itself, but rather is believed to be by the audience. In this respect extraordinary-ness and event-ness do not represent an ontological reality, but rather a social reality. For the study of the persuasive force of performative events on collective identity, this argument demonstrates that we must take the perspective of the audience into empirical consideration.

But what is *the audience*? In modern or postmodern societies, Goffman's dichotomy of stage and back stage on the one hand, and audience on the other, is too simple. Audiences are not as monolithic as they seem at first glance. The functional differentiation of the means of media productions and techniques causes a multiplication of audience on at least three different levels, which can be called first-, second-, and third-order audiences. The *first-order audience* experiences the actual performance (the crowd actually observing the kneefall, see figure 8.1); for them, in terms of speech-act theory, the fusion of time and space and of actors and audience "creates a new reality." The *second-order audience* are the media which encode the event (Hall 1980) by providing latent structures of time and space by means of textual or visual representation. The media make the "absence" of the situation possible (Derrida 1982 [1971]) and encode the event as successful or failed. The reader or viewer of the media products are the *third-order audience*, who more or less depend on these medial judgments while decoding its meaning (Hall 1980). However, it is even more complex than that: the audiences can become *actors* themselves. The first-order audience is already often included and shown on TV or in newspaper pictures. Their spontaneous utterances, their laughter, or in this case, their silence, are also taken into account by the media. Their reactions are cited by the second-order audience in order to transform a profane *occurrence* into an extraordinary *event*.[5] In modern "media democracies" not only the audiences, but also the *actors* are multifaceted (Meyer 2002). In classical theatre the actor on stage represents not himself as a person, but a *social type* of persons. The actor does not express his "real me" but a general, typological or "social me" (Eco 1977). In theatre abstract social categories are performed as if they were really happening. Thus the performance of social classifications is the central structural characteristic of

Figure 8.1   Willy Brandt kneeling in front of the Ghetto Memorial

classical theatre (Eco 1977). In contrast, television genres such as news reports or "reality TV" represent a wider scope of social reality. Here, the mediated person simultaneously refers to him- or herself both as a "real person" and to his or her social role. On television news reports he or she walks and talks not *like* a politician, but *as* a politician (Eco 1977). If, for instance, the kneeling German Chancellor is broadcasted on TV, it shows not only an actor who plays or imitates political ceremony, but someone who creates as the "real" Chancellor a new reality of commemoration by a performative act. Television's means of symbolic productions produce a multifaceted spectrum of social realities; the newer medium innovates and iterates theatre at the same time. Seen from the perspective of speech-act theory, this means that television enables real politicians to perform an act in order to transform the status or identity of the collective that they represent. In (post)modern societies *teatro mundi* is challenged by *media mundi*.

However, in order to understand the social impact of performance compre-hensively, more than just the audience and actor perspectives are required (see Alexander, this volume). Some performances are censured and changed from "above" or due to the concrete societal context cannot even take form. There-fore, power and hierarchical aspects must always be taken into account. It is a different thing if it is the leader of the opposition or the Chancellor of the country who falls to his or her knees. In the same way, it makes a difference if a private person has sexual affairs or if it is the President of the United States (see Mast, this volume). For a person holding extraordinary power, it is much more likely that his or her performance is not perceived as profane occurrence, but as extraordinary event. This is quite similar to the phenomenon of "charisma of office" (Max Weber).

Moreover, performances are embedded in "background systems of collective representations." These are general belief systems, the values on which the actual performance relies. The nation as an "imagined community" of freedom and solidarity is one of the strongest belief systems in the modern era (Anderson 1983). Narratives according to which the national identity is rooted in a heroic uprising strengthen these beliefs and transform it into a stable and latent taken-for-granted-ness (Giesen 1998).

The interrelatedness and mutuality of the different pragmatic cultural patterns such as actors, audience, representational systems, scripts, and power-structures, etc., explain the reproduction and stability of collective identity and cultural specificities. However, a salient question remains: how can these collective identities change, or how can we think of cultural change in terms of performance theory? For instance, the "guilt of nations" (Barkan 2000) was a totally new phenomenon for imagined communities.[6] There existed neither a traditional knowledge of how to remember adequately such a "counter-past," nor were there collective scripts and commemorative rituals on which one could simply rely. All these cultural techniques and representations had to be invented almost out of nothing. The kneefall was one of these inventions.

To develop patterns for the theoretical interpretation of inventions, ruptures, breaks, and rearrangements, it is necessary to take into account the phenomenon of performative "event-ness." Recent philosophical approaches to performance theory differentiate between "action" and "performance" (Mersch 2002). Whereas *actions* are intentionally driven, *performances* are events that are by definition "unintentional." Events are experienced as if they "manifest themselves," as if they "simply happen," driven by a radical "alterity" which is beyond the sphere of profane or ordinary meaning (Mersch 2002: 9, my translation). Taking up Durkheim's differentiation between the sacred and the profane, one can argue that, for modern societies, it is the uncontrived event-ness that takes on the former function of the sacred (see Giesen, this volume). Whereas sacred rites such as the communication with the divine are crucial for constructing collective identity in traditional or stable times, it is the experience of event-ness, or, to introduce another term, *meaningful contingency*, that alters rigid belief systems. Those meaningful contingencies provide a resource for the invention of new traditions, belief systems, and rituals.[7]

As the following empirical analysis will show, the presence of *meaningful contingency* is precisely why enhanced moral value is still attributed to the kneefall thirty years after it took place. For the international audience, the kneefall was unprecedented. Brandt's "invention" expressed a change in the community of perpetrators. If, in contrast, the gesture had been commented on as intended and contrived, there would be no such attributions and transformational effects.

Cultural pragmatic as public commemoration: the West German case

Before going into the detail of the kneefall's specific significance, the performative environment or the historical context of the kneefall must be roughly sketched (figure 8.2). The context can be patterned through a set of different periods in which the kneefall played an important role as turning point. Periodizations always risk over-simplification and West German history of memory in particular is characterized by fundamental ambiguities. Whenever it seems that the country's historical conscience has settled down, a new, formerly taboo issue suddenly appears as the main concern for public memory. However, by using the analytical tools of cultural pragmatics and event-ness to undertake a periodization, the principal openness, fluidity, and the subjectivity of such a categorical attempt remain transparent. It is important to note that these different periods are not mutually exclusive in a strict sense. All four acts of the German memory drama more or less overlap and are to some degree still present. Some modes of remembering continually return, some come more slowly than others to a halt (Assmann and Frevert 1999) (see table 8.1).

Throughout the 1950s and the early 1960s, most West Germans perceived themselves not as perpetrators but as victims.[8] According to them, the villain was Stalin who kept millions of German POWs in his camps and occupied German territory. The suffering of Germans has frequently been paralleled to that of the Jewish victims of the concentration camps (Moeller 1996: 1026–7).[9] Public stories portrayed German women as innocent victims of war and patriarchy (Heinemann 1996; Grossmann 1998; Schneider 1998). Yet there were some incidents which could and did indeed raise the question of guilt: war crimes trials and reparation payments to Israel. But all these public debates did not really affect the common disclaimers. Instead, these issues remained objects of contestation and resentment. The German victim-discourse was valid for both those who currently still adhered to Nazi ideology as well as for those who had regrets in retrospect. The former group usually did not feel guilt at all, whereas the latter group lived in a system of collective representations of "transcendent guilt." Guilt was transformed into an existential condition of mankind and was thus represented within the sphere of metaphysics: "Mankind is evil, thus the war and the Nazis are only one example of this evilness and we, like all others, are victims of that human nature." Within the primary script dominant at the time, Hitler was imagined as "the demon" who alone was responsible

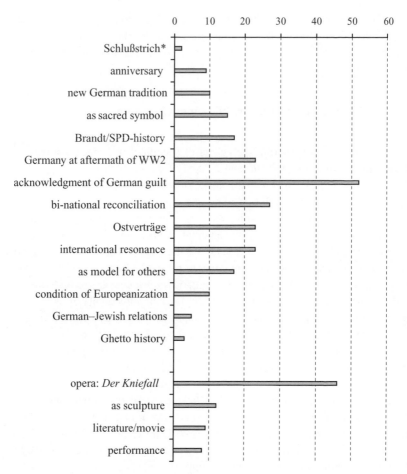

Figure 8.2   Attributed meaning and frames concerning the kneefall (n = 203)
*"Schlußstrich" means considering the kneefall as a closed object of memory.

for Auschwitz.[10] The actors in power at that time were to a great extent former National Socialists who had either changed their identity or merely kept
silent about their past.[11] It is commonly acknowledged that the continuity of
the elite within institutions such as medicine and law was almost unbroken,
but marginal fields such as, for instance, sociology, were also no exception to
this rule (Rehberg 1998). In terms of social power, it is a remarkable fact that
no surviving victim was ever given the chance to speak publicly at commemoration days (Lüdtke 1993: 554).[12] The means to symbolic production about
the extermination camps were labeled improper, although they were available.
Popular films, novels, and scholarly research depicted the general aspects as

Table 8.1 *The history of the performance of a past-as-perpetrator in the West German public sphere*

Time periods	1949–50s	Early/ mid-1960s	Late 1960s–70s	1980s–90s
Background representation	Demonization of guilt	Individualization of guilt	Gener(aliz)ation of guilt	Nationalization of guilt
Foreground scripts	Victimized Germans	Decent Germans	Resisting Germans	Victimized Jews
Actors/social power	1st generation	1st generation	1st–2nd generation	2nd–3rd generation
Public audience	Disclaim	Expulsion	Contestation	Acceptance
Means of symbolic production	Ignored, silenced	(Trans) national media coverage	Public riots, terrorism	Theatricalization of memories
Mise-en-scène	Absence	The court	The street	TV narratives

* For the theoretical model and indicators (left row) see Alexander, this volume. For historical background see Giesen 2004.

well as the specifics of Germany's "fate" (Moeller 1996). One striking example of this is that, during these years, only 4 percent of nearly 800 television documentaries on National Socialism mentioned the persecution of Jews (Classen 1999: 111). Metaphorically speaking, the only social drama performed on stage in respect to Germany's guilt and its victims, was a *mise-en-scène* of absence.

In the mid-1960s, public attention was captured by the so-called "Auschwitz trials" held in the 1960s in Frankfurt am Main. Whereas the Nuremberg trials conducted by the victorious Allies could easily be dismissed as *Siegerjustiz* ("victors' justice"), the Frankfurt trials were held before a German court.[13] In 1961, the Eichmann trial was held in Israel. The picture of the accused bureaucrat sitting in a glass chamber went around the world and was the crucial *mise-en-scène* at the time. In both cases, the accused appeared as ordinary Germans. The "banality of evil" (Arendt 1963) no longer allowed for a metaphysical demonization of guilt. Hence, the system of collective representation shifted to the crimes of individuals. Former perpetrators and bystanders were still in power and from their point of view, the criminals had to be exculpated. Thus, the individualization of guilt did not challenge the primary script of the "decent Germans." Furthermore, the trials triggered such an enormous international resonance that a new sensibility emerged in Germany as to how it should more adequately represent its past (Dubiel 1999: 105). The means of symbolic production ceased to be exclusively in the hands of the German public sphere; instead, it became clear that the perspective of the international public sphere had to be included. This new transnational tendency seems to indicate the presence of a recently identified phenomenon termed "international moral" (Barkan 2003), "moral universals" (Alexander 2002), the new international "politics of regret" (Olick and Coughlin 2003), or the transformation from "triumph to trauma" (Giesen 2004).

The trials were also observed by a new, younger generation. For this particular section of the audience, the collective representation of individual guilt versus "decent" German soldiers was unacceptable. They began to question their parents' generation (Bude 1997). In West Germany, the student movement of 1968 was directed not only against capitalism, consumerism, and societal hierarchy, but also against their parents' generation's denial of memory. The *mise-en-scène* was constituted by their "families" or demonstrations, happenings, or riots in the street. By attributing general guilt to the older generation ("gener(aliz)ation of guilt"), they, the "children," positioned themselves on the "safe" side of the generation gap. National guilt or a sense of responsibility did not exist for the students of 1968; since at the time capitalism was perceived as the ultimate cause of fascism, resistance against capitalism meant resistance against fascism. Some important participants in the student revolt were at that time already inclined towards national patriotic movements; later, they became

right-wing German nationalists (Kraushaar 2000). Latent anti-Semitic prejudices could still be identified within the cultural dramatizations (Stern 1992).[14]

It will be demonstrated in the following empirical sections that the first performative event to acknowledge national guilt was Brandt's kneefall. Another
occurrence discussed nationwide was the television series *Holocaust* of 1978.
The series raised once more the question of guilt; its performative effect lay in
the fact that this was not represented in the form of an abstract debate, but as a
narrative (Lüdtke 1993: 554f.). In general, the public's attention was above all
caught by an increase in the "theatricalization" of memory (Bodemann 2002)
and the *mise-en-scène* represented by biographical or fictitious narratives on
television. However, this period – which continues to the present day – can be
divided into several different subperiods (e.g. before and after reunification)
and is characterized by a high grade of complexity and ambiguity.[15]

The media reception of the kneefall in 1970

The kneefall occurred while Willy Brandt visited Warsaw to sign the so-called
Warsaw Treaty, one of Germany's *Ostverträge*.[16] The planned visit had been
frequently reported on by the national and international press. In the period
between November 1970 and January 1971, in France and Italy alone each
major newspaper had published around thirty articles on that topic. Within
the international public sphere, the treaties were generally viewed positively,
whereas in West Germany, the media, especially voices close to the conservative Christian Democrats and the associations of the ethnic German refugees
from Eastern Europe (*Vertriebenenverbände*) opposed the treaties furiously.
One famous slogan against Brandt's politics of reconciliation was: "Brandt up
against the wall" (*Brandt an die Wand*), which was nothing less than an appeal to
homicide. This strong opposition to the treaties had been reported on in France
and Italy, as well (e.g. *Il Messaggero*, December 7, 1970).

For the media, the kneefall was the most noteworthy event of the moment, giving it enormous international resonance. Important newspapers in Italy, France,
Switzerland, and the US (*Neue Zürcher Zeitung, Le Figaro, Le Monde, Corriere
Della Serra, Il Messaggero*, and the *New York Times*) carried a front-page photo
and feature article on this event.[17] One month later, *Time Magazine* elected
Brandt "man of the year" (*Time*, January 4, 1971). In general, the newspapers praised the gesture as an authentic symbolic admittance of responsibility
for Germany's past. For example, *Le Figaro* (December 8, 1970) subtitled the
photo an "emotional moment." Frequently, especially in Italy, the press portrayed the kneefall in a highly enthusiastic and emphatic style: "We saw Willy
Brandt kneeling and engrossed in deep reflection, lost in grief and isolated from
the world around him" (*Il Messaggero*, December 8, 1970). In almost every

newspaper, internationally as well as in the West German press, the kneefall was narrated in every detail of its performance:

The Chancellor slowly approached the monument, he paused for a moment, adjusted the ribbons of a wreath made of white carnations, then he spontaneously sank onto his knees, as if shot dead, remaining still and stony-faced in this position. (*Corriere della Sera*, December 8, 1970).

He stepped from his car and walked slowly toward the memorial between two flame-lit stone-menorahs. Mr. Brandt, who had spent the Nazi period in Scandinavia, dropped to his knees and remained that way for a full minute. He bowed his head slightly and then rose heavily. When he turned, the edge of his mouth was trembling. He joined his official party and walked slowly back, past the widely separated thin line of spectators. (*New York Times*, December 8, 1970)

Sometimes, especially in the Italian press, the kneefall was even deemed a historical moment which "drew a line under the past" (*Schlussstrich*) as either "a sign which deletes the past" (*Il Messaggero*, December 8, 1970) or as a "victory over the past" (*Corriere della Sera*, December 9, 1970). In contrast, comments in the German newspapers immediately following the event were reserved and rather reluctant. The gesture was, however, reported by the major newspapers, and mostly without any criticism.[18] The only statement questioning the kneefall was to be found in an article in the conservative newspaper *Die Welt* (December 8, 1970). It printed two pictures side by side, the kneeling Brandt and the medieval emperor Heinrich IV in Canossa. The pictures were subtitled: "self humiliation does not always eliminate the ban."

The media reception of the kneefall during the 1990s

Empirical data[19]

All articles from a period of four years (1995–9) in which the kneefall was mentioned were assembled. Out of a total retrieval of about 200 articles, 80 percent covered the kneefall as their main topic. In the remaining 20 percent, the act was mentioned in different contexts as a symbolic device, for instance in sport coverage.[20] On the most general level, the findings can first be distinguished as *memory frames* (figure 8.2: columns above) and *theatricalizations* of the kneefall (figure 8.2: columns below). The memory frames can be further subdivided into *national* frames and *international* frames.

Interpretation

In the media of the 1990s, the kneefall strongly symbolized the transformation from disclaiming the past towards an acceptance and acknowledgmen of "national guilt." This significance was not attributed immediately after the event, but at a historical distance of 25–30 years. Furthermore, the kneefall was used outside of its historical and geographical contexts as a model of appropriate recollection with respect to political gestures associated with the acknowledgment of national guilt. Framing of this kind tends to stress explicitly the characteristic meaning of such symbolic gestures. In this way, the kneefall serves as a normative point of reference in order to judge a symbolic act by the state as either "successful" or as "failed." The kneefall is iterated and re-iterated in the sense of Derrida. To give an example of a reference to the kneefall which compares it to a positively viewed, "successful" symbolic act, consider the following comment on German Federal President Herzog's speech in Guernica, Spain:

Since Willy Brandt's kneefall in front of the Warsaw Ghetto, there has not been a more touching gesture of guilt faced. The world had to wait for a long time for this. Until yesterday, neither Germany nor Spain had confessed publicly who was responsible for the destruction of the city. Finally a German broke the leaden silence about Guernica [. . .], naming the crime. (*Berliner Kurier*, April 28, 1997)

In this example the kneefall functions as an iterated, abstract model; Herzog did not perform any similar gesture, but simply gave a speech. In contrast, the kneefall has been used elsewhere in the same function, but to argue the opposite. For instance, it was applied to criticize the absence of German Chancellor Helmut Kohl on the occasion of the inauguration of the Holocaust Museum in Washington:

Willy Brandt bent his knee in the Warsaw ghetto in front of them. Though, a visible sign of German repentance would also have done well in Washington, the Germans remain guilty of the mass extermination of Jews, monstrous in its scale and execution. (*Frankfurter Allgemeine Zeitung*, April 24, 1993)

It is intriguing to see how directly the kneefall is applied within different contexts. The author did not intend to accuse Chancellor Kohl of denying German guilt, instead the contrasting comparison between Kohl's absence in Washington and the kneefall was drawn in order to emphasize – without much explanation – how an appropriate enactment of collective memory should have been performed.

National frames

Furthermore, the kneefall is referred to as a "remarkable event" in the history of the Federal Republic. The German Social Democratic Party (SPD) and Willy Brandt's biography, where the kneefall is presented on the occasion of its

25th anniversary, both attach particular importance to the kneefall in historical retrospective.

Another frame can be designated "the kneefall as *sacred symbol*." Readers of the leftist newspaper '*taz*' wrote critical letters to the editor about a satirical caricature in which the kneefall was re-enacted by Mr. Scharping, a candidate for Chancellor at that time. The caption read: "I can do that as well." The two following quotations are examples of the readers' protest:

To "estrange" Willy Brandt's kneefall in the Warsaw ghetto [. . .] is a painful blunder! On behalf of critical officers and non-commissioned officers of the German Federal Armed Forces I dissociate myself from this awful act and expect words of regret, insight and declaration of shame from the people responsible. (H. P., Retired Officer of the Federal Armed Forces (*taz*, August 22, 1994))

It's really the worst and most reactionary thing the *taz* has ever come up with, to mess with Willy Brandt's kneefall in these times of Neo-Nazism. (Member of the German Green Party (*taz*, August 15, 1994))

In response to the protests, *taz* saw itself forced to withdraw its commercial campaign. This example demonstrates that toying with the kneefall is taboo and will not be allowed, which is an indicator of the power of identification implied by the kneefall within the particular collective system of memorial representations.

Finally, two letters to the editor were coded under *Schlußstrich*, i.e. the kneefall was "considered to be a closed matter of memory." In the letter, the reader argued that in the context of the "forced labour compensation debate," Brandt's gesture had done enough penance (*Süddeutsche Zeitung*, December 29, 1999). Another letter took the opposite position (*taz*, April 10, 1993). However, due to its singularity, such argumentation does not appear to represent the main concerns of public discourse.

Transnational frames

The kneefall is mentioned again and again as a paradigm for a successful "conciliation gesture" in transnational relations, especially between Germany and Poland. For example, *Die Welt* uses the kneefall as a model of successful conciliation to comment on the state visit of President Herzog to Poland:

Herzog faced his first practical test during the months of commemoration. In Warsaw he apologized in an honest and unrestricted way for the injustice done to the Polish people by the Germans. Thereby, he may have achieved an effect as important for the relations between both nations as Willy Brandt with his historical kneefall. (*Die Welt*, July 31 1995)

In addition, there were statements in which the kneefall serves as a model for unsuccessful symbolic memory politics. The author of the following quotation combines the significance of Brandt's kneefall as a performative model with the reconciliation between Poland and Germany by proposing that it was this gesture which "suddenly gave the relationship a new basis." Brandt's *Ostpolitik*, the original context of his symbolic act, which inaugurated reconciliation on the basis of political negotiations, is simply forgotten. The power of performative acts appears much more relevant for a nation's collective memory in contrast to that of political treaties.

Nowadays, in this country the sense for symbolic action [. . .] is not very developed among politicians. The conciliatory gestures offered by Helmut Kohl to different presidents at several war cemeteries did not find uncritical approval in the public eye. With a sigh [observers] remembered Willy Brandt's kneefall in Warsaw which suddenly gave a new basis to the relationship between Poland and Germany. (*Süddeutsche Zeitung*, January 15, 1996)

Another frame is crucial for the question of the mutual interdependency of transnationalized public spheres. Here in particular, the viewpoint of others, i.e. the international resonance to the conciliatory power of the kneefall as a performative gesture, is quoted and emphasized. In this way, the *Berliner Kurier* summarized international impressions of President Herzog's visit to Warsaw:

[. . .] abroad Herzog makes a good impression. With his "plea for forgiveness" at the memorial of the Warsaw uprising, he gathered international sympathy for Germany. This awakens the memory of Willy Brandt's legendary Warsaw kneefall in 1970. (*Berliner Kurier*, July 12, 1998)

Another frame identifies the kneefall as a *model for the others*, i.e. an internationally applicable symbol "Made in Germany" and "Ready for export." This interpretation of the kneefall is suggested within the context of the Yugoslavian conflict. Additional attributions could be found within the context of post-war relations between China and Japan or Italy and Slovenia, as well as in the case of France and Algeria, Chile and Pinochet, Germany and the Czech Republic and East Germany:

A leading Croatian scientist agreed in a public discussion that, without a symbolic gesture from the Serbian side similar to Willy Brandt's kneefall in Warsaw, true normalization between aggressors and victims of aggression may not be achieved. (*Die Welt*, January 27, 1997)

China praised the Germans for coming to terms with their past and recommended it as a model for Japan. [. . .] The news agency also referred to [. . .] the kneefall of the German

Ex-Chancellor Willy Brandt in 1970 and compared it to the disputed gestures of the Japanese Prime Minister Hashimoto. (*Süddeutsche Zeitung*, August 16, 1996)

Finally, Fini demanded a formal apology from the Slovenian government for the bloodbath which Yugoslavian partisans committed [. . .] in 1945 among Italian citizens. No doubt, such an act of apology would only be possible for Slovenia if Italy were also to apologize for its fascist misdeeds, [thus] Fini's reference to Willy Brandt's kneefall in Warsaw [. . .] is misleading. (*Neue Zürcher Zeitung*, October 20, 1994)

In a few further articles, the kneefall was framed as a "necessary condition for Europeanization." The Italian journalist Franca Magnani compared the manifesto of the Italian *resistenza* with Brandt's kneefall, designating both acts as fundamental to the establishment of the European idea. In *Die Zeit* and *Süddeutsche Zeitung*, Brandt is praised as the politician to whose visions Europe should refer after the end of Cold War:

[The *resistenza*] is of a symbolic significance comparable to Willy Brandt's kneefall in the Warsaw ghetto. Therefore, one can not overlook the essential factor which applies to all countries that are characterized by resistance against National Socialism and fascism: the ethical values the struggle for freedom has created as a common point of reference for every country which is prepared for the construction of Europe. (*Die Zeit*, March 3, 1995)

The international recognition of the kneefall has been enormous; *Time* chose Willy Brandt as "Man of the Year." Since the fall of the iron curtain, he may be the only politician with a conclusive vision, the most interesting and hopeful vision of a new Europe. (*Süddeutsche Zeitung*, June 23, 1999)

The least frequent frames concern the "German–Jewish relationships" (n = 5) and the "history of the Warsaw ghetto" (n = 3). It is remarkable that the actual historical cause at which the kneefall was visually directed is so rarely featured. This infrequency highlights the relevance of "the kneefall" as an abstract iconological symbol for the history of German memory. The main focus is not the revolt in the Ghetto to which Willy Brandt's gesture literally referred. Instead, its significance is used to construct a redeemed, new German collective identity. The symbol has been removed from the historical context in which it initially appeared, in the 1990s coming to symbolize a "successful" performative act which challenged the denial of guilt within the culture of German historical memory.

Theatricalizations of the kneefall

To the group "theatricalization" or "dramatization" were attributed all those sentences which reported on the performative mimesis of Brandt's kneefall by artists, musicians, etc. Most articles were concerned with the opera *Der Kniefall von Warschau*, which had its premiere in 1997. In coverage preceding the premiere, the press responded positively to the kneefall as a theme for an opera:

The kneefall of Warsaw on 7th December, 1970 was one of the most important political symbolic acts of the century. It was readily apparent that an opera seeking to devote itself to the noble, the altruistic and the good would choose as its take-off point this great gesture before the Warsaw memorial at the very moment in which it transformed a figure of contemporary history into a hero of the theatre. (*Frankfurter Allgemeine Zeitung*, November 24, 1997)

Subsequent reviewers praised the composer's decision to have the instruments be silent during the moment at which the kneefall occurred on stage. The newspapers retold the dramatic "climax" of the opera in detail, as did for example, the *Süddeutsche Zeitung*:

The tension increases, the historical moment expands into immensity. WB [. . .] has just arranged the wreath's bows on the memorial in the former Warsaw ghetto. Now he is standing and becomes engrossed, hears from afar synagogue songs: internal music accompanying the memory of the dreadful things that came to pass here. He stands, does not kneel yet. Not until a group of young people wearing the yellow Star of David, seized by panic, comes storming up to the ramp, and they all collapse, hit by imaginary shots. Just then, as the music stops, WB kneels – "the human being becomes a myth." *Süddeutsche Zeitung*, November 24, 1997)

However, in total, critics were quite disappointed by the opera. The *Berliner Zeitung* topped off its critical review with a headline pun: "Prostration was a frustration" (*Kniefall war ein Reinfall*) (*Berliner Zeitung*, November 24, 1997). In general, the critics complain about the "hero-worship" of the work, i.e. its vocation of a "traditional heroic image" (*Berliner Zeitung*, December 3, 1997) of Willy Brandt. These reviews speak of the relative abstraction of the symbolic gesture "kneefall" in contrast to the image of Willy Brandt evoked in the opera. Whereas the act itself seems apparently suitable for the mystification, a mystification of the person Willy Brandt is viewed with skepticism and commented on with irony. Perhaps this differentiation is due to the way in which the act itself was depicted, which did not fall under the typical classical narrative presentation of a heroic protagonist. Or the criticism could also be interpreted as referring in particular to the background of traumatic memory visualized by means of a culprit/victim iconology which emphatically rejected a triumphalist hero narrative.

Another frame entails statements referring to the kneefall as a suitable subject for a stone memorial sculpture. For example, it was proposed that a sculpture of the kneefall might be appropriate for the Holocaust Museum in Washington, D.C. Elsewhere, a Social Democrat politician, Klaus von Dohnanyi, opposed a monumental Holocaust Memorial in Berlin, suggesting instead that "an artist could depict Willy Brandt's kneefall on the square before the Warsaw ghetto as a work of art" (*Berliner Zeitung*, November 11, 1997).

Occasionally, the kneefall became framed in literary contexts as an important event. In particular, it was mentioned in connection to the screen adaptation of a book by Primo Levi and readings by Günter Grass or the writer Cees Noteboom from the Netherlands (previously quoted in the introduction). In addition, references were made to the work of performance artists who presented mimetic reproductions of the kneefall. The artist Matthias Wähner placed himself beside the kneeling Brandt in a photomontage (*Frankfurter Allgemeine Zeitung*, May 13, 1994). The provocative trash artist Christoph Schlingensief dressed as an orthodox Jew and re-enacted the kneefall in front of the Statue of Liberty in New York after he had sunk a suitcase symbolizing "Germany" in the Hudson River (*Frankfurter Allgemeine Zeitung*, November 11, 1999).

Empirical and theoretical conclusions

The analysis of the media reception of the kneefall demonstrates that this short gesture has developed into a symbolic representation of a "transformed German identity." In the German media of the late 1990s, the kneefall was a continuously renarrated and emphatically recollected symbol of atonement and the acknowledgment of guilt. Symbolic representations of the acceptance of guilt are a necessary condition for reconciliation with others (Rigby 2001). In addition, the gesture became the subject of an opera and was re-enacted in various other performative art projects.

The script of the kneefall was a spontaneous invention, or had at least been convincingly represented as such.[21] The media coverage attributed to the act both authenticity and the ability to "fuse" different levels of meaning (see Alexander, this volume). The detailed retelling of the *mise-en-scène*, how "Brandt dropped to his knees," how "he rose again," how his "mouth was trembling"; all this information is provided only to prove that Brandt's authenticity fused the reality of history by "means of sudden intuitive realization." Such a "sudden intuitive realization" is the experience of extraordinary "event-ness" (see Giesen, this volume). The attribution of fusion to a performative act depends therefore on the unexpected "event-ness" of its script. However, it is neither this suddenness nor intuition alone which determined the media' interpretation of the act.

The spatial context in which the performance was enacted was the *mise-en-scène* of the Warsaw Memorial. Brandt's gesture occurred on the very squar where the hundreds of thousands of Jews of the Warsaw Ghetto were gathered to be deported to German death camps. A memorial is not the legal venue of a court room, nor is it a site of political riots like the streets of the generation of 1968. The *mise-en-scène* of a court room is juridical and the street is political, whereas the Memorial presents a moral context, and, most important of all, transcends time and space (Giesen et al. 2001). It *re*-presents to the present the victims of the past, and, in the case of the Warsaw Memorial, the heroes of the Ghetto Uprising, as well. The *mise-en-scène* represents not only an instance of guilt or heroic resistance, it also questions the nature of human existence in general in the sense of a "moral universal" (Alexander 2002).

As the Chancellor of West Germany, Willy Brandt was equipped with the maximum amount of *social power* available to a citizen of that nation. In contrast to the student revolts, the kneefall was an "act from above," performed by the highest member of the West German federal government. If a private person or a student were to have fallen to his or her knees in the same way, it would have had no societal effect. More intriguing is the significance of the kneefall for Brandt's *Ostpolitik*, as a part of which Germany renounced the entire territory east of the Oder/Neisse River. Brandt profited from the public attention given to his symbolic act. His policies were, at the time, met with strong opposition from conservatives and the right wing who still adhered to the narrative of victimization preferred by ethnic German refugees from Eastern Europe. Taking advantage of his position as Chancellor, Brandt was able to challenge symbolically this narrative of victimization without explicitly denying it. He strengthened his position by contrasting the "victimization" they claimed for themselves with that of German guilt. His performance was an indirect but nevertheless powerful way of silencing or diminishing the influence of these oppositional voices.

The collective meaning attributed to this specific location must be linked to the performing *actor* in the person of Willy Brandt. As an individual he was innocent. He had emigrated to Norway during the war and participated in the resistance movement against Nazi Germany. The actor "Willy Brandt" as individual person could in no way be suspected of hypocrisy. The paradox seems to be that only a person who individually bears no guilt that could be admitted is in the position to perform an authentic role. If a German perpetrator had acted as Brandt did, it would have reeked of strategy and calculated action. This observation brings us into the fourth and fifth part of the argumentation: the script and the systematic that lies behind collective representations.

According to the rules for the fulfillment of official scripts and systems of collective representations, the gesture represented an innovation. It was spontaneous (or at least it seemed to be spontaneous to various audiences, which the decisive factor). Its authenticity was a factor of this spontaneity. Acting unexpectedly and in an uncontrived manner, the Chancellor's kneefall symbolized the "re-fusion" of different identities. Within this moment, the "role" of the representative of the Federal Republic and the individual "real" person Willy Brandt, overwhelmed by the "sacredness of the moment," fused into one. He did what he felt, and he felt what he did, both regardless of and in regard to his official role. These "two bodies of the Chancellor," to modify Ernst Kantorowicz's (1990 [1957]) terms, are crucial to understanding the suggestive power of the script. The *individual* innocent body of the Chancellor bowed down as the representative of the *collective* body of Germany.

The innocent takes up the burden of the collectivity's "original sin," thus refounding and redeeming the nation. It is with this understanding that a former member of the Polish Resistance declared: "Within me there is no longer any hatred! He knelt down and – elevated his people [. . .] He highly elevated it in our eyes, in our hearts. I confess this as a Pole and a Christian."[22] Brandt's kneefall had a transforming or even "cathartic" effect on the audience. In terms of performance theory, it appears that Germany "has undergone a transformation of state and status, been saved, elevated or released" (Turner 1986: 81).

This example demonstrates that the performative success of Brandt's kneefall is highly dependent upon the presence of a Christian background culture in the form of "Christomimesis" (Giesen 2004). The representative of a community which is founded on the concepts of an "original sin," is him- or herself simultaneously included within and excluded from that community. The performative magic lies within this fused or trickster-like script. A person who simultaneously does and does not belong to the community of guilt is able to transform scripts in which the community's past is disclaimed. Christian myth provides both collective guilt and collective forgiveness. This might also lie behind the ease with which the German audience was able to accept Brandt's proclamation of national repentance and guilt. Since the script was decodable in accordance with Christian patterns of meaning, it claimed both collective guilt *and* forgiveness for an unforgivable past.[23]

However, the most salient impact of the kneefall is its power to challenge rigid structures in which culture was represented and with which it was identified. Rejection of the past and self-perception as victims were transformed into scripts that more and more acknowledged the past of victimizers. Why is this so? The spontaneity of the event is the key to understanding the element of potential transformation to be found even within rigid and stable cultural representations. The combination of contingency with a deeply rooted Christian culture was the condition under which a rewriting of the possible forms in which a national self could be imagined could be accomplished. If a spontaneous, contingent act resonates with existing patterns of cultural representation, and seems to fit into a system of collective representations, then this act will not be interpreted by its audience as "accidental," but instead as a manifestation of a "truer meaning." An *occurrence* is transformed in a meaningful *event*. It is the cultural meaning attributed to contingency which disentangles meaning from its either accidental or intentional, and therefore profane, significance. The power to challenge an existing script is based on this combination; on the one hand on the background presence of patterns of cultural meaning which resonate well with the challenge, and on the other hand on the meaningful contingency of a performative moment. The mutual reference between the systematic of the cultural background and occurrences transforms some of these occurrences into extraordinary events. After such a transformation "the world is seen differently." Hence, the performative event-ness enables cultural systems to alter or challenge their rigid collective self-images and paradigms.

Notes

1. *Cited in Frankfurter Allgemeine Zeitung*, November 24, 1997 (my translation). Cees Noteboom is an internationally known Dutch writer.
2. "Durfte Brandt knien?": *Der Spiegel*, December 14, 1970.
3. These assertions are not ultimately new in sociology (see also Junge, this volume). Classical frame-analysis (Goffman 1974) and the famous Thomas theorem ("if men define situations as real, then they are real in their consequences") imply very similar assumptions.
4. To put it bluntly, the aim of Derrida's argument is to prove that even action depends finally on discourse or text. Such an argument is in general at odds with social theory; however, the notion of iteration does contribute to concepts of social performance if it is interpreted as a condition for constructing "common sense."
5. For instance, Egon Bahr, Willy Brandt's counselor, stood in Warsaw behind the wall of the crowd, unable to see what was happening. Later on, he was quoted saying that suddenly the audience became absolutely silent while the journalists whispered to one another, "he's kneeling." Bahr went on to say that the rarity of moments when journalists turn silent proves the extraordinarily intense atmosphere. This is exactly the successful "re-fusion" (Alexander, this volume) of the kneefall. Thus, if we seek to understand the collective meaning of a public ritual in modern societies, we cannot avoid analyzing the media response to it (Buser and Rauer 2004).
. Karl Jaspers (2000 [1946]) was the first German intellectual to understand this new phenomenon and wrote a highly influential essay on different types of German guilt: "criminal guilt," "political guilt," "moral guilt," and "metaphysical guilt."
. The dialectical relation between change and stability is already at the core of the classical definition of performance as a means for the construction of collective identity: "Self is presented through the performance of roles, through performance that break roles, and through declaring to a given public that one has undergone a transformation of state and status, been saved or damned, elevated or released" (Turner 1986: 81).

8. At the opening session of the new German Bundestag 1949, the speaker did not mention the victims of the Germans, but instead the German Members of Parliament who had been victimized during the National Socialist period (Dubiel 1999: 37–42).

9. War criminals were euphemistically framed as "war prisoners" (*Kriegsinhaftierte*) and always seen as victims (Schildt 1998: 34f., 43). In general, "newspapers describing 'Graves and Barbed Wire: The Fate of Millions' evoked images of millions of German POWs, not millions of victims of concentration camps" (Moeller 1996: 1021, quoted in *Stuttgarter Zeitung*, October 25, 1950).

10. See the popular book *Unbewältigte Vergangenheit* by Jacob Seiler (1960) quoted in Schildt (1998: 47).

11. See, among others, the contributions in the volume edited by Loth and Rusinek (1998).

12. It is also remarkable that in the Adenauer Administration there was no "Ministry for Survivors of Nazi Persecution and Nazi Concentration Camps," but there was a "Ministry for Expellees, Refugees and War-Damaged" (Moeller 1996: 1032, 1020).

13. Some of the accused were alleged members of the SS and were accused of committing mass murder and torture in concentration camps.

14. Nevertheless, the public narrative of this movement that forced the nation to come to terms with its past is still unbroken. Marcel Reich-Ranicki (1999), a prominent German literary critic who survived the Warsaw Ghetto, writes in his memoirs that during the early 1960s, nobody ever dared to discuss his past with him. The first time a German publicly asked him to share his experience was after the Frankfurt trials at which he was called to testify. The name of the young journalist was Ulrike Meinhof, who later on became one of the most prominent figures of the 'RAF', a leftist terrorist group. The group perceived themselves as a latter-day resistance movement against fascism and capitalism.

15. See, among others, Frei (1999). Some of the many important issues were the "historians' debate" of the 1980s concerning the singularity of the Holocaust, the speech by President Weizäcker on May 8, 1985 (Dubiel 1999), and the debate concerning the Holocaust Memorial in Berlin during the 1990s (Kirsch 2001). Recent debates have focused on reparation payments to former forced labourers (*Zwangsarbeiter*), or German victimization by Allied bomb raids (triggered by the bestseller *Der Brand* by Jörg Friedrich (2002)), and on the commemoration in the form of a monument in Berlin of those who were expelled from the former Eastern territories. Whether these latter two debates could lead to a new German self-victimization (or sustain it) and if they will have strong effects on the system of collective representation cannot yet be determined.

16. Also: "East Treaties" or "treaties of reconciliation." Among others, the treaties were to confirm a West German renunciation of former territory which had become part of Poland since the end of World War Two.

17. Kneefall pictures or articles on the front pages can be found within all newspapers we selected for research: *Neue Zürcher Zeitung*: (December 8, 1970), *Le Figaro* (December 8, 1970), *Le Monde* (December 8, 1970, article, no picture), *Corriere*

Della Serra (December 8, 1970), *Il Messaggero* (December 8, 1970, article, no picture), *New York Times* (December 8, 1970).

18. In the case of the German public sphere in 1970, we analyzed the newspapers *Die Welt*, *Frankfurter Allgemeine Zeitung*, *Süddeutsche Zeitung* and the weekly journals *Der Spiegel* and *Die Zeit*. Each newspaper featured about four articles on the event at the Warsaw Memorial following its occurrence. In general, the photo was presented and at the textual level the kneefall was mentioned in a few paragraphs within coverage on the *Ostverträge*. One week later, *Der Spiegel* (December 14, 1970) covered the kneefall as a main feature. It published an opinion poll in which the majority of Germans deemed Brandt's act an exaggeration.

19. In order to analyze how the kneefall has been represented in the media thirty years later, two different methods can be used. First, one could choose the media coverage at an anniversary of the event such as December 7, 2000, when Chancellor Gerhard Schröder attended a ceremony in Warsaw in order to dedicate a new monument commemorating Brandt's symbolic kneefall. Or, this being the method I have chosen, articles are selected during a non-memorial period, i.e. a time when nothing specific happened within that memorial context. Among the newspapers sampled are agenda-setting nationally published newspapers, as well as regionally distributed newspapers: *Berliner Kurier*, *Berliner Zeitung*, *Frankfurter Allgemeine* (*FAZ*), *Neue Zürcher* (*NZZ*), *Süddeutsche Zeitung* (*SZ*), *die tageszeitung* (*taz*), *Die Welt*, and *Die Zeit*. In cases where newspapers provide an online archive reaching as far back as 1990, these articles have been included as well. The newspapers' political orientation ranges from conservative to liberal-leftist. Since all newspapers are available either as Internet archives or on CD-Rom, data retrieval was achieved by an online search strategy. In terms of methodology, a computer-assisted, quantifying frame analysis has been applied. A media discourse analysis was conducted in which Goffman's (1974) proposed method was further developed. The software "Winmax," which enables the coder to construct an inductive frame typology and to quantify the results afterwards, was used for coding.

20. "Netzer's (football) passes will stick in our memories like Brandt's kneefall in Warsaw," *taz* (May 8, 1998), quoted in *SZ* (May 11, 1998).

21. The question whether this impression of the act's spontaneity is true or not is irrelevant to its social effects due to the fact that this spontaneity was attributed by the media audience.

22. Quote in *Die Zeit* (February 4, 1977): Lew Kopelew, "Bekenntnisse eines Sowjetbürgers." The Christian symbolism of the kneefall was discussed once in an article in *Der Spiegel* (December 14, 1970). Journalists debated whether the gesture was more Protestant or Catholic. Since Brandt was an atheist, the question was irrelevant in terms of his ideological intentions. However, what was not discussed in the article was the importance of Christian symbolism from the audience's perspective.

23. The absurdity of Christian "forgiveness" in the context of the Holocaust and the problematic connotation of any Christian iconology cannot be further outlined here (cf. Bodemann 2002). See e.g. Koselleck's analysis of the cynical anti-Judaist connotation of the *Pietà*. The *Pietà* is a monument placed in Berlin's "Neue Wache"

in the year 1992 to commemorate the victims of World War Two (the statue was originally created by Käthe Kollwitz in 1937/8, referring to the victims of World War One). The monument shows a mother holding in her arms her dead son which again symbolizes Mother Mary mourning for the crucified Jesus Christ, who was, according to the anti-Judaic Christian tradition (and later for the Nazis), "murdered by the Jews" (Koselleck 2002: 78).

References

Alexander, Jeffrey C. 2002. "On the Social Construction of Moral Universals: The 'Holocaust' from War Crime to Trauma Drama." *European Journal of Social Theory*, 5, 1: 5–85.

Anderson, Benedict. 1983. *Imagined Communities*. New York: Verso.

Arendt, Hannah. 1963. *Eichmann in Jerusalem: A Report on the Banality of Evil*. New York: Viking Press.

Assmann, Aleida and Ute Frevert. 1999. *Geschichtsvergessenheit – Geschichtsversessenheit. Vom Umgang mit den deutschen Vergangenheiten nach 1945*. Stuttgart: DVA.

Austin, John L. 1957. *How To Do Things with Words*. Cambridge, Mass.: Harvard University Press.

Barkan, Elazar. 2000. *The Guilt of Nations: Restitution and Negotiating Historical Injustices*. New York: Norton & Company.

———. 2003. "Restitution and Amending Historical Injustices in International Morality," pp. 91–102 in John Torpey (ed.), *Politics of the Past: On Repairing Historical Injustices*. Oxford: Rowman & Littlefield.

Bodemann, Michal Y. 1998. "Eclipse of Memory: German Representations of Auschwitz in the Early Postwar Period." *New German Critique* 75: 57–89.

———. 2002. *In den Wogen der Erinnerung. Jüdische Existenz in Deutschland*. München: DTV.

Bourdieu, Pierre. 1991. *Language and Symbolic Power*. Cambridge, Mass.: Harvard University Press.

Bude, Heinz. 1997. *Das Altern einer Generation. Die Jahrgänge 1938 bis 1948*. Frankfurt/M: Suhrkamp.

Buser, Tina and Valentin Rauer. 2004. "Gianfranco Finis Erinnerungspolitik. Eine Medienanalyse zu den Gedenkbesuchen in den Fosse Ardeatine und in Auschwitz, pp. 239–68 in B. Giesen and C. Schneider (eds.), *Tätertrauma: Nationale Erinnerung im öffentlichen Diskurs*. Konstanz: UVK.

Classen, Christoph. 1999. *Bilder der Vergangenheit. Die Zeit des Nationalsozialismus im Fernsehen der Bundesrepublik Deutschland 1955–1965*. Köln: Böhlau.

Derrida, Jacques. 1982 [1972]. *Margins of Philosophy*. Chicago: University of Chicago Press.

Dubiel, Helmuth. 1999. *Niemand ist frei von Geschichte. Die nationalsozialistische Herrschaft in den Debatten des Deutschen Bundestages*. München: Hanser.

Eco, Umberto. 1977. "Semiotics of Theatrical Performance." *The Dramatic Review* 21: 107–17.

1987. *Streit der Interpretationen*. Konstanz: UVK.

Frei, Norbert. 1999. *Vergangenheitspolitik. Die Anfänge der Bundesrepublik und die NS-Vergangenheit*. München: DTV.

Garfinkel, Harold. 1956. "Conditions of Successful Degradation Ceremonies." *American Journal of Sociology*, 62, 5: 420–4.

Giesen, Bernhard. 1998. *Intellectuals and the Nation: Collective Identity in a German Axial Age*. Cambridge: Cambridge University Press.

2004. *Triumph and Trauma*. Boulder, CO: Paradigm Publishers.

Giesen, Bernhard, Valentin Rauer and Christoph Schneider. 2001. "Vergangenheitsentlastung durch Differenzierung," pp. 15–39 in Moritz Csáky and Peter Stachel (eds.), *Die Verortung von Gedächtnis*. Vienna: Passagen.

Grossmann, Atina. 1998. "Trauma, Memory, and Motherhood: Germans and Jewish Displaced Persons in Post-Nazi Germany, 1945–1949." *Archiv für Sozialgeschichte* 38: 215–39.

Hall, Stuart. 1980. "Encoding/Decoding," pp. 128–39 in S. Hall, D. Hobson, A. Lowe, and P. Willis (eds.), *Culture, Media, Language*. London: Hutchinson.

Heinemann, Elizabeth. 1996. "The Hour of the Woman. Memories of Germany's 'Crisis Years' and West German National Identity." *American Historical Review*, 101: 354–95.

Jaspers, Karl. 2000 [1946]. *The Question of German Guilt*. Fordham: Fordham University Press.

Kantorowicz, Ernst H. 1990 [1957]. *The King's Two Bodies: A Study of Medieval Political Theology*. Princeton: Princeton University Press.

Kirsch, Jan-Holger. 2001. "Trauer und historische Erinnerung in der Berliner Republik. Überlegungen aus Anlaß der Mahnmalsdebatte," pp. 339–74 in Burkhard Liebsch and Jörn Rüsen (eds.), *Trauer und Geschichte*. Köln: Böhlau.

Koselleck, Reinhart. 2002. "Transformation der Totenmale im 20. Jahrhundert." *Transit, Europäische Revue* 22: 59–86.

Kraushaar, Wolfgang. 2000. *1968 als Mythos, Chiffre und Zäsur*. Hamburg: HIS.

Loth, Wilfried and Bernd-A. Rusinek (eds.). 1998. *Verwandlungspolitik: NS-Eliten in der westdeutschen Nachkriegsgesellschaft*. Frankfurt/M: Campus.

Lüdtke, Alf. 1993. "'Coming to Terms with the Past': Illusions of Remembering, Ways of Forgetting Nazism in West Germany." *Journal of Modern History* 65: 542–72.

Mersch, Dieter. 2002. *Ereignis und Aura. Untersuchungen zu einer Ästhetik des Performativen*. Frankfurt/M: Suhrkamp.

Meyer, Thomas. 2002. *Media Democracy: How the Media Colonize Politics*. Cambridge: Polity Press.

Moeller, Robert G.. 1996. "War Stories: The Search for a Usable Past in the Federal Republic of Germany." *American Historical Review* 101: 1008–48.

Olick, Jeffrey K. and Brenda Coughlin. 2003. "The Politics of Regret: Analytical Frames," pp. 37–62 in John Torpey (ed.), *Politics of the Past: On Repairing Historical Injustices*. Oxford: Rowman & Littlefield.

Rehberg, Karl-Siegberg. 1998. "Verdrängung und Neuanfang: Die Soziologie nach 1945 als 'Normalfall' westdeutscher Geschichtserledigung," pp. 272–3 in Wilfried Loth and Bernd-A. Rusinek (eds.), *Verwandlungspolitik: NS-Eliten in der westdeutschen Nachkriegsgesellschaft.* Frankfurt/M: Campus.

Reich-Ranicki, Marcel. 1999. *Mein Leben.* Stuttgart: DVA.

Rigby, Andrew. 2001. *Justice and Reconciliation: After the Violence.* London: Lynne Rienner.

Schildt, Axel. 1998. "Der Umgang mit der NS-Vergangenheit in der Öffentlichkeit der Nachkriegszeit," pp. 19–54 in Wilfried Loth and Bernd-A. Rusinek (eds.), *Verwandlungspolitik: NS-Eliten in der westdeutschen Nachkriegsgesellschaft.* Frankfurt/M: Campus.

Schneider, Franka. 1998. "Ehen in Beratung," pp. 192–216 in Annette Kaminsky (ed.), *Heimkehr 1948. Geschichte und Schicksale deutscher Kriegsgefangener.* München: Beck.

Stern, Frank. 1992. "Von der Bühne auf die Straße. Der schwierige Umgang mit dem deutschen Antisemitismus in der politischen Kultur 1945 bis 1990." *Jahrbuch für Antisemitismusforschung* 1: 42–76.

Tambiah, Stanley. 1979. "A Performative Approach to Ritual." *Proceedings of the British Academy* 65: 113–69.

Turner, Victor. 1986. *The Anthropology of Performance.* New York: PAJ.

9

The promise of performance and the problem of order

Kay Junge

Introduction

The purpose of this chapter is partly historical, partly conceptual. It is an attempt to articulate the performative element implied by the metaphor of the social contract, a metaphor that served as one of the basic social paradigms in early modern and Enlightenment social thought and only a generation ago began to enjoy a revival mainly due to John Rawls' *Theory of Justice* and, to a lesser extent, the wintrier *Calculus of Consent* by Buchanan and Tullock. Though almost all of today's contractarians have taken to heart David Hume's early critique of the idea of an original contract (Hume 1948), I do not think that the exchange of promises or some equivalent performance that Hobbes and others deemed necessary for establishing a commonwealth is merely a theoretical chimera. Indeed, the particular type of consent that the earlier social contract theorists assumed people showed to their government has, as we hope to show, a strong performative element to it that deserves further theoretical attention. In particular, if sociologists with an interest in performance were to examine Hobbes' way of framing the contractual institution of a sovereign they would discover a nice interlocking of concerns relating both to problems of social fusion and the staging of collective representations (see the contributions of Alexander and Giesen in the present volume). Our reading of Hobbes will add a certain performative twist to the contractarian paradigm and will enable us to reframe some of its seemingly sterile or misplaced idealizations as the dramatic effects necessary for its successful discursive implementation.

Apart from this introduction and a short conclusion, this chapter is divided into six sections. The stage will be set in the three sections that follow, which roughly sketch some of the performative complexities characteristic to social affairs that, although acknowledged by scholars, have not always been fully integrated into sociology's conceptual canon. The first section looks at Austin's notion of the performative utterance and hints at some of its historical prede-cessors, most notably Hume's account of promises. The second section treats Goffman's more general notion of performance in the same manner, suggesting a more diverse set of authors who in a general fashion paved the way for some of his concerns and insights. In the third section we will trespass on to less secure territory in the hope of gaining perspectives on the self-referential nature of social reality, unfolding as it does through performances that give meaning to each other and through collective representations that present society to itself. After thus having set the stage, in the second half of the chapter, the main focus will fall on the contract paradigm. First, I will suggest a way to avoid the regress problem that we seem to run into when arguing that the meaning of performances is determined through their meaningful relationship with other performances. Taking a hint from Nietzsche – though not a blatantly clear one – it will be suggested that this potentially infinite expansion of contexts can be avoided if we identify sequences of performance analogous to the elements that make up a contract. It will be argued that performances that are thus framed and related to each other get transformed into interlinked performatives. The rest of the chapter consists of two further sections and will focus above all on Hobbes and the way he extended the notion of contract to the realm of society as a whole. Here we will be mainly interested in the ways he assumed fusion could be achieved and consent established in order to make social order possi-ble. The institution of a sovereign, it will be observed, depends, among many other things, on a specific distribution of the means of symbolic production that finds its parallel in the world of the theatre. The chapter will close with a short summary.

Performatives: words as deeds

Perhaps a little like Molière's Monsieur Jourdain, who spoke in prose without knowing it, we might claim that sociologists have to some extent always focused on performance without explicitly realizing that they were doing so, without having a specific term to mark the phenomenon. The two central terms, *perfor-mative utterance*, on the one hand, and *performance*, on the other, that gave us a specific grasp of these phenomena, first gained theoretical status in the late 1950s through the writings of John Austin and Erving Goffman respectively (Austin 1961; Goffman 1959). However, as will be shown below, the problems they dealt with and the phenomena they exposed had not gone unnoticed in pre-vious eras and have only much more recently acquired the status of a theoretical challenge.

It is often claimed with reference to Austin that he discovered something new, that he spotted a function of spoken language that had been overlooked or at least neglected until then. However, the idea, that – roughly – you can change the situation that you and those present are involved in simply by saying something and indeed perhaps only by saying something, and that saying something can have an effect on your own and other's future behavior has only been neglected within a very narrow field of philosophy. It had been overlooked mainly among those philosophers working within the Vienna Circle's tradition who concentrated on the concept of truth and on spoken language that reflects truth and who were at least to some tastes a little too obsessed with rejecting everything else as meaningless. Beyond that field, however, the claim that you can do things with words, and can do quite other things with words than asserting the truth or falsehood of something, would have caused no great irritation. Political philosophy knew it all along. Thomas Hobbes, for one, was well aware of other speech acts than the assertion. He extensively analyzed "how by language men work upon each other's minds" and what constitutes and distinguishes, for example, teaching and persuading, commands and counsels, or promises and threats (Hobbes 1994: 73–7). Moreover, of course, the early modern literature that addressed itself to princes and courtiers, as well as all the later literature on good manners and the art of conversation were full of advice for doing things with words. To give just one example from a classic work from the latter category: if a "controversy grows warm and noisy, endeavor to put an end to it by some genteel levity or joke" (Chesterfield 1984: 75). In choosing the title of his book, Austin (1962) obviously, though jokingly, refers to the vogue of how-to-do-manuals that has been with us for centuries.

We should also notice that Hobbes was already well aware of a certain impasse that speech-act theory quickly ran into when attempting to classify different speech acts by their grammatical form. As this did not really work, the concept of an indirect speech act had to be introduced to deal with these problematic cases. Perhaps for reasons of economy or as a matter of politeness, what we say word for word and what it means often do not match up one to one. Though Hobbes did not bother to explain why this is so, he was clear in pointing out that the meaning of our speech often cannot be reduced to the literal meaning and grammatical construction of the sentences we articulate. A request might often have the same grammatical form as a question and, if we restrict our attention to their grammatical form, the issuing of a command can often hardly be distinguished from the giving of advice and counsel (Hobbes 1960: 166f.). In order to be able to discriminate between the different meanings we might attribute to the same words, we have, as Austin vaguely suggested, to take "the total speech situation" into account (Austin 1962: 147).

But what does this situation consist of and how can we specify its limits? The binding meaning that others draw from speech acts addressed to them might at least sometimes not be discoverable within the bounds of the encounter in which these acts were uttered. To show this, we will take a look at what perhaps may be said to have become the paradigm case of a speech act, the act of promising. A pragmatic answer, sympathetic to our own concerns, to the question of what constitutes a promise and what makes it binding for the person who uttered it was first outlined by David Hume. Hume very much doubted that there is a natural obligation to be bound by one's word. He also rejected the idea that it is our intention or will that makes a promise binding, as this would only lead us into a regress of willing volition. Instead he assumed that promises are usually made out of self-interest. But, so he observes, by uttering a promise we may give our self-interest a new direction. In uttering the proper words, we willy-nilly create a new motive for us to keep the promise, because in uttering them we subject ourselves to "the penalty of never being trusted again in case of failure" (Hume 1960: 522). It is not the will that creates the obligation, but the utterance of the promise, may we will it or not. The performative act itself creates the motive to honor the promise. "The expression being once brought in as subservient to the will, soon becomes the principal part of the promise" (Hume 1960: 523). Promises, according to Hume, are a human convention which can be activated to provide security for future conduct, by redirecting interests to a group's mutual advantage. We are bound by our words because our reputation is at stake. Knowing that we care about our reputation and the obligations that go along with it, others can rely on our promises. The binding force of speech acts derives primarily from our dependence on others, not from our intentions, our resoluteness or sense of duty. A promise, if accepted by its addressee, constitutes a social fact in the Durkheimian sense and the same can be said about all other speech acts. Whenever we say something that somehow affects others, we might be held responsible for having said it, and knowing this, we will feel committed to our words.

Perhaps the real provocation in Austin's outline of what later became speech-act theory should not be sought in his distinction between a constative and performative use of language, but in his deconstruction of this distinction (Felman 1983; Fish 1989: 37–67). Though Austin changed his terminology midway, he eventually arrived at the conclusion that even constative statements have a performative component or aspect. They also affect the situation and what follows and, in doing so, bind the speaker. The distinction between saying something and doing something, the distinction Austin proceeded from, somehow collapsed in the end. The performative became ubiquitous. Whatever we say, there always is an aspect to it that affects the situation. Or, to put it in more existentialist parlance, there really is no neutral ground for us and the ideal of a non-poetic use of language is a chimera (Danto 1975: 42ff.). "To reveal is to change" (Sartre 1988: 37). Naming, blaming, and claiming are intrinsically interwoven. But one should be a bit more clear about why this is so. Of course, a committed intellectual, as Sartre pointed out, may want to fire when he speaks. But though, metaphorically speaking, words might hurt, the addressee of a speech act does not simply get hit. Being addressed puts him in a position to answer, not just to react. With reference to the propositional content of a speech act, we always have the option to say "No!" Speech acts, in both their imperative and their declarative mode, confront their addressees with a choice, to either accept or reject them, or perhaps to ask for further justification. This is the change they bring about, the difference they make, and it is only by enforcing this choice that they allow us to talk about the same things and agree or disagree with each other on the same issue (Tugendhat 1982). As we will see, performances can be distinguished from performatives in that they do not force an explicit choice on others but allow for more indirect, tacit, subtle, but also oftentimes evasive adaptations.

Performance: appearance as reality

Compared to the resonance Austin gained among philosophers, Goffman's notion of performance caused less of a stir in sociology, though it greatly influenced the development of the discipline by elevating the interactional order to a legitimate field of study. The idea that social reality shares certain characteristics with performance was not considered a new insight, as the dramaturgical view on social reality and the trope of the *theatrum mundi* has been with us at least since the Stoics. This trope was given its specific modern meaning during the late Renaissance, when man replaced God as the most important spectator of this theatre and it has been with us ever since. With the advent of modernity, it lost its force as a *memento mori*, a reminder of death, and instead began increasingly to serve as an alibi for impression management.

Like the classical sociological authors writing at the turn of the century, Goffman gave only very scant reference to those writing before him. But he did give credit to Herbert Spencer at a time almost no one was reading him anymore (Goffman 1971: vii). And indeed Spencer had already dealt extensively with the ceremonies of everyday life that were of central concern to Goffman. Among the ceremonial institutions Spencer looked at were trophies, presents, mutilations, obeisances, forms of address, titles, and fashion (Spencer 1966). He considered such ceremonies to be the earliest and most general kinds of government, long preceding civil and ecclesiastical forms of control. They are performed almost spontaneously and have till today been used to envelop the more definite restraints which church and state came to exercise in the more advanced societies later on. Spencer argued that almost all of these ceremonies have their main function in signaling subjugation. But he also observed that they are well on the way to losing much of their relevance in our contemporary society, where people, as he saw it and wished, increasingly deal with each other on a more equal footing. Unfortunately, Spencer was less interested in or sensible to the occasionally quite subtle forms of ceremonial domination, although he traced the sometimes quite curious origins of such ceremonies with great enthusiasm.

Goffman's characteristic focus on our concern for face and footing, for face-saving and face-threatening activities and for status, finds no equivalent in the more recent history of social thought. However, we may discover in the French moralists of the seventeenth century his spiritual allies (Krailsheimer 1962; Lovejoy 1961), though again many of their insights were perhaps already part and parcel of the early modern advice literature on prudent conduct and successful career-promotion at the princely courts (e.g. Gracian 2001). Rousseau later framed these observations using new premises and presented them in a more systematic, or what we might call a more one-sided and almost paranoid fashion. He observed that a gap between appearance and reality arises as soon as people become concerned about the impressions they make upon others. Man becomes alienated by scrutinizing himself in this manner and vanity and pride, or, to use Rousseau's term, *amour propre*, will inevitably follow and result in hypocrisy and inauthenticity (Rousseau 1984: 110ff.). The British moralists of the eighteenth century and the sociological classics (with the exception of Simmel) paid comparatively little attention to these subtleties and only when Goffman finally arrived on the scene did sociologists again begin to reflect on these oftentimes paradoxical intricacies.

By pointing to the dramaturgical problems that actors must face, find themselves entrapped in, or run into without recognizing, Goffman helped shift the focus of sociology from individual action to social communication. Goffman defined performance as all activities of a given participant which in some way serve to influence other participants. Wherever there is a problem of coordination, performance will arise, and wherever there are problems of mutual trust, these dramaturgical concerns will require perhaps more of our energies than we would like and occasionally might even begin to dominate the scene (Goffman 1959: 65). However, this does not mean that alienation is essential to social life, though it is certainly one of its variants (Alexander 1987: 230–7). As soon as we find ourselves in the presence of others, observing that they will make certain inferences from our behaviors, our activities will necessarily acquire a promissory character for them. Aware of this, we almost automatically will either quickly feel, though only to some extent, committed to a certain course of action or somehow feel obliged to give at least some tacit hints or even an explicit account for not being inclined or able to live up to the expectations we might have triggered and assume others to hold. This apparent conformism is not due to some intrinsic naiveté of *homo sociologicus*. It follows from the certainly quite intricate reasoning that, if we want to pursue our own goals successfully, we need to be able to predict how relevant others will react, and this we can do only if we, in turn, make ourselves predictable to them.

A further point should be added to our account of Goffman that has received only scant attention in the literature, but will be needed later in this chapter. It concerns the still only vaguely conceived difference between action – including speech acts – and performance, that we have already hinted at before. Though all our actions relating to others can acquire a performative dimension and promissory character, our performative accomplishments are not always and necessarily perceived and labeled in terms of actions. Performance seems to be a more ubiquitous phenomenon than action. Agreeing to an argument or accepting the facts that some speaker has pointed out is something we must manage to signal to our partners; it is certainly a performative accomplishment. But it is usually not perceived as goal-oriented action. We show understanding, but we do not make an act out of it. However, not having protested might be taken as an act, namely an omission, that we might be held accountable for and that might become binding on us.

Though the term suggests otherwise, interaction does not even have to begin with an intentional act. I might feel embarrassed, disgusted, hurt, humiliated, irritated, or seduced by someone else, or just take offense at his or her presence, her breath, her snoring. As I determine my own behavior accordingly and signal these feelings or ways of experiencing the situation, the other person, upon seeing this and noticing being observed this way, will find herself already somehow drawn into interaction. An encounter might already have gotten started before you intentionally become involved. You might just by chance be looking at someone, and he might react in a way that will make you feel that he thought you were staring at him. You might find yourself involved in such situations without having intended it at all and it requires specific cultural skills, e.g. of civil inattention (Goffman 1971: 304f.), to avoid traps like these. There are many circumstances where not getting involved with one another is in fact a skilled ongoing performative achievement. In heavy walking traffic, for example, we must tacitly negotiate with others our progress on the sidewalk, but again these coordinating adjustments are usually not framed as actions, but rather as routine accomplishments that go unmarked or, we might say, go noticeably unnoticed and do not require those involved to address each other explicitly. Others though, such as, for example, muggers or street vendors, have developed special skills and counter-strategies that rely on these routines only to redirect our behavior, commit us to a certain course of action, and thereby make us seemingly voluntarily run into their various traps (Katz 1988; Clark and Pinch 1995). Such are the occasional inconveniences, the sometimes quite vexing social facts of life. But even more pleasurable ventures, such as flirting, would not get underway if we could not draw on the ambiguities of translating performance into action (Sabini and Silver 1982).

Some of the varieties of performance and impression-management might already be observed in the animal kingdom. However, in order to get a conversation going or to institute more complex social arrangements, performances alone will not suffice. At least some of our behavior needs to acquire the status of performative acts that put others in a position of making an explicit choice. It is only when others can explicitly refer to our performances and either reject the intentions they attribute to the behavior in question or explicitly claim to rely on these intentions that these performances get transformed into performative acts or utterances. It is only this bifurcation that allows the establishment and negotiation of more complex social arrangements.

Self-reference, reflexivity, and reciprocation

In exposing and making us aware of our seemingly ubiquitous attempts at impression management, Goffman sometimes seems on the brink of what has been called a performative contradiction (Jay 1989). But might we not arrive at a new level of innocence and regain authenticity, at least within specific circles or on specific occasions, by openly admitting the existence of these strategies? Is not this precisely what makes Goffman's debunking of our everyday gambits so charming, so authentic? The logical problems that are lurking here have come to us in many variants. Writing at the beginning of the eighteenth century, Lord Shaftesbury gave us a slightly different version of a performative contradiction. He felt that people who only care about their private advantage "are sure to preach honesty and go to church," while those who claim to have discovered "that by nature we are all wolves," simply by saying so, give us sufficient evidence that it cannot be true and that they do not really mean it (Shaftesbury 1900: 63f.). Instead of assuming that they contradict themselves, we should understand them to mean something else. What if we read Hobbes' *homus homini lupus* not as a metaphorical description, but as a warning? If the Hobbesian warning is taken to heart, moreover, we might never find out whether it was in fact true.[1] We should not be surprised to find some people living in a Rousseauian paradise because they take a Hobbesian view of their situation, as the anthropologist Elizabeth Colson once observed (1974: 37). Sagas and tales of feuding, for example, might stand for such warnings and should not always be taken as evidence, as Max Gluckman has argued (1963: 22). Social descriptions can influence and shape what they describe, even if they engage in counterfactual reasoning or even if they are wrong. Or, indeed, as we will show later with reference to Hobbes' account of the social contract, even if they turn out to be right.

The lessons we might draw from such observations are not entirely clear. Must we avoid such paradoxes? Must sociological theories, at least those with universal ambitions, take pains to remain compatible with what they claim about their object of study because they themselves take part in it? Might the paradoxes we might run into at this juncture serve as arguments against certain variants of deconstructionism or conservative elitism claiming to be based on superior, though ineffable insights? These are the consequences Habermas wants us to draw and take to heart (Jay 1989) and it is difficult, if not impossible, to argue against them. But the puzzles just hinted at are only one aspect or variant of a more pervasive complication. So far, we have only considered which challenges we might have to face when reflecting on society from within society, i.e. when engaging in sociological theory-building. In general, however, it seems that these and similar self-referential circles are part of our human condition and cannot be avoided altogether.

It was speech-act theory in particular that made us aware of the fact that self-reference might indeed be considered to be constitutive for social affairs. A performative statement refers to the reality that, if it is felicitous, it at the same time appears to create (Felman 1983: 21f.). A promise is taken as a promise, among other things, because it says it is one. But even though performative statements are often expressed by the declarative mood of the verb, we should, of course, not overlook their imperative nuances. Performatives are not tautologies, making us run in circles, leading to nothing new. If successful, they will make a difference to other potential performers and will allow social systems to be talked into existence.

Following Judith Butler (1997), Slavoj Žižek (1989) and others (Pye 2000) and using Althusser's figure of interpellation (Althusser 1971), or choosing a slightly different path, following David Bloor (1997), and taking a look at the social world from the shoulders of Wittgenstein, one could say that social reality calls itself into existence because the words we use somehow retroactively effect what they refer to. There seems to be a "Munchhausen effect" at work in the performative creation of social reality – to recall Baron Munchhausen, who lifted himself into the air by pulling himself up by his own hair (Pêcheux 1982: 103–9). We create relevant others by addressing them or being introduced to them and thereby giving them a voice. Afterwards, we can no longer show indifference to each other as strangers would, but are forced to treat each other as friends or as foes or as something in between and thereby maintain our own social existence as well as theirs. Afterwards our future conduct will be read as performative action, as a type of conduct that contains a message that we might be held accountable for later on. Of course, speech acts often misfire almost beyond recognition. But by reciprocating each other, they can also create the felicitous conditions that mutually sustain their meanings. That the expectations that shape our conduct and action might eventually be self-fulfilling, however, should not merely be seen as an interesting curiosity or even as a pathology of social life (Merton 1968). Self-fulfilling expectations are a constitutive characteristic of all social institutions that have endured for some time (Krishna 1971).

Among the sociological classics, Georg Simmel was perhaps the most explicitly concerned with problems of reciprocation and the circular architecture of the social world, where beliefs shape behavior that in turn gives rise to an adaptation in beliefs (Simmel 1950: 309). But whereas Simmel only observed some parallels between concept formation and group formation (Simmel 1950: 96f., 254ff.), Durkheim argued that neither of them can be had independent of the other. According to Durkheim, symbolic representations first of all give form to our fluid emotions and fluctuating expectations. This patterning and fixation allows for a greater homogeneity and social cohesion among the individuals involved, which in turn is reflected and externalized in social representations demarcating group-membership (Alexander 1982: 245ff., 271ff.). Symbolic representations do not only give form to social affairs, they are constitutive for the formation of social systems – they shape them into existence. In contributing to self-knowledge, they allow people to orient themselves to each other in new ways (Greenblatt 1988: 8). It is only via such representations that we can get beyond the level of a tacit coordination of our performances and arrive at the more articulate level of performatives to make our mutual expectations more explicit.

Especially Goffman alerted us to the reflexive structure of the mutual expectations we need to assume at just those moments when individuals manage to address one another successfully. Social contact, so Goffman argues, can only occur when (1) people in fact do address themselves to one another, (2) all involved parties are simultaneously aware of this, and (3) they know that all possess this awareness (Goffman 1971: 70). But what makes these reflexive iterations necessary? If we ask ourselves how, for example, the ceremonies of subjugation that Spencer described so extensively come to function, and how they might be subverted, we should be able to grasp why such iterations are constitutive even for ritual performances. In performing ceremonies of subjugation, subjects do not only show obedience to their rulers. Being performed in public, these ceremonies also have a promissory character among the subjects themselves. By seeing each other engaging in the performance, each subject may infer that whoever stands out from the crowd will stand alone. Each subject performs on the assumption that others do likewise and each subject might know that all others will show deference to the ruler based on the same assumption. The latter would be an instance of something known to be known. But on what account can we infer that this reflexively structured assumption has in fact been made by participants? If, for example, we could observe subjects smiling at each other or grumbling during the ceremony, thereby more or less tactfully acting against the prescriptions of the ritual, such an inference might be plausible or even compelling. Observing this, we might assume a second, but partly hidden, transcript towards which they orientate themselves (Scott 1990), thus motivating and calling forth behaviors they would not dare to engage in if they were sure that at least some of them at least to some extent also only feign deference. The observable reciprocation between these subversive performances only becomes possible if we assume that such knowledge exists. A successful staging of the ritual, in which no one deviates from the set course, might of course in an analogous way depend on the fact that every one knows that everyone knows that each of them performs it with great anxiety, fearing to be sanctioned if they do not conform.

In order to be successful, the performative imputation of meaning by publicly appealing to certain collective representations of course somehow must fit the expectations of its addressees. But we should not assume that this fit needs to be total. There always seems to be some leverage. We adapt our expectations continually and might even let our performances closely follow suit. Collective representations, however, will most likely turn out to be less easily adaptable to changing circumstances. They need to remain consistent in order to provide the orientation that is fundamentally necessary. Furthermore, any change in collective representations might also undermine the standing of those known to be committed to them, who therefore will have a vested interest in upholding them. More attractive alternatives compatible with the established status distribution often cannot be invented on the spot and a certain mismatch between individually held expectations and collective representations might therefore easily develop. Such a mismatch might take on quite bizarre forms. Where proper adaptations or alternatives do not seem to be within reach, collective representations may turn into mere fictions that force all participants into an *as if* game (Kusy 1985: 163ff.) and to "live within a lie" (Havel 1985: 31). Where the mismatch becomes unbearable and breaks into the open – that is, comes to be known to be known – a double-edged situation might evolve and it is here that social drama is often most tense. A carnival ceremony might transform into rebellion and quickly lead to mayhem and massacre, as Emmanuel Le Roy Ladurie has shown (2003); or a ruler like Ceauşescu might suddenly find himself booed at (Scott 1990: 204f.).

Theoretical reflections on the performative character and self-referential nature of social reality have made us much more aware not only of the non-scripted contingencies, but more importantly also of the ontologically precarious, somehow deficient, self-referential constitution of social affairs (Felman 1983; Butler 1997). Performances are triggered and become relevant only within the type of settings that, to use a term coined by Parsons, involve a "double contingency" (1977: 167f.), settings in which our possible choices depend on each other and in which we know that they do and know that the others around us think likewise. In such settings, at least according to some, the notion of rationality is of only questionable value (e.g. Coleman 1990: 931). Attempts to derive the structure and dynamics of human affairs from other apparently more elemental, more basic givens such as interests or common values under these circumstances appear to be essentially incomplete, simplistic, and mistaken. However, the alternatives are less clear. Within sociology, a shift has clearly started towards a focus on processes, their characteristic patterns, their path-dependence and narrative emplotments, while, over the last quarter century, notions of equilibrium, homeostasis, and stability, etc., have almost disappeared from the sociologist's dictionary. Nonetheless, at present, theory-building still seems to be in a considerable muddle. To get a complete hold on the self-referential and thus always a bit arbitrary or, we might say, self-transcending character of social performance, however, might even prove impossible (see Giesen, this volume). But we can nevertheless more closely approximate possible developments and more closely determine their evolution by, for example, considering certain threshold effects (Simmel 1950: 96). We will also gain further insight if we take a closer look at a number of certain other dimensions such as the material constraints of the situation at hand, the background symbols available within a specific culture, the socially prevailing distribution of power or the distribution of the means of symbolic production (see Alexander, this volume). We will come back to these questions shortly when considering the performative nature of consent in Hobbes' scenario of the social contract. In the next section, however, we will attempt to show that we might already arrive at a more robust, more determined conceptualization of performance if we were to slightly widen our focus and conceive of the concatenation of performances as analogous to contractual negotiations.

The determination of social events and the contract paradigm

As we cannot read back from an utterance or some supposed act or omission to its intentions and as these intentions cannot directly serve as a means of checking our interpretive activities, intentions must be established discursively (Fish 1989: 296). Following Mead, we might say that the meaning of action is not an idea as traditionally conceived, but rather is something that gets developed and articulated objectively by the concatenation of the performances that follow one after the other (Mead 1962: 75–82; see also Giesen, this volume). Echoing Nietzsche (1998: 25, I. treaties, §13) and anticipating some of the more recent approaches to performance (e.g. Judith Butler 1997), early labeling theory took an even more radical stance, arguing that the apparent subject of an act is first animated through accusation and labeling and only retroactively invoked. To establish the social meaning of an action or performance, we must look beyond the moment of its occurrence and consider how others react and relate to it, and it is only by learning to anticipate such reactions and by finding out what others expect us to do that we become capable of acting intentionally and with some success.

Social performance is not only twice-behaved behavior, behavior that, in order to influence others in more or less specific ways, must rely on social conventions and some experimenting, training, and rehearsing on the part of the performer, as Schechner suggests (1985: 36). It is also twice-described behavior. The ways others react to what we have done permits us to construe another, second description of the meaning of our behavior (Schneider 2000; Heritage 1984: 255) and this, in turn, gives us the opportunity to correct them or to agree with them. The meaning of action or the forces that possibly might be inherent to a speech act only become observable and articulated as part of a *mise-en-scène*. As long as participants do not explicitly correct the way they assume to have been understood by others, these others can proceed on the tacit assumption that they have understood correctly. That a social consensus can be achieved by this type of social feedback and tacit confirmation has been a central insight elaborated upon within the pragmatist tradition (Dewey 1988: 106; Mead 1962: 75f.; Warriner 1970: 110f.).

A cultural pragmatics of performance forces us to treat the problem of mutual understanding as a problem that is already inherent to our object domain. Meanings become determined by socially mediated attributions and communicative feedback. It is the explicit accounts and the tacit confirmations that produce the necessary informational redundancy that help those involved orient to each other, calibrate their meanings and arrive at some working consensus. The question to be dealt with next is: how many steps does it take to agree on a specific account and arrive at such a consensus? What concatenation of events can be taken to establish social fusion?

In his *Genealogy of Morality*, Nietzsche argued that it was contract law that first of all made us morally responsible persons, capable of feelings of guilt, bad consciousness, and resentment (Nietzsche 1998: 41, II. treaties, §6). Criminal law, which apparently inspired Weber's definition of action (Bendix 1977: 267), he felt, was not a good starting point to understand these phenomena. Taking our license from Nietzsche, we will seek an alternative to Max Weber's individualist manner of framing action in terms of an *actus reus* and a *mens rea*. It will be argued that we might more sensibly determine the meanings of social events by identifying certain self-encapsulating sequences of performance in analogy to the juridical notion of implied contract. The exchange of promises and the making of contracts served not only the early modern natural lawyers as a basic tool to think about social relations and obligations. As we will see, it still serves some of our more contemporary social thinkers as a hidden prototype to frame their unit of analysis and account for social order. The concept of contract suggests a useful set of abstractions allowing us to specify our unit of analysis in a way most fitting to a pragmatics of performance. Contracts have just the right size and structure to be taken as exemplary instances of performances giving meaning to one another.

As is well known, the contract paradigm's disrepute among sociologists is due to its ideological overtones, its political commitments, and its conceptually misplaced concreteness (for a history of contract law that reflects these points see: Atiyah 1979; see also Durkheim 1983a: 192–237; Alexander 1982: 277f.). These criticisms must of course be taken into account in order to appreciate more adequately what still might count as the valuable insights offered by this tradition. However, that would lead us too far within this context, so that we have decided to concentrate on what has been left intact by these criticisms. As we hope to show in a moment, there are important traces not only within the history of sociology, but even among some of our contemporary thinkers that indicate that the contract paradigm has served and still serves as a tacit master trope.

Usually, contracts are defined in terms either of agreements or of promises, but there are many different ways to conceive of contracts and their constitutive elements. A contract might be defined as an offer coupled with an acceptance or as a pair of promises or as an exchange of rights or as a promise given for a reasonable consideration or in return for an act. A contract can also take many different forms. It can be written, oral, or implied from conduct, though, depending on the type of transaction, legal validity is often only conferred when specific requirements in deed or writing are fulfilled. In comparison to the sociological accounts discussed below, we should notice that the definitions of contract that prevail among legal scholars often conceive of contracts in a seemingly more restricted or, we might say, more reified fashion. This is partly due to the problem of having to present evidence in courts. But it is, though for quite different reasons, also due to the so-called "will theory" of contractual obligations that became dominant during the eighteenth century and still prevails in many places (for a critique of this theory, see Atiyah 1979). However, as we have seen above, David Hume already made clear that more than the mere will of the parties is required to account for the binding force of promises and contracts. Promises would neither be made nor relied on nor performed if there were no social world beyond them.

Marcel Mauss, George Herbert Mead, and Erving Goffman have all suggested theoretical schemes that could be said to be modeled on the paradigm of contract or on fragments of this paradigm. Marcel Mauss observed a sequential structure, analogous to our paradigm, at work in the cycles of gift exchange. Gift exchange is characterized by three obligations: to give, to receive, and to reciprocate (Mauss 1990: 39ff.). It can be said to set in with the transfer of a gift, followed by its reception, and is completed by the return of a similarly valued gift. As Marshall Sahlins pointed out: "The *Essai sur le don* is a kind of social contract for the primitives" (Sahlins 1972: 169). George Herbert Mead gave us a much more abstract and equally well-known account of the concatenation and specification of acts (Mead 1962: 76f.). He also observed a threefold relationship constituting a matrix that allows us to account for the articulation of meaning in interaction. Mead's unit of analysis, too, is divided into three successive phases. It starts with a gesture or offer, followed by a response to that first gesture by its addressee, and a subsequent phase that we might call a response to the response by which the act is completed. Mead conceives of these responses not in behaviorist terms, but rather takes them to be delayed, in other words well-considered responses (Tugendhat 1982). In Goffman's writings, the contract paradigm most explicitly surfaces in his analysis of remedial interchanges in which people become involved when their "territories of self" are at stake (Goffman 1971: 95–187). Such interchanges can take the form of accounts, apologies, or requests. In Goffman's work, we can again find a specific concatenation of moves that make up such an interchange. Apologies, for example, can often be seen as being embedded in a sequence of four steps. The sequence might begin with a priming move, whereby the victim calls attention to the other's misconduct and the work that needs to be done. Picking up on this, the offender then might offer an apology, which in turn might be accepted by the person to whom this offering was made. The whole sequence then might conclude by the offender showing signs of gratitude. In the case of requests, the parallel to contractual agreements is even more obvious, as requests occur before the "offending" act. If the person thus addressed accepts the request and licenses the intended act, she usually will be paid back through signs of gratitude.

More contemporary, and again on a more general level, in two of our most advanced attempts to theorize social communication, i.e. in the works of Jürgen Habermas and Niklas Luhmann, we can also see the contract paradigm at work, orienting the analysis as a background metaphor. Inspired by Mead, Habermas reconstructs what to Karl Bühler and later to Austin seemed to be different aspects of a single act or as different acts performed simultaneously, as the implicit validity claims inhering in a speech act that others may take up, question, or reject or agree to (for some of the contractualist intuitions in Habermas see Heath 2001: 34, 211f.). Luhmann maps these aspects on to the sequential uptake and synthesis of a communication, which again is seen as putting its addressee in the position to either reject or accept what has thus been put forward as a premise for his or her own future conduct (Luhmann 1995: 137–75).

The implied contractual agreements established by these multistep concatenation of events can, however, take many different forms. If an agreement is arrived at by symbolic communication, it will of course suit the notion of contract best. This, though, should not come as a surprise, as the ancient Greek notion of *symbolon* originally meant a physical object intended as a material indication of identification or agreement, and its cognate term *symbolaion* meant agreement and contract. But the degree of fusion represented by such an agreement can also vary in more than one dimension. An agreement can consist in grudging or halfhearted consent where more attractive options are apparently not feasible, but it might also be a wholeheartedly embraced emphatic agreement. It can be based on the bracketing of areas of disagreement or even consist in a tacit agreement not to agree and keep on quarreling. It can consist in the sequential formation of a consensus or the step-by-step negotiation of some compromise and there are probably many other variants. Arriving at such an agreement or working consensus must be seen as a performative achievement and the agreement itself should be understood as social fact in the Durkheimian sense, not necessarily implying a close meeting of minds (Gilbert 1994). The binding effect of such a consensus, however, comes about only by leaving it up to participants to renegotiate and reject it; it comes about, ironically as Habermas (1987: 73f.) observes, precisely through the fact that participants could have said "No!"

Formally contractual arrangements are not restricted to two parties. But are there pragmatic limits to the number of participants? Does the heuristic power of the contract paradigm diminish when we shift our attention from dyadic arrangements to larger settings (Giesen 1998: 46ff.)? And what would consent mean in instances where it is obvious that not everyone has the same say in setting up the contract?

Tacit consent and the problem of order

Through the common legal technique of analogical extension, the notion of contract can easily be applied to society at large to account for the establishment of social order. From their conduct we might then be inclined to infer that people have indeed entered a social contract to escape the state of nature. This is at least what Hobbes argued and by the route thus sketched he thought that the so-called "problem of order" could be solved. From Hobbes to Parsons the problem of order has been put in many different ways. Hobbes' scenario went like this (Hobbes 1960: 81): men, being equal, desire the same things. As these things are scarce, there will be competition for them. Competition, in turn, will lead to mistrust. To secure oneself under these circumstances, some might be expected to try to build up a reputation of being tough and this in turn will force everyone else into a hostile defensive posture, creating a situation of mutual mistrust and fear. For Hobbes, the problem of order is a problem of mistrust that reduces all promises that might be made in the state of nature to mere words and ineffective cheap talk. A sovereign is needed to create a situation of trust where people can rely on the promises they make to each other.

But how can such a sovereign be instituted? Doesn't Hobbes' train of arguments run in a circle? If the institution of the sovereign derives from a contract among his people, can the sovereign then also be the one who gives binding force to this contract in the first place? Hobbes considered society, or more precisely, government to be an artifact and a product of man, indeed assuming it to have a somewhat circular structure because man is both the matter and the artificer of his commonwealth (Hobbes 1960: 5).

Unfortunately, he was not able to show us how by small steps man might leave the state of nature and establish a commonwealth. What we need is an account of how the problem of order can be solved step by step by the actors themselves, by their own strategizing, their inventiveness, and their ways of typifying the situation (for this trifocal conceptualization of action, see: Alexander 1988: 312ff.). It has become customary to model the state of nature as a repeated prisoners' dilemma and it has been often enough demonstrated that under these circumstances, cooperation might evolve quite naturally. However, Hobbes' state of nature is not a two-person game where rules of direct reciprocity might easily be implemented. The state of nature, as conceived of by Hobbes, poses a dilemma that involves a multitude of people and thus requires more intricate arrangements to resolve. Though little attention has been paid to it, Hobbes outlined a highly inventive schema that he hoped could help man escape the state of nature. It might be said to involve a performative leap, or, as Parsons might have called it, an "operation bootstrap" (1967: 275) and it will occupy us for the rest of this chapter.

Hobbes knew very well that "there is scarce a commonwealth in the world, whose beginnings can in conscience be justified" (Hobbes 1960: 463),[2] but he nevertheless thought it wise and prudent that once some government is established that does protect its citizens from injuring each other and from foreign invasion and allows them to live more or less contentedly, we should consent to it under these conditions. Obedience is conditional on the granting of protection (Hobbes 1960: 144). But here again, we apparently run into an impasse, because only a power that can grant security deserves consent, while only a power that is based on consent will be strong enough to grant security. Knowing that "the power of the mighty hath no foundation but in the opinion and belief of the people" and being well aware of Juvenal's problem of who will guard the guardians, the problem of "what shall force the army?" if the army is meant to force men to obey the law (Hobbes 1990: 16, 59), Hobbes put his finger on a performative gambit by which the prudence of each person could be transformed into a collectively binding representation of all.

Instead of sketching Hobbes' argument *in toto*, I will describe only those certain details of his schema that directly relate to problems of performance and staging. The reason for reading Hobbes from this perspective is not just historical curiosity. It is the limitations and deficits of today's two most prevailing views on political legitimacy that should make us alert to possible alternatives or compensatory devices. Within the field of public choice, it has long been observed that the aggregation of individual preferences to determine a specific form of government cannot dispense with some arbitrary element. Whatever arrangement is chosen, it will in principle and to some extent always lack complete democratic legitimacy as understood in terms of preference aggregation. Discourse ethics, perhaps its most important theoretical alternative, suffers from more pragmatic deficits. Those who pursue discourse ethics, quite frankly admitting its contra-factual claims, have so far mainly shown that it is easier to withdraw legitimacy from a political regime than to achieve public agreement on a more adequate one.[3] Somehow contrary to both of these accounts, however, we see many regimes, and not only democratic ones, that are able to make collectively binding decisions and achieve social fusion. We should therefore ask ourselves what allows them to do so. Hobbes offers us at least three hints which can help us get a little closer to an answer. In the rest of this section, I will first attend to Hobbes' view on tacit consent, then I will touch on Hobbes' use of the "as-if" device to establish social fusion and legitimate government. In the section that follows, I will then draw on certain parallels between the world of the theatre and the world of politics as Hobbes sees them and that should allow us to conceive of problems of representation and social fusion as performative accomplishments possibly superseding problems of individual aggregation and communicative rationality.

Hobbes distinguishes between two ways of establishing sovereign power: force and agreement. He calls the former a commonwealth by acquisition and the latter a commonwealth by institution (Hobbes 1960: 112ff.). Men consent to either of the two types of commonwealths that Hobbes distinguishes out of fear. If a commonwealth is instituted by the agreement of a multitude, this agreement is the result of the fear that people carry of one another; if a commonwealth is acquired by force, people subject themselves to their sovereign because they fear the sovereign himself. In both cases, the covenant proceeds from fear of death and violence (Hobbes 1960: 130). Though Hobbes did not exclude the possibility that a commonwealth might indeed be instituted by some mutual agreement, it was obvious to him that this road was much less traveled. However he claimed that even a commonwealth by acquisition is based on consent. If sovereign power is attained by force and the sovereign, having the power to destroy those he has conquered, grants those willing to become his subjects their lives and does not physically bind them, then, so Hobbes assumes, they can be said to have consented to him and authorized him to govern and protect them (Hobbes 1960: 129f.).

The idea that there can be other signs of consent besides spoken and written words, is central, though not original, to Hobbes. Hugo Grotius, for example, who like Hobbes distinguished between consent established by association and consent due to subjection (Grotius 1925: 234, 258), discussed many such cases where silence or mute signs or actions imply consent or the acceptance of certain premises (Grotius 1925: 14 f., 857ff.). Here Hobbes follows closely by distinguishing between two kinds of signs that allow for the mutual transfer of rights to make a contract (Hobbes 1960: 87f.). These signs can either be what he calls express and consist in what we now call a performative speech act or they can be signs by inference, being the implied consequences of words or the consequences of keeping silent or the consequences of actions or omissions. Remaining silent can be an "argument of consent" (Hobbes 1960: 174). Rousseau subsequently held the similar view that in some cases "general silence may be held to imply the People's consent" (Rousseau 1948: 191).

Tacit or implied consent might be difficult to observe and therefore the more easily assumed. Contract law has always tried to harness the ambiguities that might result from such impositions by insisting on certain formalities and declaring other assumed contracts void. But it could not dispense altogether with assumptions about things that go without saying, could not dispense with such notions as implied contract or quasi-contract. The ambiguities involved in the notions of implied contract and tacit consent allow Hobbes to infer in respect to the subjects and sovereigns reading him that if those subjects are publicly taken to have consented and, if they do not openly object to this imposition, then they have in fact consented. Any subject confronted with this argument, or, if you like, rhetorical trap or appellative gambit, cannot escape the conclusion that he has chosen his lot and should therefore feel committed by his consent.[4] Silence is taken as implying consent, and the giving of consent is, of course, a performative act.

Hobbes' apparent over-attributions or "as-if" impositions give his endeavor a certain ideological tinge. Hobbes assumes that the institution of a common power that is able to protect its subjects from one another and from outside invasion is only possible when the subjects give up certain of their natural rights. By nature they will only do so on the condition that all relevant others will do the same. But in the state of nature, we can never be sure of this. In the state of nature, "covenants . . . are but words, and of no strength to secure a man" (Hobbes 1960: 109, 92). However, should a sovereign power come to be instituted, then this event could be looked upon "in such a manner *as if* every man should say to every man I authorize and give up my right of governing myself, to this man, or this assembly of men, on this condition, that thou give up thy right to him, and authorize all his actions in like manner" (Hobbes 1960: 112, emphasis added). The "as-if" assumption here is central to Hobbes' project. People are observed to behave as if they had contracted with each other no longer to live in war with each other. The sovereign can be seen as a third-party beneficiary of this contract that he in turn is meant to enforce. That we might not find any written contract testifying this assumption does not prove this assumption to be mistaken. We do not even need words for proof, for it suffices if we can see an implied contract being performed, a contract implied by the behavior of the contracting parties and successfully enforced by the sovereign.

Hobbes looked at his demonstration and making evident, what precisely was implied by the multitude made one in submitting to the sword of a sovereign, as being arrived at *more geometrico*. But his schema nevertheless, or even more so because of the appeal of such a conclusive method, has a strong performative aspect. Hobbes endeavored to make evident and explicit, what before was only implied and vaguely conceived of. By doing so, he intended to change the image the subjects have of themselves. The request to his readers to "read thyself!" figured as the leading motif to his book (1960: 6). There is certainly a strong inventive element in Hobbes' narrative. It makes the sovereign's subjects see themselves and each other as covenanters and attempts to make them adopt and act from this role. Likewise, the mirror Hobbes holds up to the sovereign makes the sovereign see himself as being only authorized by his people to regulate their affairs and reminds him not to risk this trust again by some dubious endeavors.

Extending the notion of contract to society at large might, of course, easily turn into an absurdity. It does so if this interpellation (Butler 1997: 24ff.) fails to constitute the subjects it is addressed to. Hobbes' hypothetical "as-if" contract might be taken as an implied contract and, if taken this way by those who start to reflect upon it, then his theoretical project will indeed fit the facts it has helped to shape.[5] We know thanks to Durkheim that representations of the social realm are not only externalizations of prior expectations, but that, by assuming public status, by becoming common and communicable, by giving orientation to our behavior and by allowing in turn for their internalization collective representations almost inevitably transform and transfigure what they are taken to represent (Durkheim 1983b: 87; Alexander 1988: 314). Durkheim's argument elucidates what Hobbes' argumentation does, and being well trained in the art of rhetoric, we might read him as if, indeed, he knew what he was doing.

Sovereign performance and social fusion

There is a third element in Hobbes that is of interest to us, relating to the worlds of politics and the staging of collective representations (Alexander and Giesen, this volume). The world of the theatre that had acquired its specific modern shape and institutional form during the seventeenth century (Agnew 1986) already at this time served contemporaries as a master metaphor to conceive of the reign of Queen Elizabeth and Louis XIV in new ways, thus allowing them to account for their performative fabrication (Orgel 1975; Pye 1990; Burke 1992; Goldberg 1983). It also served Hobbes as a model for political representation (Agnew 1986). While the medieval theatre allowed actors to refer directly to their spectators, often asking for immediate feedback, the Renaissance stage became a much more autonomous space. The audience was no longer addressed directly, but fashioned in the role of mere spectators separate from the performance on stage. The world of the theatre supplied Hobbes with some of the distinctions he needed to frame the problem of collective representation in a new manner. It allowed him to conceptualize the relation between subject and sovereign in analogy to the relationship that exists between author and actor and to treat authorship in parallel with ownership, the domain where contract law first attained its modern contours and where it has been extensively developed ever since.

Like Durkheim, Hobbes argued that a collective representation is constitutive for the collectivity it represents. Representation, as we understand it today, is an essentially modern concept. To the Romans, the Latin word *representare* meant the literal bringing into presence of something previously absent, or the embodiment of an abstraction in an object. During the thirteenth and fourteenth centuries, a wider meaning became attached to the word. Now it could also mean that something could stand for something else, that one person could stand for another or a group of others, or one person could act for or on behalf of others (Agnew 1986: 102). It is here that Hobbes' argument sets in, making the idea of the social contract much more adaptable to large-scale anonymous settings. Hobbes sets in with the distinction between natural and artificial persons. In Latin, as Hobbes reminds his reader, the word "person" signifies the disguise or outward appearance of a man counterfeited on stage. A person, according to him, is the same as an actor, both on stage and in common conversation. To personify and to act are the same things. Natural persons are persons whose words are considered their own, while artificial persons represent the words or actions of another. Artificial persons are actors, while those in whose commission or by whose license they act or speak are authors. Just as goods and possessions have owners, so do words and actions have authors, and as the right of possession is called dominion, so, according to Hobbes, the right of doing any action, is called authority. An artificial person can perform things a natural person cannot and this is the most decisive point in Hobbes' argument. An artificial person may represent and act by the authority of a multitude of men, who are made one only through the unity of this representer. It is only due to this artificial person that the contracting multitude becomes a real unity (Hobbes 1960: 105–8).[6] This distinguishes Hobbes radically from most of the contractarians after him. For Locke, the government is only a trustee to the community and for Rousseau a people exists and can be identified before it might or might not surrender to or choose a king. But for Hobbes, the multitude is not one, but many and it is only by being represented by one man or an assembly of men that it constitutes a unity.

In a time where communal rituals had lost much of their efficacy, and the advent of the daily newspapers that were to create a more or less homogeneous nationwide public sphere was not yet clearly in sight, the new world of the theatre appeared to Hobbes as an inspiring model for thinking about collective representation and politics. This was especially so as its institutional structures could also be realigned to questions of contract law. We easily, though certainly not completely, attribute what the actors do on stage to the author of a play; what the sovereign or sovereign assembly does, Hobbes argues, should be attributed likewise, namely to his people. Continuing this analogy, we might say that just as an author could be imagined to be among the audience of his play and approve or disapprove of the performance in some way or another, so also those following the sovereign's performance without tumult can be said to have consented to him by their silence or by their action, e.g. by applauding.

The people as authors of the sovereign were "invented" or "interpellated" on stage, i.e. by the monarch or sovereign assembly (see also Morgan 1988). Hobbes' *Leviathan* contains a somewhat elliptic script for how a multitude might be politically united by authorizing a sovereign as the third-party beneficiary of a contract he in turn is meant to enforce. This theory of authorization is genuine to Hobbes' *Leviathan* of 1651 (1960: 105–8) and should be considered a definite advance in comparison to his previous writings. It centers on a cleverly conceived and historically tested performative triangulation *mise-en-scène*. Unfortunately, only little attention has been paid to this dramaturgical aspect of his theory. Perhaps this is so because these *mise-en-scène* happenings were perceived as knife-edge situations with many imponderables where so much might depend on so little that general conclusions seemed out of reach. A sociological analysis of such a seemingly ill-balanced setting therefore runs the risk of remaining indeterminate if it limits itself to what is taking place within the *mise-en-scène*. However, taking some of the other dimensions outlined by Alexander (this volume) into account, we should arrive at a more complete and determinate picture as the variables they define influence what can possibly happen and what can succeed within a given *mise-en-scène*. In order to do so, we will take a brief look at two structurally similar performative triangulations that likewise can be said to transform a multitude into a group, but that partly differ with reference to these other dimensions. The first originates with James Coleman (1990: 203–18, 899–931), though most of the argument can already be found in Roger Brown (1965: 709–63), the second with Jean Paul Sartre (1976: 345–404).

Coleman is concerned with the question of what might account for the sometimes different dynamics of bank-runs as compared to escape panics. If a bank is expected to become insolvent, it is rational to withdraw your money as quickly as possible, as you can expect that others will do the same and the bank therefore will indeed become insolvent. In this scenario, the customers have no chance to control each other's actions. Coleman's other scenario is concerned with the world of the stage, or, to put it in a less ironic form, with what might happen inside a theatre if a fire breaks out. Here, the situation the audience finds itself in very quickly might begin to resemble a Hobbesian state of nature, as everyone might start rushing to the doors, trampling others down and making a more orderly and more efficient evacuation of the place impossible. However, as Coleman observes, this need not be so. Those in the audience might let their behavior be controlled or correlated by a third party, perhaps by one of the actors on stage, by someone visible to all of them and known to be visible to all of them. This is what makes the situation different from his first scenario where we can find no such focal player. There is a tiny chance that this person might be able to control the crowd by giving directions and making people proceed calmly to the exits. But each member of the audience will only follow the instructions of the actor on stage if he or she can be confident that almost all others will do likewise. The members of the audience, so we might say, enter an implied contract each with each other to let themselves be directed by this actor. By thus authorizing him to direct them, they avoid a possible inferno. This scenario almost exactly matches Hobbes' script for how to exit the state of nature. The main structural difference is, that the orderly evacuation in Coleman's scenario might unravel near the exits, as some people nevertheless might start running. Anticipating this, the performance on stage might get too little attention right from the start and the actor will not be given the authority he needs. Seen from this perspective, his attempts could easily fail.

If the performance were to succeed, however, this success, though still contingent on what is happening in the *mise-en-scène*, will also depend on some of the givens of the situation. It apparently presupposes, first, a spatial separation between those on stage and those in the audience, which implies a highly uneven distribution of the most rudimentary means of symbolic production. Only those who are professionally aligned to the theatre will be able to position themselves in a place that allows them to catch everyone's attention and only they might be taken to know how to make their voice heard. Second, it presupposes a more or less clear-cut and well-established differentiation between the roles of actors and audience, which implies that those in the audience are not allowed to play an active part and therefore will probably not be expected to supply any contenders for the organization of the crowd.

But there are still at least two other important aspects that need to be taken into account if we want to come closer to Hobbes' scenario. These will become apparent in our next scenario, which had become the paradigm of Sartre's concept of the *groupe en fusion*, the group in fusion. Like Hobbes, Sartre seeks an explanation for how a multiplicity of people can become a group (Laing and Cooper 1971: 129ff.). Sartre's scenario parallels Coleman's, but it is more conducive to the development of cooperation and, in this, it is closer to Hobbes'. Sartre focuses on what led up to the storming of the Bastille during the French Revolution. He starts by considering a fleeing crowd, cowardly, almost in panic, threatened by a common enemy and gathering in a public space. As the members of the crowd become aware of each other, of their situation and their possible power to defend themselves if only they could unite, and as more and more people begin to join the crowd, observing others doing the same, sooner or later a moment will be reached where one of them starts to address those around him and, by this sovereign performance, transforms this multitude into a group, into the People of Paris capable of fighting back. But in order to defend themselves they know that they need weapons, they need to storm the Bastille. And so they did, etc. For today's tastes, this might sound a bit too romantic and we should at least add that, what here certainly appears as a liberating move, as the cathartic revelation of a hidden transcript, to use James Scott's (1990: 202ff.) terminology again, could also be conceived of in quite other terms. As the history of the French Revolution later showed, the successful declaration and imposition of a new public script does not always and not necessarily have to reflect the actual feelings and intentions of those taken to consent to it. But what should concern us here, however, is again those features that frame, make possible, and partly structure what is happening within the *mise-en-scène*. First, once again the means of symbolic production are only partly distributed equally. Everyone might be taken to participate in the rumor driving the crowds, but the coming together of the people also depends on the topography of the city and its open spaces, as Sartre carefully points out. Second, though in the beginning there is a redundancy of potential command and though Sartre assumes that in the process of fusion everyone conceives of himself as being in the position of the third, mediating the process and giving direction to those around him, those eventually addressing the crowd will certainly have to position themselves somehow above street level, thereby creating a distance between themselves and their audience. If everyone spoke, no one could be listened to. Only if there is some focal player attracting everyone's attention, will those he addresses himself to be prepared to delegate the control of their behaviors to him, because only under these conditions can they expect that others will follow suit. This differentiation between actor and audience itself implies a new distribution of the means of symbolic production. They become centralized by those who manage to attract everyone's attention, acquire a name, and create a stage for themselves. The peculiar authority of the focal players in this context does not derive from their personalities or the offices they might hold, though both will certainly also contribute to their success. In the beginning, at least, it is primarily their positioning that gives them a voice that is heard. Once established, the differentiation between actors and audience will, however, make it more difficult for those in the audience to coordinate any alternative arrangement. Not all people will have an equal say in the formation of the general will, but they nevertheless might support it.

We have already spotted both of these elements, the unequal distribution of the means of symbolic production and the differentiation between actors and audience, in Coleman's scenario. But here we have encountered two further aspects that Coleman had no need to be concerned with, but which Sartre could hardly neglect. The first relates to the problem of power. Here it is basically represented by the power of numbers and the need for weapons. If the group is not immediately to dissolve again, however, questions of institutionalization and differentiation also will need to be dealt with, processes that according to Sartre will necessarily lead to a certain petrifaction of the group. The other aspect relates to the sphere of symbols, their emotional power and imaginary value. The Bastille does not stand for just another fortress, but is a synonym for the *ancien régime*, the places of the city have their names, and the crowd is elevated into "The People of Paris." The group, initially only negatively designated, eventually reorganizes itself reflexively to fight its divisive tendencies by introducing some form of a public pledge (Sartre 1976: 419–28) serving as a common signaling device and facilitating mutual monitoring and collective sanctioning.

We can observe all these aspects in Hobbes' scenario of the performative fabrication of a sovereign, as well. For such a performance to be successful, there must be, first, an unequal distribution of the means of symbolic production. Second, there must be a differentiation between actors and audience. And third, the background symbols Hobbes has chosen to make us conceive of the commonwealth in a specific way are of course also not chosen arbitrarily, but are taken from the Bible. The Leviathan is taken to be a mortal God, a God that man should fear (see also Giesen, this volume). But fourth, and most importantly, the sovereign's success does, of course, not only depend on his staging and performance in the *mise-en-scène*, but also on his power to use his sword. Though the power of government, as Hobbes knew very well (Hobbes 1990: 16), has its foundation in the opinion and belief of the governed, it is not merely symbolic, it is not all theatre. The sovereign must be capable of defending himself successfully at least against small deviations. For this, he at least sometimes might have to rely on force, on his sword. Otherwise people would think differently about the protection he can offer and the power he claims and, they thinking so, he would therefore quickly lose it again. But as long as they expect him to be able to handle such smaller affairs, he will have sufficient resources to do so. His words will be heeded and taken for more than being merely suggestions. With all these background variables properly set, the public fabrication of sovereign power becomes a far less uncertain performance. Its contingencies, at least within limits become manageable, actors can prepare, and sociologists, properly equipped, can later on depict and reconstruct what happened.

Conclusion

For Hobbes, the theoretical and also moral challenge was to determine how man could escape the state of nature. About 300 years later, Parsons reformulated this problem in much more abstract terms as the problem of "double contingency." To many, however, his answer to this problem looked a bit like begging the question. But nevertheless, we feel inclined to say that in a situation of double contingency, whatever those involved do or omit to do will have a promissory dimension attached to it, it will contain a communicative element, and might acquire a performative character. In retrospect, it therefore comes close to a tautology when we claim that, if man again and again has managed to leave the state of nature behind, he has done so by a performative turn. In way of a summary I will quickly retrace our argument, giving hints where we feel to have touched on something new.

The argument has taken the following course: if we conceive of the elements of social systems in terms of performance and communication, we must relate what people do primarily to other performances, albeit without denying their subjective references. Following Durkheim's methodological maxims, we must relate people's behavior to something exterior to the individual human mind and available in the public domain. Instead of looking for a fusion of minds and a correspondence of sentiments, cultural analysts have therefore increasingly turned to focus on performance, the mutual determination and cross-reference between performances and the processes of fusion and fission on the level of communication and symbolic behavior. By thinking of performances relating to each other as analogous to the successful or unsuccessful tacit or open negotiation of contracts, we can specify our units of analysis, as units of performative fission or fusion.

In the early modern period, when the face-to-face society of old began to lose its contours, Hobbes and others looked at the world of the theatre, which just a little earlier had acquired its specifically modern shape, as an attractive model to think about certain features of politics and representation. It was through this trope alone that Hobbes was able to extend the contract paradigm to society at large without reducing it to a mere metaphor. A little later, though, with the rapidly increasing circulation of print media, on the one hand, and the expansion of public administration and diverse other government agencies, on the other, the stage became a less and less plausible model of politics, covering less and less of what was going on. Within the newly established, print-based public sphere it also became obvious that the performative imposition of a consensus by the sovereign might not really or not always be backed by public opinion, making social fusion much more difficult to achieve. However, during the first half of the last century with the advent of mass movements, large-scale mobilization, and nationwide public radio broadcasting, the metaphor of the stage again began to recommend itself. It fascinated both authors from the right like Carl Schmitt and from the left like Bertolt Brecht, but later on also began to be reconsidered as an analytical tool for sociological thought. The public stagings and spectacles that now became media events (Dayan and Katz 1992) could no longer be seen just as epiphenomena or anachronisms. Foucault's claim that power itself has become invisible in the modern area (Foucault 1979: 214) certainly seems mistaken when seen in this context. If we identify political power with collectively binding decision-making, it certainly needs to be made public, and if democracies depend on political competition, the contestants will certainly have to appear before those they compete for. That these performative stagings and strategies of discursive control depend on, and are made possible only by a specific institutional and material infrastructure has been central to our argument. Moreover, that there is of course more to modern politics than public performances should go without saying. The fact, however, that these stagings seek and compete for public approval, that political actors need to proceed on the assumption of political consent and occasionally even appeal explicitly to the social contract, that is said to authorize them, should make us reconsider the question of how this authority is gained and legitimated. The paradigm of the social contract offers a classical answer to this question. But the contract paradigm is usually understood only as a retrospective rationalization or mere metaphor. A retooling and amendment of the contractarian tradition by the schemes and concepts of a cultural pragmatics of performance should make it more fitting to capture the intricacies of staging political authority and make it more sensible to its situational contingencies. But perhaps most of all, it

310   Social Performance

should enable us to see its seemingly misplaced individualistic concreteness as a performative rhetorical device. In its Hobbesian variant it encourages citizens to impose responsibility upon one another and to treat each other as consenting wherever they do not openly oppose. In what came to be its Rousseauian variant, however (which, for lack of space, we could not deal with here), the underlying script insinuates a much more active involvement on the interactional order, according to which the responsible citizen suspects dissent wherever people do not openly participate in public rituals and prove their loyalty. With reference to the latter, no one has ever doubted that consent is a matter of performance. In Hobbes' scenario, however, consent is equally a matter of performance, though it might be a performance that goes unmarked, that does not go beyond a noticeable silence. Social fusion need not necessarily be driven by effervescence and enthusiasm, but may nevertheless have a performative dimension.

Notes

1. And, on the other hand and for matters of completeness, if this warning is not heeded at all, there might be no one left in a position giving him enough safety to put it into a book.
2. For the challenge this insight poses for the formation of collective identities, see Giesen (2004).
3. Too little attention has yet been paid to another feature of discourse ethics, namely that it might silence certain positions on the behalf of which no one might have the courage to speak up (but see Moon 1993: 91f.).
4. The use of such rhetorical devices was characteristic of many Renaissance writers (Malloch 1956) and even had its parallels in painting (Pye 2000: 65–104).
5. Such constellations are less absurd and more common than it might at first seem. Stanislavsky's system of actor training (Alexander, this volume) also works by an "as-if" clause. It teaches actors to act out the consequences of the roles assigned to them, as if these roles were their natural persons. But Stanislavsky's system is not only used to help actors prepare for the stage. It has also been successfully implemented in Soviet collectives (Kahrkordin 1999: 273ff.) and in the modern marketplace (Hochschild 1983). In contrast to these arrangements, Hobbes' argument will certainly look much less bizarre.
6. Which is nicely depicted by the famous frontispiece of Hobbes' *Leviathan*.

References

Agnew, Jean-Christophe. 1986. *Worlds Apart. The Market and the Theater in Anglo American Thought, 1550–1750*. Cambridge: Cambridge University Press.
Alexander, Jeffrey C. 1982. *The Antinomies of Classical Thought: Marx and Durkheim* (Theoretical Logic in Sociology, vol. II). Berkeley: University of California Press.
1987. *Twenty Lectures: Sociological Theory Since World War II*, New York: Columbia University Press.

1988. "Action and its Environments," pp. 301–33 in *Action and its Environments*. New York: Columbia University Press.

Althusser, Louis. 1971. "Ideology and Ideological State Apparatus," pp. 121–73 in *Lenin and Philosophy and other Essays*, London: New Left Books.

Aristotle. 1985. *The Politics*. Chicago: University of Chicago Press.

Atiyah, Pattric S. 1979. *The Rise and Fall of Freedom of Contract*. Oxford: Clarendon Press.

Austin, John L. 1961. "Performative Utterances," pp. 220–39 in *Philosophical Papers*. Oxford: Clarendon Press.

1962. *How to Do Things With Words*. Oxford: Clarendon Press.

Barker, Ernest (ed.) 1948. *Social Contract: Essays by Locke, Hume, and Rousseau*. New York: Oxford University Press.

Bendix, Reinhard. 1977. *Max Weber: An Intellectual Portrait*. Berkeley: University of California Press.

Bloor, David. 1997. *Wittgenstein, Rules and Institutions*. London Routledge.

Brown, Roger. 1965. *Social Psychology*. New York: Free Press.

Burke, Peter. 1992. *The Fabrication of Louis XIV*. New Haven: Yale University Press.

Butler, Judith. 1997. *Excitable Speech: A Politics of the Performative*. New York: Routledge.

Chesterfield, Lord. 1984. *Letters to His Son and Others*. London: Everyman's Library.

Clark, Colin and Trevor Pinch. 1995. *The Hard Sell: The Language and Lessons of Street-wise Marketing*. London: HarperCollins.

Coleman, James S. 1990. *Foundations of Social Theory*. Cambridge, Mass.: Harvard University Press.

Colson, Elizabeth. 1974. *Tradition and Contract: The Problem of Order*. Chicago: Aldine.

Danto, Arthur C. 1975. *Sartre*. Glasgow: Fontana.

Davidson, Donald. 1980. *Essays on Action and Events*. Oxford: Clarendon Press.

Dayan, Danile and Elihu Katz. 1992. *Media Events: The Live Brodcasting of History*. Cambridge, Mass.: Harvard University Press.

Dewey, John. 1988 [1922]. *Human Nature and Conduct*. Carbondale: Southern Illinois University Press.

Durkheim, Émile. 1964. *The Division of Labor in Society*. New York: Free Press.

1983a. *Durkheim and the Law*. Oxford: Oxford University Press.

1983b. *Pragmatism and Sociology*. Cambridge: Cambridge University Press.

Felman, Shoshana. 1983. *The Literary Speech Act: Don Juan with J. L. Austin, or Seduction in Two Languages*. Ithaca: Cornell University Press.

Fish, Stanley. 1989. *Doing what Comes Naturally: Change, Rhetoric, and the Practice of Theory in Literary and Legal Studies*. Durham: Duke University Press.

Foucault, Michel. 1979. *Discipline and Punish: The Birth of the Prison*. Harmondsworth: Penguin.

Giesen, Bernhard. 1998. *Intellectuals and the Nation: Collective Identity in a German Axial Age*. Cambridge: Cambridge University Press.

2004. *Triumph and Trauma*. Boulder, CO: Paradigm Publishers.

Gilbert, Margaret. 1994. "Durkheim and Social Facts," pp. 86–109 in W. S. F. Pickering and H. Martins (eds.), *Debating Durkheim*. London: Routledge.

Gluckman, Max. 1963. *Custom and Conflict in Africa*. Oxford: Blackwell.

Goffman, Erving. 1959. *The Presentation of Self in Everyday Life*. New York: The Overlook Press.

1971. *Relations in Public*. New York: Basic Books.

Goldberg, Jonathan. 1983. *James I and the Politics of Literature*. Baltimore: Johns Hopkins University Press.

Gracian, Balthasar. 2001. *The Art of Worldly Wisdom*. New York: Random House.

Greenblatt, Stephen. 1988. *Shakespearean Negotiations: The Circulation of Social Energy in Renaissance England*. Berkeley: University of California Press.

Grotius, Hugo. 1925. *The Law of War and Peace*. Oxford: Clarendon Press.

Habermas, Jürgen. 1987. *The Theory of Communicative Action*, vol. II: *Lifeworld and System: A Critique of Functionalist Reason*. Boston, Mass.: Beacon Press.

Havel, Václav. 1985. "The Power of the Powerless," pp. 23–96 in Václav Havel et al. (eds.), *The Power of the Powerless*. London: Hutchinson.

Heath, Joseph. 2001. *Communicative Action and Rational Choice*. Cambridge, Mass.: MIT Press.

Heritage, John. 1984. *Garfinkel and Ethnomethodology*. Cambridge: Polity Press.

Hobbes, Thomas. 1960. *Leviathan or the Matter, Forme and Power of a Commonwealth Ecclesiasticall and Civil*. Oxford: Blackwell.

1990. *Behemoth or the Long Parliament*. Chicago: University of Chicago Press.

1994. *Human Nature and De Corpore Politico*. Oxford: Oxford University Press.

1998. *Man and Citizen*. Indianapolis: Hackett Publishing Company.

Hochschield, Arlie Russel. 1983. *The Managed Heart: Commercialization of Human Feeling*. Berkeley: University of California Press.

Hume, David. 1948. "Of the Original Contract," pp. 147–66 in Ernest Barker (ed.), *Social Contract: Essays by Locke, Hume, and Rousseau*. New York: Oxford University Press.

1960. *A Treatise of Human Nature*. Oxford: Clarendon Press.

1975. *Enquiries concerning Human Understanding and concerning the Principles of Morals*. Oxford: Clarendon Press.

Jay, Martin. 1989. "The Debate over Performative Contradiction: Habermas vs. the Post-structuralists," pp. 171–89 in Axel Honneth et al. (eds.), *Zwischenbetrachtungen im Prozeß der Aufklärung: Jürgen Habermas zum 60. Geburtstag*. Frankfurt: Suhrkamp.

Katz, Jack. 1988. *Seductions of Crime: Moral and Sensual Attractions in Doing Evil*. New York: Basic Books.

Kharkhordin, Oleg. 1999. *The Collective and the Individual in Russia*. Berkeley: University of California Press.

Krailsheimer, Alban J. 1962. *Studies in Self-Interest: From Descartes to La Bruyère*. Oxford: Oxford University Press.

Krishna, Daya. 1971. "'The Self-fulfilling Prophecy' and the Nature of Society," *American Sociological Review* 36: 1104–7.

Kusy, Miroslav. 1985. "Chartism and 'Real Socialism'," pp. 152–77 in Václav Havel et al. (eds.), *The Power of the Powerless*. London: Hutchinson.

Laing, Ronald D. and David G. Cooper. 1971. *Reason and Violence: A Decade of Sartre's Philosophy 1950–1960*. New York: Pantheon Books.

Le Roy Ladurie, Emmanuel. 2003. *Carnival in Romans*. New York: Weidenfeld & Nicolson.

Lovejoy, Arthur. 1961. *Reflections on Human Nature*. Baltimore: Johns Hopkins University Press.

Luhmann, Niklas. 1990. *Essays on Self-Reference*. New York: Columbia University Press.

1995. *Social Systems*. Stanford, CA: Stanford University Press.

Malloch, A. E. 1956. "The Technique and Function of the Renaissance Paradox," *Studies in Philology* 53: 191–203.

Mauss, Marcel. 1990. *The Gift: The Form and Reason for Exchange in Archaic Societies*. New York: W. W. Norton.

Mead, George Herbert. 1962. *Mind, Self, and Society*. Chicago: University of Chicago Press.

Merton, Robert K. 1968. "The Self-Fulfilling Prophecy," pp. 475–90 in *Social Structure and Social Theory*, 2nd edn. New York: Free Press.

Moon, J. Donald. 1993. *Constructing Community: Moral Pluralism and Tragic Conflicts*. Princeton: Princeton University Press.

Morgan, Edmund S. 1988. *Inventing the People: The Rise of Popular Sovereignty in England and America*. New York: W. W. Norton.

Nietzsche, Friedrich. 1998. *On the Genealogy of Morality*. Indianapolis: Hackett Publishing Company.

Orgel, Stephen. 1975. *The Illusion of Power: Political Theater in the English Renaissance*. Berkeley: University of California Press.

Parsons, Talcott. 1967. "Some Reflections on the Place of Force in Social Process," pp. 264–96 in *Sociological Theory and Modern Society*. New York: Free Press.

1968. *The Structure of Social Action*, 2nd edn, vol. I.. New York: Free Press.

1977. *Social Systems and the Evolution of Action Theory*. New York: Free Press.

Pêcheux, Michel. 1982. *Language, Semantics and Ideology: Stating the Obvious*. London: Macmillan.

Pye, Christopher. 1990. *The Regal Phantasm: Shakespeare and the Politics of Spectacle*. London: Routledge.

2000. *The Vanishing: Shakespeare, the Subject, and Early Modern Culture*. Durham: Duke University Press.

Rousseau, Jean-Jacques. 1948. "The Social Contract," pp. 169–307 in Ernest Barker (ed.), *Social Contract: Essays by Locke, Hume, and Rousseau*. New York: Oxford University Press.

1984. *Discourse on Inequality*. New York: Penguin Books.

Sabini, John and Maury Silver. 1982. "Flirtation and Ambiguity," pp. 107–23 in *Moralities of Everyday Life*. Oxford: Oxford University Press.

Sahlins, Marshall. 1972. *Stone Age Economics*. Chicago: Aldine.

Sartre, Jean Paul. 1976. *Critique of Dialectical Reason*. London: New Left Books.
1988. *"What is Literature?" and Other Essays*. Cambridge, Mass.: Harvard University Press.

Schechner, Richard. 1985. "Restoration of Behavior," pp. 35–116 in *Between Theater and Anthropology*. Philadelphia: University of Pennsylvania Press.

Schneider, Wolfgang L. 2000. "The Sequential Production of Acts in Conversation," *Human Studies* 23, 2: 123–44.

Scott, James C. 1990. *Domination and the Arts of Resistance: Hidden Transcripts*. New Haven: Yale University Press.

Shaftesbury, Anthony, Earl of. 1900. *Characteristics of Men, Manners, Opinions, Times, etc.* Vol. I. London: Grant Richards.

Simmel. Georg. 1950. *The Sociology of Georg Simmel*, ed. Kurt H. Wolf. New York: Free Press.

Spencer, Herbert. 1966. "Ceremonial Institutions," pp. 1–225 in *The Principles of Sociology*. Vol. II. Osnabrück: Otto Zeller.

Tugendhat, Ernst. 1982. *Traditional and Analytic Philosophy: Lectures on the Philosophy of Language*. Cambridge: Cambridge University Press.

Warriner, Charles K. 1970. *The Emergence of Society*. Homewood, Il: The Dorsey Press.

Weber, Max. 1964. *The Theory of Social and Economic Organization*. New York: Free Press.

Žižek, Slavoj. 1989. *The Sublime Object of Ideology*. London: Verso.

10

Performance art

Bernhard Giesen

Introduction

"Performance art" is a collective term covering a range of artistic activities and movements, that, from the 1960s onwards, appeared in different domains such as the visual arts (Joseph Beuys, Christo, Gilbert and George, Rebecca Horn, Dan Graham, Bruce Naumann, Hermann Nitsch), dance (Pina Bausch), theatre (Robert Wilson, Richard Foreman, Richard Schechner, Peter Brooks, Vito Acconci, Antonin Artaud, Chris Burden), circus (Jerome Savary, the Performance Vaudevillians), music (John Cage, Philip Glass), and pop culture (Laurie Anderson, Yoko Ono). Most performance art resists the attempt at neat classification by reference to traditional branches of art and turns this crossing and fusing of boundaries into a distinctive feature. A range of programmatic statements and descriptive accounts of performance art is available (e.g. Lance Carlson 1990; RoseLee Goldberg 1988), but a systematic reconstruction is still missing. The following remarks attempt such a systematic outline of performance art rather than a historical reconstruction of its development.

Although quite heterogeneous and manifold, the field of performance art might be demarcated by the following programmatic commitments:

(a) Performance art shifts the focus of artistic activity from the completion of an enduring piece ("the work") to the volatile event of a corporeal performance. This move beyond text and picture towards *eventness* and *corporeality* is the most distinctive feature of performance art (Bruce Naumann, Chris Burden, Vito Acconci). It links many performances closer to theatre than to the visual arts. However, unlike traditional theatrical performances most performance art does not separate actor from stage director and script from performance. In many cases it tries to overcome the model of theatrical illusion and to return to the ritual roots of theatre (Schechner 1977; Artaud 1958).

(b) Performance art aims at the *destruction* of conventional narratives, genres, and structures of meaning to open up a space for new and surprising, frequently provocative and even deliberately absurd happenings (e.g. John Cage's famous "Untitled event"). In this respect performance art continues the tradition-smashing heritage of *modernism* and, in particular, of futurism (Marinetti: "Let us burn down the museums"). It is, however, less militant than futurism. In particular in its postmodern version it relies more on irony and parody than on direct destruction.

(c) Performance art tries to blur the boundaries between art and reality, artist and spectator (Joseph Beuys: "Everything is art, everybody is an artist." Vito Acconci: "Performance is setting up a field in which . . . the audience became a part of what I was doing"). It is neither the creative intention of the artist nor the substantial quality of the piece of art or the conventional symbolism that constitutes art but, instead, the perspective of the spectator or the audience on it that turns something into art. We may call this focus on reception and perspectivity the *postmodern* thrust in performance art.

In spite of its ultramodernist pretension for breakthrough and novelty we will, in the following remarks, try to connect different elements of performance art to some basic problematiques and paradigms in the visual arts and relate the different strands of performance art to their predecessors in the history of art. For the sake of simplicity we will mention only four of these basic paradigms and point to their relations to different aspects of performance art. Obviously, the following remarks cannot and do not claim to provide an exhaustive account of performative art or to cover every aspect of it. Instead, because of the lack of a generally acknowledged treatise on performance art, they are to serve as a basis for further discussion.

Symbolic or iconic art

Symbolic or iconic art refers to the collective identity, the history or the sacred items of a particular community: totems, gods, demons, historical or religious events and stories, rulers and other icons of collective identity. Symbolic art in this sense ranges from so called "primitive art" (e.g. African masks, heraldic signs, totems), via religious and mythological art (e.g. statues and pictures of gods and saints, of heroes and mythical events, of allegorical and metaphorical representations), monuments and representations of major historical events (e.g. portraits of rulers, representations of battles, triumphant victories or tragic defeats), to the representation of beauty according to conventional taste: sunset mountains, flowers, pets, nudes, kids. In symbolic art the artist or the artful execution of the piece do matter less than the topic that is represented. The artist's creative intention is largely irrelevant for understanding the meaning of symbolic art; he or she can even be unknown as in the case of "primitive" or early religious art or of commercial art for home decoration (kitsch). Whoever has carved the crucifix or painted the sunset on the ocean does not matter. Symbolic art is embedded in the familiar symbolic universe of a social community – every member of the respective community is able to understand its language, the narrative is obvious and plain, the emotional impact is clear. Only for outsiders has it an enigmatic quality, only outsiders will ask questions, only outsiders will start to collect it as an "exotic" item. Therefore symbolic art is widely spread and highly accepted within the respective community. Its value is not set by craftsmanship, novelty, or rarity, but by the iconic quality of the symbols represented.

Performance art borders occasionally the domain of symbolic art, but it rarely does so in a plain and familiar way. Instead, it uses traditional symbols and rituals deliberately in an alienating, desacralizing, and subversive mode. Hermann Nitsch slaughtered lambs on stage, dispersed the bloody entrails on the naked bodies of actors, and performed sexual acts on the corpses; old sacrificial blood rituals and elements of Catholic liturgy are merged into a frightening new performance that, however, turns the conventional symbolic elements upside down. Antonin Artaud's Theater of Cruelty, too, used elements of torture and of Catholic liturgy. Joseph Beuys, in one of his most striking performances ("How to explain paintings to a dead hare," 1965), carried a dead hare in his arms in order to hint at Dürer's famous etching, the mass reproduction of which has been turned into a standard decoration of German homes. On another occasion ("I like America and America likes Me" 1974) he lived together with a live coyote for three days in a gallery thus referring to the world of Native Americans, etc. Performance art subverts or even perverts symbolic traditions, runs counter to the conventional interpretation of symbols, shocks the spectators (at least the unprepared ones), and aims at the destruction of everything that is fixed, established, and well accepted. One of the most famous groups of performance art called itself "Fluxus."

Illusionary art

Illusionary art, as it emerged in classical antiquity (Pheidias and Praxiteles in sculpture, Roman painting) and as it was rediscovered in early modern times fifteenth century) in Europe, grounded its artistic ambition and pretension less on the symbolic content but on the sensual refinement and accuracy of representing reality. It aimed at the perfect illusion even of symbolically unimportant or ugly parts of reality. The representation of three-dimensionality and perspective, of details and colour, later on of texture and surface, finally of the light itself, became the major concern and ambition of painting. Vasari already reconstructed the art of the Renaissance as a gradual approximation to such a perfect representation of reality (Vasari 1996). The summit of illusionary art is marked by the *trompe l'œil* in the case of which we cannot distinguish – at least from the regular distance – whether we see a two-dimensional painting or a three-dimensional sculpture, a representation or the real thing. Ideally even the artist should surrender to the illusion and take it for true reality. At the end he – like Pygmalion – could fall in love with his own creation.

But, in order to be successful, the illusion has to hide the fact that it is just an illusion. If the surface is too perfect and too polished the suspicion of deceptive illusion rises – at least for the experienced spectator. In contrast, the veiling or visual covering of the surface seduces the viewer to assume a hidden reality behind it. Therefore, sometimes the intentionally blurred rendition of contours and the darkening of colours can be used to conceal the illusion and to heighten the sense of realness at which illusionary art aims. The *sfumato* of Leonardo da Vinci and Andrea del Sarto at the beginning of the sixteenth century or the somber and fuzzy manner of Courbet and other *tenebristes* of the nineteenth century worked in this direction. Similar modes of deceiving the suspicious eye can be found in modern photography. The out-of-focus photo conveys more sense of the real event than the ultra-sharp one (see, for example, Gerhard Richter's series of photos of the "Baader-Meinhof"gang), whereas the ultra-accurate rendition of a moment gives it a weird sense of surrealism. The observer assumes something hidden behind the slick and accurately reproduced surface. This effect is thoroughly used by photorealism. Fuzziness and sombriety are, however, not to be mixed up with slurrish execution. Traces of the process of production have to be avoided in the final work of art since they disturb the illusion.

This illusionary function of art is referred to by contemporary performance art in several ways. Some artists focus on the moment of *iteration* and theatricality and play with the tension between role and identity: Cindy Sherman takes photos of herself in different historical costumes or poses in the manner of movie-stills thus producing the illusion of an illusion. The illusion is insurmountable, there is nothing behind the mask, but another mask.

Others take the opposite direction and expose their own bodies and their most intimate private behavior, i.e. their ultimate living reality, on stage: Manzoni exposed himself as "living creature" in an art gallery as early as 1961; Gilbert and George presented themselves in frozen gestures as "living sculptures" in 1969; Vito Acconci masturbated in a gallery in the presence of visitors in 1971; Yoko Ono and John Lennon invited the public to watch them in the famous performance "Bed Peace" in 1974; Chris Burden had himself shot in the arm onstage and crucified on a Volkswagen Beetle, etc. (Sharp 1979). Reality and theatrical illusion cannot be clearly separated any more. The happening on stage is real and reality is just another happening. In Chris Burden's phrasing: "getting shot is for real . . . there is no element of pretense or make believe in it."

But also the visual trick of veiling an object in order to let the viewer assume a secret reality is used by performance artists. Christo's collective actions of wrapping famous buildings are only the most widely known cases in point. Wrapping and concealing allow one not only to assume a hidden reality but also to present the reality as renewed and recreated after the veils and wrappings are undone (furthermore, wrapping and unwrapping are core procedures of a visual *rite de passage*).

Expressive art

Expressive art, too, focuses the problem of representation. It centers, however, not on illusion but on authenticity. Assuming a Platonic or idealist model of representation expressive art separates the transcendental aesthetic idea from the material document of the creative act. True art can hardly do more than display the traces of the creative genius in a material substance. The sacralized reference of this type of art is neither the reality of natural things nor the collective identity of a community; instead it is the individual person of the artist in distinction and even opposition to the conventions of society and the requirements of descriptive accuracy. This romantic idea of the creative genius dominated the nineteenth and early twentieth centuries, but it started already with Michelangelo's and Leonardo's *nonfinito* in the early sixteenth century, it continued with Titian's, Velasquez's and Rembrandt's use of crude brushstrokes in their later work, it extended until Vincent van Gogh, the Fauves and the German expressionists' coarse and sketchy mode of painting, and it ended with Jackson Pollock's or George Matthieu's action painting or Yves Klein's body painting in the 1950s.

According to the expressionist or romantic conception of art the visible material work is just an imperfect document of an ingenious creative moment. The aesthetic idea itself is spiritual and transcends any finite and tangible embodiment. Hence, the fragment, the rough surface that does not conceal the difference between the visible document and the invisible form, is a much more authentic and fascinating piece of art than the immaculate surface and the perfect form. Sketchy brushstrokes on a painting hint at the moment of creation and activity of the artist. Performance is, here, the creative performance of the individual artist. This line can be extended to performance art. Here art is viewed to be an ephemeral and volatile event that can be conserved only in its material traces.

Thus, Christo wraps public buildings and sells multiples of the photos or scrapbooks of the event, Beuys spends hours with a dead hare on his lap and signs photos of this event, etc. The volatile creative event marks the center of the aesthetic experience, the material documentation is hardly more than a souvenir – whatever the art market will set as a price for these "souvenirs." The relatively high prices that the documents of the volatile event will achieve (Beuys sometimes sold just his bare signature on a piece of paper) relate paradoxically to the programmatic commitments of the artists.

Another link to the general paradigm of performativity is established by the representation of *identity* that is at the core of many activities of performance art. By displaying their own – often naked – bodies in public performance artists expose their corporeal identity, sometimes their scars (in 1977 one of Beuys' exhibitions had the title: "Show your wounds") but they also use their bodies as expressive signs in a theatrical performance. The reference of this bodily sign, however, escapes description. "What is it, identity?" asked Yamamoto in one of his fashion statements. This reference to identity and corporeality is stronger in early performance art than in its later, more postmodern, versions that centered irony, parody, and iteration.

Postmodern art

Postmodern art disregards the creative process of expression and devalues the technical skills of the artful illusion as well as the familiar universe of symbols. Although, as outlined above, performance art reaches back to elements of illusionary as well as of expressionist art, its proper domain is postmodern art. Postmodern art is a matter less of the artist than of the spectator, less of production than of reception, less of artful illusion of reality than of watching an *event*. The *audience* takes center-stage. This turn from production towards reception is sometimes reflected by special mirror arrangements (e.g. Dan Graham) that present the spectator as the actual piece on exhibition. The piece of art has no message on its own, it is just reflecting the viewer. Transforming the mind of the spectator and turning the spectator into an artist is one of the declared objectives – e.g. of Beuys' so-called "extended conception of art" (*erweiterter Kunstbegriff*). After the postmodern turn the roles of artist and spectator are exchangeable: the artist is just another spectator responding to a performance by another performance, the creativity of the heroic genius is gone, iteration replaces originality. This relates effortlessly to the general paradigm of performance, to iteration and audience.

Iteration in postmodem art is, however, not to be mixed up with perfect duplication or illusionary representation. Instead every act of iteration not only repeats other events but also produces estrangement and *alienation*. Postmodern art is the result of aesthetic alienation. Quite ordinary objects, bodily move-ments, or processes can be turned into art if they are taken out of their ordinary context, get stripped of their regular meaning and familiar function and are presented under purely aesthetic premises – which is certainly not to be mixed up with decoration or conventional beauty. Instead of resulting from an under-standable symbolic universe, art is here produced by tearing apart the common web of meaning. What was plain and obvious before is turned into something enigmatic and absurd. Surrealism and Dada were already pointing to the weird absurdity behind the surface of familiar objects: Kurt Schwitter's Merztowers and Marcel Duchamp's famous Readymades are early examples of this turn towards decontextualization. Pop art continued the line: Andy Warhol presents banal icons of everyday life as art; Daniel Spoerri turns the remainders of a dinner into a sculpture; Arman works with carwrecks; Joseph Beuys and the Artepovera discovered the beauty of junk, felt, fat, earth, and other seemingly "poor" materials, etc.

If symbolic art relied on given structures of meaning which are accessible to all members of a community, postmodern performance art aims at the very erosion and *subversion* of these structures of meaning. If successful, it not only breaks down the conventional modes of using and interpreting things, but it opens up a space where surprising sensations and moments of encountering transcendence can occur. These experiences escape familiar narratives, they are difficult to describe by reference to the classificatory grid of profane language. They are sublime. Sometimes this subversive turn alienates familiar objects by irony and absurdity, by decontextualization, by blown-up proportions, or by screaming loudness. Other forms of performance art represent the void, the nothingness, the weird and even dreadful lack of meaning by an empty stage, by extreme slowness of movements (Wilson), by the complete absence of events, by monotonous continuity (Warhol's movies, especially *Empire State Building* which shows the famous high-rise for hours without changing perspective). More modernist early strands of performance art aimed at producing the sub-lime moment thus supporting a sophisticated metaphysics of presence that, from a radical postmodern point of view, has to be replaced by the incessant dance of iteration, by irony and parody as the prime mover of performance. Whether performance art is phrased in more modernist or in more postmod-ernist philosophical terminology, it is provocative, subversive, and enigmatic, it tries to trespass the limits of reason and decency, and thus to produce a cri-sis, a state of exception, a dissolution of text and language in order to allow a new and sublime perception before language and law can freeze the order of things.

But this thrust to run counter to the expectations of the audience – or in another phrasing to be an event – has its own risks. Performance art can exist only if there is an audience. However, this audience will be very small if attending the performative event requires strenuous intellectual efforts or results in a banal and boring experience. In many cases only those habitués who are familiar with the unfamiliar experience and whose perspective, therefore, cannot be subverted any more will attend the performative event. In order to attract public attention and a larger audience, but also to present the performance as a real event instead of an artful illusion, performance art often relies on violence, disgust, and shocks (Graver 1995): Chris Burden is shot on stage; Hermann Nitsch and Otto Mühl slaughter animals on stage; Paul McCarthy copulates with a dead pig; the attack on the Twin Towers is declared to be a great event of performance art, etc. Other performance artists succeed in attracting large audiences not by sensational shocks, but by the surprising beauty and poetic quality of their performances: Rebecca Horn, Robert Wilson, Christo and Pina Bausch are cases in point.

Because performance art consists of events instead of fixed objects it can dispense – to a certain degree at least – with the material frame that separates the conventional painting from its surrounding environment. This frame marks, in a literal way, also the boundary between the realm of art and the realm of everyday life where considerations of function and use, reason and truth, apply. Abstract expressionism had already removed this confining and containing frame – the art expanded into "real life," the sizes of the paintings were blown up to gigantic proportions, the only remaining frame of art was the museum itself. The museum was no longer just a showcase, but a sacral space permeated with the aura of the art. Performance art could proceed even further in this "decontainment" of art. The performative event could happen everywhere, in public places where people were turned into an audience without their consent (Mason 1992) as well as in private meetings where outsiders could be excluded. Beuys' Extended Conception of Art aimed, indeed, at a total aestheticization of society, assuming, in the best of the Romantic tradition, that the reign of art would cure political and social malaises. By its very structure performance art was liberated from containment and could reach out to permeate life, and art, in its turn, could take on the volatile nature of life.

But this spatial decontainment of performance art comes at a price. The limitations of performance art are temporal ones – after some repetitions the event becomes routinized, the attention of the spectators turns to other attractions, the practice of performance is turned into an almost banal experience. And this is exactly what happened to some famous forms of performance art: Gilbert and George's frozen gestures and living sculptures are today part of the repertory of street performers all over the world; Robert Wilson's theatrical inventions are used by stage directors everywhere; Christo's wrappings are turned into decorative events supported by the local office for tourism etc. Performance art is gradually transformed into a regular branch of the established field of arts. What was the cutting edge of the avant garde before is now turned into a chapter of art history that ranges among others and that itself represents an iteration in a historical sequence. Yesterday this happened to Dada and futurism, and it happens today to performance art.

References

Artaud, Antonin. 1958. *The Theater and Its Double*, trans. Mary Caroline Richards. New York: Grove Press.

Auslander, Philip. 1994. *Presence and Resistance: Postmodernism and Cultural Politics in Contemporary American Performance*. Ann Arbor: University of Michigan Press.

Bauman, Richard. 1977. *Verbal Art as Performance*. Rowley, Mass.: Newbury House.

1986. *Story, Performance and Event: Contextual Studies in Oral Narrative*. New York: Cambridge University Press.

Carlson, Lance. 1990. "Performance Art as Political Activism," *Artweek* 22: 23–4.

Chambers, Ross. 1980. "Le Masque et le miroir: Vers une théorie relationnelle du théâtre," *Études littéraires* 13.

Derrida, Jacques. 1982. *Margins of Philosophy*. trans. Alan Bass. Chicago: University of Chicago Press.

Diamond, Elin. 1989. "Mimesis, Mimicry, and the 'True-Real'," *Modern Drama* 32: 58–72.

Erickson, Jon. 1990. "Appropriation and Transgression in Contemporary American Performance," *Theatre Journal* 42, 2: 225–36.

Féral, Josette. 1992. "What is Left of Performance Art? Autopsy of a Function, Birth of a Genre," *Discourse* 25: 142–62.

Fluxus. 1963. *Fluxus: An Anthology*, ed. George Maciunas. New York: ReFlux Editions.

Foreman, Richard. 1976. *Plays and Manifestos*. ed. Kate Davy. New York: New York University Press.

Garner, Stanton B., Jr. 1994. *Bodied Spaces: Phenomenology and Performance in Contemporary Drama*. Ithaca: Cornell University Press.

Garvin, Harry R. (ed.). 1980. "Romanticism, Modernism, Postmodernism," *Bucknell Review*, special issue, vol. 25.

Goldberg, RoseLee. 1988. *Performance Art: From Futurism to the Present*. New York: Harry N. Abrams.

Graver, David. 1995. "Violent Theatricality: Displayed Enactments of Aggression and Pain," *Theatre Journal* 47: 43–64.

Hassan, Ihab. 1971. *The Dismemberment of Orpheus: Towards a Postmodern Literature*. Madison: University of Wisconsin Press.

Huizinga, Johan. 1950. *Homo Ludens*. New York: Beacon Press.

Kostelanetz, Richard. 1994. *On Innovative Performance(s): Three Decades of Recollections on Alternative Theater*. Jefferson, NC: McFarland.

Mason, Bim. 1992. *Street Theatre and Other Outdoor Performance*. London: Routledge.

Pratt, Mary Louise. 1977. *Toward a Speech-Act Theory of Literary Discourse.* Bloomington: Indiana University Press.

Schechner, Richard. 1965. *Rites and Symbols of Initiation.* New York: Harper.

1970. "Guerrilla Theatre: May 1970," *TDR* 17: 5–36.

1977. *Essays on Performance Theory 1970–76.* New York: Drama Book Specialists.

1985. *Between Theater and Anthropology.* Philadelphia: University of Pennsylvania Press.

Sharp, Willowby. 1979. "Body Works: A Pre-critical, Non-definitive Survey of Very Recent Works Using the Human Body or Parts Thereof," *Avalanche* 1: 14–17.

Shyer, Laurence. 1989. *Robert Wilson and his Collaborators.* New York: Theatre Communications Group.

Stern, Carol Simpson and Bruce Henderson. 1993. *Performance: Texts and Contexts.* White Plains, NY: Longmans.

Wiles, Timothy. 1980. *The Theater Event: Modern Theories of Performance.* Chicago: University of Chicago Press.

Vasari, Giorgio. 1996. *Lives of the Painters, Sculptors and Architects*, 2 vols. Oxford: Everyman's Library Classics.

11

Performing the sacred: a Durkheimian perspective on the performative turn in the social sciences

Bernhard Giesen

Introduction

Although generating a logic and scholarly sophistication of its own, social theory has always gained additional power and plausibility when grounded in pre-scientific paradigms and commonsense images of social reality. In this way the classical social theory of the eighteenth century started with the idea of society as a normative constitution based on contract; later on it imagined society as a coercive organization, as an organized division of labor or as a market. During the so-called cultural turn of the 1980s, social reality was conceived as a text that is interpreted by other texts. Meanwhile the focus has shifted from the structure of the text to the process of narrating it, from the normative constitution to the rituals of contracting, from the coercive organization and the revolutionary movement to the rituals of staging authority and the rituals of rebellion: social theory is going to take a performative turn.

Of course, this turn to performance is not entirely new. It has been preluded by the debate about the primacy of ritual over myth in classical anthropology (Smith 1927; Frazer 1922), it borrows from the theory of drama (Burke 1965; Schechner 1976), from the theory of speech acts (Searle 1970; Austin 1975), from the ethnomethodological thrust to dissolve institutional structures into modes of practices (Garfinkel 1989), and, most important of all, it has been programmatically introduced, some decades ago, by Victor Turner (Turner 1969, 1974, 1982) and Erving Goffman into sociology (Goffman 1959, 1986). Goffman's concepts – e.g. identity and representation, role play and role distance, backstage and frontstage, faceworking and framing – have, most certainly, set the stage for a dramatological perspective on social reality, and Victor Turner's notions of liminality, communitas, social drama, etc., provide the starting point for every sociological account of performance. In many respects contemporary contributions can hardly surpass the conceptual architecture created by these founding fathers of the performative turn. However, as stimulating and path-breaking as the contributions of Turner and Goffman may be, they fall short of offering a fully fledged theoretical paradigm that relates to core themes of classical social theory. Goffman fails to extend his paradigm to macro-sociological domains, he rarely deals with the mediation of performances through television and cinema, and, when imagining the construction of social reality, he takes mostly the perspective of the actor instead of the point of view of the audience. Furthermore, he can hardly conceal that he assumes mostly strategic motivations driving the presentation of the self.[1] Turner avoids falling into this trap, but he is too much confined by his anthropological domain to develop a truly sociological model that could cover also fields of contemporary society and its new media of communication (Gusfield 1981). Recent contributions (Alexander, this volume; Wagner-Pacifici 1986) have successfully attempted to broaden the scope of the emerging new paradigm of performativity within the social sciences, not only by relating it to general cultural evolution as well as to classical issues of social theory, but also by centering mass media and the audience as the arena where the meaning of a performance is created. Thus they allow us not only to extend the dramatological model to the macro-sociological domain but also to embrace a postmodern "receptionist" perspective on performance.

The following remarks follow this path. Stimulated by ideas from the general history of religion and from the theory of ritual they try to outline an elementary conception of performativity and to explore its contribution to social theory. They converge with many parts of the conceptual architecture outlined by Alexander in his programmatic chapter in this volume but they also differ from it in some respects. Most important among these differences is the central reference to the Durkheimian distinction between the sacred and the profane. Other oppositions could, of course, as well have been used as conceptual starting points – language and speech act, frame and event, identity and representation, eternal ideas and temporal objects, transcendental subject and real object, theoria and praxis, rule and exception, etc. These oppositions – although differing from each other in many respects – hint, partially at least, at a similar domain. They separate an invisible and non-contingent "internal" world that is exempted from limitations of time and space, that is neither caused nor produced, and that allows to assume identity and meaning because it stands for the totality of the world, from a visible and tangible "external" realm that is treated as "real" and that is submitted to the distinctions and dissections of time and space. This classical distinction between subject and object, between a presupposed, but invisible internal world and the varying phenomena of the external reality, provides the basic conceptual architecture of the following essay on performance. Its main theme is the mediation between both opposites by different modes of performance. This shift to the issue of mediation presupposes that the thrust for immediate access to the external or internal world, to identity or to the things as such has been given up and replaced by the more melancholic question of how, if immediacy is impossible, we can refer to it in the world of signs and communication.[2] At the same time modern literary theory, however, discovers immediacy and suddenness as a special mode of aesthetic perception (Bohrer 2003).

We will return to this issue in the next section of this chapter when dealing with symbolic objects and moments of epiphany as representations of the sacred in the world. Here performance is related to an extraordinary "epiphanic" or "hierophanic" (Eliade 1985) symbolic event in contrast to the banal continuity of social order and everyday life. This epiphanic event resists being told to outsiders. Then, in the third section, we will deal with rituals as the elementary "poesis" of social reality. Here, performance appears as the iterative social construction of order that allows us to frame the extraordinary event and to cope with the challenge of chaos and absurdity. We will argue that ritual performances constitute social reality and do not allow us yet to question the performance with reference to a reality or a script independent from it. Performance and reality are still "fused" as Alexander underlines in his programmatic account of the performative turn. Rituals are carried by a community that tries to mark the boundary between inside and outside and to keep outsiders at a distance. The fourth section will present the theatrical mimesis as a special mode of performance that has not only to blend the performative event into the script and to merge performance and reality – as the constitutive ritual does – but it has also to connect the performance on stage to the audience in front of the stage. While rituals are treated as "second-order events" that frame and tame the impact of unmediated (epiphanic) events, theatrical performances add an additional frame to rituals – they have to catch the attention of outsiders and turn them into a fascinated audience. Hence they may be regarded as a "third-order event": the theatrical performance itself is an event that frames ritual events on stage that, in their turn, try to interpret "extraordinary" or "immediate" events by integrating them into a story or a mythical narrative. Finally, the fifth section will outline the moral drama (Turner 1969, 1981, 1990; Wagner-Pacifici 1986; Alexander, this volume) as an even more complex mode of performance that, in addition to the exigencies of eventness, fusion and fascination, refers also to the "internal reality" of the actors: in moral drama the actors have to present themselves on stage in an authentic way, they are expected to speak the unconditional truth, they have to disregard their own interests as well as the special expectations of the audience, they have to take on a universalist and almost divine perspective, they are to speak out "parusiah." This requirement of moral drama is illustrated by the case of modern politics. Moral drama, theatrical mimesis, constitutive rituals, and symbolic events are treated as ideal types of increasing complexity. The concluding remarks will return to the idea of the sacred and present the relationship between audience and performance as a new model of the origin of social order.

Sacred objects and moments of epiphany: performance as an extraordinary event

The basic distinction

The following remarks start with the distinction between the sacred and the profane. Referring to the sacred as a basic concept setting needs justification. After discarding the idea of a personal God, modern secularized cultures convey a certain oddity to the concept. Its meaning is, however, not to be exhausted by the imagination of transcendence as a personal God. The concept becomes truly obsolete only if we subscribe to a rigorous positivism. In a modern context "the sacred" denotes extraordinary moments or experiences that escape ordinary classification and that can be referred to by texts only in an indirect way. Notions like "aura" or "shock" in Benjamin, "alterity" in Levinas, "event" or "now" in Heidegger, or the "sublime" in Lyotard refer to such shocking perceptions or extraordinary experiences that occur immediately and suddenly, but resist comprehension and language because their wholeness escapes linguistic distinctions. These sudden experiences of the unspeakable have fascinated modern literary authors already since the nineteenth century (Bohrer 2003). Nietzsche's "suddenness of perception" or his "Dionysian moment," in which self-awareness is lost, Baudelaire's "extase" in contrast to the banality of ordinary life, Proust's moments of "mémoire involontaire" in his *Recherche du Temps Perdu*, "moments of being" in Virginia Woolf's *Sketch of the Past*, James Joyce's "suddenness of epiphany" in his *Portrait of the Artist as a Young Man*, or Robert Musil's "daylight mysticism" in which the immediacy of the ideal now is not yet replaced by the "déjà vu," were only some of many phrasings of a transcendence without a divine reference. In a modern context transcendence is – in a seemingly paradoxical twist – a kind of "profane revelation" (Benjamin).

This fascination by the shocking experience of immediacy and transcendence was not confined to reflections on aesthetics but extended also to classical social theory. Concepts like "charisma" in Weber (1990), "liminality" in van Gennep (1977), "antistructure" in Victor Turner (1969), or "state of exception" in Carl Schmitt refer explicitly to transcendence of the regular social order and this transcendence differs strongly from the one implied in the classical notions of "state of nature" or of "sovereignty" that were at the core of early modern political theory. Durkheimian sociology uses the term "sacred" for this transcendence (Durkheim 1960; Caillois 1994). It denotes not just a personal moment of epiphany as in the aesthetic experience or an extraordinary, pre-social and counterfactual situation as in early modern political philosophy but, instead, it took a new reflexive turn on social reality: the sacred stands for the collective identity of a social community, i.e. the general mode by which a community refers to itself in distinction to the sum of its individual members.[3] This reference to the collective self is an extraordinary complex operation, because the self – individual or collective – is *intransparent* to itself. The basic intransparency of the self results from the difficulty of being subject and object at the same time.

In order to overcome this problem we can either change the point of view of the subject and take – for the moment of this operation – the perspective of the other or we can disguise and transform the referential object and translate it into something different from us. The first solution leads to concepts like Mead's "generalized other" (1934) or to Habermas' idea of a universalist attitude in an ideal discourse (Habermas 1985). The second solution of the problem of self-reference translates collective identity into something that seems to be different from the actual and visible representations of the collectivity. The result of this translation is the sacred in the broadest meaning of the term. By this translation the collective identity of the community is presented as radical alterity.

We will use the Durkheimian term "sacred" because we want to account for this basic translation of the collective self. The term "collective identity," as used by many authors, tends, unfortunately, to blur the distinction between self-referentiality, i.e. identity in the strict sense, and its representations in social interaction (Brubaker 1996; Wagner 1998; Giesen 2004). The following remarks about the sacred and the profane can, therefore, also be taken as an essay on collective identity and its representations. At the end of this discussion we will return to this conception of the sacred as an indirect or "translated" phrasing of collective identity.

If we account for the complexity of self-reference it is hardly a surprise that the direct encounter with what is called "the sacred" is rare and exceptional. It is the contrary to the empirical perception of profane objects. These are experienced because we dispose of categories, words, textual grids into which they seem to fit effortlessly, while the sacred is experienced because and insofar as it *cannot* be inserted into the grid of profane classification. The sacred is not perceived as a regular "case of . . .", it escapes profane typification and classification as such, it is the opposite to "déjà vu." It means the wholeness of the world (or of the community) instead of particular phenomena within this world. It "occurs" to us instead of being produced by us. It is considered to be incomparable and unique, it cannot be conceived by numbers. We are used to refer indexically to ourselves by using pronouns like "we" or "ourselves," but we can hardly stand the moment when we have to face the direct encounter with our mind in a mirrorlike setting (Freud 1963). When it happens, the extraordinary complexity of this operation breaks down the structure of ordinary life. We are taken over by a state of suspense, vertigo, and awe. It is the moment of crisis, in which we desperately struggle to find an exceptional point of view from which we are able to consider as an object what was, before, itself such an exceptional point of view and as such the presupposition of objectification and order.

In its most elementary form the encounter with the sacred does allow to be classified as positive or negative: the "spirits" in original religions hint at this axiologically undifferentiated impact of the sacred. However, Durkheim has already noted that, in most cultures, the sacred as opposed to the profane is itself split up into two mutually counteracting forces: 1. the "positive," redeeming, and charismatic force that is the ultimate source of the cosmic order and identity, and 2. the "demonic" that aims at decay and chaos, at the dissolution of order and structure, at pollution and evil (Durkheim 1960). Thus, the mundane world of everyday acting and profane things is framed by two transcendent references, the cosmogonic sacred marking the center on the one side, and the demonic force, the chaos, the evil on the other side.

This opposition between cosmos and chaos can be translated into different languages. Religions refer to it as acting persons like gods and devils or as spheres like heaven and hell; psychoanalytic theory rephrases it as the opposition between Eros and Thanatos; Heideggerian philosophy refers to it as "being" and "nothingness" etc.[4]

Since the encounter with both, with the sacred as well as with the demonic, is experienced as shocking and frightening, it suspends the compromises of the ordinary lifeworld and disrupts the mundane social structure. It is interpreted as the event as such and because of this it can be remembered again and again whereas the continuous banal flow of profane phenomena not only escapes our attention, but also does not intrude into our memory (Proust). When we recall the past, our memory refers not to the empty continuity of the past where everything seems to be an iteration of the past, but, instead, it constructs events that interrupted the flow of profane time.[5]

This encounter with identity, with the sacred or with "being" in the Heideggerian sense has been largely neglected by contemporary social theory. Sociological constructivism, thrusting to overcome the positivist account of the social world as measurable facts, has paid much attention to the social processes by which the lifeworld is perceived as profane, i.e. by which the world is fitted into a grid of classification and by which it can be taken for granted (Schütz 1964; Luckmann and Schütz 1974; Garfinkel 1989). The linguistic or semiotic turn in the humanities has radicalized this insistence on the impossibility of an unmediated experience of the world – there is no world outside of the text

(Derrida 1978). Luhmann's theory of communication points to a similar direction – autopoetic social systems can dispense even with the reference to acting subjects (Luhmann 1999).

The general constructivist thrust to overcome the positivist naiveté has been largely successful. Today even the advocates of hardcore quantitative analysis concede that facts are not directly accessible, but only via observational statements. But while the profane world has been discovered as a social construction, its opposite, the sacred, has been rarely turned into the object of contemporary sociological analysis.[6] The following remarks try to contribute to the analysis of the social construction of the sacred. They start with a typology of different modes of relating the sacred to the profane, the realm of identity to the realm of mundane things, the uniqueness of the moment to the rule or the repetition of a pattern etc.

At the core of this typology is the concept of representation. Symbols and signs represent something else – they hint at something invisible that is, however, no less real than the visible things at hand. They represent something that, although invisible, is the key for understanding the visible situation. In this respect symbols differ strongly, however, from simple signs or indexical gestures (Langer 1967). Signs can just hint at other signs, which, in their turn, refer to other signs etc. – an infinite process of signification that can never be anchored in a real world. This postmodern perspective conceives of signification as an endless dance that can never touch the ground. The intended referential world appears, from this point of view, only as an illusion without which we could not act, but nevertheless as an illusion.

In contrast, a phenomenological perspective centers *indexical gestures* that produce meaning by pointing to the "unquestionable" givens of the present and local world out there: here, this, now, we (Schütz 1964; Garfinkel 1989). Hinting at the (supposedly) visible, tangible, and immediately perceptible situation at hand anchors the signifier in the empirical world, connects it to a seemingly immutable and unquestionable basis and, thus, generates profane meaning and a sense of reality. The signified is just out there, it is taken for being plain and immediately perceptible. This reference to the immediately given observable reality is also the referential anchor of descriptive representations – even if they do not hint at an empirical situation at hand, they presuppose that in principle they can – at least partially – be translated into indexical gestures or empirical operations (Bridgeman 1991).

Symbols take the opposite way to signification and meaning: they anchor the visible in the invisible, they explain the plain, local, and present phenomena by reference to an invisible reality behind it. This perspective on a realm that transcends the plain and present reality is generated by the reflexive capacity of the human mind. We can question the visible phenomena, imagine possible states of the world, invent an alternative reality and ask "What is it really?" if faced with the plain and obvious.

However, this reflexive capacity of the human mind not only opens up spaces of imagination and gives way to the movement of the spirit, but – in principle – it also renders the world around us fragile, malleable, and uncertain. Symbols counteract this fragility and arbitrariness of the world. They relate the visible, contingent, and plain phenomena not just to other empirical phenomena that are only incidentally invisible and absent, but to an absolute reference, i.e. to a totality and wholeness that transcends any finite accounts of the world and sets the indispensable starting point for orientation. Without this Archimedean point not only the perception of spatial and temporal differences, but also the assumption of sameness and voluntary action, would be impossible. The absolute transcendental reference cannot be deduced from particular mundane reasoning, it cannot be reduced to contingent empirical phenomena, it cannot be classified and described – to the contrary: it defies reason and it cannot be confined into any particular locality and moment. By hinting at absolute transcendence or – in a different phrasing by referring to totality or identity – symbols not only generate meaning, but they also can be taken as a non-contingent backbone of reality – they prevent the dissolution of order into chaos, they shield us from falling into the abyss of unregulated violence, they hold us before we relapse into the state of nature, they prevent us being overwhelmed by the shocking immediacy of the sublime. Thus, they not only bridge the fundamental chasm between the immediately perceived world at hand and the possible worlds imagined in our mind, but they also mediate between those realms that Durkheim has called the sacred and the profane.[7]

The following remarks disregard aesthetic signs as well as indexical gestures and their way of producing a cultural order. Instead, they center different modes by which symbols mediate between the present and perceptible world and the transcendence – or in another phrasing, in which they represent the sacred in the profane world.

Sacred objects

In a first attempt we can distinguish between spatial and temporal modes of symbolic representation of the sacred. Spatial modes of symbolic representation assume that there are particular material objects or places that are fused with sacrality, that recall past worlds or promise future ones and thus embody collective identity – in distinction to other places and objects that are considered as profane, as cases of a kind, as objects that can be used and consumed exploited and destroyed and that, above all, are the sites and materials for mundane everyday interaction. The bones of the ancestors, the relics of important individuals, the statues of the gods, the site of temples and the memorial monuments of a nation, but also flags of sports clubs or cherished pieces of art are such material embodiments of the sacred. These material symbols are not just conventional signs that can easily be replaced by others. Nor are they mere allegories and metaphors that represent the sacred but admit that they are just artificial and changeable imaginations of something that essentially defies any imagination (Kurz 1997). Instead, true symbols are sacred by themselves and this sacredness prevents any profane use or trade.

The charismatic sacred objects or places are the center of society, the firm ground from which the perspective extends to the horizon, the source for the poesis of meaning (Shils 1979). They have a cosmogonic force – they create a meaningful and orderly realm: the cosmos of the community (Eliade 1959). This permeating and radiating quality of sacred objects is their aura. The members of a community try to be close to its sacred objects in order to partake in this aura. Proximity to a sacred object is experienced as an extraordinary situation – it evokes feelings of excitement and bans mundane activities to a certain degree. A burial ground may not be used for growing crops, in the temple there should be no commercial trade, a flag should not be used to clean the floor etc.

In its most elementary forms the sacred was not yet imagined as firmly located in particular objects. Instead it was conceived of as an overwhelming force and frightening phenomenon that was beyond human disposition and communication. The thunder, the sun, the mountain, the burning tree, the rock, the wind are such phenomena of nature that are treated as sacred, as the voice of the superhuman, as the embodiment of supernatural force. Magical practices and the sheer and absolute submission of humans up to the sacrifice of human lives were the only modes to stand and to cope with this diffuse and terrifying sacred force.

In distinction to these conceptions of the sacred as a supernatural force there are visible representations of the sacred that are intentionally produced by men: statues and images of gods and deities, sacred symbols, temples and altars that are set apart from the space of profane objects and exempted from regular use for profane purposes. These anthropogonic constructions of the sacred as represented by the Homeric world of Olympic gods do not yet dissolve the material symbol into mere metaphors. Although there may exist many statues of the same god, these statues are sacred by themselves and cannot be used for profane purposes. Destroying the material representation of the sacred does not affect directly the existence of the deity but it is considered as a pollution that requires purification, as an offense that urges for revenge.

The mode of representing the sacred in manmade objects leaves its imprints in its content: the gods usually have human traits and act like humans. Here, the sacred is not just an unstructured superhuman force, but it is a person, with whom humans can communicate, to whom they can pray and promise offerings, who is, even as a divine person, subjected to passions and rivalries, who, although immortal, lives through stories that can be narrated, who can commit adultery and fall in love with humans, who is revengeful and compassionate, who helps and saves, etc. These gods are persons, who walk on the surface of the earth and who differ from humans mainly in their immortality and their power to work miracles. The dialogue between gods and humans starts: prayer and grace, suffering and sin, covenant and promise, sacrifice and salvation, get their original meaning.

The anthropogonic constructions of the sacred have their counterpart in the charismatization of the exceptional individual – as the gods have a human face, the humans aspire for divinity. The hero who does the extraordinary, who stands above the rules, who defies profane reason, becomes the archetype of human perfection – as warrior or prophet, genius or ruler (Campbell 1993). In between the realm of the sacred forces and the realm of profane proceedings a zone of mixed creatures emerges – gods who have human traits, heroes who are semi-divine, monsters who are partly animal and partly human, devils and witches who are demons in a human body, etc. Following Turner (1969) this location betwixt and between in a third position that escapes the ordinary classification and structure is also the embodiment of communitas and liminality, i.e. in our phrasing: of the sacred.

The charismatization of the exceptional individual, the anthropogonic construction of the sacred and the dialogue between gods and humans prepare the stage for a theatrical conception of performance. The gods and the exceptional individual human being are ideal persons who provide the exemplar of the right and virtuous life and, thus, uplift ordinary persons above their everyday life. The mythical stories of gods and heroes are not only narrated again and again but also re-enacted in human action. They provide the frame and backbone of history.

No community can entirely dispense with these symbols that relate the past to the present, the profane to the sacred, the visible objects to the invisible identity. Some religious communities, however, reject the immanence of the sacred, i.e. the assumption of an uneven distribution of sacredness within the visible and tangible world. According to their doctrines and convictions, sacredness exists only in a strictly separated realm, whereas the things of this world have to be regarded as fundamentally and irredeemably unholy and profane objects. Any attempt at blurring the boundary between the sacred and the profane by imputing a sacred aura to material objects or by representing the invisible god or the sacred by pictures or statues has to be treated as blasphemy, idolatry, or a ridiculous superstition.[8] The profane world out there has, according to the "axial age civilizations" (Eisenstadt 1986), an order of its own that is radically different from the transcendental order. It is "disenchanted" and thus may be explored with respect to the principles governing their domains (Weber 1988). At the end, the spirit of modernity takes over the world. From now on magical practices are to be banned as well as anthropogonic representations of the sacred. Whoever tries to identify the principled order of the sacred in the visible things of the world will be accused of falling back behind the progress of the Enlightenment. The iconoclastic zeal of radical reformatory Protestantism, of post-Mosaic Judaism or of Islam, that prepared the ground for the principled order of modernity, does, however, not only ban polytheism and exempt God from any earthly imagination, but it also extends to the identity of those living human beings who are chosen by God and who consequently carry his charisma. Images of human beings are banned and mirrors are considered to be an invention of the devil. The representation of the individual person is also a duplication and as such it challenges the uniqueness, the identity, the sacrality of the person. A haunting awareness of this challenge to identity and sacredness may also drive our feeling of uneasiness with "Doppelgängers," doubles, and lookalikes. Many simple societies used to kill twins because they were seen as demonic and impure. Identity is not a case of a category, it exists as a unique and incomparable totality and wholeness. An iconoclastic perspective removes the representation of identity almost completely from the world of visible and tangible things. If this world is seen as irredeemably profane, ascetic abstention and retreat from it should be the proper motive of those who aspire for salvation.

Sacred time: epiphanic events

However, even in the most iconoclastic religions, the knowledge about transcendence, about the totality, about the sacred, has to be revealed and this revelation occurs, sometimes fostered by special methods and arrangements, in a particular moment of epiphany when the sacred is turned into words and texts.[9] Judaism and, later on, Christianity and Islam have oriented their religious activity not only to the interpretation of the word of God, but also towards the eschatological expectation of a future epiphany, towards the advent of the Messiah, towards the return of the Savior, or – on an individual level – towards a personal encounter with God in mysticism and meditation. Buddhism and Hinduism are driven by the longing to retreat from the fractured and fragmented mundane existence, to escape from the eternal circle of death and rebirth in order to become part of the all-one, nirvana, brahma etc. Even the ancient Greek philosophy opted for theoria and sophia as the true concern of the free citizen in contrast to mere praxis, i.e. the laborious pursuit of mundane affairs.

While the popular religious practice is mostly focused on sacred objects, relics and fetishes, or on fixed and common sacred times of festivities, the religious life of the virtuosi, of prophets, monks, and sacred men and women centers increasingly on the elusive moment when the sacred is revealed to the human being. Because the moment of encountering your own self or the wholeness of the world is absolutely unique and incomparable, it is difficult to describe, to report, and to narrate (Swinburne 1989). It is a matter of absolute presence, of liminality, of intensive and overwhelming feeling that affects deeply the person who experiences it. The yogic "samadhi" in Hinduism, the "satori" in Zen Buddhism or the "unio mystica" in Christian thinking, the "sublime" in modern aesthetics refer to this extraordinary experience (Rappaport 1999). We have already mentioned Nietzsche, Baudelaire, Joyce, Benjamin, and Musil as modern bearers of evidence for this experience of immediacy and epiphany beyond any reference to God. In contrast to these authors who focused the sudden individual personal experience the sociological classics frequently underline that the encounter with the extraordinary is often a collective experience. Weber's "charismatic leadership" is a collective construction of the followers, Durkheim's moments of "effervescence" are based on mutual contagion, Turner's "communitas" can be conceived of only as a collective phenomenon, etc. (Weber 1988; Durkheim 1960; Turner 1982). We follow them in assuming that the encounter with the sacred is a culturally mediated collective construction and that the stories of epiphany reported by individual persons are just narrative mediations of an originally collective relationship.

The exceptional encounter with the sacred is fostered by a certain readiness and sensitivity for liminality on the part of the collectivity – mundane expectations have to fade away, everyday rules have to be disregarded, differences of social status have to be forgotten. Social order recedes and opens up the space for communitas. Charismatic individuals like prophets break up the firmly entrenched social order; they have to tell the message of God even to a community that by itself would not give up their mundane ways of living. They establish communitas even among those who resist listening.[10] These charismatic individuals are mostly cut off from positions in the regular and profane social structure. They are exempted from ordinary social life, they have no family like monks, they do not care for profane well-being like mendicant travelers, they do not account for mundane reasoning and caution like fools or geniuses, sometimes they are just strangers without ties to the community.

In many religious narratives the extraordinariness of the epiphanic moment is marked by the reference to violence – God asks Abraham to sacrifice Isaac, Christ is tortured and crucified to redeem his people, Saint Paul is hit by a divine stroke, etc. The importance of violence for the moment of epiphany results not only from its unexpectedness in ordinary life, but also from its location in the boundary zone between common social life and the outlands – it represents the ultimate exception from rules of everyday life, it is the event at such. The exceptional nature of violence conveys a sense of utmost veracity and authenticity, it is grounded in a realm beyond volatile communication, fragile conventions, and faked pretentions: it has an absolute presence. René Girard has pointed to this rootedness of the social order in a constitutive violence: the social bond is created by the violent act of sacrificing an innocent victim (Girard 1977).[11] Because it is unexpected and unique the violent event is difficult to explain by referring to rules and reasons. Its source and cause escape description, its generation is not guided by reason or utility, it is not caused by something else, instead it constitutes itself like a sovereign subject – what we can describe are only its effects and impact on our regular life, its traces in reality.

But the encounter with the sacred in moments of epiphany is not confined to religious practices. These moments of epiphany may occur also in seemingly secularized spheres such as politics or private life where they appear as turning points of biographies and histories that, later on, are remembered as traumata or as triumphant moments of sovereign subjectivity (Alexander et al. 2004; Giesen 2004). Proust, in his pursuit of the problem of immediate recalling of the past, focuses on these personal and private memories of feelings and sentiments that by their epiphanic nature resist communication (Proust 1996). Immediacy of experience or memory seems to exclude sharedness and communication in a paradoxical way.

Collective memory is also structured by these extraordinary events that are recalled and re-enacted as collective traumata or collective triumphs. The great revolutions are telling examples of these epiphanic moments of national history. When they occurred the lived experience of violence and victory often escaped description. Only later on, from a distance and from the outside, the epiphanic event when the demos opened up the state of nature and encountered its identity could be represented and remembered.

Another domain where these moments of epiphany occur is the experience of art. The reality of art starts beyond the confines of functional purposes and social order – in the sublime that escapes conventional narratives and ordinary patterns. The intensive moment, the absolute presence, the sublime experience of something that escapes ordinary interpretation, are at the core of the modern aesthetic experience. We have referred to Benjamin's notion of "shock" and "profane revelation," to Musil's immediacy of the "ideal now" that is not yet replaced by the "déjà vu," and to Joyce's "suddenness of epiphany" in his *Portrait of the Artist as a Young Man*. Barnett Newman's famous phrase "The sublime is now" catches this reference for the realm of visual arts. Immediacy and suddenness are also a central concern of what today is called performance art. Performance art (Phelan 1993) is based on a general feature of performances: performances are – unlike texts or social institutions – temporally located between a before and an after. They are *events* (Fischer-Lichte 2002). As events they are unique and only those who are present can participate in them. This uniqueness of the event is not only due to the simple fact that every moment is volatile and will never come back, but it also results from the perception of the event as extraordinary and unexpected. Events are commonly perceived only in contrast to an unchanging and continuous background. Although the degree of extraordinariness and discontinuity that is associated with events varies greatly, no performance will be noticed and catch attention if nothing extraordinary happens. The event of encountering identity or the sacred does not fit into a sequence or a rule, it occurs suddenly and strikingly like the intervention of God or the outburst of the demonic in everyday life. Extraordinary events like miracles or catastrophes intrude suddenly and violently into the regular life and their violent nature produces awe and trembling on the part of those who experience them. In a paradoxical turn this moment of encountering the sacred is experienced as a time out of time, as eternal.

Postmodern performance theatre tries to produce this intensive experience of the extraordinary event that escapes any common experiences and familiar narratives. Here, the theatrical performance has not yet a script and a story and the question of right or wrong cannot yet be asked. The corporeal gestures and bodily movements of the performance may even appear absurd because they do not repeat or represent a well-known story or represent familiar characters. Shattering and destroying the common patterns, rules, and narratives is the very aim of these theatrical performances. At its extreme the performance presents nothing but the aura of the extraordinary event, the epiphany of presence, the kairos of happenings that fascinate because they do not fit into regular categories and profane narratives. Elementary gestures and archaic acts like screaming and bloodshed, torture and terror create a violent reality on stage that is beyond understanding and before language and storytelling and that conveys an utmost sense of veracity and authenticity.[12] In this respect postmodern theatre tries to strip off the theatrical frame and to return to the roots of performance: to the epiphany of the sacred that occurs suddenly and defies any profane reasoning.[13]

Constitutive rituals: performativity as the iterative poesis of social reality

Iteration and sharedness

Ritual performances are not just events, but iterations of events. They repeat events that have happened before. Only by this reference to the past can the ritual become visible as a standardized performance. This standardization and formalism are at the core of the ritual process. Like all other social performance, the ritual too has an essential doubleness (Baumann 1986). A performance is no just an action performed by particular actors at a particular location. Instead this action follows a rule, it refers to a script, it recalls previous events, it transcends the reality at hand. But the performance is never completely controlled and instructed by this script, it is never pure transcendence, it is never just the role and nothing else. It is also a concrete, visible, particular event that catches the attention of those who attend it. In this merging of the particular event and the ritual pattern, in the iteration of events, the ritual constructs meaning. The meaning of an event results from its reference to another event, which, in its turn, also receives its meaning from the reference to other events and so forth.

In the iteration of previous events the ritual performance appears as a second-order event, an event that represents another event or that allows us to frame and bracket the occurrence of an event. Thus it blurs the frightening impact of the original event, it softens the edge of suddenness of true events, it pales down the dread of the original epiphany, it allows us to cope with the extraordinary as something that has happened before. The passage of boundaries, the transformation of identities, and the encounter with the sacred do not disrupt and shatter the social order any more, but it is regulated and integrated into this order by the ritual performance.

Rituals differ from moments of epiphany also in another respect. They always involve several actors – unlike the moments of epiphany that – although culturally mediated – can also occur to an individual person. Rituals bridge the gap between different individual perspectives to construct a shared social reality (Bell 1997, 1992; Tambiah 1981; Douglas 1973). They achieve this by a temporal sequence of coordinated and rule-guided actions in which each action refers not only to the preceding, but also to the subsequent actions. By participating in a ritual the actors cope not only with the possible difference between their individual perspectives but also with the fundamental problem of change, uncertainty, and boundaries. Rituals perform an order; in relating events to each other they construct, for the moment of performance, an insurmountable and immutable reality.[14]

Rituals differ from mere habits although they share with them the strong relation to embodiment and corporeality. Habits cannot be wrong – they are just embodied regular behavioral sequences that do not follow a rule and that are therefore not necessarily subject to reflection. Unlike habits, the performance of a ritual can be criticized for deviating from the rule and, therefore, failing to create reality. Because rituals presuppose an awareness of rules and mistakes they represent reflexive interaction in its most elementary form. As a rule-governed activity the ritual can never be confined to a single individual – whereas a habit can be displayed by an individual actor alone. Following a rule presupposes the perspective of the observer who is able to decide about mistakes and correct performances because he or she is a competent member of the respective community (Wittgenstein 1976; Winch 1999).

The poesis of social reality

In their most elementary form rituals do not just describe or imitate an order of the external world that is also available by other representations. Instead, the ritual performance is the poesis of order and this order exists only because it is performed. Rituals are constitutive performances in the Searleian sense. When, for example, we are dancing tango, we do not consider the performance of the dance to be just a weaker imitation of some external reality, but, instead, the performance *is* the reality and the dance is only real insofar as it is performed. People who are greeting each other do not regard this interaction as a play in contrast to reality: they see themselves as truly greeting each other and the act of greeting has no outside reference except to the interaction order it displays. This constitutive performativity concerns not only simple everyday rituals, but also solemn rituals of passage. People who are marrying each other cannot, later on, invalidate the marriage by simply claiming that they had been just playing bride and groom when they were solemnly declaring "I do" in front of their families and the representative of the community – it is just by this declaration that the act of marriage is performed.[15] In this respect the ritual performance is similar to the performative speech act in the Searleian and Austinian sense of the term. Ritual performances are, however, not coextensive with speech acts: rituals are frequently muted bodily actions and many speech acts lack the power of rituals.

It is the solemn and serious attitude of the participants that sets the ritual performance apart from the "non-serious" process of probing, learning, or quoting a procedure or ceremony. The same iterative bodily procedure can be framed as a play, as a probing, as a mockery, as a quotation, or as a serious ritual performance. Thus, the ritual performance results neither from the inner attitude of the individual actor nor from the bodily behavior alone. Instead, it is generated by the collective definition of the performance as serious and this seriousness is related to the sacred basis of their social bond: the ritual actors would put their collective identity and the core of their social order at stake if they would afterwards, invalidate a serious ritual performance.

No construction of social reality can entirely dispense with this constitutive poesis of the social – there has to be an ultimate horizon where we simply give up the doubts as to whether the action is staged or spontaneous, artificial or authentic, true or false, and where we ignore any further questions and take the performance for real.[16]

We can find this constitutive poesis in all sorts of rituals: in everyday ritual like greeting each other that establish an interaction order among persons present in a local site, in aesthetic rituals like wearing a dress or displaying a sign of a particular style, and in sacred rituals like religious ceremonies or burial rituals (Becker 1973).[17] For similar reasons that brought us to focus on symbols in the last section we will, however, center sacred rituals instead of aesthetic or everyday rituals in the following remarks. This is not to deny the importance of style and everyday rituals for the constitution of social reality. Our focus on the mediation between the sacred and the profane, however, demands a special regard of the performative construction of the sacred. The sacred is believed to be present and effective if particular rituals are properly performed by actors who are authorized to do this. In the ritual of praying the faithful do not just play at encountering God, but they believe that they really do address him. In burial ceremonies we do not just play a theatrical performance, but instead we really perform the passage of the dead body from the community of the living to the realm of the dead, etc. However, this ritual "poesis" of social reality works only if performed by actors who are competent or authorized to do this. Unauthorized ritual performances are labeled as caricature, theatre, madness, or sacrilege by the insiders.

Rituals, whether sacred or not, differ strongly from techniques or from the logic of "work." Techniques refer to an external reality that is available by other descriptions and which can be improved and criticized with reference to this external reality (Malinowski 1960; Tambiah 2002). Work results from the attempt to spend as little energy as necessary in order to achieve a desired state of the external world. In contrast, rituals are beyond considerations of utility and functional improvements – they refer to collective identity, to an unquestionable and invisible core reference of social reality. This core is exempted from direct criticism – criticism can only refer to the actual performance of the ritual. Thus we, as insiders, may question the perfection of an aesthetic performance, the dignity of a religious performance, or the mode of performing an everyday ritual, but the binding force and validity of the ritual form can be questioned only from an outside perspective.[18]

Like symbols being not just conventional signs, rituals are finally not to be mixed with conventional rules that regulate and coordinate behavior and that can be exchanged against other rules without hampering the effects of coordination. The display of the Christian cross cannot be replaced by the display of a circle, the ritual of consecration cannot be substituted by filling out a bureaucratic form. In this respect rituals differ also from games or plays that are to follow certain rules. These rules can – under certain circumstances – be modified or partially replaced by other rules without risking disrupting the performance of the game. If we are playing a game, we do not only know the difference between rules and rule-guided actions, but we view the other players from a strategic point of view – we assume a difference of interests, different roles, different options to respond to the actions of others etc. In playing a game we are also able to fake an intention, to be suspicious, to criticize a strategic move, and to improve our performance. In contrast, rituals suspend and disregard the differences and divisions between the participating actors and establish communality. The collective reality of the ritual is an ultimate one – there is no way of relativizing it, changing it, criticizing it with reference to a higher order frame. Rituals resist rational arguments and are exempted from discursive fluidification. Similar to what indexical gestures and symbols achieve with respect to the relation between signs and reality, the ritual provides the basic performative construction of the social world. It constructs the elementary "communitas" that transcends social cleavages and unites the body social before social order and social structure can take over. Beyond the constitutive ritual there is only a frightening reality that is devoid of any form – the sacred or the demonic in its pure and unbearable existence. Rituals shield social reality from facing the unspeakable – in the case of religious rituals from the direct encounter with the sacred or the demonic, in the case of everyday rituals from the crisis of absurdity, disorientation, and uncertainty.

Rituals provide answers to the question of beginning as well as the question of death, they create foundations and horizons beyond which nobody should try to go. In this respect rituals are the performative counterpart to myth. In myth the genesis of the world or of a human group or the decay of order and the transformation of history into chaos are narrated as a story that presents ruptures as meaningful changes, the horrible as the heroic, the inconceivable as the plausible course of action. Myth provides a frame for imagining stories in the real and historical world, but this mythical frame itself is not submitted to the constraints of reality (Campbell 1981). Instead of being controlled by the rules of reality, it constitutes them. In a similar way, rituals are exempted from constraints of technological efficiency. They provide the ultimate anchor for connecting actions, they refer to the construction of meaning itself.

Corporeality

This fundamental nature of rituals is rooted into their corporeality. Rituals do not exist like texts or institutions as structures of signification or dispositions of power and control. Instead, they exist as embodied performances, as events produced and experienced bodily by actors in a shared situation and in a local site. They center bodily procedures – singing, dancing, moving, marching, signs, painful violations of the body, or even killing a living being in a sacrificial rite. A sacred ritual without any reference to the corporeality of the participants is hard to imagine.

In the ritual coordination of bodily movements the participants experience themselves as mirrored by others – individual differences are disregarded in and even banned from the ritual performance. The ritual opens up the space for communitas (Turner 1982) or for collective identity in its most elementary form. There is also almost no separation between the acting person and his or her role – both are merged in the ritual performance. Thus, the constitutive rituals produce a collectively shared embodied reality that is beyond any question and doubt, exempted from fluidification and negation, but also no longer driven by the imperatives of nature. In between nature and discourse the original ritual does not yet allow for the question of authenticity that vexes the modern mind (see also Alexander et al. 2004).

This feeling of authenticity is enhanced by the violent event that is at the core of many original rituals. The ritual frames, sublimates, and purifies the archaic violence that lurks behind the surface of everyday life. The Hobbesian metaphor of "war of all against all" in the "state of nature" hints at this archaic violence as well as the Freudian concept of aggression. Instead of ignoring, denying, or repressing this violence entirely, the ritual extracts the violence from the members of the community, shifts it to an isolated and regulated space, and frames it by its opposite – order (Girard 1977). Like the shamanistic practice takes the evil from the individual person and bans it into a particular object, the sacrificial ritual concentrates the dangerous violence on the victim and thus purifies the community: when the bloody sacrifice of the victim or the ritual fight between antagonists is finished, the audience mostly leaves the site with a feeling of deep relief and even internal peace: catharsis (Douglas 1966).

Although the ritual community considers the basic pattern of a ritual to be immutable, there are moments and spaces of contingency and variation in every-day rituals as well as in sacred rituals. The scene, the actors and agencies may differ and vary, and the outcome of the ritual action may be open – the person addressed in an everyday ritual may respond in a disturbing and unexpected way, the verdict of the court of law is unpredictable, the sacrifice or prayer may not produce the results desired, oracles may tell strange messages, the devil may resist simple exorcism, etc. Some rituals are even set up to produce and frame contingent outcomes – oracles, proclamations of authoritative decisions, etc. Thus rituals not only reiterate previous events, but also add an event-ness of their own to this. They are second-order events that generate moments of epiphany and chance in which the unpredictable occurs in a predictable frame, the extraordinary happens in a rule-guided setting, the exception contrasts to a rule.[19]

The exclusion of outsiders

All rituals are collective endeavors that draw a boundary between inside and outside. They achieve their construction of collective identity best by excluding outsiders. Though similar in this exclusive and defensive attitude rituals differ in their sensitivity to the actual presence of outsiders, i.e. of persons who do not participate in the ritual process. Here again we have to distinguish between profane everyday rituals like greeting or addressing other persons in communication, aesthetic rituals like wearing a special dress, having the hair cut in a special way or displaying another particular sign of style, and sacred rituals like religious services or burial ceremonies. In most profane everyday rituals the ritual actors disregard largely uninvolved third parties. Outsiders are not yet taken into account. If outside observers are watching the ritual of greeting between two actors or if the participants of the greeting are alone it does not matter for the validity of the ritual performance. This disregard with respect to the presence of outsiders is a mark of everyday rituals by which a profane interaction order is produced.

In contrast, aesthetic rituals take the presence of outsiders into account – the display of style aims at distinction, at demarcating the boundary between insiders who are alike and outsiders who are different. The presence of outsiders enhances this distinction and is sometimes even deliberately sought for in order to integrate the aesthetic community by disdain for the outsider. Outsiders who try to pass the boundary and display aesthetic signs without being a competent member of the aesthetic community are frequently mocked: Japanese tourists wearing Bavarian folk dresses or seniors with a punk hair cut are viewed not as dangerous intruders but as ridiculous figures.

This situation changes, however, if we consider the third group of ritual performances: solemn ceremonies that allow us to address the sacred. Outsiders can destroy the taken-for-granted assumption of the presence of the sacred that is produced by the constitutive poesis. They do not know how to continue the ritual action, and their very presence seems to contaminate the aura of the sacred. Outsiders who refuse to participate in the ritual process represent the regular and profane order of everyday life – they prevent the generation of the ritual communitas and the emergence of the sacred (Turner 1969). Therefore solemn ceremonial rituals try to exclude these profane outsiders physically or socially from the scene. The performance of the ritual is shielded from the eyes and ears of outsiders or their presence is bound to strict rules of respect that allow the ritual actors to ignore it. Sometimes, however, outsiders cannot be excluded and their presence cannot be ignored because, instead of being silent bystanders, they ask the wrong questions, mock serious things, and interrupt the performance. Faced by these disturbances of profanity, the ritual community mostly responds violently and tries to remove the outsiders from the site of the ritual. This sensitivity towards outsiders seems to limit the existence of rituals in societies in which the encounter between strangers becomes a regular situation. Modern urban societies are, hence, bound to establish new forms of shielding and boundary construction in order to provide spaces for sacred rituals without risking violence.

In distinction to these profane outsiders there is also the position of the sacred outsider who participates in and even structures the ritual process. Priests monks, and officials are cases of such figures who are stripped down from regular social, sexual, or political attributes and who, by the very exemption from a position in the regular and profane order, are able to construct liminality (Turner 1969). These sacred outsiders represent an essential thirdness that breaks down the profane order, and opens up the space for communitas and the encounter with the sacred. A special case of this thirdness is the homo sacer (Agamben 1995) who is ceremonially sacrificed in order to constitute the social order. This sacrificial constitution of the social order presupposes that the homo sacer is an outsider, an individual who is exempted from the profane social order. If the homo sacer had a position within the social structure his death would inevitably engender a vicious circle of violent revenge and retaliation. The group of the killed person would respond violently even if this person was considered guilty of a crime. Because the attribution of guilt requires an assumption of norms and obligations that are valid only for members of the community, the sacrificial victim has to be innocent. Thus the ceremonial killing of the innocent outsider prevents or stops the circle of violence within the community (Girard 1977).

In a similar way as ceremonial rituals are sensitive to the presence of profane outsiders, they have also to overcome disorder and evil by banning, expelling, defeating, or destroying it. Most ritual communities are haunted by the fear that the evil outside could cross the boundary, invade the bodies of its members, and be present within the community, although in a disguised way. This is the origin of beliefs in witchcraft, in devils, soul stealers, and body snatchers. Hence rituals of purification, exorcism, and sacrifice try to remove, ban, or expel the impure, demonic, and evil from the body of the ritual community. Because the ritual constitutes reality, the opposite of order may only be performed and embodied by being overcome and destroyed in an exemplary way: if it could not be expelled or purified, the evil would threaten and destroy the order. Therefore the ritual performance cannot have a tragic ending – in contrast to theatrical performances.

In distinction to sacred rituals that have to ban the evil by special precautions, everyday rituals can cope with disorder by simply ignoring it. In everyday life we act mostly as if mistakes could not exist, as if everything could be normal and regular, as if the acting of others could be a case of a well-known type – and in doing so we produce the social order. In a similar way aesthetic rituals can disregard those elements that do not fit into the pattern: they are shifted to the background, considered as noise, or treated as unimportant.

Theatre: performance as mimetic representation

Fascination: audience and actors

Like rituals, theatrical performances, too, are a collective endeavor. They require, however, not only performing actors but also an audience that evaluates the performance and judges whether the rules have been properly observed. The audience represents the public, it embodies society as a third-party perspective on social life.

The position of this audience, however, varies greatly. It ranges from the other actors who cease to act for a moment and watch the actor performing his part to large audiences that are excluded from participating or intervening in the performance. We call these performances that require the presence of a non-acting third party "theatre" (Nietzsche 1994).

In a certain way the audience of a theatrical performance is situated in between the outsider and the participant. It is in an ambivalent situation: like outsiders, the audience is excluded from direct participation and can hence not be totally involved in the binding magic of the ritual action. Though unquestionably present, it is largely prevented from developing a social reality on its own that could draw the attention from the performance on stage. The core problem in the relation between actors and audience is this inequality of access to performing the theatrical reality. It is usually the actors who have the right and duty to construct the theatrical reality, whereas the audience, although excluded from active participation, is to be overwhelmed, fascinated, and carried away by the event on stage. There are, of course, many transitions from the total exclusion of outsiders in constitutive rituals to the inclusion of a silent and non participant audience by a theatrical performance – the chorus in ancient Greek tragedy, the loud interventions of spectators to folk plays, the narrator on stage who introduces and comments on the play, etc.[20]

The power of the theatrical performance results from being an event for an audience: it interrupts the continuity of profane reality, it presents something unexpected and extraordinary, it opens up a space for the encounter with what we have called collective identity or the sacred. In this respect the theatrical reality has to differ strictly from mundane everyday life – nobody would watch if there were not a breach within the flow of ordinary reality. Showing an empty stage does not attract an audience – although modern performance art, in its thrust to run counter to the expectations of spectators, often aims at the void of the stage.

Fusion and defusion: performance and reality

Ideally, not only the actors in a ritual, but also the audience of a theatrical performance should take the performance not just for an illusion but for reality. This reality of the theatrical performance has, however, to be distinguished from the ordinary reality of everyday life – in a similar way as the reality of art or of dreams is usually not mixed up with the reality of mundane life. Even if the spectators are carried away by a brilliant performance, they will not intervene when a murder is presented on stage. They know that it is just a theatrical performance and not "real life" just as they know how to distinguish between a mock fight and a real one or between dream and reality (Goffman 1982; Schütz 1964). As adult and competent members of a community we use the frame "dream," "art," or "theatre" in order to connect the extraordinary content of a poem, a painting, or a theatrical performance to our regular lifeworld.

Because of its intermediate position between outsider and participant, between the exclusion from action and the imposed demand of attention, the spectators will view the events on stage mostly as "second-order" events, as an event that – however fascinating the illusion might be – pretends to be another event. However, if a theatrical performance never comes close to a moment of fusion, if the spectators never forget, for a moment, that it is just theatrical blunder, if they cannot indulge for a moment the experience of an extraordinary reality, then the performance is a failure. When we disregard the frame and surrender to the content, when we get immersed into the story, when we experience "flow" (Turner 1969) or fusion, then the ideal now of immediacy and intensity occurs to us: the contingencies of experience and the experiencing subject are forgotten. We encounter an extraordinary reality that is even stronger than our familiar and banal reality of everyday life. These moments of intensive encounter with an extraordinary reality may be rare and elusive, but they are the ideal the actors strive for. The moment of fusion is the moment when the actor's construction of reality is imposed upon the audience: the audience surrenders to the domination by the stage. (The extraordinary reality on stage can have an emotional impact that is even stronger than the ordinary non-theatrical reality. Hard-nosed members of the audience who would rarely come to tears in real life can be deeply moved when watching a movie or attending an opera performance. The artificial reality on stage can represent their emotional world in an undiluted way, without the restrictions of strategic consideration and cunning – emotionally it has more immediacy than real life.)

In classical theatrical performances the audience watches real events of coreally present actors on stage – even if these theatrical events try to simulate another reality. This presence of real actors is lacking in movie theatres. Movie performances present a second-order illusion: they imagine the presence of actors who pretend to be the person in a role. Here, additional performative twists are required in order to produce a moment of flow and fusion. Most important among them is perhaps the blurring of the distinction between audience and stage. The movie theatre is darkened, hence the viewers cannot see their co-viewers; the movie figures on scene are larger than life; the changing perspective of the movie camera (which is also the perspective of the viewer) simulating a position on stage: this viewer is surged into the stage and is turned into a silent co-actor (Woody Allen's movie *The Purple Rose of Cairo* reverses this move to the stage – the actors leave the screen and become a part of the audience). Television images, in contrast, are usually small and the persons watching TV are hardly forgetting that they are in their familiar surroundings at home. If the TV performance is to catch the attention of viewers it has to rely on additional attractions: the events presented on TV claim to be live, authentic, real-time events in distinction to mere theatrical illusions or cinematographic recordings. This engenders a new logic of authentic performance that we will deal with in the next section.

When moving back and forth between the ideal of fusion and the awareness of theatrical illusion, the audience responds to its ambivalent situation in a similar way as adult actors in everyday life do. They, too, rarely surrender to the illusion that every single action is a true and authentic expression of the actor, they know that there may be faked presentation and artificial staging. But it is hard to continue an interaction when nothing can be taken for granted in a Schützian natural attitude. If everything – including the frame in which an action is discovered as faked – has to be treated as unauthentic, then social reality collapses and the flow of communication stops.

Therefore, theatrical performances – even if they are taken for plays – cannot dispense with a ritual framing that constitutes the particular reality of the theatre but is not part of the theatrical mimesis in the strict sense: when, for example the curtain opens at the beginning of the performance or when the audience is giving applause at the end, then the person opening the curtain does not play a being a curtain opener and the audience is not playing at clapping their hands - instead they are performing a constitutive ritual that frames a theatrical mimesis Thus theatrical mimesis, in order to fascinate the audience, has to be framed by rituals that not only, by their very nature, avoid the question of authenticity but that also embrace audience and actors on stage alike. These embracing ritual or modulations in the Goffmanian sense (taking seats after the gong sounds being silent after the light is dimmed, giving applause when the curtain falls etc.) are events on their own, but they also iterate previous events of theatrical rituals, etc. (Goffman 1982).

Script: staging the sacred and the demonic

While theatrical performances are events of their own, they also follow a script a model that exists independently from the performance itself. Alexander et a (2004) distinguishes between foreground scripts and background symbols. Ou concept of "script" refers only to the foreground script that instructs the playin on stage. In a most elementary way rituals, too, are scripted performances they follow rules, participants and competent observers are aware of violation of these rules, etc. But, in many cases, the script of the ritual exists only in i performative reproduction. Like the competent speaker of a language notices immediately the mistakes of grammar, but is unable to specify the rules of grammar, we are, in most cases, able to identify the deviations from the ritual rules, but we cannot specify the abstract principle of the ritual. In contrast, theatrical performances are usually based on an abstract script that can be reproduced or is available independent from its realization in an actual performance. The theatrical performance translates the script into a sequence of events, and even if it is not based on a written text, it uses a repertory of well-known topics, rhetorical figures, narratives, masks, etc., in order to tell a story. The script allows for coordination between the expectations of the audience and the actual performance on stage.

Although the script shields the performance against facing directly the frightening transcendence or the chaos of absurdity, it does not alleviate the tension between potentiality and actual representation completely. As detailed as the script may be, there is always space for varying interpretations and creativity – no theatrical performance will exhaust the meaning of a dramatic text completely and no theatrical performance can entirely be reduced to the script. Like constitutive rituals theatrical performances, too, allow for contingencies. Stage directors can control these interpretations of the script, the availability of *mise-en-scène* can change it (Alexander, this volume), and the expectations of the audience can influence it. Thus theatrical performances are events on their own, although they iterate previous performances and repeat a well-known story. Only because of this very iteration can they be experienced as a unique and contingent event that cannot be predicted entirely by the script.

Theatrical performances do not just represent an ordered reality in a narrative format, but they represent also its counterpart – disorder: the drama presents gods and demons, kings and enemies, the familiar people and the unknown strangers, good guys and bad guys, etc. In constitutive rituals, disturbances of order, the threat of pollution, the power of evil, and the existence of outsiders have explicitly to be banned and be defeated – their continuous existence would destroy the social reality created in the ritual as the uncorrected performance of mistakes will disrupt the rule. In carnival the ritual reversal of positions can be performed only because it will be ended after some time and the actors will return to normality. In theatrical performances, however, they can persist and survive – the encounters with the devil, the crime, the vices, the insanity, are not ultimately real, they are not even ritually framed and tamed events, but just theatrical representations of events. Hence, in contrast to rituals, the theatrical performance can have a tragic ending – the evil can prevail. Similar to the existence of outsiders that may disturb the ritual construction of collective identity, but is turned into the audience of theatrical performances, also the existence of disorder, that may disrupt the poetic construction of reality in rituals, is staged in theatrical performances as the necessary opposite of order. Thus the theatrical performance allows us – in a more explicit way than rituals can do – to present the invisible and implicit structure of a social community – the sacred and the demonic, purity and danger, the hero and the villain, the good people and their enemies.

However, the presentation of order and its opposite in the performance engenders the problem of it mediating the opposition. Therefore, the theatrical performance mostly presents, in between the representatives of order and the representatives of disorder, a third person, a trickster, a clown, a jester, a stranger, a person in a liminal situation that mediates between the opposites, moves the action, and alleviates the tension by unexpected and surprising turns (Turner 1969). If theatrical performances do not introduce these liminal positions, they have to present liminality in a temporal mode, as crisis, as a situation of uncertainty, as an external intervention, an unexpected moment that turns the action and allows for a rearrangement of the opposition and a solution of the tension.

Thus, the script, too, has, by dramatic means, to construct a mediation that constitutes performance – as fusion mediates between the performance and reality and fascination mediates between the audience and the actors on stage – or, on a more general level, as sacred rituals mediate between mundane communication and the unspeakable, and as moments of epiphany mediate between the sacred and the profane.

The epiphany represented the sacred in a unique event that thrusted forward and seemed to demand being told to others, but the outside observers could hardly partake in the experience of the unique moment; sacred rituals aim to construct a shared reality between several actors, but this fragile reality is sensitive to the presence of outsiders. Theatrical performances, in contrast, require the presence of "outside" observers and thereby allow for the inclusion of a large number of passive participants. This inclusion comes, however, at a price: it presupposes distinctions between the privilege to act and the exclusion from it, between script and performance, structure and anti-structure, and these distinctions engender additional demands on mediation, interpretation and translation.

Moral drama: performance as authentic presentation

The following remarks will explore the concept of moral drama as a new paradigm for the analysis of politics and the production of democratic consensus. Moral drama is a mode of performance that shares many features with symbolic events, constitutive rituals, and theatrical performances, but it adds to their basic structure the reference to the inner state of the actor. Dramas are driven by the question of whether the actor's performance expresses his true inner feelings, convictions, and intentions or whether it is faked intention, deceitful behavior, and feigned feelings. In classical theatrical performances, by contrast, this question never comes to the fore. To the contrary: the art of the actor consists in disguising his true identity behind the mask, in concealing the individual person of the actor behind the role (Stanislavsky 1980). Since it is just theatre, the audience wants to be captivated by the illusion and the rhetoric. If the audience cannot forget the inconvenient question "Does the actor really mean what he is speaking?," then the theatrical performance is – strictly speaking – a failure. This situation changes profoundly in moral drama. Illusion, the aim of the theatrical performance, is here turned into deception. Trust and authenticity replace artful feigning, morality and personal integrity take center stage. This reference to "parusiah," to the unconditional revelation of the truth, differs from the fascination and fusion in theatrical performances and it differs also from the poesis of social reality in constitutive rituals. In moral dramas the audience knows about the possible inconsistency between the overt performance and the true convictions and feelings of the actor and it is moved by the question "Can we trust him or her?" The quest for signs of and hints at authenticity adds a new reference to the boundary between inside and outside as constructed by rituals, and to the audience as aimed at by theatrical performances. The moral drama refers to the hidden moral interior of the acting individual, it transforms actors into persons with feelings.

This quest for authenticity has a special affinity to a particular medium of communication. It is the force driving the TV presentation of live events. Live TV reports are – although watched in a familiar home setting – taken for real by the viewers because they are presented real-time, because they have unpredictable outcomes, and because the viewers know that a multitude of other invisible viewers are also watching the event. In this respect TV presentations of life events differ from cinematographic performances that are perfectly scripted and dispense with the requirement of real-time reports and imagined co-presence of the audience. Because of the imagined co-presence and of the real-time reporting the isolated viewers can forget that they are not attending the real event but watching a screen.

In the following section we will, however, explore this special reference of drama in the field of politics. Although the moral drama is by no means confined to the field of politics, but can be found also in other domains of social reality (e.g. personal relations), it is politics on TV that gives special salience to the question of authenticity, trust, and morality. Hence it fits particularly well into the frame of a moral drama. First, we will briefly outline the basic structural features which politics has in common with symbolic events, rituals, and theatrical performances.

Politics as a symbolic event

If politics is to attract an audience it has to be an event. The continuous flow of ordinary life can hardly catch the attention of a large number of people. It mostly goes on unnoticed. To shift the attention from pursuing private concerns to public affairs, politics has to present itself as a breach of the ordinary and mundane affairs, as something extraordinary, as the response to danger, risk, and demons, as a call to heroism.

Hardly anybody will watch what is happening on stage if the play, the actors, the set are known for years. The actors on stage do not have to be competent, but they should never be boring. Similar to a theatrical production that, even if it is excellent, will be taken from stage after a time, the well-known and experienced leader, too, has to be replaced by a young and fresh successor who has not yet had the chance to be incompetent or boring. Hence the sudden loss of popularity of political leaders and scandal-driven turnover of political elites is rendered plausible if we consider politics as the production of symbolic events. If political leadership were based mainly on personal commitment to a leader, on expertise and training, or on traditional legitimacy, then a rapid decay of authority would rarely occur – only if the leader is discovered to be a traitor or if his claims to authority are disclosed as fraud would we expect him to be ousted from office. If, however, the bond between leader and people is based on the fascination by a spectacle, then a sudden fall from grace is a regular phenomenon: the audience that boos at an actor does not question its former enthusiastic support of the same actor.

Political leadership (not office) is based on charisma, i.e. on a collective belief that a person is embodying the sacred, the extraordinary, the divine. This belief is – as Weber has noted very early – a projection of the charismatic community and it fades quickly away if the charismatic leader fails to work the expected miracles and turns out to be a common and ordinary person. Only totalitarian and authoritarian leaders can prevent this discovery of their ordinary nature for some time. In democracies, however, where the persons on center-stage are closely watched by the media the decay of charisma is unavoidable. New leader will replace the old ones, if these are not able to reconstruct the charismatic situation by staging new dangers and demons, new challenges and promises i a believable way.

Politics as ritual

Ritual aspects of political ceremonies have been noticed before (Shils 1979 State funerals and coronations, visits of political leaders at national memorial the pageantry of the prince appearing solemnly in public, triumphant marche of victorious warlords in the capital city, party conventions or military parade at memorial days, but also rallies against the government and fights between protesters and police are, evidently, not rational deliberations about the common good or strategic choices in a power game. The paradigm of contract, the paradigm of rational choice, or the paradigm of public discourse fail to grasp the basic features of these processes. They are not rational decisions between independent citizens, but ritual constructions of community or of authority. Fighting the police in the streets is not for gaining strategic advantages and occupying territories, parliamentary debates are not for convincing political opponents, coronations are not for deciding about political leadership, military parades are not for evaluating the armed forces, carrying flags in a rally is not for providing orientation in a crowd, etc. They are rituals. These rituals are about the visible and tangible representation of a collective identity that is essentially invisible – the political community. Because political communities cannot be touched upon like individual persons they have to be represented by symbols and rituals. Their existence relies on symbolic representations and ritual performances that renarrate the triumphant or traumatic foundation of the community, recall their heroic moments and stage the threatening outside, the enemy, the danger against which the community has to stand united. Thus participation in ritual performances constitutes and constructs the fundamental boundary between inside and outside without which no community can exist.[21]

Politics as theatre

Theatrical performances are not confined to the field of dramatic arts. Since Goffman we know that the pattern of theatrical performance can be found in many interactions that include a large number of persons but reserve the privilege to act and to communicate to few of them. Since it allows for a non-violent and seemingly non-repressive form of domination the theatrical performance is especially apt to be used in politics. Theatrical forms of staging power by public appearances, processions, and gatherings are indispensable for any construction of political authority (Geertz 1980). As such political authority is an invisible disposition and the political community extends, in most cases, far beyond the group of people present in a locality. Therefore the invisible body politic has to be staged in a visible form. Monuments and pictures, coins and heraldic signs represent the absent ruler in the everyday life of his people, the people hail and cheer the leader if he appears among them, the pageantry of power is displayed in public events, etc.

This need for representation holds true also for modern democracies. The theatrical performance in modern democracies can avoid the costs of repression and the toils of an open public debate in which every citizen can participate and the outcome of which can hardly be controlled. In contrast to constitutive political rituals that can disregard the presence of third parties, political theatre addresses mainly the audience, the people, the crowd, the outside observers watching the ceremony in public spaces, in the streets or even on TV. This inclusive tendency of political performances is only limited by the material media of representation – it exceeds by far the range of rational discourse. Rational discourse can be performed only among a limited number of participants – as long as every citizen is to have a fairly equal chance of participation. Large populations can hardly participate in a public discourse that allows everybody to present his or her opinion to everybody else. Therefore, modern democracies have to face an inconvenient alternative: either participation in public discourse will be limited to a few priviledged voices – which violates the ideal of equality; or equality prevails at a price: it has to be watered down to voting at the ballots and thus to give up the idea of discourse. Pitted against the reality of modern democracies the idea of public discourse appears as a pious illusion or as a highly inaccessible ideal (Habermas 1989). If, however, democratic politics is conceived of as a theatrical performance, then the inclusion of large populations into the political process has almost no limits.

In these theatrical performances of political power the impressive surface and the presence at the site of the event matter more than the actual intentions of the actors on the political stage. The actors on stage may perform morality plays, but their actual acting has not necessarily to be moved by personal moral concerns. The audience is carried away by costumes and choreography, by rhetoric and rave, by splendor and salutes. Neither the audience nor the actors will raise questions referring to the true intentions underlying the behavior of, for example, waving leaders and hailing followers in a public parade. These political performances are spectacles and as such they have to be fascinating and eye-catching displays of power. The question of truth is not at the core of the theatrical performance in politics.

Politics as moral drama

When, however, in modern democracies (but also in traditional political regimes), politicians present their cause in order to convince a public audience, a problem that had only marginal salience in dramatic arts may take center-stage: the question of authenticity. In theatrical performances the actor try artfully to hide their true identity as persons behind the role and the audience is mostly not interested in the person behind the mask. Whether the acting on stage is a true expression of the actor's personality or whether it is just artful presentation, does not matter. Questions of authenticity are not asked. Moral dramas differ strongly from this. The audience evaluates politicians according to the degree to which they play their role in an authentic way.

The thrust for authenticity goes beyond the mere requirement of fusion. The audience wants the political actors not just to stage a theatrical illusion, for example, to behave as if they were trusting in the strength of the movement during a party convention, fighting for the common good or defending the cause of the people, expecting victory or urging them to be on the alert, etc., but they want to know if they are really and truly mourning, trusting, rejoicing etc. This thrust for authenticity is the mark of the moral drama performed in the non-media.

In moral drama the actors claim that their acting is – to a certain degree at least – an expression of their true inner feelings irrespective of the expectations and exigencies of the situation. They claim their performance to be authentic and believable. What is a virtue in the theatrical performance – artful deception and illusion – is turned into a vice in social drama. While theatrical performances are driven by a hermeneutics of illusion, social dramas are moved by a hermeneutics of suspicion: the audience suspects the politicians possibly to be deceitful and to hide their true motives. People distrust the rhetoric, the "metis," the cunning reason of politicians, because they believe that there is more at stake than sheer entertainment and that politics is about real concerns. In a social drama they consider themselves to be not just an audience, but, instead, to be participant actors. The transformation of outsiders into audience and of audience into participants affects profoundly the nature of the performed reality. Participants expect this reality to be an unconditional one, undistorted by personal interests and the illusions of the moment. Since modern democratic politics reaches out to diverse lifeworlds and unknown situative backgrounds, only those political claims that disregard personal interests can expect to attract a wide support. The logic of ideal discourse, of truth claims and their validation, of universalistic standards of argumentation, could enter the stage, but unfortunately the very size of the addressed group that, on the one hand, requires the universalism of argument prevents, on the other hand, its rational debate. Thus all is left again to the tides of trust and suspicion.

Politicians, on their part, respond to this suspicion by presenting themselves on TV in a way that, assumedly, cannot be faked – more with the tone of the voice than with the content of the talk, more with spontaneous gestures than with ceremonial procedures, etc. In playing to be overwhelmed by emotions, as members of the people, as one of them, however, they push the illusion just to a new level of refinement. In staging themselves as an authentic representative of the people they blur the constitutive distinction between actors and audience, which coincides, in this case, with the opposition between leaders and followers, rulers and people. Thereby they pretend to include the people into a community of participants, in which some are just more visible than others, but all are sharing the same reality.

This blurring of the boundary corresponds to the people's efforts to open up the curtain separating front stage and back stage where the actors put off their masks, disregard their roles, show their true faces and act authentically i.e. presenting their true selves (see Mast's chapter, this volume). However, sociology after the performative turn has to disappoint this longing for authenticity. The back stage, the true self, is not only invisible and inaccessible for the spectators, but it is, in principle, inaccessible even for the actors themselves. Identity is intransparent to itself as we have pointed out at the beginning of this chapter. But it is also intransparent to the outside observers. What we, the audience, can perceive is only the performance on front stage, the mask, the acting in a role, the presentation in a performance. As soon as we take off the mask, we discover only another mask behind it, and behind this mask there is, again, another mask, etc. A radical theory of performativity, therefore, insists that the ultimate back stage, the true unmasked face, the identity of the individual person, are beyond perception (Goffman 1959). Thus, moral drama cannot dispense with the theatre – as theatre cannot dispense with a ritual construction and rituals cannot dispense with events. We cannot act without assuming that there is something hidden that would bring our search for authenticity to an end, but ultimately we have to admit that we are talking about varying presentations, documents, and façades performed in front of us. The mask, the façade, the performance is constitutive for our communication. Only when and if we are masked can we understand each other. And even the actor who tries ruthlessly to discover his or her true self cannot rely on more than his or her memory of past actions, thoughts, and feelings. His picture of his self will certainly be more complete than the one available to others but his present perspective inescapably limits it.

The relation of the TV performance to the true self of the politician is, however, only a special case of the more general problem of representing the sacred in the profane. In modern societies the sacred is commonly related to the identity of individual persons, but it can also be conceived of as a personal God who is represented by, for example, a mask. In ancient theatrical rituals gods were played by actors and they interacted with humans. However, the mask or the actor representing the sacred in the visible world of the theatre did not claim that the sacred was fully converted into visible and tangible performance – there is always the invisible back stage, the ineffable source of identity, the existence of potentiality and transcendence – even if for a moment the sacred is actually represented on front stage. The actual representation of transcendence is only a partial one, inevitably distorted and misleading. And this reference to something that transcends any actual representation is constitutive for the logic of performance.

The readiness to confirm and support the indispensable illusion of authenticity separates insiders from outsiders. Followers of a political leader or members of the political community accept his political performance as believable fascinating, and authentic while outsiders, foreigners, and non-members perceive these performances as unauthentic, as fake, even as fraudulent or as ridiculous (Alexander et al. 2004).

In between the core of devoted followers and the group of sceptical outsiders is, however, the position of the ambivalent audience, of bystanders who could possibly join the marching people, who could possibly be fascinated, and who could possibly be included. Thus the moral drama of politics aims not only at constructing a boundary between inside and outside, but also at including as many additional supporters and followers as possible. And in doing so it corresponds to the universalistic thrust of democracy.

Conclusion

This perspective on the audience of a spectacle also sheds new light on the relation between collective identity and the sacred as presented at the beginning of this chapter. "Sacred" commonly refers to an ultimately unconceivable "spirit," a "substance," or a "force" that is seen as prior to the grid of classification and the order of language. In this regard it is similar to the audience of a theatrical performance.

The audience is in a situation of "communitas" – to use Turner's term – muted, unstructured, undefined, and beyond the regular order of everyday social life. It is not only, for the time of the performance, exempted from the obligations that govern the ordinary life, but it is also not yet part of the order performed on stage with rules and social positions of its own. Instead, it is excluded from participating in the action on stage, even its expression of approval, admiration, or disappointment for the performance is restricted to pre-linguistic gestures and utterances. The audience remains in a position of before and beyond. This state of exception and shapelessness comes, indeed, close to what we have called the "sacred" or – to use another Durkheimian phrase – to the "conscience collective." There are, certainly, deeply engraved memories and expectations, fears and hopes in this conscience collective, but they are devoid of a fixed form, they exist like dreams or nightmares that can be told only under special circumstances and that need the assistance of others to be represented and narrated.

Theatrical rituals and performances refer to these diffuse dispositions of the collective consciousness and respond to it by presenting a regular story. The performance is the performance of an order. This order exists only and insofar as there is an audience that expects, observes, interprets, and identifies with the performance. Without an audience the performance would be pointless, without a performance the audience would dissolve. This mutual referentiality is the core of the performative process. In the performance on stage the undefined and ineffable sacred reflected in the communitas of the audience is represented in the visible world, as a regular sequence of actions. And this performed order is taken by the audience as a true and authentic representation of its own longings, hopes, fears, and obsessions. *This* is the real moment of fusion. It would be misleading to assume that fusion is generated by an accurate representation of the external world.[22] A mere assembly of detailed facts would fail to attract and fascinate as long as it did not resonate with the conscience collective of the audience. The audience would respond by asking "So what?" and turn away. Instead, fusion in Alexander's use of the term results from surrendering to the performance because the audience takes it to be an authentic representation of its own internal world, recognizes it unconsciously to be an expression of its conscience collective, accepts it as a representation of its collective identity.

In order to be effective, this reference to the conscience collective has, however, to be kept *latent*. It is largely prevented from entering the mind of the spectator and it can hardly be represented directly on stage. Even if there is a role or a position representing the audience in the performance on stage (e.g. a commentator or a chorus), the representation of collective identity has to be concealed or couched in an indirect way. If it were presented in an unmediated and explicit way, if the people in the audience were confronted directly with their own collective consciousness, fascination would fade away, fusion would collapse. Instead they would feel embarrassed and uneasy. Whoever has to face directly the representation of his or her identity without having resort to denying the accuracy of the representation will feel cornered and trapped. This embarrassment happens also when we have to face photographical portraits that reveal our identity in an unmasked and undistorted way. We cannot stand the direct encounter with our own identity. This frightening impact of the direct encounter with our identity is also the reason why identity has to be *translated* into something different that we call, in the Durkheimian tradition, "the sacred." Even this translation of identity is mostly disguised, mystified, banned from direct representation. Representations can refer to identity only in an indirect way, mediated by symbol, myth, ritual, theatre, etc. The sacred is indeed a translation of collective identity into a language that keeps the direct reference to identity latent. Collective identity can perceive itself only as a projection on the world and the performance is one of the most important of these projections.[23]

This indirect, covered and latent correspondence between the conscience collective of the audience and the performed order on stage resembles the general nature of interaction. Here, too, we have no direct access to the identity of the other. For the moment of interaction we have, to a certain degree at least, to ignore the dark motives driving our actions, we have to take the actions of others as authentic expressions of their intentions, we have to ignore the possibility of misunderstanding, we have to assume that we know what is going on, etc. Of course, from a critical distance we can debunk all these assumptions as illusions. But even in this debunking gesture we have to presuppose a layer of reality that is, for the moment, exempted from these illusions. The illusion is constitutive and unavoidable. If we could never embrace in these counterfactual assumptions, social interaction would dissolve – as the theatrical performance cannot dispense with the fusion between the performance on stage and the collective consciousness of the audience. Viewed from this perspective, the moment of fusion denotes the origin of social order.

However, as constitutive and indispensable they are, the bonds between audience and stage are fragile, the moment of fusion between the sacred communitas and its performative representation is volatile. Like other representations of the sacred the theatrical performance, too, can hardly avoid gradual profanization. The extraordinary event, if it occurs too often, becomes an ordinary element of our everyday world – the fusion fades away because the audience is bored. And this dissolution of fusion is the origin of change. If we never slid out of the state of fusion, if we surrendered incessantly to the flow of the performance, if there were never a mistaken representation, then, indeed, the social order would be permanent and frictionless.

But fusion is not only dissolved by gradual profanization, it is also disrupted by unexpected disturbances and unintended mistakes, by – to use the Durkheimian phrasing – the sudden appearance of subversive "demons" that can never be finally banned. No performance can avoid entirely the occurrence of misunderstandings, disturbances, mistakes that interrupt the smooth proceeding of the performance and subvert its illusion. In this case the audience is not bored – on the contrary: the disturbance attracts attention because it is a subversive mimetical event. Such subversive events shatter the structure of meaning and allow for a glimpse into the abyss of the inconceivable identity – the audience takes a step back and laughs because the taken-for-granted distinctions are eroded (Butler 1990).

A third challenge to fusion results from the longing for parusiah and the question of authenticity that emerges with the advent of axial-age civilizations. Are the actors on stage just presenting a feigned, artificial, rhetorically brilliant reality thus disguising cynically their true beliefs and convictions, or are they speaking the truth without any reservation, deception, or distortion? These questions cannot be asked in a world in which the individual persons are not yet separated from the social roles they are playing, in which individual guilt and voluntary action are not yet separated from demonic forces and bodily defilements, in which social order needs no further legitimation because it is the only valid orientation, in which the moral realm of conscience is not yet distinguished from external pressures and inescapable fate. If, however, the fascination by the perfect illusion is replaced by the quest for truth and the reflexive turn towards the inner conscience, if rhetoric is replaced by sophia, if the tragic entanglement of Oedipus is replaced by Socrates' moral rationalism or Paulus' anti-legalism, than the field opens up for the moral drama (Ricoeur 1967). The moral drama is not only driven by the urge to represent the collective identity of the audience on stage, but, in addition to this, it is driven by the thrust to penetrate the illusionary surface of the performance and to represent the individual identity of the participants. But this anti-theatrical thrust for parusiah and morality can hardly escape, in its turn, the pitfalls of deceit and hypocrisy. Illusion and disillusion, theatre and parusiah, metis and sophia, are inseparably locked to each other.

Thus, the distinctions between the collective consciousness of the audience and the performance of the actors on stage, as well as the distinction between the performance of the actors and their inner reality, provide a new paradigm for a classical issue of social theory. The conscience collective of the audience in a state of communitas refers to a transcendence that classical political theory called the "state of nature" or "the original anarchy," that in psychoanalysis is referred to as the "unconscious" or the "drives," that vitalism phrases as "energy" or as "life," or what is called the "sublime" or the "lived experience" (*Erlebnis*) in the theory of art. As Cassirer has put it in his famous debate with Heidegger in Davos: "The human subject has to convert everything that is unstructured 'Erlebnis' (lived experience) within him into some objective form." What holds true for the symbolizing activity of the human individual, does also apply to the emergence of social order out of the unstructured conscience collective of the audience. Both are inseparably connected to each other – there is no communitas that can resist being translated into structure, and there is no social order and social structure that can dispense with any spaces for communitas; there is no collective identity that can endure without being represented in stories, rituals, myths, and symbols, and there is no performance or story that does not presuppose any collective identity of the audience.

A similar claim could be made with respect to the distinction between the performance and the inner reality of the individual actors, the oppositions between the individual person and the realm of social action and social order or the contrast between the changing social conventions and the universal truth are at the core of modern social theory. Both oppositions have frequently been linked to each other – the individual person was presented as the site of universal reason and rights and contrasted to the historical variations of social order. Again, both sides of the opposition can only be conceived as constituted by mutual reference. These constitutive mutual references have to be represented and the theatrical performance is a promising new paradigm of this reference. Constitutive rituals, theatrical performances, and moral dramas are different basic models within this paradigm – different in complexity, different in their reference to audience and outsiders, different in their reference to authenticity and illusion, different in their reference to reality and fusion.

Notes

1. Thus, Goffman can – to a certain extent at least – be colonized by rational choice theory.
2. This, too, is a classical issue that has been treated before – e.g. in Plato and Kant as the problem of knowledge, in Proust as the problem of memory, or, in Weber, as the problem of salvation. Unlike Weber, however, we will not focus on historical religions as the field of mediation between the sacred and the profane – or in Weber's phrasing: between *Diesseits* und *Jenseits* (this-worldly and other-worldly).
3. Durkheim uses the notion of "conscience collective." Following Shils we have, in translating the Durkheimian term, to distinguish between the collective consciousness and collective self-consciousness. The first concept refers to the shared symbolic culture of a community, the second concept denotes the reflexive image a community develops of itself.
4. The opposition between two sacred forces allows us not only to construe the spatial structure of the world, but also the structure of time and history. History occurs between the sacred time of the beginnings, of paradise and mythical unity, and the apocalyptic end of times, when the profane order dissolves and the chaos takes over (Eliade 1985; van der Leeuw 1950). In the same way as space can only be measured and perceived if a referential point is presupposed, the telling of stories has to assume a beginning and an end, a before and after, and these categorical distinctions are a priori to any particular story.
5. The frightening impact of the sudden event is certainly true for the appearance of the demonic chaos, but it may sound less plausible with respect to a charismatic sacred. However, the immediate encounter with the cosmogonic and redeeming sacred is also frightening. This has been noted before. Rudolf Otto (1917) described the impact of the sacred on ordinary human beings as "fascinancs, tremendum et numinosum." Max Weber (1990), outlining his concept of charismatic authority, stressed this incompatibility of charisma with the regular order of mundane everyday acting – charisma will shatter established rules and the charisma, in its turn, risks fading away if it is turned into routine.
6. In contrast, the classics have paid due attention to it: cf. Durkheim (1960) and Weber (1988); contemporary exceptions are: Callois (1994); Shils (1977); Eliade (1953); Ricoeur (1967).
7. In order to complete this (very sketchy) typology of science we should also mention a third category of signs that neither relate to an external world of profane, common, and ordinary phenomena like indexical gestures or descriptive signs do, nor relate to the inner world of the sacred, the unique, and the extra-ordinary as symbols do. We may call these signs aesthetic signs like melody and rhythm of a song or the decorative pattern of a surface exist as pure forms. Even if they are sometimes used

to depict or represent an external reality, to hint at the sacred or to mark collective identity the aesthetic sign as such refers to nothing else than other aesthetic signs. In its purist mode it means "difference" or "form" without denoting a referential world or expressing an identity. But this purity of the aesthetic sign can only be perceived when contrasted to a background – the visual decoration has to be inscribed into a carrier material, the music can be listened to only if there is silence, etc. Thus the background substitutes, in a way, the referential world.

8. As, for example, Greek philosophy mocking at the anthropogonic imagination of gods.

9. History starts with this shift from local or spatial to temporal modes of representing the sacred. They set not only to the beginning of history, but also at its end. They set the frame for the narration of stories although the epiphanic event itself is beyond any reasonable account. It can hardly be expected, it defies rules and sequential order, it breaks any narrative pattern. Instead, it starts history the order of which is basically a repetition of the original event. This is the meaning of the sacred tradition: a reiteration of the cosmogonic event (Eliade 1953). Even the moment of salvation when the time of merging the sacred and the profane matters is over, and this sacred and the saved will again be clearly separated from its opposite, repeats this original mediation of the sacred and the profane.

10. But the fragile moment of encountering the sacred cannot be made accessible to everyone. The divine message has to be frozen into holy scriptures, the epiphanic moment has to be turned into "doxa" that can be controlled, institutionalized, and administered by a trained elite of scholars, priests and intellectuals. The Brahmins in Hinduism, the Buddhist Sangha, the Islamic Ulema and the Christian Monks were such learned scholars mediating between the sacred scriptures and the laic commoners (cf. Eisenstadt's work (1986) on the Axial Age civilizations).

11. A similar figure appears in Freud's story of patricide as the transition between familiy and society (Freud 1969).

12. Artaud's theatre of cruelty: Chris Burden has put the authenticity of the violent event to the extreme by shooting himself on stage.

13. Just to complete the analytical distinction, a third mode of mediation between the sacred and the profane should be mentioned. The opposites can not only be connected spatially or temporally, but also by referring to them internally when projecting an action: actions refer not only and exclusively to ultimate sacred or moral ends but have also to take into account profane means and situational contingencies, and even the most profane and utility-minded choice has to limit its horizon by some vague reference to ultimate ends.

14. Garfinkel's ethnomethodology has centered this perspective on order as practice: "doing order" replaces the assumption of structure as a presupposition of action.

15. Searle was the first to introduce this difference between regulative and constitutive rules (Searle 1970; Austin 1975, 1979).

16. Caillois has called this the moment of "vertigo" or "ilinx" in rituals – the moment when the participants of a ritual performance surrender to the illusion in voluptuous feeling of panic and destabilization. Turner uses the term "flow" for this moment,

Huizinga speaks of "enchantment" or "captivation," Geertz distinguishes superficial "shallow play" from "deep play" in which the actors forget their personal identity and surrender to the ritual. Alexander uses the term "fusion" for the surrender to the illusion of the performance. A similar reference – although this time with respect to everyday interaction – is the "taken for granted" that Garfinkel centers as the mark of the lifeworld (Garfinkel 1989; Caillois 1994).

17. Schechner uses a similar distinction in *The Future of Ritual* (1993).
18. Evans-Pritchard's Azande could therefore, after performing the rain magic, attribute the missing rain to a failed performance instead of questioning the ritual. Western observers, in contrast, mistook the ritual for a technique that can be questioned and improved.
19. Caillois (1994) has called this feature of rituals "alea."
20. Modern theatrical performances try occasionally to bridge the gap between actors on stage and spectators in front of it by positioning actors within the audience or by inviting spectators to join the actors on stage. The exclusion of the audience can, however, go even beyond the non-intervention and the norms of silence – e.g. watching a live performance on TV does not allow the audience to be present in the location of the performance. Here the sheer knowledge that an important ritual event occurs at the time when it is watched by the spectators is sufficient to catch their attention. The millions of spectators all over the world watching rituals like state funerals, princely weddings, or the eastern blessings of the Pope in Saint Peter's Square testify to this magic of imagined co-presence via TV.
21. The new institutionalism in political and social science accounts for the rule-guided and non-rational nature of political processes, but it fails to relate this to the implicit construction of community inherent in politics.
22. Sometimes Jeffrey Alexander, when he uses the term for the merging of performance and "reality," seems to assume this. See Alexander (2003).
23. However, some modern theories of drama, e.g. Brecht, demand exactly this disillusion of the audience: the audience should be aware that it is just theatre in order to stay at a critical distance to the performance on stage.

References

Agamben, Giorgio. 1995. *Homo Sacer*. Stanford: Stanford University Press.
Alexander, Jeffrey C. and Philip Smith. 2001. "The Strong Program in Cultural Theory: Elements of a Structural Hermeneutics," pp. 135–51 in Jonathan H. Turner (ed.), *Handbook of Sociological Theory*. New York: Kluwer Academic/Plenum Publisher.
Alexander, Jeffrey C., Ron Eyerman, Bernhard Giesen, Neil J. Smelser, and Piotr Sztompka, eds. 2004. *Cultural Trauma and Collective Identity*. Berkeley: University of California Press.
Artaud, Antonini. 1958. *The Theater and Its Double*, trans. Mary Caroline Richards. New York: Grove Press.
Austin, John L. 1975. *How to Do Things with Words*. Cambridge, Mass.: Harvard University Press.

1979. *Philosophical Papers*. Oxford: Oxford University Press.

Bakhtin, Mikhail. 1965. *Rabelais and His World*, trans. Helen Iswolsky. Cambridge, Mass.: MIT Press.

1986. *Speech Genres and Other Late Essays*, trans. Vern W. McGee. Austin, TX: University of Texas Press.

Bateson, Gregory. 1972. *Steps to an Ecology of Mind*. San Francisco: Chandler.

Baumann, Richard. 1986. *Story, Performance, and Event: Contextual Studies in Oral Narrative*. New York: Cambridge University Press.

Becker, Howard S. 1973. *Outsiders: Studies in the Sociology of Deviance*. New York: Free Press.

Bell, Catherine M. 1992. *Ritual Theory, Ritual Practice*. New York: Oxford University Press.

1997. *Ritual: Perspectives and Dimensions*. New York: Oxford University Press.

Berger, Peter L. and Luckmann, Thomas. 1967. *The Social Construction of Reality*. Garden City, NY: Doubleday.

Bohrer, Karl H. 2003. *Ekstasen der Zeit*. Vienna: Hanser.

Bridgeman, Percy. 1991. "The Operational Character of Scientific Concepts," pp. 57–69 in Richard Boyd (ed.), *The Philosophy of Science*. Cambridge, Mass.: MIT Press.

Brubaker, Rogers. 1996. *Citizenship and Nationhood in France and Germany*. Cambridge, Mass.: Harvard University Press.

Burke, Kenneth. 1957. *The Philosophy of Literary Form*. New York: Vintage Books.

1962. *A Grammar of Motives*. Cleveland, Ohio: Meridian.

1965. "Dramatism," pp. 445–51 in *Encyclopedia of the Social Sciences*, vol. VII.

Butler, Judith. 1990. *Gender Trouble*. New York: Routledge.

Caillois, Roger. 1994. *L'homme et le sacré*. Paris: Gallimard.

Campbell, Joseph. 1981. *The Mythic Image*. Princeton: Princeton University Press.

1988. *The Power of Myth*. New York: Doubleday.

1993. *The Hero with a Thousand Faces*. London: Fontana.

Carlson, Marvin. 1996. *Performance: A Critical Introduction*. London: Routledge.

Chambers, Ross. 1980. "Le Masque et le miroir: Vers une théorie relationnelle du théâtre," *Études littéraires* 13: 397–412.

Derrida, Jacques. 1978. *Writing and Difference*, trans. Alan Bass. Chicago: University of Chicago Press.

1982. *Margins of Philosophy*, trans. Alan Bass. Chicago: University of Chicago Press.

Diamond, Elin. 1989. "Mimesis, Mimicry, and the 'True-Real'," *Modern Drama* 32: 58–72.

Douglas, Mary. 1966. *Purity and Danger: An Analysis of Concepts of Pollution and Taboo*. London: Routledge.

1973. *Natural Symbols*. London: Barrie and Jenkins.

Durkheim, Émile. 1960. *Les Formes Élémentaires de la Vie Réligieuse. Le Système Totémique en Australie*. Paris: Presses Universitaire de France.

Eisenstadt, Shmuel Noah. 1986. *The Origins and Diversity of Axial Age Civilizations*. Albany, NY: State University of New York Press.

1992. *Max Weber on Charisma and Institution Building: Selected Papers.* Chicago: University of Chicago Press.

Eliade, Mircea. 1959. *The Sacred and the Profane: The Nature of Religion.* New York: Harcourt.

1985. *Symbolism, the Sacred and the Arts.* New York: Crossroad.

Evans-Pritchard, Edward E. 1937. *Witchcraft, Oracles and Magic among the Azande.* Oxford: Clarendon Press.

Felman, Shoshana. 1983. *The Literary Speech Act: Don Juan with Austin, or Seduction in Two Languages*, trans. Catherine Porter. Ithaca, NY: Cornell University Press.

Fischer-Lichte, Erika. 2002. *Politik als Inszenierung: Vortragsabend mit der Akademie der Wissenschaften zu Göttingen im Niedersächsischen Landtag am 12. November 2001.* Hannover: Hahn.

Frazer, James G. 1922. *The Golden Bough: A Study in Magic and Religion.* London: Macmillan.

Freud, Sigmund. 1963. *Das Unheimliche. Aufsätze zur Literatur.* Frankfurt am Main: Fischer.

1969. *Gesammelte Werke.* Frankfurt am Main: Fischer.

Garfinkel, Harold. 1989. *Studies in Ethnomethodology.* Cambridge: Polity Press.

Garner, Stanton B., Jr. 1994. *Bodied Spaces: Phenomenology and Performance in Contemporary Drama.* Ithaca, NY: Cornell University Press.

Geertz, Clifford. 1972. "Deep Play. Notes on the Balinese Cockfight," *Daedalus* 101: 1–37.

1980. *Negara: The Theatre State in Nineteenth-Century Bali.* Princeton: Princeton University Press.

Gennep, Arnold van. 1977. *The Rites of Passage.* London: Routledge.

Giesen, Bernhard. 1999. *Kollektive Identität.* Frankfurt am Main: Suhrkamp.

2004. *Triumph and Trauma.* Boulder, CO: Paradigm Publishers.

Giesen, Bernhard and Daniel Suber. 2005. *Cultural Perspectives on Politics and Religion.* Leiden: Brill Academic Publishers.

Girard, René. 1977. *Violence and the Sacred.* Baltimore, MD: Johns Hopkins University Press.

Goffman, Erving. 1955. "On Facework: An Analysis of Ritual Elements in Social Interaction," *Psychiatry*, 18: 213–31.

1959. *The Presentation of Self in Everyday Life.* Garden City, NY: Doubleday.

1963. *Stigma: Notes on the Management of Spoiled Identity.* Englewood Cliffs, NJ: Prentice-Hall.

1982. *Interaction Ritual: Essays on Face-to-Face Behavior.* New York: Pantheon Books.

1986. *Frame Analysis: An Essay on the Organization of Experience.* Boston, Mass.: Northeastern University Press.

Gusfield, Joseph R. 1981. *The Culture of Public Problems: Drinking-Driving and the Symbolic Order.* Chicago: University of Chicago Press.

Habermas, Jürgen. 1985. *The Theory of Communicative Action: Reason and the Rationalization of Society.* 2 vols. Boston, Mass.: Beacon Press.

1989. *The Structural Transformation of the Public Sphere: An Inquiry into a Category of Bourgeois Society*. Cambridge, Mass.: MIT Press.

Hassan, Ihab. 1971. *The Dismemberment of Orpheus: Towards a Postmodern Literature*. Madison: University of Wisconsin Press.

Heidegger, Martin. 1984. *Sein und Zeit*. Tübingen: Niemeyer.

Huizinga, Johan. 1950. *Homo Ludens*. New York: Beacon Press.

Kristeva, Julia. 1980. *Desire in Language: A Semiotic Approach to Literature and Art*. Oxford: Blackwell.

Kurz, Gerhard. 1997. *Metapher, Allegorie, Symbol*. Göttingen: Vandenhoeck & Ruprecht.

Langer, Susanne K. 1967. *Philosophy in a New Key: A Study in the Symbolism of Reason, Rite and Art*. Cambridge, Mass.: Harvard University Press.

Luhmann, Niklas. 1999. *Soziale Systeme: Grundriß einer allgemeinen Theorie*. Frankfurt am Main: Suhrkamp.

Luckmann, Thomas and Peter L. Berger. 1987. *The Social Construction of Reality*. Harmondsworth: Penguin.

Luckmann, Thomas and Alfred Schütz. 1974. *Structures of the Life-World*. London: Heinemann.

Lyotard, Jean-François. 1999. *The Postmodern Condition: A Report on Knowledge*. Minneapolis: University of Minnesota Press.

Malinowski, Bronislaw. 1960. *Argonauts of the Western Pacific: An Account of Native Enterprise and Adventure in the Archipelagoes of Melanesian New Guinea*. New York: Dutton.

Mead, George H. 1934. *Mind, Self and Society*. Chicago: University of Chicago Press.

Mersch, Dieter. 2002. *Ereignis und Aura: Untersuchungen zu einer Ästhetik des Performativen*. Frankfurt am Main: Suhrkamp.

Morris, Charles W. 1938. "Foundations of the Theory of Signs," *The International Encyclopedia of Unified Science*, 1, 2. Chicago: University of Chicago Press.

Nietzsche, Friedrich. 1994. *Geburt der Tragödie: Schriften zur Literatur und Philosophie der Griechen*. Frankfurt am Main: Insel-Verlag.

Otto, Rudolf. 1917. *Das Heilige: Über das Irrationale in der Idee des Göttlichen und sein Verhältnis zum Rationalen*. Breslau: Trewendt und Granier.

Phelan, Peggy. 1993. *Unmarked: The Politics of Performance*. London: Routledge.

Pratt, Mary Louise. 1977. *Toward a Speech-Act Theory of Literary Discourse*. Bloomington, IN: Indiana University Press.

Proust, Marcel. 1996. *In Search of Lost Time: The Guermantes Way*. London: Vintage.

Rappaport, Roy A. 1999. *Ritual and Religion in the Making of Humanity*. New York: Cambridge University Press.

Ricoeur, Paul. 1967. *The Symbolism of Evil*. New York: Harper.

Schechner, Richard. 1965. *Rites and Symbols of Initiation*. New York: Harper.

ed. 1976. *Ritual, Play and Performance. Readings in the Social Sciences: Theatre*. New York: Seabury Press.

1985. *Between Theater and Anthropology*. Philadelphia, PA: University of Pennsylvania Press.

1993. *The Future of Ritual: Writings on Culture and Performance*. London: Routledge.

Schneider, Christoph. 2003. "Symbolizität und Authentizität." Zur Kommunikation von Gefühlen in der Lebenswelt," pp. 101–34 in Bernhard Giesen, Jürgen Osterhammel, and Rudolf Schlögl (eds.), *Die Wirklichkeit der Symbole*. Konstanz: UVK.

Schütz, Alfred. 1964. *Collected Papers. Vol. II: Studies in Social Theory*. The Hague: Martinus Nijhoff.

Searle, John R. 1970. *Speech Acts: An Essay in the Philosophy of Language*. Cambridge: Cambridge University Press.

Shils, Edward Albert. 1979. *Center and Periphery: Essays in Macrosociology*. Chicago: University of Chicago Press.

Smith, William Robertson. 1927. *Lectures on the Religion of the Semites: The Fundamental Institutions*. London: Black.

Stanislavsky, Konstantin S. 1980. *An Actor Prepares*, trans. Elizabeth Reynolds Hapgood. London: Methuen.

Swinburne, Richard. 1989. *Miracles*. New York: Collier-McMillan.

Tambiah, Stanley J. 1981. *A Performative Approach to Ritual*. London: Oxford University Press.

2002. "Form and Meanings of Magical Acts," pp. 340–57 in Michael Lambek (ed.), *A Reader in the Anthropology of Religion*. Malden, Mass.: Blackwell Publishers.

Turner, Victor M. 1969. *The Ritual Process: Structure and Anti-Structure*. Chicago: Aldine Publishing Company.

1974. *Dramas, Fields and Metaphors*. Ithaca, NY: Cornell University Press.

1981. "Social Dramas and Stories about Them," pp. 137–64 in W. J. T. Mitchell (ed.), *On Narrative*. Chicago: University of Chicago Press.

1982. *From Ritual to Theatre*. New York: Performing Arts Journal Publications.

1990. "Are There Universals of Performance in Myth, Ritual and Drama?" pp. 8–18 in Richard Schechner and Willa Appel (eds.), *By Means of Performance: Intercultural Studies of Theatre and Ritual*. New York: Cambridge University Press.

Van der Leeuw, Gerardus. 1950. "Urzeit und Endzeit," *Eranos-Jahrbuch* 18: 11–51.

Wagner, Peter. 1998. "Fest-Stellungen. Beobachtungen zur sozialwissenschaftlichen Diskussion über Identität," pp. 44–72 in Aleida Assmann and Friese Heidrun (eds.), *Identitäten. Erinnerung, Geschichte, Identität 3*. Frankfurt am Main: Suhrkamp.

Wagner-Pacifici, Robin Erica. 1986. *The Moro Morality Play: Terrorism as Social Drama*. Chicago: University of Chicago Press.

Weber, Max. 1988. *Gesammelte Aufsätze zur Religionssoziologie*. Tübingen: Mohr.

1990. *Wirtschaft und Gesellschaft. Grundriβder verstehenden Soziologie*. Tübingen: Mohr.

Winch, Peter. 1999. *The Idea of a Social Science and its Relation to Philosophy*. London: Routledge.

Wittgenstein, Ludwig. 1976. *Philosophische Untersuchungen*. Frankfurt am Main: Suhrkamp.

Index